*Praise for*

# THE UNPROTECTED CLASS

"In a country where being racist is the ultimate sin, how has our ruling class gotten away with attacking the majority of Americans on the basis of their race? And what exactly is the purpose of anti-white hate? The answer is scary, and this outstanding book explains."
—Tucker Carlson

"Jeremy Carl bravely exposes, documents, and names the racialist ideology that is tearing America apart. This book shows that left-wing race politics is a dead end and offers America a better way forward: A system based on the principle of color-blind equality. A must-read as America enters a pivotal phase of the Culture War."
—Christopher Rufo, senior fellow, the Manhattan Institute, and author of *America's Cultural Revolution*

"A stunning work of exceedingly rare bravery, and indeed of patriotism. Jeremy Carl tells urgent truths that, until now, few if any intellectuals of his stature have had the courage to say publicly, out of fear for their own livelihoods. If we don't act now to reverse the injustices detailed in this prophetic book, America as the home of liberty and justice for all will cease to exist."
—Rod Dreher, author of *Live Not By Lies*

"Most Americans concede that there is a virulent but largely exempt racial demonization of so-called whites as a collective. Yet they are afraid to confront the perpetrators of such pernicious and incoherent bias and hatred. Not Jeremy Carl. In his meticulously researched and carefully argued analysis of this pathology, Carl astutely reviews the symptoms of the malady, diagnoses its root causes—from careerism to racial chauvinism—offers concrete courses of action, and then warns of a bleak prognosis to a racially obsessed America if it does not desist from its current premodern and suicidal obsession. A prescient, landmark book that finally calls out those who for far too long have claimed victimhood even as they fueled a toxic brand of tribal chauvinism."
—Victor Davis Hanson, senior fellow, The Hoover Institution, Stanford University, and author of *The Dying Citizen*

"What a great book! Jeremy Carl confronts the ahistorical racialist rot presently eating at the core of the American Experiment. *The Unprotected Class* demolishes the false narratives about race that have captured many American institutions and provides essential intellectual ammunition to refute such lies."

—Peter Kirsanow, commissioner, United States Commission on Civil Rights

"There is a pathological war on white people in America. It's time decent people wake up and fight against it. Read this book to figure out how."

—Charlie Kirk, founder and president, Turning Point USA

"There are few greater taboos in public discourse than using the word 'white' non-pejoratively. Jeremy Carl explains this taboo—and breaks it, in the hope of saving the U.S. from a future of ever-worsening race relations. Discontent is growing surreptitiously among whites regarding their scapegoat status. Carl provides a language with which this 'unprotected class' can reject its own demonization and set the country on a better course."

—Heather Mac Donald, author of *When Race Trumps Merit*

"Anti-white racism is a growing global trend. But its rise to cultural dominance in a non-racist nation like the U.S. needs a particular kind of explanation, criticism . . . and careful handling. When St. Paul describes charity as not being provoked to anger, devising no evil, not rejoicing over iniquity, but rejoicing in truth, he describes the spirit in which Carl's honest, well-researched but inevitably controversial book is written. It deserves to be read in the same spirit."

—John O'Sullivan, president, the Danube Institute, and former editor-in-chief, *National Review*

"Jeremy Carl brings to bear his unique insights into the central quandary of our time: the people whose ancestors carved America out of the wilderness are now strangers in their own land, ashamed of their history, and abused by the institutions their forefathers built. White Americans are dispossessed, disrespected, and discriminated against. As a scholar, activist, and government official who has lived and worked in the trenches for decades, Carl navigates the dark waters of taboo topics with ease and shows how the crusade against racism has only given rise to hate by a different name, trampling freedom and equality under the law."

—Pedro Gonzalez, proprietor, *Contra* and former Associate Editor, *Chronicles Magazine*

"White people, and especially white men, are now the only group of people who fall outside the framework of civil rights law. This excellent book argues that although in principle the civil rights regime protects all races, in practice 'anti-racist' means anti-white. *The Unprotected Class* explains how the nostrums of critical race theory such as reverse racism, affirmative action, and diversity have constructed race as a foundation for legal and political entitlements, displacing the individual liberties enshrined in the U.S. Constitution such as freedom of expression and the right to private property. The powerful message of this book will resonate with all who are concerned with justice and peaceful co-existence."

—Wanjiru Njoya, scholar-in-residence, Ludwig von Mises Institute, and former lecturer, Oxford University and the London School of Economics

"Young Americans will suffer the dire consequences of the racial spoils system poisoning American institutions. This book is the best attempt yet to shake Americans awake ahead of the coming competency crisis."

—Saurabh Sharma, president, American Moment

"Finally, a book that has the courage to call wokeness what it is: anti-white. *The Unprotected Class* should allow well-intentioned readers of all races to see how widespread and unjust anti-white discrimination is in contemporary America."

—David Azerrad, assistant professor, Van Andel School of Government, Hillsdale College

# The Unprotected Class

# The Unprotected Class

## How Anti-White Racism Is Tearing America Apart

# Jeremy Carl

*Since 1947*
**REGNERY**
*An Imprint of Skyhorse Publishing, Inc.*

Published in the United States by Regnery, an imprint of Skyhorse Publishing, Inc.

Regnery® is a registered trademark and its colophon is a trademark of Skyhorse Publishing Inc.®, a Delaware corporation.

Visit our website at www.regnery.com.
Please follow our publisher Tony Lyons on Instagram @tonylyonsisuncertain.

10 9 8 7 6 5 4 3 2 1

Library of Congress Cataloging-in-Publication Data is available on file.

Print ISBN: 978-1-68451-458-8
eBook ISBN: 978-1-68451-559-2

Cover design by John Caruso
Cover photograph courtesy of the Pacifica, California, Police Department

Regnery books may be purchased in bulk at special discounts for sales promotion, corporate gifts, fund-raising, or educational purposes. Special editions can also be created to specifications. For details, contact the Special Sales Department, Regnery, 307 West 36th Street, 11th Floor, New York, NY 10018 or info@skyhorsepublishing.com.

Printed in the United States of America

*For my children: may they be treated equally*
*as they pursue their dreams.*

# CONTENTS

# INTRODUCTION

> *"The white race is the cancer of human history."*
> —Susan Sontag, *Partisan Review*

> *"Sooner or later, one has to take sides, if one is to remain human."*
> —Graham Greene, *The Quiet American*

Minneapolis Mayor Jacob Frey knelt before George Floyd's 24K gold-plated casket and wept.

His body heaved as though he were mourning the loss of his own son. A week earlier, Floyd, a small-to-medium-time career criminal who had once held a gun to the belly of a woman in front of her toddler during a home invasion, had died in the course of an arrest. Floyd was high on methamphetamine at the time and had three to four times what could be a lethal dose of fentanyl in his system.

The now well-known events that led to Floyd's death began when Floyd was accused by a local store owner of passing a counterfeit bill. The police were called, and among those who responded was Derek Chauvin, a white officer. Floyd, who was African American, would utter his soon-to-be-famous comment "I can't breathe" numerous times before police even touched him (difficulty breathing is a common side effect of fentanyl intoxication[1]). After Floyd resisted arrest, Chauvin knelt on his neck for an extended period. A jury would later determine amid a politically tense trial that this had caused Floyd's death, leading to a conviction of Chauvin on a count of second-degree murder.

The Chauvin trial took place in the wake of the most financially destructive riots in American history, which killed at least nineteen people, led to more than seventeen thousand arrests, injured more than two thousand officers, and gave rise to more than twenty-four hundred incidents of looting. In total, rioters caused more than $2 billion in damages.

One was, of course, not permitted to ask whether Chauvin received a fair trial, or whether the jury was swayed by the days of deadly riots, overt threats of violence, and massive demonstrations just outside the courthouse. As one prospective juror explained about his reluctance to serve, "It's more from a safety, security standpoint. . . . I just wouldn't want any issues or harm to come to my wife or my family."[2]

Regardless of your opinion as to whether the jury got it right, the broader context of the trial was apparent to many. As commentator Tucker Carlson noted at the time, "Americans have been told that George Floyd's death was a racist murder, and they're responsible for it."[3]

The fiery eulogy for Floyd was delivered by the Reverend Al Sharpton, a career race-baiter (and frequent Obama White House visitor) who first came to prominence in the late 1980s in New York City when he was the leading promoter of a fabricated hate crime invented by an African American teenager, Tawana Brawley, who falsely accused multiple white men, including a police officer, of raping her.[4] Sharpton nonetheless became a mainstream political figure without ever apologizing for his leading role in the Brawley hoax or subsequent incitement of a fatal anti-Semitic riot in New York City. In his Floyd eulogy, Sharpton demanded to a crowd packed with celebrities and politicians (Joe Biden addressed the group by video) that America "get your knee off [black people's] necks."[5]

Minneapolis would go on to pay Floyd's family $27 million.[6]

In conjunction with the protests, which occurred at the height of public health lockdowns over COVID, nearly thirteen hundred public health officials declared racism and white supremacy "a public health crisis" that justified mass rallies. They were supported by men such as Tom Frieden, the former head of the Centers for Disease Control under President Obama.

Ignoring any presumption of innocence prior to the trial, Joe Biden weighed in and commented that Floyd's death "sends a very clear message to the black community and black lives that are under threat every single day," a comment he made at an online "event" held with Pennsylvania Gov. Tom Wolf. Or, as he later said at a campaign speech in Wilmington, Delaware, "They speak to a nation where too often just the color of your skin puts your life at risk."[7]

Biden, needless to say, did not provide any data or evidence for this assertion, largely because it was factually absurd.

Nor was it ever explained why African American officer Alex Kueng (who had frequently expressed concerns about racial issues in policing) or Asian-American officer Tou Thao had chosen to idly stand by while Officer Chauvin committed a racist murder. No evidence emerged during his trial that Chauvin had ever engaged in racist conduct or bore racial animus.

But Chauvin was white, Floyd was black, and the video was viral.

And that was enough.

◆ ◆ ◆

Grace Church School in Manhattan (tuition and fees approximately $63,000 per year) is one of the many ferociously competitive schools that serve the children of New York City's elite. Like its brethren, after George Floyd's death, Grace Church embraced an "anti-racist" curriculum that included separating white students into groups that didn't include non-whites.

At Manhattan's ultra-elite Dalton School, the interim school director wrote a "racial biography" interrogating her own white privilege. Over one hundred students at Dalton proposed an "anti-racism" curriculum in which any gap between black and non-black students in advanced course performance would have led to course cancelation. The equally tony Brearley School added mandatory anti-racism training for all students and staff.

These measures have not been enough for some. A prominent "diversity consultant" attacked the schools for having "insidious whiteness" and being "built to replicate the plantation mentality." He compared some white parents at Dalton opposed to his race-based policies to those who attacked the Capitol building on January 6, 2021.[8]

Similar programs have taken place at virtually every other elite New York City private school. Some parents were disturbed, but they almost universally refused to go on the record criticizing the schools, out of fear that doing so would torpedo their children's chances of being accepted to an elite university. They knew, in the 2020s, where racial privilege lay—and it wasn't in whiteness.

As the then-head of Grace Church School put it in a secretly recorded conversation in 2021: "We're demonizing white people for being born," adding, "We're using language that makes them feel less than [others], for nothing that they are personally responsible [for]."[9]

Despite this, the policies have not changed, and in fact, most elite schools have doubled down on anti-white rhetoric. Examinations of the class privilege of those parents who can afford to shell out $60,000-plus per year for school tuition are somewhat more difficult to come by.

◆   ◆   ◆

The George Floyd trial and "anti-racism" curricula in our schools are very different issues, but they are tied together by a common thread: the stigmatization of white Americans and "whiteness" in the service of justifying blatant racial discrimination.

White Americans increasingly are second-class citizens in a country their ancestors founded and in which, until recently, they were the overwhelming majority of the population. We've come a long way from the days when we were "securing the blessings of liberty for ourselves and our posterity," as the Preamble to the Constitution puts it.

How did we get here?

How did the civil rights revolution, begun with largely sincere intentions, run so badly off the rails?

How can we correct course?

And why is it necessary that we do so?

It is to these questions that this book is dedicated.

◆ ◆ ◆

Any book is difficult to write, and this book was no exception.

This book was difficult to write, however, not because its thesis was difficult to prove. Rather, it was difficult because demonstrating the thesis's accuracy is politically and socially fraught. It goes against the grain of what many Americans are taught by our media, education system, and cultural apparatus about the so-called "white privilege" that supposedly rules America. While I believe this narrative is rapidly changing, that much of what sounds provocative in this book today will be acknowledged as obviously true by large numbers of Americans in the coming years, the fact remains that this book's argument runs against officially approved narratives.

Adding to the challenge is that there is also a certain *noblesse oblige*, particularly among traditional white elites, that is repelled by any notion that whites would acknowledge real threats to their status or rights. To bemoan discrimination against one's group is simply, as that arch-symbol of wealthy conservative white privilege William F. Buckley Jr. would have said, *infra dignitatem.*

Another challenge is that while Democratic politicians have increasingly waged an all-out assault on the rights of white Americans, Republicans have been tepid defenders of them at best. While some GOP lawmakers have stiffened their spines in recent years, and an increasing number of GOP political and media figures have called out anti-white racism in direct terms (Tucker Carlson, Charlie Kirk, and Matt Walsh have been particular stalwarts), the default Republican response to repeated racial insult has been to say, "I don't see race/color," even in the face of obvious anti-white animus.

Yet while this book is written to explain the current situation of white people in America, I have not written it only for a white audience. Racial reconciliation must be done in a spirit of truth, and that truth must be received and accepted by all Americans—not simply whites. I hope that non-white audiences will engage with this book and see their own complex interrelationship with whites in a new light.

I am largely in agreement with those who warn that a "politics of whiteness" is both tactically and morally inferior to a focus on the unalienable rights in the Declaration of Independence that all Americans should enjoy. Yet as a practical matter, issues of anti-white discrimination and racism must be discussed as issues involving whites as a whole, not just as issues of individual discrimination.

The political reality is one in which non-whites have organized and made powerful group demands, while whites have focused on broad, gauzy appeals to those unalienable universal rights, appeals that have been almost completely ineffective in stopping the Left's long racist march through the institutions.

Simply put, it is foolish to pretend the wrongs being done to white people under our current system aren't being done because they are white. To vindicate individual natural rights, *groups* of people must organize *as groups* to claim them. Martin Luther King Jr. secured the individual natural rights of African Americans, but he amassed the political force to do so by organizing African Americans (and allied whites) as a group.

◆ ◆ ◆

I wish at the outset to discuss my qualifications to write this book, to answer some possible objections to my thesis, and, most important, to explain why this book is necessary.

I've been involved in American politics as a scholar, activist, government official, and advisor for almost three decades.

I've served in the federal government at a senior level as a presidential appointee and been appointed by the president of the United States and my state's governor to various boards, where I've watched the national media attempt to introduce anti-white hostility into work that had little or nothing to do with race.

I've also served for many years as a think-tank scholar at Stanford University's Hoover Institution and subsequently at my current employer, the Claremont Institute, where I've regularly written and spoken about issues of race, immigration, and national identity.

I've traveled extensively and have lived abroad over a period of several years, which has allowed me to view America's racial issues in a global context. Indeed, it was living in India two decades ago, where conflicts around caste, religion, and tribe often served as proxies for American conflicts around race, that first spurred me to think about racial issues more seriously.

I've observed firsthand how the Left casually throws around allegations of racism to further its political goals, and how conservatives often self-censor, afraid of the political consequences of speaking out. That has to end.

In writing a book asserting that anti-white racism is the predominant and most politically powerful form of racism in America today, I am not denying in any way the racism in America's past or that other forms of racism and discrimination currently exist in our society. But one surprising finding in this book is just how long we have had "reverse discrimination" in some areas of American life—in many cases starting as far back as sixty years ago. Today, the advantages white Americans have are mostly informal and evanescent cultural legacies. The discrimination they experience is also sometimes informal but is increasingly legal and formal.

I do not claim this book is a comprehensive treatment of the issue of anti-white racism and discrimination in current society. And, indeed, entire books have been written about many of the subjects I cover in a single chapter here. While I am familiar with each subject area that I profile, experts in individual subjects may find themselves frustrated over what I have included, or what I have chosen to leave out.

I can only ask for their indulgence. This is very much a survey that looks at discrimination in highly disparate areas and shows that this discrimination has common intellectual and political roots. Most of the books specializing in these areas describe in great detail for the proverbial blind man a particular part of the elephant they are touching. My goal in writing this book is to show that the elephant is, in fact, an elephant.

Finally, I am not looking to place primary blame on non-whites for our current, sad situation. In fact, while political leaders of many minority groups have played leading roles in getting us to where we are today, a small number of elite liberal whites are disproportionately involved in maintaining our current system. These elites are, in the words of the conservative African American writer and anthropologist Zora Neale Hurston, "my race but not my taste. . . . My skinfolks but not my kinfolks."[10] Or, as Cassius says to Brutus in Shakespeare's *Julius Caesar*, "The fault, dear Brutus, is not in our stars, But in ourselves."[11]

This book will begin by presenting an overall "lay of the land" on where anti-white discrimination is today. Then we'll move on to our current civil rights regime because both it and its offshoots explain why anti-white discrimination has become so prevalent. From there, we'll look at how anti-white animus manifests itself in a variety of areas, from education to crime to entertainment. The themes of each of these subject matter chapters are intertwined, and they are designed to be read as a whole, but a reader pressed for time can select only chapters of particular interest to read without missing the book's overarching argument. Finally, I will conclude with what is necessarily some speculative discussion on why we have arrived at this place and the political and social motivations of those taking us there. I will also offer concrete steps we can take to get us off our present path and onto one that can build a sustainable and bright future for all Americans.

Finally, a few words as to why this book is necessary: America is in the midst of a rapid demographic and even civilizational transformation. Large numbers of whites, living either in disproportionately white areas or white enclaves in more diverse areas, are in denial about the degree to which they have been replaced as the dominant ethnic group across much of America. While election integrity is a serious and real issue, much of the cry we've heard lately about ballot fraud is really at its heart a complaint about "America fraud"—the fact that many whites cannot acknowledge that a combination of the civil rights revolution and a flood of immigrants over the last sixty years, many from places with thin-to-nonexistent ties to America's core ethnic communities and cultural and social traditions, now wield tremendous political power, which they are using to advantage their groups over whites.

What happens when those largely historically responsible for building American society and its institutions go from a dominant position to just one group among many, and a legally and culturally disfavored group at that?

Simply put, what does a post-white America look like, especially when that post-white America actively denigrates much of the cultural, political, and social legacy that built the country?

And can America and its institutions survive such a transformation?

If we do not correct the course we are on, I fear we are headed for the civil strife and racial violence that has characterized so many other multiracial countries over the centuries, including, in the past, our own.

# CHAPTER 1

# The Lay of the Land

*"In America, the majority raises formidable barriers around the liberty of opinion; within these barriers, an author may write what he pleases, but woe to him if he goes beyond them... Before making public his opinions he thought he had sympathizers; now it seems to him that he has none any more since he revealed himself to everyone; then those who blame him criticize him loudly and those who think as he does keep quiet and move away without courage."*
—Alexis de Tocqueville, *Democracy in America*

*"It is never worth a first-class man's time to express a majority opinion. By definition, there are plenty of others to do that."*
—G. H. Hardy, *A Mathematician's Apology*

Over the last six decades, America has rapidly become a multiethnic, multiracial, and multicultural country.

We take this for granted today, forgetting it was not always true. At the time of the American Revolution, America's free population was not just overwhelmingly white, but overwhelmingly of British origin. Somewhat less than 2 percent were free African Americans[1] (very few of whom could vote) and Native Americans (who were not taxed and were only counted if they were living as part of a white political community, and few were[2]). Other groups were so small as to scarcely even be measurable.

According to one estimate, of the population of Americans on the eve of the Revolution, almost 170 years after the first European settlements in what is now the United States, an estimated 85 percent were of British origin.[3] America's initial political community was not simply white but, in its basic demographics, remarkably homogenous.[4]

Over the next two centuries, American demographics went through various permutations and combinations of settlement and immigration[5] (which I chronicle later in the book). In 1970, the year of the first Census following the 1965 Hart-Celler immigration law—which led to a rapid change in America's demographics—America was 83 percent white non-Hispanic and 11 percent African American. Of the 4.5 percent estimated Hispanic population that made up most of those not captured in the first two groups, 80 percent were native born (as opposed to about 60 percent today).

Much of the Hispanic population of America in 1970 was therefore fairly assimilated into the white majority culture. Some, such as many residents of New Mexico, had histories in America that went back to even before the Pilgrims.[6] Others, such as the Tejanos in Texas and Californios in California, again had settlement patterns that predated the United States, and they maintained their traditions while often marrying into prominent Anglo families over time. In other words, America in 1970, at least judged by the standards of today, was fairly demographically unified—at least in its self-conception.

In examining the racial demographics of America, we should note that while the public concept of race has a basis in shared genetic heritage, it is also a product of social convention. "Whiteness" was hardly a murky or arbitrarily invented concept (the original Nationality Act of 1790 specifically restricted American citizenship to "free white persons"[7] without any particular lack of clarity as to who was being referred to: Jews, for example, were considered white and entitled to citizenship).

Early America had informal hierarchies within the white community, of course. One can find historical instances of "No Irish need apply" and similar insults to newly arrived or otherwise disfavored white ethnic groups. But overall, American society in the eighteenth, nineteenth, and early twentieth centuries classified the same groups of people as white that we classify as white today.

That "white supremacy" is now proclaimed by the White House, Hollywood, and many major corporations to be the greatest threat to America is proof that, in fact, white supremacy no longer holds great sway in America at all and hasn't for quite some time. You can speak of Kim Jong Un's totalitarianism in North Korea only if you don't live under it. Indeed, it is not a coincidence that the term "white privilege" originated in 1988 with Wellesley College women's studies professor Peggy McIntosh, just as it was becoming clear that whiteness was now a legal and social disability in much of American life.[8]

Indeed, denying this alleged "privilege" will inevitably result in being called a racist or being accused of defensiveness or denial—or "white fragility." But this is mere projection. I, as with many other whites, would be happy to acknowledge that I have been the beneficiary of many unearned privileges in life, from being raised by good parents to enjoying good health to benefiting from a good education. But whiteness does not happen to be one of my privileges.

The demand for "racism" among political activists continues to increase even as the supply of racism diminishes: 93 percent of whites approve of interracial marriage, essentially identical to the 96 percent of non-whites who approve of it, with almost all of the tiny minority who disapprove being senior citizens.[9] (Just 4 percent approved in 1958.) At the same time, the Gallup Poll shows, record low numbers of Americans see an improvement in the civil rights of black Americans during their lifetimes (59 percent in 2020, down from the mid-to-high 80s from the 1990s until the start of the so-called "Great Awokening" (the early 2010s rise of "woke culture").[10]

A recent survey of Asian Americans found that almost 80 percent did not "completely agree" that they belonged in the United States, with higher percentages feeling that way among younger cohorts who grew up in a much more diverse and accepting America.[11] Older generations, likely to be actual immigrants with lower language skills and less engagement with American culture, are more likely to believe they belong in America. These findings should give us pause and lead us to examine the public discourse around race in America today and why it has veered so far from reality.

Instances of past racism in America were deplorable, but from a cross-cultural perspective they were also not particularly exceptional. Majority groups have discriminated against minority groups in virtually all societies from time immemorial. Indeed, what is unusual about America is, in comparison with most other countries, the incredible historical openness of many white Americans to welcoming new groups into the American family. This global migration, on a scale never before seen, is a testament to the generosity of America's historical Euro-American majority.

## The Unprotected Class

In civil rights law, we refer to groups as a "protected class" if they have legal protection from discrimination based on various characteristics, which can include sex, disability, veteran status, and so on.[12] But practically speaking, the most socially important of these protected classes is race.

In principle, whites are protected from legal discrimination because of their race.[13] But in practice, they are often an unprotected class, both formally and informally.

In the culture, they are often subject to extreme attacks. Louis Farrakhan can declare that "white people are potential humans, they haven't evolved yet" and still meet with Barack Obama and share a stage with Bill Clinton.[14] Salon.com can print an article headlined "White Men Must Be Stopped: The Future of Mankind Depends on It."[15] Nikole Hannah-Jones, the *New York Times* journalist and founder of the 1619 Project, a well-funded and highly-influential effort that re-focuses American history around slavery, can write that "the white race is the biggest murderer, rapist, pillager, and thief of the modern world."[16] Her 1619 Project can still make its way into countless American schools and curricula despite its conclusions and methods being attacked by historians on the Right and the Left.[17]

Hannah-Jones wasn't even the only unrepentant white-hater on the *New York Times* staff: Sarah Jeong, once a member of the *Times* editorial board and later an opinion columnist, tweeted, "Oh man it's kind of sick how much joy I get out of being cruel to old white men."[18] When the *Times* editorial page was alerted to this and other anti-white writings of Jeong's, they shrugged them off.

Nor do the anti-white forces believe that sitting on the sidelines is an option. Ibram X. Kendi, one of the most prominent academic supporters of Critical Race Theory, believes any federal policy can be defined as racist or anti-racist and that you are racist if you support a racist policy "through action **or inaction** [my emphasis]."[19]

Robin DiAngelo, author of the bestseller *White Fragility,* one of the central texts of Critical Race Theory, believes that today's white people aren't any better than their grandparents. "I am often asked if I think the younger generation is less racist," she writes, "No, I don't. In some ways, racism's adaptations over time are more sinister than concrete rules such as Jim Crow."[20]

Yet these supposedly powerful and unreconstructedly racist whites are just 58 percent of America's population and are rapidly declining in population share. Soon, we will be left attempting to explain why the rights of a white minority are less important than those of other minorities. This is not politically or ethically tenable long-term.

One of the common objections to the notion that America systemically discriminates against whites is to compare some element of the social status of white Americans to Hispanics and, in particular, African Americans. Conveniently, this erases the almost 7 percent of our population that is Asian-American.

Yet Asian Americans do far better than whites on the vast majority of social and economic metrics, despite many of them having arrived in America with little in the way of assets.

This multiethnic success is not even limited to East and South Asian Americans. Iranians, Lebanese, and Turkish Americans have substantially higher median household incomes than the average white American. American-born Argentinian, Ecuadorian, and Cuban Americans have higher incomes than white Americans.[21] Ghanaians, Nigerians, and Egyptians have incomes just slightly below the average white American.[22]

If we were able to split up Nigerians into particularly successful and education-focused groups like the Igbos, those Nigerians would almost certainly have substantially higher education and income profiles than white Americans.[23] Needless to say, those who attribute racial and ethnic disparities in outcomes to racism do not have compelling answers for why these groups seem to do so well in America while other similarly hued groups do less well.

How did we get here—to a place where our discourse around race is so blatantly at odds with reality?

And why does it matter?

One reason it matters is that white people are increasingly struggling with social dysfunctions. In recent years, there has been a dramatic increase among white Americans in what Nobel Prize–winning economist Angus Deaton and his wife and fellow economist Anne Case have categorized as "deaths of despair" (suicides, drug overdoses), concentrated particularly among middle-aged white Americans.[24]

Whites suffer from downward economic mobility, declining fertility (excluding Asians, they have the lowest average fertility of any major ethnic group in America),[25] rising drug addiction and depression, and narrowing opportunities, all piled onto a false presumption of privilege and combined with the general collapse of socialization that Harvard sociologist Robert Putnam describes in *Bowling Alone*.

## The Flight from White

Additionally, if whiteness is an advantage, it is strange that so many whites have been clamoring to obtain a non-white identity. Journalist and commentator Steve Sailer has referred to this as "the flight from white."[26] The number of Hispanics identifying solely as "white" dropped by almost 53 percent between the 2010 and 2020 censuses.[27] Hispanics have realized that whiteness is stigmatized and disadvantaged, whereas a multicultural identity is sacralized.

Likewise, the Native American population ballooned from 5.3 million to 9.7 million between 2010 and 2020.[28] That amounted to almost 3 percent of the American population, compared to 0.4 percent in 1970. This is not due to a Native American fertility explosion but primarily to an explosion of benefits, both formal and informal, for identifying as Native American and penalties for being white.

Some of these changes may reflect how questions on the census were asked, but much of it reflects the increasing cultural and legal advantages to being classed as an ethnic minority. As one scholar who has studied white-to-native race-shifting put it, "These people are not fleeing from political and social persecution, but from whiteness," with race-shifters associating whiteness with "racial and cultural emptiness."[29] Such feelings arise from a broader cultural zeitgeist and messaging.

This has long been a trend. Identifying as Native American for purposes of education and employment is a huge advantage, regardless of the other disadvantages you might experience. And for many, obtaining that advantage is easier than it might seem. To enjoy the benefits of Cherokee tribal enrollment, for example, you need to be of only one sixty-fourth Cherokee descent. If white supremacy actually reigned in America, this would be laughable. In days when it did reign, "Aryans" from India claimed whiteness before the Supreme Court, while many light-skinned African Americans looked to "pass" as white (captured in non-fiction books and novels such as James Weldon Johnson's 1912 *Autobiography of an Ex-Colored Man*).

This change in racial attitudes is happening amid a breathtaking demographic transformation. As of 2020, nearly 53 percent of Americans under the age of eighteen were "minorities."[30] Within twenty years, whites are projected to be a minority in America and one older than most other racial groups on average.[31] America's youth figures to be heavily multiracial and multicultural. California has long been held up as the future, and there just 23 percent of children are white.[32] As people who, for better or worse, are soon to be just another patch in the American quilt, whites need to be able to speak up unapologetically for their own rights.

Those such as this author who criticize America's strategy of diversity do not hate America's diverse populations. Accusing us of such hatred is a classic example of the composition fallacy, whereby we mistakenly generalize from the part to the whole or vice-versa.

Race and ethnicity scholar Eric Kaufmann offers examples of this fallacy, such as: because I believe "immigration should be controlled for the benefit of the country," then I believe "Raul, an immigrant, should be prevented from entering the country because he will harm it." Or if I believe that "America's ethnic majority should not decline too rapidly because it is part of the nation's identity," then I must also believe "Indira, an ethnic minority, is not fully American.

. . . Progressives thus collapse a complex discussion about collective entities into a debate about the treatment of individuals," Kaufmann writes in *City Journal*.[33]

I have lived in India and spent additional years of my life traveling in the developing world, doing everything from volunteering for weeks at a Tanzanian orphanage to hobnobbing with rural indigenous Bolivians. That I am criticizing the way America has sacralized diversity does not mean I hate the diverse groups of people who call themselves Americans. It means I hate the social dynamics we are creating through anti-white discrimination, unfettered immigration, and a declining focus on cultural assimilation.

## Some Final Thoughts

For middle-class and working-class whites, and even for an increasing number of upper-class whites, this anti-white discrimination and racism is deadly—we might even say the problems it causes are intersectional. Anti-white racism interacts with lower incomes, unsafe neighborhoods, or an inability to send one's kids to a good school (or all of the above) to create a toxic brew.

And while confrontation around these issues is sometimes unpleasant, cowardly avoidance is far more dangerous. If we continue to let the Left engage in continuous and rampant race baiting without resistance, tensions will increase until they ultimately boil over, likely with terrible consequences. To combat anti-white discrimination is not something we should do for whites but for all Americans, because if we don't change the course we are on, we are all going to suffer.

To borrow a Cold War analogy, the only way we will achieve peace in our current era of racial strife is for people of every race to adopt a policy of Mutually Assured Destruction (MAD). Simply put, the Left must learn that when they use racist tactics, the blowback will be fierce, immediate, and extremely painful for them.

In writing this book, I have attempted to set an example of what the Ancient Greeks called *parrhesia*, or speaking the truth candidly for the common good, even at personal risk—a danger of taking on a highly charged subject about which Americans of all political stripes may have decided views.

But as Ambrose Redmoon observed, "Courage is not the absence of fear, but the judgment that something else is more important than fear." This subject is indeed more important than our fear of discussing it, for the future of both ourselves and our country is on the line.

And with that, let's get down to business.

# CHAPTER 2

# Civil Wrongs

*"Experience should teach us to be most on our guard to pro-tect liberty when the government's purposes are beneficent. Men born to freedom are naturally alert to repel invasion of their liberty by evil-minded rulers. The greatest dangers to liberty lurk in insidious encroachment by men of zeal, well-meaning but without understanding."*

—Justice Louis Brandeis, dissent in
*Olmstead v. United States*

*"I will eat my hat if anyone can find language which pro-vides that an employer will have to hire on the basis of per-centage or quota related to color, race, religion or national origin."*

—Senator Hubert Humphrey, during the debate over
the Civil Rights Act of 1964

From small beginnings, great mischief can grow. Affirmative action began in 1965 under President Lyndon Johnson with the seemingly harmless Executive Order 11246, which required all contractors that conducted more than $10,000 worth of business with the government to "take affirmative action to ensure that applicants are employed and that employees are treated during employment, without regard to their race, color, religion, sex or national origin."[1] From this small statement, an understandable reaction against racial discrimination in some U.S. unions at the time, a giant civil rights bureaucracy grew—ironically one that very much required employers to give special weight to just those characteristics.

In 1978, a sharply divided Supreme Court (the nine justices issued six separate opinions) ruled in the case of *Regents of the University of California v. Bakke* that, while specific racial quotas for university admissions were impermissible, it was permissible to use race as a factor in admissions in so-called affirmative action policies.

This would later be more firmly but narrowly upheld in 2003 in *Grutter v. Bollinger* before finally being overturned in 2023 by the Court in *Students for Fair Admissions v. Harvard.*

While some are familiar with the original *Bakke* case as a generality, far fewer are familiar with the underlying facts or what happened to the plaintiff Bakke, and those who were admitted in his place, afterward. Their story is worth telling because it reveals so much about the diversity regime that has ruled us for many decades and how it discriminates against white Americans—and the consequences that discrimination causes for society as a whole. Until Justice Lewis Powell provided the key vote for it in *Bakke*, nobody realized that diversity could be a compelling state interest. After he did, ensuring the magic blessings of diversity (which, as we will see later, inevitably means, in practice, anti-white discrimination) became a necessity for many institutions.

Even Republican politicians, in the wake of the *Bakke* case, embraced the benefits of diversity. The phrase "diversity is our strength" appears to have originated with former vice president Dan Quayle, who used it in the wake of the deadly Los Angeles riots in the early 1990s: "I was asked many times in Japan about the recent events in Los Angeles," Quayle said. "From the perspective of many Japanese, the ethnic diversity of our culture is a weakness compared to their homogeneous society. I begged to differ with my hosts. I explained that our diversity is our strength."[2]

Alan Bakke, and other whites harmed by America's diversity ideology, might not agree. Bakke was a Vietnam combat veteran and engineer in his early thirties who had graduated from the University of Minnesota. Bakke's Medical College Admissions Test (MCAT) scores were outstanding: 97th percentile in scientific knowledge, 96th percentile in verbal, 94th percentile in quantitative, and 72nd percentile in general knowledge. His faculty interviewer at the University of California at Davis thought he was "a well-qualified candidate . . . a very desirable applicant, and I shall so recommend him."[3]

Nonetheless, Bakke was rejected by UC-Davis in favor of non-white applicants with far inferior credentials. Bakke eventually sued UC Davis and was ultimately ordered admitted by the courts. Vicious protests greeted his arrival at medical school, and Bakke refused to grant press interviews. He eventually became an anesthesiologist working in his home state of Minnesota at the Mayo Clinic, where he presumably had a respected professional career (if he had fallen short, some liberal journalist surely would have discovered it).

One of the students who took Bakke's place at UC-Davis Medical School in the year he was originally rejected was Patrick Chavis. Indeed, Chavis was often cited in media accounts as *the* student who took Bakke's place. Chavis's grades and test scores (generally in the 35th percentile nationally) were vastly lower than Bakke's.[4]

In the years after his graduation, Chavis became something of a medical celebrity. In 1996, Senator Ted Kennedy cited him as a "perfect example" of how affirmative action worked, a statement that was far more apt than Kennedy was aware.[5] He received a glowing 10-page profile and a cover appearance in *New York Times Magazine*, among write-ups in many other publications, highlighting his work as an obstetrician delivering thousands of babies (and performing thousands of abortions) in an "underserved community"[6] in the Los Angeles area.

Shortly after these write-ups appeared, the bloom came off of Chavis's rose. Having expanded his practice into liposuction for women looking to lose weight postpartum, in 1998, the Medical Board of California suspended his license for "gross negligence, incompetence and repeated negligent acts." It cited his "inability to perform some of the most basic duties required of a physician."[7] He was sued for malpractice by at least twenty-one patients and their families, at least one of whom died after Dr. Chavis physically abandoned her after a failed liposuction procedure. In 2002, Chavis was killed in what prosecutors described as a presumed failed attempted carjacking in Hawthorne, California. His assailants were never found.

The fact that *Bakke* has at long last been overturned (at least on paper) after almost half a century does not change its status as an exemplar of the regime we live under. Even today, universities and businesses are plotting to get around the *Students for Fair Admissions* decision or obey the letter of the law while violating its spirit. *Bakke*'s underlying logic was fiercely endorsed not only by every one of the Court's three liberal justices who dissented in *Students for Fair Admissions,* but by the media, every Democratic leader of Congress, and the president, as well as in impassioned statements by Barack and Michelle Obama, among many others. Virtually nobody supported *Students for Fair Admissions* except for American voters. Even in liberal California, the movement to restore affirmative action to universities (where it had been banned) went down to a 57–42 percent defeat, despite having the endorsement of almost every Democratic politician and despite outspending its opposition overwhelmingly.[8]

Leading universities (including Harvard, one of the defendants in *Students for Fair Admissions*) issued public statements in the immediate wake of the decision explaining how they intended to get around its substance, something they had been planning in recent years by removing objective standards such as test scores and class ranks from admissions consideration. Absent a conservative Supreme Court that was the product of a hotly contested 2016 election, *Bakke* would still be the law of the land.

The *Bakke* case is a stark example of the stakes of our current debates over anti-white discrimination. The discrimination against Bakke did not just hurt him personally but society as a whole, including the host of largely minority women who were victims of the incompetence of Dr. Chavis. Removing anti-white discrimination can literally be a matter of life and death. That is the system the Left passionately defends today.

## Understanding the Civil Rights Regime

Before we examine the individual subject areas of anti-white discrimination, it is useful first to understand our overall civil rights regime, of which the affirmative action decision in *Bakke* was a part, that grew out of the Civil Rights Act of 1964. This regime provides the intellectual superstructure that overarches many of the anti-white developments we see in American life.

Our current anti-white civil rights law rests on three pillars, which will be discussed at greater length below:

1. Affirmative action
2. Disparate impact
3. The removal of free association.

In developing my analysis, I am particularly indebted to my Claremont colleague Christopher Caldwell, whose magisterial book *The Age of Entitlement* sees our "Constitution of 1964," enshrined in the Civil Rights Act, as, however well-intentioned, essentially canceling many of the fundamental rights and liberties guaranteed to Americans by our original Constitution of 1789.[9]

Caldwell writes: "Civil rights ideology, especially when it hardened into a body of legislation, became, most unexpectedly, the model for an entirely new system of constantly churning political reform."[10] We are still in the midst of that "constantly churning political reform" and will continue to be until we fundamentally re-center our civil rights laws. As Caldwell noted, the law, meant to target "Southern bigots," eventually put many if not most American institutions at risk for discrimination lawsuits.[11]

Caldwell sees the two constitutions as frequently incompatible, a reality that has worsened with each new civil rights law that has passed, or, more notably, with each new interpretation of the law from activist bureaucracy and judges. The Civil Rights Act of 1964 banned discrimination in the voting booth, in public schools, in restaurants, and other similar public facilities. But more important, it built out a large supervisory apparatus with increasing power to regulate companies, organizations—anyone who potentially fell afoul of its dictates.

It created an army of bureaucrats, lawyers, and others who became its enforcement arm. And when expanded into the Fair Housing Act of 1968, it increasingly controlled even the minutiae of how and where Americans lived. Not for nothing, as Caldwell notes, did Yale's great civil rights historian C. Vann Woodward refer to the civil rights acts as America's second Reconstruction.[12]

This disparate impact, if you will, of the civil rights laws themselves is increasingly visible throughout American society. Between 2007 and 2016, non-whites gained ten million jobs while whites lost seven hundred thousand, a trend that only temporarily reversed itself under Trump before resuming under Biden. This distribution of employment was no accident but a reflection of the fundamental power dynamics of the new America: "You could see rainbow flags flying alongside Black Lives Matter posters in rich and academic neighborhoods," writes Caldwell. "The antithesis between 'the regime' and 'the street' was fading." The losers from these arrangements were whites, and in particular white men, whom the laws were technically not designed to hurt, but as they helped everyone else, Caldwell argues, it amounted to the same thing.[13]

Civil rights law also served the instrumental purpose of demoralizing whites, the effects of which we will see in later chapters: "They fell asleep thinking of themselves as the people who build the country and woke up to find themselves occupying the bottom rung of an official hierarchy of races," says Caldwell.[14] Indeed, in this new regime, whites are almost beneath mention: "Twenty-first-century suburban whites were not protagonists of the nation's moral narrative. Indeed, they barely figured in it."[15]

Alan Bakke would heartily agree.

## The Two Constitutions

Caldwell believes, as does this author, that much of our current struggle is over a question of which of our constitutions will ultimately reign supreme. Our struggle against anti-minority racism, represented in the Constitution of 1964, has swallowed every other consideration of what makes a successful society.

This presents challenges for me, for while racism is important and anti-white racism is the all-but-official ideology of our ruling regime, highlighting it so prominently arguably reinforces the pre-eminence of racism and discrimination in determining what constitutes good government.

Racial discrimination is a serious problem in any society, but there are many sins committed by our government (for example, fiscal profligacy, foreign military adventurism, a failure to educate its citizens, a failure to keep citizens safe from criminals) that are, in this author's opinion, even worse than presiding over unequal racial outcomes. Unfortunately, because America has put "racism" at the center of our legal regime, whites labor under a profound disability.

## Disparate Impact

Along with affirmative action, the demerits of which were so clearly demonstrated in the *Bakke* case, disparate impact has been a pillar of the anti-white discrimination enforced in American civil rights law.

Disparate impact was born in a 1971 Supreme Court ruling, *Griggs v. Duke Power*.[16] While little known by the public, almost no ruling has enabled more anti-white discrimination than *Griggs*. It arose in response to the actions of Duke Power, a large North Carolina–based company that had enacted IQ and mechanical aptitude tests as part of an assessment for employee advancement.

No racial component to this test was alleged, nor was evidence offered that it had been done with an intent to discriminate by race. Yet white employees passed it at a substantially higher rate than black employees. The Supreme Court ruled this to be a violation of the Civil Rights Act and in doing so introduced the concept of "disparate impact" into U.S. law, declaring that a process with an outcome that varied by race could potentially be illegal even if no racial discrimination was intended.

It was ultimately up to the party in question to prove a business necessity or similar compelling interest in using the test. Until then, they were guilty until proven innocent. Today, disparate impact theory affects not just employment law, but housing policy, education, and criminal background and credit checks, discriminating against whites in almost every instance.

Even the very liberal Supreme Court of that time soon realized that *Griggs* had gone too far. In 1989, they effectively gutted *Griggs* in *Wards Cove Packing Company v. Atonio*, ruling that only a "business justification"[17] was needed to avoid running afoul of disparate impact law, a relatively easy thing to demonstrate. But in 1991, establishment Republican President George H. W. Bush, in a shameful and short-sighted political capitulation, effectively reversed *Wards Cove* in a deal with Democrats, putting the burden of proof back on employers.[18]

As conservative civil rights activist (and then Department of Justice employee) Roger Clegg later wrote, "The reaction to the Supreme Court's decisions was predictable and typified the later debate: shrill condemnation from civil rights groups followed with a tentative defense by the Bush administration."[19] Conservatives in the administration knew how bad overturning *Wards Cove* was, but they were stymied by political pressures and, ultimately, the cowardice of political leadership.

Disparate impact is how the state enforces anti-white discrimination, as Gail Heriot, a politically independent member of the U.S. Commission on Civil Rights, noted in an article, "Title VII Disparate Impact Liability Makes Virtually Everything Presumptively Illegal."[20] As a result, companies and other private entities are essentially at the mercy of the whims of the Civil Rights Division of the Department of Justice, an institution that is politically liberal under Republican presidents and politically radical under Democratic presidents (since virtually all career attorneys in the division are on the Left to Far Left).

It wasn't supposed to be this way. Based on her detailed analysis of the debates that surrounded the legislation, Heriot claims it is "virtually certain"[21] that disparate impact would not have been endorsed by the sponsors of the 1964 Civil Rights Act. In fact, the Senate floor managers explicitly committed that their legislation would not stop employment tests, the very item at issue in *Griggs*. But raw politics often does not care about legislative intent.

As with the Hart-Celler immigration legislation in 1965 (which we will discuss later) and any number of other social issues, those who were mocked brutally by the political and journalistic establishment for worrying about the extent or pace of change proposed under the Civil Rights Act were ultimately vindicated. It is almost as if there is a pattern here.

This illustrates a key aspect of contemporary civil rights law. In addition to the inherent problems within the legislation itself,

over the years the liberal bureaucracy has dramatically expanded its
scope, often without congressional authorization, and, with the help
of activist judges, has even subverted the clear intent and language of
the Civil Rights Act, often in service of an anti-white agenda.

As Heriot noted bluntly, "Members of the 88th Congress tried
much harder than they should have needed to in order to ensure they
would not be misunderstood. But in establishing disparate impact
liability, the EEOC and the *Griggs* Court saw to it those efforts
would be for naught."[22]

Disparate impact has been used exhaustively to deprive whites
of jobs they would have otherwise earned. Much of this happens
not overtly, but due to the ubiquitous looming threat of a disparate
impact lawsuit. Companies simply won't try to implement policies
that might inadvertently give an advantage to whites, even if there
is a compelling non-racial rationale for their use. Most companies,
above all, loathe legal risk. The internet is filled with websites advis-
ing employers on how to avoid *unintentional* disparate impact in
their employment practices.[23]

As the late Justice Thurgood Marshall wrote in a different context, "The value of the sword of Damocles is that it hangs—not that
it drops."[24]

## Freedom of Association

Beyond affirmative action and disparate impact, the third pillar of
modern anti-white civil rights laws has been the removal of freedom
of association, a bulwark of America's original Constitution, as a
legally valid concept. As Caldwell notes in *The Age of Entitlement*,
"Eliminating freedom of association from the Constitution changed
everything."[25]

There are two compelling rights at stake concerning freedom of
association—first, the right of people to obtain goods and services,
and second, the right of a business or individual to choose who he or

she wants as customers, just as any customer is free to choose what businesses he or she wants to patronize.

With respect to public goods and services, few would dispute that the government must provide them on an equal basis to all Americans. But with private businesses, the situation is more complicated, something the libertarian-leaning Senator Rand Paul tried to express in 2014: "I don't like the idea of telling private business owners—I abhor racism. . . . I do believe in private ownership."[26] Paul later hedged his remarks in the wake of attacks from the Left.

In making this fundamental distinction between the public and private spheres, Paul was following the lead of the late political philosopher Leo Strauss, himself a Jewish refugee from Nazism, who noted the dangers of attacking private "discrimination." According to Strauss, this would entail "The abolition of the private sphere, the denial of the difference between the state and society, in a word, the destruction of liberal society."[27] This is just what our civil rights regime has done.

In the well-known case of the Colorado baker who refused to bake a cake for a gay wedding (while happily serving gay customers who asked for cakes that didn't violate his religious beliefs), there were any number of other local bakers who would have been happy to serve the gay couple in question. In fact, the business owner was specifically targeted for his deeply held religious views. Under our current legal regime, the victims are often effectively perpetrators.

One possible solution would be to create a legal framework that preserves a strong right for all Americans to obtain goods and services while requiring someone to show that the failure of a particular provider to offer goods and services to a particular customer was both intentionally discriminatory AND placed an undue burden on a consumer. This would do wonders in terms of restoring freedom of association and eliminating frivolous lawsuits. Until then, expect the plaintiffs' bar to get rich at the expense of any sufficiently unsympathetic white defendant.

## Penumbras and Emanations

While Caldwell sees the Civil Rights Act of 1964 as the major culprit behind this new constitution, political scientist Richard Hanania, the president of the Center for the Study of Partisanship and Ideology, and others see subsequent meddling by diversity bureaucrats as perhaps an even larger problem.

The Department of Justice's civil rights division has grown overwhelmingly over the years, as have the number of people who claim, genuinely or dubiously, to belong to a protected class. In numerous cases, from Raquel Saraswati[28] to Rachel Dolezal to Senator Elizabeth Warren, white people have attempted to claim minority identities to get bonus points in our society. In the past, when society was structurally racist in the opposite direction, numerous people, from African Americans to Hispanics to Asians, attempted to pass for white. Today, attempts to pass for another race invariably go in the opposite direction.

Hanania writes, "For so many public intellectuals and politicians to be anti-woke but indifferent to civil rights law struck me as similar to worrying about global warming but not bothering to know anything about energy policy."[29]

Hanania argues that much of the diversity regime we have today is a function of DOJ rulings and procedures set decades ago, not simply the Civil Rights Act of 1964. "The triumph of this ideology over the last ten years in public discourse is simply culture catching up to law."[30]

He details how, in 2019, the Equal Employment Opportunity Commission (EEOC) sued the retail store chain Dollar General for doing criminal background checks (these had a disproportionate effect on black applicants). The government eventually settled for $6 million. He also notes how the Obama administration punished schools that had differential rates of punishment for black and white students, ignoring the fact that these reflected different underlying patterns of behavior.[31] The latter policy was instrumental in the failure to discipline and ultimately prosecute a Florida teen named Trayvon Martin for a theft he committed. Martin would later be shot and killed after an encounter with neighborhood watch volunteer George Zimmerman and his family would portray him as an innocent victim. It was out of this incident that the Black Lives Matter movement first arose.

Modern governmental interpretation of the Civil Rights Act also created the concept of a "hostile work environment," which gave birth to the modern corporate HR department. As Eugene Volokh of UCLA Law School has noted, the growth of these departments can be traced directly to federal race and gender policies.[32]

In 1955, fewer than 30 percent of organizations had HR offices, but by 1985, this had grown to 70 percent. Forty percent had an affirmative action office in 1985, up from zero in 1967.[33]

Soon enough, anti-white discrimination was entrenched. When the Reagan administration attempted to weaken the enforcement of these laws, they were dismayed to find the business community opposing them. The new reality had already been baked in by the administrative state and activist judges. This is a problem that still plagues us.

The Trump administration thought about undoing disparate impact but didn't even approach the issue until early January 2021, long after it should have been addressed.[34] The next GOP president, whoever it may be, should have such reforms on the front burner.

## Judicial Review: The Enforcers

Rules and procedures are only useful if they have a powerful enforcement arm.

This is why the final necessary product of the civil rights apparatus is control of the judiciary. It's why the Left has campaigned so ferociously to control the judiciary, the governmental branch they used to remake society before the Trump administration's appointments gave us a solidly right-leaning Supreme Court for the first time in living memory. It's why even at the top levels of their party (Joe Biden declined to disavow it during his campaign), the Democrats have legitimized "packing the Supreme Court," a tool so radical that it was dramatically and overwhelmingly rejected by Democrats in the 1930s, even when FDR was demanding it and they had a 3–1 supermajority in Congress.

To enforce the civil rights regime's rules against white Americans, one needs compliant judges. Little wonder, then, that President Biden's remaking of the judicial branch has been one of the starkest examples of anti-white racism in recent policymaking. The corruption is powerful because the judiciary increasingly acts as a super-legislature, and left-wing judges are entirely unmoored from the Constitution.

While Biden was certainly not the first president, formally or informally, to appoint someone to the court based on demographics, his efforts went far beyond even the racial tokenism of Bill Clinton and Barack Obama to an entirely new level of cynicism.

Most egregious was his pledge, casually accepted at the time with little pushback except from a few quarters of the Right, to appoint a black woman to the Supreme Court. In doing so, he was proposing to elevate, to arguably the most powerful position in our government outside of the presidency, someone from a group that made up less than 2 percent of lawyers overall, and an even smaller percentage of truly outstanding attorneys that ought to be considered for such an honor.

Most people think of affirmative action as a "thumb on the scale," but in reality, it's more like a ton of bricks, particularly at the elite level. In one recent cohort, just 29 African Americans scored over 170 on the LSAT, an average score for a top ten law school (note that this average itself is depressed by affirmative action admissions). In that same year, more than 1,900 white applicants received this 170+ score, a more than 60–1 ratio.[35] (Of course, for a Supreme

Court justice, you would want someone of far higher acuity than that of just an "average" student at a top law school.)

Assume those scores are divided equally among men and women, and you are looking at perhaps fourteen black women per year with the performance to even be considered average students at a top ten law school, much less a standout at the level of a Supreme Court justice. Little wonder that one judge nominated by Biden was exposed as not knowing, among other things, what Article II and Article V of the Constitution were—which should be elementary for any law student, much less someone seeking to become a federal judge.[36]

Yet of the ninety-seven federal judges Biden approved during the first two years of his term, just five were white men (a group that, in addition to scoring highly, makes up 50 percent of total attorneys), while twenty-two were black women.[37] So roughly 23 percent of Biden's judges were coming from a group that (generously) might have had 0.5 percent of the highly qualified candidates for the position.

Such extreme discrimination cannot even be excused on the grounds of political expedience or representation of one's electoral coalition (neither of which, to be clear, are good reasons to racially discriminate). Biden's coalition of voters in 2020 was made up of approximately 27 percent white men, more than five times the rate that he selected to be judges in the first two years of his term.[38]

Even white women, who fared "better," comprised 29 percent of Biden's voters but just 23 percent of his judges. And 11 percent of federal judges are African American, a number representing just 4.5 percent of the legal profession, suggesting blacks are 2.5 times overrepresented among judges as compared to their representation as lawyers—and that's not even taking into account judge quality and legal achievements.[39] President Trump, by contrast, had a percentage of minority judges that was almost identical to the percentage of minority voters in his electoral coalition.

Meanwhile, the standards that would normally be used for judicial selection—scholarly output (virtually no minority women are listed among the most cited law professors), big law firm partnership (less than 2 percent were black and Latina women despite aggressive affirmative action)—were nowhere to be found. And this shows up in decisions.

Justice Sonia Sotomayor clearly does not understand some basic distinctions between state and federal powers.[40] In her unimpressive dissent in *Students for Fair Admissions*, Judge Ketanji Brown Jackson made basic errors of fact and had an interpretation that was devoid of legal reasoning and history at times, looking silly in comparison to Clarence Thomas's evisceration of her position.[41]

Biden's affirmative action judiciary was a disaster for the country, but not for Biden—since he was most concerned with finding judges who would maintain America's anti-white legal edifice. And these judges judge racially, mistaking their own political preferences for the Constitution.

Nowhere was this more apparent than in Biden's selection of Nancy Abudu for the 11th Circuit Court of Appeals. Abudu came directly from a career at the Southern Poverty Law Center (SPLC), a far-left group that has made a career out of smearing conservatives and attacking whites who will not toe the leftist line on racial matters. Not for nothing did *National Review* refer to Abudu as a "concession to the far left." More than fifty prominent individuals and groups signed a letter opposing her nomination, arguing that Abudu works "for a disreputable organization that has no business being a feeder for positions to any judicial office—not even of a traffic court—let alone the second highest court system in the United States. She is a political activist not a jurist and is unfit to serve at the federal appellate level."[42]

According to the Family Research Council, "Senator Ted Cruz was one of the most vocal critics of Abudu, drilling her on her record, highlighting her time at the SPLC *and* the ACLU: 'You've never served as a judge. You've spent your entire life as an advocate and as an advocate on the extreme left. There has been a pattern of nominee after nominee that had been extreme zealots. But I have to say, your nomination, when I look at your record, I find deeply concerning. The Southern Poverty Law Center is a hateful and extreme place. And their hate, among other things, has led to horrific violence.'"[43]

"I can't believe you've been nominated for this position," Senator Josh Hawley said. "I can't believe that the president of the United States would nominate someone from this organization with this record. And I can't believe that you would sit here today and refuse to condemn this hateful, frankly violent rhetoric from this organization with this record. It's astounding to me."[44]

Nonetheless, on a party-line vote, Abudu was confirmed to the court of appeals. What Hawley and Cruz viewed as an obvious demerit in Abudu's ability to judge impartially, Biden and the Democrats viewed as an asset. The president was looking for reliable troops to entrench a racial caste system in America, not dispassionate fair-minded jurists.

The Left has made it clear that if the courts lack their preferred ethnic composition, it means they may not be legitimate. "Trump's appointments have made the federal judiciary less diverse. And our research as scholars of judicial politics suggests that could erode the legitimacy of the judicial system," wrote the authors of one influential paper.[45] Having judges that follow the Constitution is strictly suckers' talk. Having judges with the right amount of melanin is the new name of the game.

The paper's authors go on to note that this "could damage the court's ability to serve its function as a neutral arbiter of the law in American politics and society."[46] In other words, if you aren't the right race, you can't arbitrate about race. This is the legal equivalent of saying, "Nice courts, it would be a shame if something happened to them." Such intellectual mafiosi tactics increasingly characterize the legal Left today. The civil rights behemoth is at the center of its power, and anyone who threatens its authority can expect a ferocious challenge.

Having set the stage by discussing the legal framework that undergirds anti-white power, we will next explore how that framework and other assets have been used to discriminate against and punish white Americans in many different areas of society.

# CHAPTER 3

# Crime and Punishment

*"Show me the man, and I will find you the crime."*
—Lavrentiy Beria, head of Stalin's secret police

*"Every assistant D.A. in the Bronx, from the youngest Italian just out of St. John's law to the oldest Irish bureau chief . . . shared Captain Ahab's Mania for the Great White Defendant. For a start, it was not pleasant to go through life telling yourself, 'What I do for a living is, I pack blacks and Latins off to jail.'"*
—Tom Wolfe, *Bonfire of The Vanities*

On August 23, 2020, several officers in Kenosha, Wisconsin, a small city on the banks of Lake Michigan situated almost equidistantly between Chicago and Milwaukee, went to serve an arrest warrant on a man named Jacob Blake after his girlfriend and the mother of his children, who had recently taken out a restraining order against him, called the police and let them know Blake was trespassing and hassling her.

As it turned out, Blake had taken his girlfriend's car (and their children) without permission. In addition to the restraining order, police arriving on the scene knew Blake had already had warrants served against him for sexual assault in July and for trespassing and disorderly conduct in May. As they attempted to serve the warrants, Blake violently resisted, continuing to fight even after being Tased twice and putting one of the officers in a headlock. He finally lunged at police with a knife, at which point he was shot seven times by Rusten Sheskey, a white police officer on the scene, paralyzing him partially from the waist down.[1]

Despite Blake having open warrants for his arrest (a fact known to the officers) and having on camera clearly resisted arrest and lunged with a knife at the officers, under political pressure, prosecutors seriously considered charging Officer Sheskey with a crime (before declining to do so).[2]

Blake's family then hired attorney Benjamin Crump, a notorious lawyer in many racially-charged cases who had previously worked with, among others, the families of Trayvon Martin and Michael Brown (in Martin's case, his killer was acquitted, and in Brown's case, the police officer accused of murdering him was not even charged and later completely exonerated by Obama's Justice Department though not before his life and career had been ruined).[3] By October 2021, even Biden's radical DOJ declined to charge Sheskey, knowing there was no case against him. Yet this did not stop the anti-white and anti-police rhetoric from flowing freely.

In the immediate aftermath of the shooting, protests erupted. These quickly turned violent, and police cars were damaged. That night, there were violent riots as misinformation spread throughout the community. A car dealership was set on fire along with the front of the local courthouse and several other buildings. The next day, the governor, a Democrat, called out the National Guard, rail service into Kenosha was suspended, and freeway exits were closed. The following day, rioters attempted to attack the police station and burn down a gas station and several other buildings. Overall, the rioting saw forty businesses destroyed and more than one hundred damaged.[4] The story quickly went national. The WNBA canceled their games over multiple days in protest.[5] Improbably, Jacob Blake, sexual assaulter and thug, had become yet another victim of "racist policing."

Within a day, a "Kenosha Guard" Facebook page, started by a former Kenosha alderman, arose, calling on residents to protect property and businesses from rioters. After a little more than a day, they'd accumulated five thousand names. The next day, rioters repeatedly attempted to breach the courthouse and the protest became even more violent.[6]

That night, a seventeen-year-old white boy from just over the state line in Illinois named Kyle Rittenhouse appeared on the scene. Rittenhouse, who would later say in an interview with Tucker Carlson that he supported the BLM movement and peaceful protests, had always admired the police and had joined a public safety cadet program at the age of fifteen. During the riots, he was recorded on video being thanked by police and others for helping to protect property from rioters. He had a first aid kit with him to treat injuries.[7]

Rittenhouse would later shoot three rioters in self-defense as they attacked him while he sought to defend local property. Two of the rioters died and one was injured. Fortunately for Rittenhouse, all of the people he'd shot were white—and all had extensive criminal records.[8] The first rioter killed was a child rapist and violent felon who had spent fourteen years in prison; the second was a domestic abuser with multiple felony convictions. The injured assailant, Gaige Grosskreutz, had been arrested for multiple violent crimes including one against his own grandmother.[9] Even in the current system, the "victims" were hardly sympathetic.

Despite these facts working in his favor, as well as multiple videos of the shooting that clearly showed him acting in self-defense, Rittenhouse was arrested and charged with murder. He was also tarred as a racist and a white supremacist on numerous occasions, including by the president of the United States and numerous celebrities, on the basis of little to no evidence.[10] Perhaps the most egregious slanderer of Rittenhouse was Representative Ayanna Presley, a member of the so-called "Squad" of young left-wing House members, who called Rittenhouse a "white supremacist domestic terrorist" in a tweet that was viewed millions of times.[11] If you're looking for an example of institutional racism, it would be hard to find a better one.

Though advised to stay away by some officials, President Trump toured the riot-affected areas and offered support for the victims. As a result, in 2020, even as Trump's vote went down nationally and in Wisconsin, he became the first Republican to win a majority in Kenosha County since 1972.[12]

The Democrats reacted differently. In her first campaign trip after accepting the nomination to be Biden's running mate, Kamala Harris flew to Kenosha to meet with Blake's legal team and family (Blake joined from the hospital by phone). She called them "incredible" (not the first word one might use to describe the parents of a multiple-time violent felon) and discussed with them various "anti-racist" police training programs she would implement once in office.[13] Needless to say, she did not visit Kyle Rittenhouse and his family, despite Rittenhouse's attempt to protect property and lack of a criminal record. Rittenhouse is white, and Blake is black, and that was what counted.

On November 19, 2021, Kyle Rittenhouse was acquitted of all charges in a trial in Kenosha. Just two days after his acquittal, a black career criminal just out on bail named Darrell Brooks in nearby Waukesha, a heavily white and very Republican suburb of Milwaukee, intentionally drove a car into a Christmas parade, murdering six people and injuring sixty-two others including seventeen children, nine of whom were critically injured. Four of the dead were members of the "Milwaukee Dancing Grannies."[14]

One might have expected a terrorist attack that killed and seriously injured numerous grandmothers and little children during a Christmas parade to receive wall-to-wall coverage (say, more than that of a single black felon lawfully shot by police while in the process of committing another crime—or three white defendants with serious criminal records being shot). But while it certainly received significant media coverage, it was mentioned just a fraction of the times that Kyle Rittenhouse's assailants were. A Google search for "Milwaukee Dancing Grannies" turned up 20,000 results while Gaige Grosskreutz turned up 283,000. Jackson Sparks, the eight-year-old who was killed by Brooks, had 38,700 mentions, while Joseph Rosenbaum, the violent pedophile rapist that Rittenhouse killed, had 127,000. And, of course, all of these were dwarfed by Jacob Blake, who was mentioned in 333,000 Google searches.

Brooks was a supporter of the radical anti-Semitic and anti-white Black Hebrew Israelites group. He had an extensive criminal record, and his Facebook page contained numerous racist posts. Just the day before the attack, he had domestically abused his girlfriend. He had been released on an absurdly low $1,000 bail two weeks before the attack for (surprise) running over a woman. And no wonder: John Chisolm, the Milwaukee County D.A., a George Soros–supported prosecutor who had praised San Francisco D.A. Chesa Boudin (a politician so radical he was recalled by San Franciscans) in his campaign for office, had called for "proportional outcomes"—that is, letting criminals go free if they're of the right race.[15]

Jill Biden arrived in Waukesha on December 15, several weeks after the incident and with far more than honoring the victims on her agenda, as her press office was eager to point out. Meanwhile, after a similarly horrific mass casualty incident that saw a racist white gunman kill ten African Americans in a Buffalo supermarket, the president himself visited within seventy-two hours.[16]

The false specter of white supremacy hung over the Biden administration's response.[17] "It's the reason Biden immediately went to Buffalo after a white mass shooter attacked a predominately black supermarket—yet couldn't find the time to visit the victims and their families, who were predominantly white, of the black assailant of the Waukesha, Wis., parade massacre; some tragedies are more equal than others," observed Adam Coleman, a politically independent African American writer.[18]

But perhaps most damning of all throughout the unrest in Wisconsin was the response of GOP officialdom, who again abandoned their most loyal voters in favor of staying "above the fray." Wisconsin Senator Ron Johnson (generally one of the better GOP senators) issued a joint letter with Democrat Senator Tammy Baldwin urging groups not to "exploit the tragedy that occurred last Sunday in Waukesha for their own political purposes."[19] But this is pure defeatist sophistry. From the pillorying of the white police officer who had shot Jacob Blake to the vilifying of Kyle Rittenhouse to the Waukesha massacre, all of this had been shamelessly used by the Left for political purposes, an orgy of radical anti-white activism riled up by the worst elements in our society. To demand a just accounting for these outrages is not to exploit a tragedy—it is to learn from it in the hopes of avoiding future tragedies.

Far more shameful was the silence of Paul Ryan, the avatar of the GOP establishment, who not much earlier had represented in Congress the district where all of these crimes had taken place. He may have commented on these incidents at some point, but even a fairly extensive search comes up with nothing. Googling Paul Ryan and Waukesha reveals endless political speeches, disinviting Trump, appearing with Mitt Romney—but nothing in the first few dozen results on the racist anti-white murder in his own backyard. Ryan represents the cowardice of the GOP in defending its white voters from overtly racist criminal attacks. As we will see, this was part of an enduring pattern.

## The Numbers on Crime

Perhaps in no area of public policy is anti-whiteness more evident than in our response to crime. Many of the subjects this book will discuss flow directly from the anti-white way that crime is dealt with in America. Anti-white crime leads to white flight, which leads to collapsing schools (school integration peaked in 1988 and has fallen substantially since[20]) and ultimately anti-white racism in education. It's hard to make sense of race relations in America without first grappling with the issue of crime.

Anti-white crime functions as a twenty-first-century *de facto* pogrom, driving whites out of areas where they have lived for decades, even centuries, as can be documented in a large number of cities since the mid–twentieth century, as I will show in the following chapter.

While crimes committed by minorities are frequently minimized or ignored by elites, especially if whites are the victims, any crime or plausible similar activity that can be blamed on whites in which minorities are victims, from "White Hispanic" George Zimmerman to any number of white policemen, is often the subject of wall-to-wall coverage.

Virtually everything that is said in the media and Hollywood about race and crime is incorrect and usually is the exact opposite of the truth.

In fact, the list of prominent fake "hate crimes" in which whites are falsely accused is almost endless. Political scientist Wilfred Reilly investigated more than 350 alleged hate crimes in his 2019 book *Hate Crime Hoax* and determined less than one-third were genuine. Reilly writes that "a huge percentage of the horrific hate crimes cited as evidence of contemporary bigotry are fakes," and adds that these are done specifically in service of leftist narratives about white supremacy and similar issues.[21]

An academic paper that examined the TV show *Law and Order* and its various spinoffs found that African Americans and, to a lesser degree, Hispanics were dramatically underrepresented among criminals versus their proportion in committing real-world crimes. Whites, of course, were substantially over-represented (though to be fair, the study also found that whites were substantially over-represented

among victims).[22] Debuting in 1990, *Law and Order* is the longest-
-running scripted drama in the history of television and has been
profoundly influential on how Americans see crime.

This trend toward desperately looking for white criminals to
both charge and cover in the media has been so pervasive and so
longstanding that the late, brilliant author and cultural critic Tom
Wolfe dubbed it "the hunt for the great white defendant"[23] in his
1987 novel *The Bonfire of the Vanities*. One of the most acclaimed
works of its era, the novel features a New York district attorney,
Abe Weiss, who has the sobriquet "Captain Ahab" because, as Ahab
hunted for the Great White Whale in *Moby-Dick*, Weiss obsessively
searches for "The Great White Defendant."

The Great White Defendant Appears in numerous instances,
whether Kyle Rittenhouse in Kenosha, Jussie Smollett in Chicago
(supposedly attacked by white men shouting, "This is MAGA country!"), or the infamous Duke lacrosse case in 2006, in which white
lacrosse players were baselessly accused of rape by a black woman
and tried and convicted in the media. In that case, the story was so
big, and the prosecutorial misconduct so severe, that the prosecutor
was disbarred.[24]

In a Townhall op-ed, conservative African American columnist
Larry Elder labeled Derek Chauvin, the officer convicted of killing George Floyd, the ultimate great white defendant whose trial
was turned into a morality play in which (according to one news
network) "America's soul is on trial."[25] At least those in America
who mocked Floyd's death were not arrested for committing a hate
crime, as happened in the UK to a group of teenagers who subsequently required police protection from the death threats they
received.[26]

Chauvin was hardly given a fair trial, as we noted in the introduction. Nor was Floyd's case, for all of its attendant publicity, unique.
Edward Bronstein, a white man police arrested after a routine traffic
stop, was non-compliant as police attempted to draw blood and died

under similar circumstances. But with Bronstein, the official cause of death was acute methamphetamine intoxication. Video shows several officers forcing Bronstein down onto a mat as he shouts, "I'll do it willingly! I'll do it willingly, I promise!" At least five officers continue to hold him down.[27] Yet this was a one-day story.

Tony Timpa, a white trucking executive who told officers he had schizophrenia and was off his medications, was killed in a similar way in Dallas, Texas, in 2016, repeatedly calling out, "You're gonna kill me!" as police attempted to restrain him. When he fell unconscious, officers laughed and joked. Timpa's death was ruled a combination of cocaine intoxication and stress of restraint. Video evidence of the killing was not made available for three years, and there was no public outcry. Most of the officers were initially given qualified immunity by the trial court, though litigation is ongoing, and in the wake of the Floyd trial bringing new publicity to the case, $1 million was awarded to Timpa's son, seven years after the event.[28]

These deaths fit a pattern—white defendants in prominent cases are hunted down while the stories of white victims are minimized. African Americans, who represent just 13 percent of the population, are perpetrators of 33 percent of non-fatal violent crimes. In 2021, in the wake of George Floyd's death, blacks made up more than 60 percent of murder offenders, a substantial increase from earlier numbers.[29]

The numbers are far greater for multiple assailant crimes, which are more likely to involve strangers. In these crimes, 43 percent of assailants were black, 38 percent were white, and 16 percent were Hispanic.[30] (Note these numbers were generated before the George Floyd era, when minority crime increased substantially but white crime did not.)

While crime data on interracial stranger homicides is harder to obtain (in part due to the reluctance of many scholars to investigate a sensitive area of criminal justice), one study looking at nine cities found that whites are more likely to be victims of such crimes than perpetrators. In these cities, 74 percent of white victims in stranger homicides were killed by African Americans (60 percent) or Hispanics (14 percent), while for crimes in which the victim was black or Hispanic, just over 10 percent were killed by whites.[31] When the average upstanding citizen worries about crime, he usually isn't worried about being attacked by friends or family. He's worried about strangers, and it's clear from the data that whites in great disproportion are the victims and not the perpetrators of these attacks. Yet the media only focuses on rare instances of the latter.

More recent data, compiled anonymously by a popular online quantitative analyst who goes by the pseudonym "Datahazard" (@ fentasyl) paints a similar picture. Combing through more than five decades of official violent crime statistics, he found blacks at least 9.8 times more likely to commit interracial murder than whites. And this was probably a substantial underestimate due to the limitations of data, which lump in whites with Hispanics, a group that is significantly more crime-involved than whites on average. Since 1968, according to FBI statistics, there have been approximately 193,500 interracial murders, with more than 75 percent of those being white victims of black murderers.[32]

Among women, who are even more likely to be pure victims as opposed to those who may have been murdered as a result of violent two-way conflict, the statistics are even more extreme. More than 85 percent of female victims of interracial murder are white victims of black murderers. And the interracial murder "gap" between white/black and black/white interracial murders has actually dropped substantially from much higher peaks in the mid-1970s.[33] That the number is this low is a function of residential segregation, which keeps populations largely separate. According to Datahazard's calculations, if racial populations were fully integrated, interracial murder numbers for blacks would be as high as sixty-five times the number for whites. Between 1976 and 2007, blacks also committed 98 percent of interracial rape-murders of the elderly and 88 percent of all interracial rape murders, according to the same source, citing data derived from the FBIs uniform crime reports.[34]

## Prison Challenges and Police Violence

The interracial disparities persist once perpetrators are incarcerated. Again, politically correct academia and NGOs have ensured these controversial subjects are rarely studied, but as a 2001 report from the left-wing NGO Human Rights Watch detailed, "both black and white prisoners emphasized the importance placed on racial distinctions in prison. A white prisoner asserted: 'I hate to say this but if you weren't racist when you came to prison more than likely you will be when you leave.'"[35]

An African American prisoner who said he was "relatively oblivious to racial distinctions before entering prison" warned, "When a white man comes to prison, the blacks see him as a target."[36]

Or as one study of prison rape in 2018 put it, "whites proportionally and numerically constitute the largest victim groups. The literature on prison rape in the past few decades have [sic] indicated that whites make up the majority of the rape victims at the hand of black perpetrators."[37]

Despite this, and the fact that, on average, only about ten unarmed African Americans are killed by police each year (a far cry from the thousands per year that liberal activists believe are killed, according to surveys), blacks report record anxiety from police violence.[38] This false and anti-white impression is relentlessly reinforced by journalists and liberal politicians who stoke false fears.

Meanwhile, significant crime trends that target whites go largely ignored. These include "polar bear hunting," in which minority youths (usually African American) attempt to knock out whites randomly on the street with a single sucker punch. The actor Rick Moranis was a victim of one such attack.[39] Visibly observant Jewish whites have been particularly targeted while warnings have gone largely ignored by the mainstream press and the Left.[40]

"Hands up, don't shoot," the slogan that emerged out of the Michael Brown case in Ferguson, Missouri, was a fiction. But when Elon Musk tweeted out this indisputable fact along with the report (agreed to even by Obama's DOJ) that exonerated Officer Darren Wilson, who was accused of murdering Brown, he ultimately deleted his tweet amid a firestorm of protest, with St. Louis's mayor going so far as to quit Twitter.[41] Consider the level of anti-white racism we must have in our society, that the richest man in the world can't even tweet out the truth about a famous crime on a platform he owns.

Of course, such trends are hardly new, and neither are liberal white apologists for black criminal behavior, often aided by nefarious outside forces. As the African American writer and anthropologist Zora Neale Hurston wrote to a friend in 1945,

> Crime in Harlem is rampant and the police are helpless because New Deal–promoted Negro politicians immediately let out a scream that Negroes are being persecuted the minute a Negro thug is arrested. I was there, I know what happened about that race riot in 1936. Mayor LaGuardia and the New Deal gang passed if off as something that happened because the 'poor Negroes were so hungry and downtrodden.' But I happen to know that it was promoted by the Communists and nothing was said about it because they had all pledged to vote for Roosevelt in the 1936 election.[42]

George Floyd had a fatal dose of fentanyl in his system when he died (several times a fatal dose, actually). George Zimmerman was convicted by the media before being correctly acquitted by a jury, perhaps because both eyewitnesses and physical evidence showed that Trayvon Martin was pounding his head into the pavement at the time Zimmerman (a Democrat who voted for Obama) shot him in self-defense. The media's categorization of Zimmerman as a "white Hispanic" was perhaps the most blatant element of anti-white racism around the case.

The media looked at Zimmerman's last name, assumed he was white, and then desperately attempted to manufacture a white versus black narrative. It turned out that Zimmerman had not just a Hispanic mother but Afro-Peruvian heritage. "Let's talk about the elephant in the room. I'm black, okay?" one neighbor of Zimmerman's said, speaking anonymously because she feared a backlash. "There were black boys robbing houses in this neighborhood. That's why George was suspicious of Trayvon Martin."[43] It was a desperate attempt to manufacture an anti-white narrative around Zimmerman that led to his labeling.

Little wonder that the Left's celebration of criminals and excoriation of cops in the wake of George Floyd led to killings and assaults of law enforcement officers, reaching a twenty-five-year high in 2021.[44]

## The Narrative of Guilt

When a case is racially charged and involves an accused minority, even the most famous so-called "exonerations" often turn out to be anything but. The anti-white bias of law enforcement coverage can also be seen in the so-called "Central Park 5," the horrific 1989 violent rape and near-murder of a jogger in Central Park that became one of the most notorious crimes of the last several decades. Five young black men were sentenced to lengthy prison terms (a sentence actively and publicly supported by then-New York City businessman Donald Trump), only to later be "exonerated," while Linda Fairstein, the attorney who prosecuted them, was exiled from polite society.[45]

Fairstein was most recently attacked in the Netflix series *When They See Us*, which focused on the events and was utterly slanted in favor of the defendants.[46]

Many years after the attack, another criminal confessed to the crime with matched DNA evidence, but it was always known that there were other rapists and attackers besides those arrested. The Central Park Five, most of whom confessed to the crime that night and several of whom provided self-incriminating evidence, went free. In what was truly a miscarriage of justice, these five young men (four African Americans and one Hispanic) were collectively paid $41 million by the city of New York.[47]

As conservative commentator Ann Coulter, who studied the case in detail, noted, "What the police had against the Central Park Five were detailed confessions, on videotape, given in the presence of their parents or adult relatives; the deeply incriminating statements of at least a half-dozen of their friends and acquaintances; and the defendants' knowledge of facts about the crime that only the perpetrators would know."[48] There's even a website showing their videotaped confessions and detailing the evidence against them, but the truth is sometimes powerless against the narrative.[49]

It is beyond question that the Central Park Five were involved in "wilding" that night—they'd admitted to randomly attacking eight other people, two of whom were beaten so badly as to be sent to the hospital.

One of those victims, a schoolteacher named John Loughlin, was later described by a police officer who arrived at the scene as "look[ing] like he was dunked in a bucket of blood," after being robbed, assaulted, and temporarily knocked out after being hit in the head with a metal pipe, cracking his skull. The assailants (or possible bystanders) yelled "Whitey" and "F---ing white people," while attempting to prevent his escape.

Nevertheless, the Netflix film *As They See Us* creates a false narrative, inventing a theatrical fantasy in which the Central Park Five were deprived of food and parental contact and forced to confess.[50] Fairstein, who had become a successful crime novelist and who never backed down from the validity of her prosecution, was dropped by her publisher amid the flood of moral outrage that followed the release of *As They See Us*.[51]

The film also ignores incriminating evidence surrounding the possession of an attack weapon. For example, one boy picked up in the park told the cops without prompting that he knew the name of the "murderer," fingering one of the defendants. All of them confessed to attacking the jogger, but none to raping her (though in the context of the crime, all admitted to enough criminal activity to secure a rape conviction).[52]

Two of the defendants independently brought investigators to the precise location where the attack took place. The victim herself, who was so brutally beaten that she had no memory of the crime, believed she'd had multiple assailants and opposed the settlement.[53]

As Coulter put it searingly on the eve of the massive payout, "But now [NYC Mayor Bill] de Blasio, who had run a racially charged campaign to win the mayorship, wants to hold down our legs while the 'Central Park Five' rape us, again."[54]

Or as one detective who worked on the case wrote, "The five of them went to Central Park to beat up people and they ended up with millions of dollars and they're heroes and civil rights icons. . . . It's appalling."[55]

The anti-white nature of the criminal justice system is not just a black-and-white issue. Whites are also victimized, even by groups with very low rates of criminal offenses. In particular, whites have been blamed for anti-Asian hate crimes under the #StopAsianHate hashtag, a charge that constitutes a blood libel. This is supposed to be the result of comments that Trump made about COVID, which allegedly stirred up the antagonism of whites toward Asians.[56]

Interracial violence against Asians is predominantly of the black-on-Asian variety. Yet because acknowledging this would upset the political coalition between black and Asian anti-white racial activists, this truth must be disguised while crime is blamed on right-wing whites. As the *San Francisco Chronicle* documented as early as

2010, 85 percent of the three hundred assaults they examined in San Francisco were black-on-Asian—despite African Americans being just 6 percent of the population and Asian Americans 33 percent.[57]

As I wrote in a 2021 profile of the shameless behavior of Asian-American activists, "Clearly, the much-publicized horrific attacks on Asian Americans, largely at the hands of young African American men, long preceded Donald Trump's administration and obviously have nothing to do with 'white supremacist terrorism.' Community leaders knew it then. They know it now. The pattern hasn't changed."[58]

Yet Princeton professor Anne Cheng wrote in the *New York Times* (without evidence), "This recent onslaught of anti-Asian violence can be partly attributed to our former President, who spoke nonstop of the 'Chinese Virus' and even 'Kung Flu.'"[59] Cheng somehow failed to explain why this rhetoric from Trump would spur blacks (overwhelmingly Democrats) rather than whites to violence, or why the violence spiked especially in Democratic communities rather than Republican ones. Another leading Asian-American activist said during the peak of the #StopAsianHate campaign that "Supporting our Asian community is not about dividing us. This support is for all of us suffering under white supremacy."[60]

Perhaps best exemplifying the mentality among Asian-American leaders was a statement of seventy-two Asian-American community activist organizations condemning the violence: "We are committed to working with Black, Indigenous, Latinx, and Pacific Islander communities for long-term shared vision and solutions to stop violence in all of our communities." Whites were curiously absent from this list, nor did it escape careful readers that in their calls to not "scapegoat any community of color," the scapegoating of whites went unremarked upon.[61]

Tina Tchen, Michelle Obama's former chief of staff and later an apparatchik at the Southern Poverty Law Center, also blamed "white supremacy" for the attacks on Asians.[62] (Ironically, Tchen's own father, who overstayed his visa and was thus in America illegally, had been saved from deportation to China in 1956 by the ultra-conservative Ohio Senator John Bricker, who was white.[63])

Nor was the anti-white blood libel confined to the activist class. Asian-American business leaders, who should have known better, joined the pile-on. Asian-American executives, primarily from the tech world, raised over $20 million and placed a full-page ad in the *Wall Street Journal* denouncing anti-Asian hate crimes. The ad listed the tragic murders of eight people (six of them Asian) in an Atlanta massage parlor in 2021, despite the assailant explicitly denying any racial motive for the murders and no evidence being produced for one. The assailant was a Christian fundamentalist deeply troubled by his sex addiction and its conflict with his religious beliefs.[64] Numerous other Asian-American politicians made statements linking the shootings to Trump's rhetoric, as did many prominent athletes.[65] Marilyn Strickland, a Korean-American congresswoman from Washington State, dismissed the gunman's own account of his motivation, saying he was "making excuses and rebranding it as economic anxiety or sexual addiction."[66]

The same ad declared, "It is critical that we also acknowledge that the violence we are experiencing has been the daily reality for our Black, Latinx, Indigenous and LGBTQ communities."[67] But this isn't objectively true, nor is the strong implication that the group that was left off of the list—whites—is to blame.

The leaders criticized Trump's rhetoric, saying, "Those words were an open invitation to hate and the result has been a 150% rise over the past year in reported hate crimes against the Asian American community"[68]—but there is no evidence this is true. As previously discussed, the majority of street crimes committed against Asian Americans are committed by African Americans. It is important to note that this statement wasn't issued by some marginal far-left activist group but one that represents some of America's most prominent Asian-American business leaders. Evidently, when it comes to racially scapegoating whites, there isn't much difference.

Back in the real world, anti-Asian violence continued, and whites statistically continued to be a small part of the problem on a population-proportion basis. The Rapper YG's song "Meet the Flockers," which celebrates attacking vulnerable Asian Americans and caused an outcry in 2021, was still up on YouTube in 2023.[69] Some communities are held to different standards than others.

"First, you find a house and scope it out," the song instructs. "Find a Chinese neighborhood 'cause they don't believe in bank accounts."[70] Even when Asian American leaders criticized YG's rhetoric, they did not do anything so foolish as to blame the African American community for it. Instead, they blamed the white community. "YG's ignorant and hateful lyrics undermine the momentum the historical Black Lives Matter movement has generated to challenge systems of oppression," said one prominent Asian-American activist.[71] "Systems of oppression," of course, are implicitly built by white people.

As for YG, in 2019, he humiliated a young white kid attending one of his concerts who refused to say, "Fuck Donald Trump," after being brought onstage, calling the kid a racist and causing him to receive online threats.[72] In January 2020, YG was arrested on robbery charges just two days before he was scheduled to perform at the Grammys.[73] It is interesting to note that his substantial criminal record and overt racist rantings didn't prevent him from being featured at the music industry's premier award ceremony.

There have been many notable voices in the Asian-American community pushing back against this narrative, such as Ying Ma, author of *Chinese Girl in the Ghetto*, an autobiographical experience of growing up in Oakland that talks frankly about the realities of black-on-Asian crime and harassment. Another such voice is Melissa Chen, a noted libertarian-leaning pundit. When Alexandria Ocasio-Cortez said of Trump in a Twitter thread that crimes against Asian Americans had been "amplified by the actions of our last President," Chen pointed out that many of the statistics were being inflated by liberal activist groups based on self-reporting. She also pointed out, as I did elsewhere, that the overwhelming growth of these crimes had been in "progressive" cities like San Francisco and New York, not in more conservative cities such as Houston, which also had substantial Asian-American populations.[74]

Chen noted, "How curious is it that using race as a shield (btw China is NOT a race) only serves the CCP's interest to obfuscate the association between the virus and its origins in Wuhan."[75]

## Defining Hate Down

The very concept of a hate crime is prone to anti-white abuse. For example, in 2020, there were a total of 2,871 anti-black hate crimes, according to FBI statistics. During that same time, there were just 869 reported anti-white hate crimes and 279 anti-Asian hate crimes.[76] Yet we know that blacks commit vastly more interracial crimes than whites. While it is theoretically possible that somehow this situation is dramatically reversed for hate crimes, it is much more likely that rules or reporting incentives are being manipulated to punish (presumably white) defendants.

We know, for example, in urban environments, that young black men target Asian-American victims (and to a lesser extent white victims) for crimes because they are seen as easy targets. Are these "hate crimes"? Victims are certainly picked according to their race. But it seems such episodes are rarely categorized as such. Instead, the criteria for what constitutes a "hate crime" ultimately serve the interests only of those in power.

While the category of a hate crime sounds appealing—attacking someone because you hate a group they belong to is a particularly reprehensible act—in reality, it is ripe for abuse. And at the times when hate crime charges are most needed, they often end up being superfluous. Just as I was turning in the initial draft of this book, Robert Bowers was convicted of numerous federal hate crimes charges for the mass murder of eleven congregants at the Tree of Life Synagogue in Pittsburgh.[77] The failure of our justice system is that it took four and a half years to convict someone of crimes that had scores of eyewitnesses—and that it took federal "hate crimes" statutes like "obstruction of free exercise of religious beliefs resulting in a death." The man unquestionably committed murder, for which he should be eligible for the death penalty.

Yet just three months after the death of George Floyd, Cannon Hinnant, a five-year-old white child, was intentionally gunned down without warning by an African American man while riding his bike in front of his siblings. The killer's girlfriend was charged as an accessory after the fact.[78] While the absolutely horrific nature of the crime did ensure it received some notice, it was a small fraction of the attention received by Floyd, even though Floyd was a convicted felon high on drugs and resisting arrest while Hinnant was an innocent young child riding his bike. The shooter was convicted of murder and sentenced to life in prison, but no "hate crime" charges were ever brought nor did the prosecution ever present a motive.

The contrast between the treatments of Cannon Hinnant and George Floyd is as stark an example as you will see that when it comes to white Americans, the criminal system is simply institutionalized injustice.

# CHAPTER 4

# There Goes the Neighborhood

*"Every man's house is his castle."*

—Sir Edward Corke, 1644

*"You know, I want to remind white folks that y'all were running from us—this family with all the values that you've read about. You were running from us. And you're still running."*

—Michelle Obama, 2019[1]

In a 2019 speech celebrating the release of her autobiography, Michelle Obama criticized the white families that had fled her Chicago neighborhood shortly after African American families such as hers arrived.[2]

Michelle Obama grew up in South Shore, a Chicago neighborhood that borders Lake Michigan, just a few short miles from tony Hyde Park, home of the University of Chicago, where she and her husband would make their home before Barack Obama was elected to the presidency.[3]

The story that Michelle Obama tells is a common one: racist whites selfishly fleeing noble desegregation efforts, mortgage redlining denying blacks and other minorities opportunities. And like so many stories we tell about public policy injustices, there is a grain of truth in it. But what this chapter will show is that this is just one narrative about a turbulent era in our history—and not necessarily the most accurate one. However, it's one that has served a left-wing goal of anti-whiteness, used to shake down the white middle class economically while humiliating them socially.

This chapter will give a more complete narrative of America's housing history and take a look at how radical left-wing activists are attempting to control where white people can live even today.

The South Shore of Michelle Obama's youth had a remarkably rapid transformation, going from 96 percent white in 1950 to 94 percent black in 1980. In 1960, just four years before Michelle Obama was born, South Shore was still almost 90 percent white, and by 1970 it was 70 percent black.[4]

Today, South Shore is listed as one of the ten most dangerous neighborhoods in Chicago (itself one of America's most dangerous cities) where, according to one source, "robbery and assault are common [and] murder and gun violence are much higher than the national average."[5] What caused this rapid transformation, and what were its long-term effects?

A fuller picture of South Shore and Michelle Obama's story there was provided by my Claremont colleague William Voegeli in a perceptive 2019 article in *City Journal*. Voegeli recounts the story of Carlo Rotella, the son of immigrants, who lived just a few blocks from Obama. Rotella, who wrote a book about growing up as a white ethnic in South Shore, recounts stories of crimes such as murder, rape, and robbery that were three times more frequent in the South Shore than in an average Chicago neighborhood.

Rotella argues that whites' fear of crime in South Shore "wasn't unfounded, nor was it simply reducible to white people reacting to the arrival of black people." Whites were responding to real events that were making their lives in South Shore harder. But, as Rotella recounts, "the way the story of their departure got told often took

the form of 'enough is enough' after a gunpoint robbery, home invasion, or similar last-straw outrage."[6]

Rotella's memoir highlights a major turning point in 1970, when
Manny Lazar, a beloved local South Shore toy store owner, was
gunned down by a young black male during a robbery. According
to Rotella, this was the "last straw" for many white South Shore
residents.

Voegeli notes that, as "South Shore changed from a white neighborhood to a black one, it also changed from a safe neighborhood to
a dangerous one." Further, as Voegeli explains, racial turnover had
already come to other Chicago neighborhoods in previous decades,
and so white people were aware of a disquieting pattern—rapid
demographic change went hand in hand with higher crime, and as a
result, lower property values. To notice this was simple awareness of
reality, not racism.[7]

Chicago's murder rate of 10.5 per 100,000 residents in 1960
exploded to 28.7 by 1980 and continued to rise from there. While
victims of this crime wave were of every race, the white victims, feeling abandoned by the government, became part of President Nixon's
so-called silent majority pushing for greater law and order in cities.
And no wonder. During that time, Chicago went from 86-plus percent white in 1950 to a white minority in 1980. Today, it is less than
one-third white non-Hispanic.[8]

Nor are urban crime stories like Rotella's limited to Chicago or
to white victims. Civil rights icon Rosa Parks was famously assaulted
by a young African American man in her own home in Detroit. After
eventually being released from prison twenty-six years later, he was
back to committing home invasion crimes elsewhere in Michigan.[9]

Voegeli tells of the more recent "black flight" from Southfield,
Michigan, a formerly middle-class city near Detroit. As poor blacks
from Detroit flooded into Southfield and brought with them various
antisocial behaviors, middle-class blacks moved out. Like white residents decades earlier, some middle-class black Southfield residents

moved out of Southfield, even if that meant selling their homes at a financial loss. Such trends were not limited to metro Detroit. Demographer William Frey at the Brookings Institution noted that the percentage of blacks in "urban cores" in the ten largest cities fell more than 10 percent over a twenty-seven-year period between 1990 and 2017, driven in part by white gentrification in more prosperous cities, and, in part, in less prosperous cities (St. Louis, Detroit, Cleveland, et cetera) by the departure of more affluent African Americans, who fled for the same reasons whites had in previous decades.

Voegeli quotes the late African American economist Walter Williams: "It turns out that blacks, like whites, want better and safer schools for their kids and don't like to be mugged or have their property vandalized."

As for the many commentators who condemned the whites who fled, as Voegeli said, "It would then follow that the white owners of homes and businesses there had a *duty* to stay, risking solvency and safety, for the sake of their new black neighbors. To state such propositions is to demonstrate their unreality."[10] There has been a great deal of unreality around the subject of whites' housing choices in recent decades.

The narrative never changes: the white homeowners who left are always incipient Klansmen or other hardcore racists—not just middle- and working-class people seeking a neighborhood that's safe and comfortable for them and their families.

Outside of the fantasies of left-wing academics, very few people voluntarily abandon their stores, their churches, their families, their favorite restaurants, and their communities, which have existed for decades or even centuries, unless they're under extreme duress. Many books have been written about the phenomenon of "white flight," but most of them are either seen through the lens of African Americans and Hispanics, or, if told from the perspective of the whites who fled, are told in a not-especially-sympathetic way.

Something harsher but closer to the actual empirical reality of white flight (and in many ways a metaphor for race relations in America) is the rather pathetic spectacle of groups of non-whites following whites as whites move like vagabonds from place to place, looking for a community free from crime and chaos—all while the non-whites yell at whites about how racist they are. Of course, if whites later move back into the heavily minority neighborhoods they once left, they are accused of "gentrifying" them.

As the story of Michelle Obama shows, it is impossible to tell the story of white flight in America and the general racial re-composition of American neighborhoods without telling the story of crime, as we did in the previous chapter. It was the rampant rise of crime, not rampant racism, that was the core motivation for white flight in America.

## The History of Block-Busting

There is a long history of the American real estate industry victimizing the white middle class. Unscrupulous real estate agents have often worked hand-in-glove with bad government mandates, with devastating effects.

After World War II, as racial barriers to home ownership were broken down, a practice jump-started by the Supreme Court declaring unanimously (and correctly) in *Shelley v. Kraemer* (1948) that racially restrictive covenants were legally unenforceable,[11] there was an epidemic of so-called block-busting. This occurred when unscrupulous real estate agents (who rarely, if ever, lived in the affected areas) frightened existing white homeowners, including by hiring black women with baby carriages, starting simulated fights in neighborhoods, selling houses in middle-class white neighborhoods to black families with the explicit goal of generating panic sales among whites, and offering flyers advertising cash for houses.

While all this played to many whites' fears and prejudices, such fears and prejudices would not have taken hold had they not been rooted in social reality. As we discussed in the examination of Michelle Obama's comments, many of these areas did become dilapidated and crime-ridden as minorities moved in. It is evident that even for the many homeowners who were not racially prejudiced and wanted to stay in their old neighborhoods with their new neighbors, they could be ruined economically by block-busting practices. And given that, in cities like Chicago, many of these block-busted areas subsequently became places where dozens of shootings a weekend were the norm, it is difficult to say their fears were unjustified.

The practice of displacing whites from central city neighborhoods was best outlined in a notorious article in the July 1962 issue of the *Saturday Evening Post* entitled "Confessions of a Block-Buster," which exposed the practice to a national audience.[12] Interestingly, in 1972, a case went all the way to federal district court in which African Americans attempted to sue the journalist who had written the article, arguing they had been forced to pay inflated prices for their homes (which had presumably gone down sharply in value in the intervening years) and attempting to get the name of the real estate agent who had engaged in block-busting so he could also be sued.[13] But of course, the decline in property values was ultimately due to the degradation of the neighborhood, which was largely not the fault of the whites who had fled, nor of the journalist who had documented it.

Middle and working-class whites, however, had no legal recourse for what was happening to them (anti-block-busting laws would not be passed until after much of the damage had already been done). They had to sell their houses at a massive loss due to an intentionally racialized campaign to dispossess them by unscrupulous speculators. Decades after it began, white flight resembles ethnic cleansing, but we blame the victims rather than the perpetrators. Princeton University economist Leah Boustan examined seventy metropolitan areas and found that between 1940 and 1970, two white families moved out for every black family that moved in.[14]

Motivated in part by completely valid fears for their safety, whites fled inner-city neighborhoods and the homes and businesses they had built there, losing billions of dollars of capital that their ancestors had worked decades and even centuries to accumulate. My own family, living primarily in the so-called Rust Belt, fled cities like Cleveland, Detroit, and Akron for safer suburbs, losing out on the "generational wealth" that activists claim minorities were deprived of. Today, my earliest ancestors who came to the United States in the 1840s are buried in a cemetery under lock and key, as it is in a "bad" area of a major midwestern city and would otherwise be at risk of vandalism.

The urban white middle class became America's internal refugees from crime. In the wake of the Civil Rights Act and its adjunct provisions between 1964 and 1969, there were hundreds of riots in cities, disproportionately harming the property of white-owned businesses that, in many cases, were specifically targeted by the rioters, according to the government's Kerner Commission report that came out in 1968.[15]

According to a study from Boston University economist Robert Margo cited in the *New York Times*, between 1964 and 1971, there were more than 750 riots in American cities, which killed 228 people and injured more than 12,000.[16] Nor were these simple crimes of desperation, what Martin Luther King Jr. called "the language of the unheard."[17] As the Kerner Commission documented, most of those arrested for rioting had jobs.[18] The riots predictably had devastating effects on property values in affected areas that hurt both black and white homeowners and broke down social trust.

Between 1940 and 1970, homes owned and occupied by blacks in central cities jumped to 69 percent of the value of white-owned homes (up from 51 percent in 1940). But by 1990, the ratio had gone back down to 53 percent. This collapse in value was not a product of redlining, but of riots and a generally unsafe environment.[19]

The driving factor in this decline was the decisions, made largely by some blacks, to burn their own neighborhoods in civil disturbances, and the moral failure of the leadership in these communities and among their white liberal allies to effectively condemn and stop the disorder. As the Kerner Commission put it, "The civil disorders of 1967 involved Negroes acting against local symbols of white American society, authority and property in Negro neighborhoods."[20]

This only accelerated with the riots after the assassination of Martin Luther King in April of 1968. The National Bureau of Economic Research, in a 2004 retrospective study on the damages that the riots caused in African American communities, commented that after 1970 there was a great slowing in the racial convergence in earnings because so many black males were no longer working full-time.[21]

Partly as a result, and partly as a result of white flight from riots and violence, there was an increase in residential segregation in African American neighborhoods. Because many blacks were no longer working full-time, the proportion living in high-poverty urban neighborhoods increased, with residential segregation leading to increasingly poor social and economic outcomes among black youth. Overall, the riots "significantly depressed the median value of black-owned property between 1960 and 1970."[22] Facing uncontrolled violence, whites retreated from cities. In Detroit, whites collapsed from 70 percent of the population in 1960 to just 34 percent in 1980.[23] Today, Detroit's population is just 11 percent non-Hispanic white, and the overall population is just one-third of its 1950 peak.[24]

While the Fair Housing Act of 1968 implemented various rules to eliminate blockbusting as a practice, by then it was too late. Decades of social and physical capital had been turned over to real estate speculators for pennies on the dollar. Families went bankrupt. Indeed, many of the early, more modest suburbs might be seen as refugee camps for the urban white middle class, places where they could buy a modest home in a safe and culturally familiar environment from what was left of the equity they maintained after selling their former homes in the city.

"Confessions of a Block-Buster," the *Saturday Evening Post* exposé, details the victims of this practice and reads like a soliloquy for forgotten white America: "Among them were a widow who had been living alone and had no assets but her home, and the parents of four young children who feared what 'change' might mean to the youngsters' safety." The family with four children "sold out at a sizeable loss," according to the article.[25]

Block-busters were busy in cities such as Baltimore, Philadelphia, Cleveland, Detroit, and St. Louis. Many of these cities would later become among the most dangerous in the country. According to one block-buster, they moved to "change" an average of two to three blocks per week and over one hundred block-busters were operating in Chicago alone.[26]

"It would be impossible to exclude explicit, individual racism from the housing riots of the first half of the 20th century, but economic fears driven by the state unquestionably played a role,"[27] wrote Elaine Lewinnek in her history of Chicago suburbanization, *The Working Man's Reward*. Immigrants' families had invested heavily in neighborhoods they would now abandon.

The speculators dealt in emotional abuse. They preferred to buy in places where minorities were already encroaching: "Whites already there have been conditioned to insecurity by the inexorable march of the color line in their direction. This makes these blocks setups for the quick turnover, large volume, and the large profits I like," said one speculator actively involved in block-busting.[28]

While this chapter necessarily focuses on the white experience, in no way does it deny that bad things happened to African Americans and other minorities as a result of block-busting—threats and violence often accompanied racial turnover. But those stories have already been told with more volume, reach, and sympathy (witness Michelle Obama's bestselling memoir) than those told of whites, who were largely erased from history or treated as mindless bigots.

This fact was acknowledged by the block-buster in his "confession" (which, despite its candor, could still be printed in the early 1960s in a mainstream magazine like the *Saturday Evening Post*): "Actually, block-busting probably is tougher on the whites than the Negroes. Nobody who has lived in a neighborhood for years, seen his children grow up there, remodeled his home exactly to his liking and become accustomed to nearby school, church, and shopping facilities likes to be uprooted. . . . Several elderly persons have died because of the anguish and upheaval involved. . . . Once a block has been busted, some white owners simply stare, almost dumbfounded, as we draw up sale papers for them. Others break down and cry."[29]

As a result of the bad reputation of block-busting, so-called open housing became unpopular everywhere. A stark example of this can be seen in the popular response to the Rumford Fair Housing Act, passed by the California legislature in 1963. The act dramatically reduced the ability of people to do what they wished with their own property by putting racial non-discrimination requirements on home sales.

Democrat governor Pat Brown was in favor of it, while then gubernatorial candidate Ronald Reagan deplored racial bigotry but said prejudice could not be prevented through the law. He said all persons in a free society have a "basic and cherished right" to do as they pleased with their property. He opposed the Rumford bill *and* racially restrictive covenants (restrictions on property deeds that said property could not be sold to certain groups, often blacks and Jews), both of which he felt were fundamental restrictions on property rights.[30]

California Prop 14, which was set to repeal the Rumford bill, passed with 65.3 percent of the vote, winning all but tiny Modoc County (including uber-liberal bastions like Marin and San Francisco), despite Governor Brown (father of future governor Jerry

Brown) comparing its proponents to Nazis. Not for the first time on racial issues, politicians would be wildly out of step with their voters. And not for the first time on racial issues, unaccountable left-wing elites ignored the voters' wishes.

In an early case of what would become a pattern of the federal government bringing voters to heel, the federal government cut off all federal housing funds to California. Later, in a narrow 5–4 decision in *Reitman v. Mulkey*, the ultra-liberal Warren Court found Prop 14 unconstitutional. Reagan lamented the decision, declaring during a talk to California real estate agents, "I oppose the Rumford Act for the same reason I oppose restrictive covenants. Freedom is based on the right of an individual to personal ownership of property and this basic human right cannot be infringed on by majority rule."[31]

But it was not just race that led to white flight. In the mid-twentieth century, substantial suburbanization of middle-class whites happened even in cities like Minneapolis, where there was very little new minority presence. People wanted larger houses and backyards as the mass arrival of the affordable automobile opened up the countryside to many more Americans.

## Life after White Flight

Amid the Left's outrage, the conditions that drove white flight are not frequently examined, and when they are, they are rarely reported on with any prominence, because they make elite white liberals and minority leaders uncomfortable.

But one particularly compelling account is Scott Cummings's book *Left Behind in Rosedale: Race Relations and the Collapse of Community Institutions*. An academic and community organizer who had worked in "Rosedale," Cummings's account of white flight in a community in the Dallas-Fort Worth Metroplex in the late 1970s and early 1980s makes for harrowing reading. From 1960 to 1990, whites collapsed from 98 percent of Rosedale's population to just 12 percent. Cummings discusses how white elderly residents became regularly victimized in racialized crimes. He explains that older white residents of Rosedale lived in "constant fear" and inter-racial rapes were common.[32]

The demographic transition had a devastating impact on Rosedale's remaining white residents, as the elderly, left behind, had no opportunity to move. Cummings describes the situation as "comparable to a natural disaster" that brought about "collec-tive trauma" and "extreme grief" among both residents and for-mer residents as community organizations and support networks disappeared.[33]

"Fear dominates them emotionally and spiritually," he says of the few remaining elderly whites left in Rosedale. They have "converted their homes into fortresses." "On the streets, black adolescents seize the personal possessions of the elderly. Like predators, they forcibly overwhelm them and steal bags of groceries, wristwatches, purses, wallets, cash, and social security checks. The elderly are pushed down, shoved, and beaten. . . . Many robberies are accompanied by violent assault, rape or murder."[34]

Rosedale had seventy-nine rapes reported to the police in 1982 alone, which the author says is only a small percentage of the rapes that took place in the city. Other white Rosedale residents describe being victims of random violence. One mass rapist discussed the racial revenge present in Alex Haley's famous book and miniseries *Roots* (a fictionalized account of the author's family history during times of slavery) as he was raping his elderly victim, showing the key interlinkage between media-based racial incitement and subsequent anti-white crime.[35]

Hate crime hoaxes were devised to allow criminals to get away with their crimes. One assailant who broke into the home of a younger white woman with the intent of raping her was shot by the woman, who had been sleeping with a gun by her bed. By his own account, he subsequently reported (falsely) to the police that a motorist had called him a "motherfuckin' nigger" [*sic*] and shot him unprovoked.[36]

Forty-six elderly white victims were attacked in Rosedale by African Americans between June and September 1982 alone. One in four homes was eventually vacant, and investors and landlords stopped maintaining them.[37]

While Rosedale was not the universal experience in neighborhoods with large racial turnover, its horrific account is far from unique. In such bleak circumstances, it is hardly surprising that whites did flee, and that in many situations, they did not wait to see how things would turn out before they left.

Similar stories could be told about other places. Senator Dick Durbin, the Democrats' white Senate majority whip, grew up in East St. Louis, Illinois. Today, East St. Louis is almost entirely black and just 1 percent white, having shed nearly all of its white population (and the overwhelming majority of its population generally).[38] East St. Louis is now one of the most impoverished and dangerous towns in America.[39]

Why did Durbin's family leave and move to Springfield, Illinois? Durbin is a leading Democrat politician, at the forefront of the party that pushed these policies, so you'd think he would be asked about this regularly. Yet you would be wrong. Perhaps he moved because Springfield was more than 90 percent white in the 1970 census.[40]

Durbin's peregrination was like that of many other Democrat politicians. That includes Nancy Pelosi, whose father and brother ran Baltimore as mayors during its precipitous decline, then moved to San Francisco as its moderate-sized black population collapsed. Even today, in uber-diverse California, Pelosi chooses to live in an overwhelmingly white neighborhood that is just 3 percent black and 8 percent Hispanic.[41]

Most damningly, recent research shows that white flight is actually the norm for white progressives, who busily condemn everyone else for what they do themselves.

In a recent scholarly article, Eric Kaufmann documents how white progressives in both America and Great Britain, 60 percent of whom support increasing immigration, who strongly believe "increasing the number of people of many different races, ethnic groups and nationalities" makes the country better, and who say that they believe whites are less intelligent, lazier, and more violent than blacks, do not practice, to put it mildly, what they preach.[42]

What we see when we look at the data from recent years is that whiter cities (Kaufmann cites Salt Lake City and Boise) tend to experience more white population growth, while less white cities such as Houston and almost any city in California experience even greater white decline. According to Kaufmann's elegantly designed study, whites who strongly oppose Trump and whites who strongly support him move to equally white localities. And liberal whites who support higher immigration and diversity policies at the national level move away from diversity at the same rate as conservative whites who oppose higher immigration.

As Kaufmann puts it bluntly, "White progressives champion greater diversity but vote with their feet against it." They have engineered one America for the white middle and working classes, but choose to live in a different America. As he notes, white neighborhoods retain white population share while "more diverse" neighborhoods rapidly lose white share.[43]

Another study shows that highly educated whites had more "progressive" views on race but were also more likely to move their children to a heavily white area than other whites when the percentage of African American students became elevated.[44] This phenomenon of silent white flight was nicely captured by the liberal African American scholar Rich Benjamin in his perceptive 2009 book *Searching for Whitopia*, which profiled fast-growing, heavily white areas of the country (usually located far from traditional metro areas). In a later update to the book, Benjamin would note that Trump carried 94 percent of Whitopian counties and won 67 percent of the votes in those counties.[45]

## From Redlining to Reparations

Redlining is considered one of the great historical sins of white racism, allegedly having deprived minorities of "generational wealth," as the left-wing narrative goes. When cities like San Francisco and states like California demand that taxpayers pay reparations to African Americans, redlining is often explicitly stated as a justification.

Yet the redlining story is again something of an anti-white myth, as John McWhorter, a prominent African American public intellectual and professor at Columbia University, has documented. Redlining, which declared some neighborhoods too risky for traditional mortgage lending, was at least as much about social class as race. Ninety-two percent of homes in the lowest-rated areas for redlining between 1930 and 1940 were owned by whites.[46] Redlining did not just represent blind prejudice but real payback risks.[47]

While blacks were overwhelmingly resident in redlined urban areas, as opposed to other parts of the city, there was far more than racism at play. Neither McWhorter nor I would claim that racial discrimination was not present in lending at that time nor that other racial factors didn't contribute to the income disparities of that era. But as McWhorter puts it, "The Redlining 101 story—that cigar-chomping bigots in suspenders drew lines around where Black people happened to live while giving loans to poor whites, doesn't fully hold up."[48]

As McWhorter notes, the number of whites in redlined neighborhoods far exceeded the number of blacks, and they got stuck in the redlined areas too. These families, often without home equity and disconnected from the changing community, had to move in with their adult children who had moved elsewhere. "We just don't hear that part of the story," McWhorter writes.[49]

## Forced Busing

When whites attempted to flee to safety, liberals and government bureaucrats were there to make sure they were penalized. Another manifestation of the attack on the white middle class, and an indication of the hypocrisy of white elites, was forced busing, a practice whose ramifications are still being felt today. In *Swann v. Charlotte Mecklenburg Board of Education*, in 1971, the Supreme Court unanimously said courts could use the forced busing of children from their neighborhood school to a more distant school to achieve desegregation. This decision caused a firestorm in white communities, as they did not want to send their children to distant, often unsafe schools where little learning took place.

Busing was one of the most explosive issues in the 1970s, and it boiled down to whether people could choose where to live and go to school or not. It should come as little surprise that there was little sympathy among elites for the large number of middle-class and working-class whites who were affected.

Forced busing led to the deaths of neighborhood schools and the further dissolution of predominantly white communities, particularly, though not exclusively, urban ones. It is not a coincidence that overall, the elites (largely in the Northeast) who forced busing on others (largely in the South) and patted themselves on the back for their progressivism soon became patrons of some of the most segregated schools in the country. I personally attended highly integrated Southern public schools and graduated at a time when the Southern United States had the most integrated schools of any region at any time in modern American history.

Yet forced busing led to further neighborhood collapse. As late as 2019, letters to the editor in even the *New York Times* about a story by Nikole Hannah-Jones were full of poignant stories about neighborhoods ruined by busing.[50]

Unable to provide a safe learning environment for their children in cities, white parents were forced to pay massive amounts of money for their kids to go to private schools. Again, the media portrays this not as a massive and unfair tax on whites, who were forced to subsidize government schools that they did not use, but as awful racism on the part of whites. And as the percentage of minorities increased in these areas, white parents also ended up paying a disproportionate amount in tax dollars for failing public schools they often didn't send their own children to.

Whites are only about 14 percent of New York City and San Francisco public school students, but their parents make up the bulk of the wealthiest taxpayers, and they bear an enormous portion of these cities' budgets (about half in New York City). This, of course, is true for almost all city services, which benefit all residents but are paid for in great disproportion by white taxpayers.

Interestingly, Joe Biden, as a young senator, was a strong opponent of forced busing, only to betray his constituents in later years as he burnished his reputation as an advocate for racial justice in his desperate and all-consuming push for power. According to the *New York Times*, Biden became the Senate's "leading anti-busing crusader in the 1970s." "No issue has consumed more of my time and energies," he said in a 1981 Senate hearing. "We want to stop court-ordered busing."[51]

So important was busing to Biden that in 1975, according to the *New York Times,* he floated a constitutional amendment to eliminate forced busing. Biden would eventually join forces with arch-conservative North Carolina Senator Jesse Helms to offer an amendment to a 1975 school funding bill that would have banned busing. He would later attempt to bar the Department of Justice from effectively mandating court-ordered busing.[52] Biden would even co-sponsor a bill in 1976 to eliminate the role of federal courts in enforcing desegregation, transferring jurisdiction to state courts.[53]

"The new integration plans being offered are really just quota-systems to assure a certain number of blacks, Chicanos, or whatever in each school," Biden told a television interviewer in the late 1970s, adding, "That, to me, is the most racist concept you can come up with. What it says is, in order for your child with curly black hair, brown eyes, and dark skin to be able to learn anything, he needs to sit next to my blond-haired, blue-eyed son. That's racist! Who the hell do we think we are, that the only way a black man or woman can learn is if they rub shoulders with my white child?"[54]

This is an eminently sensible statement, but it directly contradicted the logic of *Brown v. Board of Education.* (*Brown* was correctly decided on substance in that the schools involved were clearly separate for the purposes of being unequal, but some of its underlying logic was flawed, a defect Biden intuitively understood in his early career and one that haunts civil rights law to this day.) Needless to say, this sort of thinking is verboten in 2024 Democrat circles. But the Democrat Party has changed, and Biden now supports the Democrats' busing proposals, completely reversing himself on the signature issue of his early political career.

In the person of Joe Biden, one sees how once-moderate white Democrats have become anti-white extremists as the price of staying in power. If they had any dignity at all, they would be embarrassed by this spectacle.

## Gentrification

The polar opposite of the story of redlining and white flight is the story of gentrification. The discussion of gentrification is another pillar of anti-white rhetoric in urban policy. Gentrification occurs when people (usually mostly white) settle in a formerly depressed area, help to improve its amenities, and ultimately raise home prices by making it a more attractive place to live (and, as a result, drive out some poorer, more heavily minority renters).

The white fight/gentrification paradigm are the two poles of anti-white structural racism in our current debate. If whites move back to an area they formerly abandoned, that is gentrification, to be deplored. "Gentrification is rooted in colonialism and white supremacy," in the words of one activist group.[55]

The *New Republic*, one of the Left's most respected magazines, declared that gentrification was "about profit and power, racism and violence on a massive scale."[56]

And here we see the ultimate irony: whites are condemned if they leave, and they are condemned if they return; the only consistency is that whites are condemned. That's why a 2020 Stanford study found that gentrification predominantly hurts minorities (though it did not mention minority homeowners in gentrifying neighborhoods who bought their homes cheaply and may sell for an enormous profit).[57] There are, in fact, a raft of academic studies on gentrification, most of which deplore the practice at some level and blame it for perpetuating racism. Gentrification is not seen as improving well-located and once-blighted real estate—but as a "problem" to be solved.

A rather remarkable article in the *New York Times* highlighted the anti-white double standard in our gentrification debate—though, to be fair, the *Times* writer seems to have a far more radical view of it than the minority homeowners themselves, who are understanding of neighborhood change and appreciative of the huge financial windfall they will receive when they sell their homes to white gentrifiers.[58]

One story spotlighted by the *Times* centers on a seventy-four-year-old retired transit bus operator and his multimillion-dollar Crown Heights brownstone, which he has lived in for fifty-eight years. He acknowledges attempting to sell it to a black friend at a discount to the market price, but even then, the friend couldn't qualify for the necessary mortgage. The article laments that the homeowner cannot sell his home in a racially exclusive way thanks to the loss of "community"—ironically, the very same factors that originally caused the white middle class to flee.[59] One, of course, cannot imagine the *New York Times* having the least bit of sympathy for white victims of racial neighborhood turnover.

Jeremie Greer, the co-founder and executive director of a "racial justice" nonprofit, mentions that the Affirmatively Fair Housing Initiative (AFFH)—about which we will have more to say later—can be used to provide down-payment boosts and low-interest loans to minority homebuyers.[60] (Again, can you imagine if the races were reversed?) Yet as one study showed, "As neighborhoods gentrify, they also improve in many ways that may be as appreciated by their disadvantaged residents as by their more affluent ones."[61]

Criticizing Chinese for living in Chinatown, Hispanics in the barrio, or African Americans in Harlem would be rightly seen as ludicrous. Nor would China, India, or any place in Africa tolerate the level of ethnic displacement that American whites are told to welcome. Only whites are expected to cheer their own ethnic mass displacement—and then, once displaced, never consider returning.

Yet some white gentrifiers are standing up to these attacks. In an article in *Philadelphia* magazine, a writer discusses the repurposing of an old school into a restaurant that had attracted mostly white hipsters into a previously dilapidated area. One new white resident refreshingly refuses to be shamed.

"I don't feel guilty," he says. "Cities change. They always change."[62]

## How Whites Paid for the Minority Housing Bailout

White flight, crime, and gentrification are far from the only ways that the housing market has discriminated against whites. The idea that as Americans we ought to be able to live where we please in the type of housing we desire (up to the limits of our budget) is a fundamental part of the American dream. Indeed, this assertion is what motivated some of the court rulings we touched on earlier in this chapter.

But what started as a reasonable attempt by the government to ensure that people did not discriminate turned into an elaborate scheme that devastated the wealth of America's white middle and working classes.

This didn't just happen during the years of redlining but during the great housing bubble, which was caused by the government stepping in and massively subsidizing the housing markets in majority-minority areas. After the resulting economic crash that caused the Great Recession of 2008, most of the tab was picked up by (predominantly white) taxpayers.

Furthermore, those receiving massive mortgage bailouts after the dust had settled—again paid for by a predominantly white tax base—were disproportionately black and especially Hispanic. Overall, the bailouts would cost taxpayers an estimated half-trillion dollars and lead to the most significant economic downturn in America since the Great Depression, one that still echoes dramatically throughout our public policy.

How did we get there? The Bush administration was operating under a *noblesse oblige* mindset that ignored the realities of twenty-first-century power politics. The White House, under constant pressure from civil rights groups, set up a program called Increasing Minority Home Ownership between 2002 and 2004. The program's goal was simple: it sought to create an "ownership society" and boost home ownership amongst minorities by pushing banks to lend more to them regardless of their creditworthiness.[63]

As the *New York Times* explained in 2008, "Bush pushed hard to expand home ownership, especially among minority groups, an initiative that dovetailed with both his ambition to expand Republican appeal and the business interests of some of his biggest donors. But his housing policies and hands-off approach to regulation encouraged lax lending standards."[64] Not for the first time or the last, wealthy, predominantly white elites worked with non-white "racial justice" advocates to pursue the supposed interests of minorities at the expense of the white middle class.

According to former Bush Treasury Secretary John Snow, the Bush administration took a lot of pride that minority home ownership had reached historic highs. "But what we forgot in the process was that it has to be done in the context of people being able to afford their house," Snow said. "We now realize there was a high cost."[65] That qualifies as an understatement.

The results: a study by real estate marketing firm Zillow showed that, amid the bubble, housing in heavily Hispanic neighborhoods had the largest price rise followed by the sharpest fall. After Hispanic neighborhoods came Asian-American neighborhoods, with white and black Americans bringing up the rear. While this appreciation pattern devastated those who bought in these neighborhoods at the peak, it also greatly benefitted those who used their homes as ATMs after huge price increases, before ultimately being unable to pay back their second or sometimes third mortgages. That mortgage debt in many cases was then partially or totally forgiven.[66]

More than four times as many Hispanics, by percentage of population, were delinquent on their mortgages than whites. By modifying these mortgages, the Obama administration essentially handed hundreds of billions of dollars to these debtors.[67] Ethnic minorities had a hugely disproportionate share of the so-called subprime mortgages that were at the heart of the mortgage crisis. Default rates on mortgages issued between 2004 and 2007, which would form the heart of the subprime crisis, were issued to Hispanics at 31 percent, blacks at 28.2 percent, Asians at 14.7 percent, and whites at 12.1 percent.[68] Alleged debunkers of the borrower-centric blame narrative point to Wall Street and mortgage banker greed as the precipitating factors of the crisis, but both scenarios can be true—the greed was real, but corrupt government policies, as well as well-meaning but destructive government policies, enabled predominantly minority homeowners to make poor borrowing decisions. Regardless, the deck was stacked against the white middle class.

It was no accident that so many non-creditworthy minorities got expensive mortgages they could not pay back. There was an active government policy to promote this kind of lending. As Christopher Caldwell describes it succinctly, the mortgage banks' 'off-balance sheet liabilities' of the finance crisis were largely those of the civil rights revolution." [69]

Much of this was done with stated-income loans (informally referred to as "liar loans") that abused historical standards of credit-worthiness. The government wanted loans to minorities, and banks were only too eager to comply to get government benefits in other policy areas of interest.

Overall, minority buyers were happy to overstate their income to get loans, and banks were happy to please federal officials by complying.[70] During the bailout that followed, favoritism was also shown to banks on an explicitly racial basis. OneUnited, which markets itself as the nation's largest black-owned bank, was given unique assistance by the government and was still benefitting more than a decade after the bailout had ended. Representative Barney Frank, then the most powerful Democrat on the House Banking Committee, inserted a provision into the original bailout bill to ensure OneUnited was rescued, and Representative Maxine Waters, whose husband was on the bank's board, faced ethics charges over intervening with regulators to help the bank.[71]

But it was not just black-owned banks that benefited. According to one study of California's housing market, even after adjusting for income and credit score, African Americans were 3.3 times more likely to be in foreclosure than whites, while Hispanics were 2.5 times and Asian Americans were 1.6 times. Presumably, similar ratios prevailed for those who were ultimately bailed out by the government.[72]

## Affirmatively Destroying Mostly White Communities

The real estate war on white Americans wasn't limited to the housing bailout. Affirmatively Furthering Fair Housing (AFFH), a radical policy begun under President Obama and restored by the Biden administration after being canceled (appropriately) by the Trump administration,[73] was another anti-white initiative that effectively attempts to turn the federal government into a national zoning board by forcing high-density zoning on cities and letting federal bureaucrats decide the ethnic and racial compositions of communities.[74] *National Review*'s Stanley Kurtz called it "arguably the most radical, transformative" initiative undertaken by the Obama administration, which, given the number of radical initiatives taken under Obama, was quite a statement.[75] Yet it received relatively little public attention.

AFFH is a blatant rewriting of the Fair Housing Act of 1968 that has no relationship to the act's original intent. The original Fair Housing Act, part of the Civil Rights Act of 1968 (which itself was a part of President Johnson's so-called "Great Society"), prevented housing discrimination based on race, religion, or national origin, adding other categories of protection subsequently.

AFFH does the exact opposite, mandating state-based and state-funded housing discrimination to appeal to core Democrat constituencies. It forces any city taking federal housing funds (which is to say basically all cities) to develop elaborate protocols for increasing residential density. It also points the way to race-based housing resettlement policies. While Biden has eliminated the current analysis of residential segregation, the rule also pressures home appraisers to artificially inflate prices in heavily minority neighborhoods.[76] Here was another direct, though highly opaque, attempt by the government to put money in minority pockets at the expense of whites.

AFFH requires towns that the government feels are too white to build high-density, low-income housing, regardless of their wishes, and to engage in the aggressive recruitment of non-whites to such housing. In heavily white Dubuque, Iowa, rather than give preference to their own residents in public housing, they must advertise to African American residents from several hours away in Chicago. Simply put, if your community is "too white" for HUD, you can expect to be targeted.

As Peter Kirsanow of the U.S. Commission on Civil Rights wrote to then HUD Secretary Ben Carson in a critique of AFFH during the Trump administration, "The approach outlined by Justice Kennedy envisions the use of race as a last resort in remedying disparate impact claims. AFFH uses race first, last, and always. Even if under your leadership, HUD does not enforce AFFH, private plaintiffs will rely on it."[77]

This is where we have gone on national housing policy: from preventing discrimination based on race to demanding it.

## CHAPTER 5

# School Daze

*"Education is a weapon, whose effect depends on who holds it in his hands and at whom it is aimed."*

—Joseph Stalin

*"Experience keeps a dear school, but fools will learn in no other."*

—Benjamin Franklin, *Poor Richard's Almanac*, 1743

There will be many controversial statements made in this book, but hopefully observing that most parents love their children will not be among them. And there is perhaps no area in which parents are more concerned about their children than schooling.

So there are few things more dismaying to parents than seeing their children discriminated against in a school setting. Yet whites are discriminated against systematically in a variety of ways in our educational system, from kindergarten to college.

Schools, of course, are very connected to city and neighborhood patterns of settlement, which we discussed in the previous chapter. And these patterns of settlement are highly related to prevailing levels of crime, which we discussed in the chapter before that. As cities became unsafe, whites moved, and as they moved the composition of schools changed. School discipline, diversity-obsessed curricula, and Critical Race Theory are a result of a school system that struggles to mask substantial achievement disparities between races. As white students flee school systems that discriminate against them, the same problems emerge.

## Critical Race Theory

Taking a cue from the inspired work of such activists as Chris Rufo, parents in 2020 began fighting back against Critical Race Theory in their children's schools. While the discipline has its origins in radical academic theory, it was Rufo who first put Critical Race Theory, a form of racial indoctrination that assigns "guilt" or "innocence" based on race, on the political map. In the 2021 gubernatorial campaign in Virginia, Republican Glenn Youngkin, recognizing a hot issue, cleverly picked it up, and defeated former governor Terry McAuliffe in a state that Joe Biden had carried by 10 percent of the vote.

Indicating the issue's importance to votes, Youngkin's first act as Virginia governor was to bar the teaching of Critical Race Theory in schools.

"Inherently divisive concepts, like Critical Race Theory and its progeny, instruct students to only view life through the lens of race and presumes [*sic*] that some students are consciously or unconsciously racist, sexist, or oppressive, and that other students are victims," wrote Youngkin in his executive order enforcing the ban.[1]

Yet Critical Race Theory was commonplace in schools before 2020 and remains commonplace in many schools today. It's part of a generalized anti-white discourse that has increasingly taken over American education.

At the university level, the comments of an Indian-American psychiatrist who spoke at Yale are illustrative: "I had fantasies of unloading a revolver into the head of any white person that got in my way, burying their body and wiping my bloody hands as I walked away relatively guiltless with a bounce in my step. Like I did the world a fucking favor," Aruna Khilanani told the medical students who had gathered to hear her lecture.[2]

Critical Race Theory is regularly being taught in schools. A 2021 YouGov survey found that 85 percent of Democrats thought America was systemically racist, while 72 percent felt that all differences between blacks and whites were caused by discrimination. A 2022 survey by the Manhattan Institute's Zach Goldberg and Eric Kaufmann was likewise illuminating. Kaufmann and Goldberg surveyed more than 1,500 eighteen-to-twenty-year-olds and found heavy usage of Critical Race Theory in schools. Sixty-two percent said they thought America was systemically racist, while 69 percent were taught that white people have white privilege. Sixty-seven percent were taught that America was built on stolen land.[3]

Overall, 90 percent of those surveyed acknowledged being taught about at least one of the CRT concepts surveyed by Kaufmann and Goldberg. Perhaps more importantly, 68 percent had been taught that there were no—or at least no respectable---arguments against CRT, a number that did not meaningfully differ according to the race of the respondent (that is, it was not respondent bias that suggested these counterarguments were not made). Furthermore, those who were taught these concepts, particularly those without counterarguments, were significantly more likely to believe them than those who had not been taught CRT.

The survey also indicated that white students in particular had been taught racial shame, and that the teaching had been effective. "Whereas 39 percent of whites who did not report any CRT-related classroom exposure indicated feeling 'guilty about the social inequalities between white and black Americans,' this share rises to about 45 percent among whites who reported being taught one or two

CRT-related concepts, and to between 54 percent and 58 percent among whites who reported being taught three or more concepts."[4]

Propaganda works, which is why it's used.

## School Funding

But problems of anti-whiteness aren't just limited to the classroom.

Contrary to popular belief, school district expenditures are essentially identical across races,[5] a fact that the Left constantly disguises when they attempt to portray minority-heavy schools as underfunded. This equality of funding is all the more remarkable given that most schools tend to be funded by local taxes, of which white parents on average are paying far larger amounts than blacks and Hispanics.

Nor does expenditure equal outcome. The author sends his five children to a highly rated public school system that spends less than the national average on instruction and far less than a number of disastrously underperforming districts. One reason for this is that, in many areas, state and federal funds (again, disproportionately paid for by white taxpayers) provide massive boosts to schools without extensive local funding.

But even when the government has compelled dramatic changes in school funding, there has been little change in relative student performance. The most dramatic case of attempting massive racial "equity" spending was in the Kansas City, Missouri, schools in the early 1980s as a result of a court case called *Missouri v. Jenkins*.[6] (The case would go through several iterations before finally, in 1995, the U.S. Supreme Court overturned some of the more aggressive rulings, though payments continued until 2003.)

Between 1985 and 2003, federal judges ordered the payment of an incredible $2 billion to the Kansas City school system (roughly $4 billion in today's dollars) in an aggressive attempt to remove self-segregation by race from its schools. Local property taxes were doubled, and a special income tax surcharge was levied on everyone who either lived or worked in Kansas City—an enormous imposition, especially in a city in which whites already paid the overwhelming majority of taxes. Spectacular new facilities were built at Kansas City schools—a new classical Greek magnet school had an Olympic-sized swimming pool and racquetball facilities, among other luxuries.[7]

Yet test scores dropped, and white students continued to flee the system. Activist judges continued to prescribe dramatic penalties on local schools, while for some time the Supreme Court refused to step in.

The judges had been seduced by left-wing education experts who insisted their extravagant spending would eliminate racial achievement gaps. They didn't—not even close. By 1990, corruption and incompetence ensured that the school district was spending less than half of its budget on actually teaching kids. Equipment thefts were rampant. Eventually, the judicial activists gave up. Today, Kansas City schools are 54 percent black, 27 percent Hispanic, and just 10 percent white. A predominantly white tax base was taxed massively to fund a school system they didn't even use. A substantial part of that tax base, tired of being used as racial cash cows (or guinea pigs, if you prefer), fled Kansas City entirely.[8]

## School Discipline

The reporting and use of school discipline is another area of systemic bias that hurts white students.

Attempts to reduce the numbers of suspensions of African Americans (in particular) and Hispanics, who are suspended at far higher ratios than white students, lead to racially unjust policies because these suspensions are invariably a result of different disciplinary offense rates by race. (Asian-American students are suspended at even lower rates than whites but also make up a much lower percentage of students, and thus for this and other political reasons tend to be less a part of the conversation around school discipline.)

Federal bureaucrats, however, are on a mission to make suspension numbers by race equal in the name of "equity," though the behaviors of these groups are different. Thus, white students, and disproportionately white teachers, are put at substantial risk.

To use one prominent example where real-world school disciplinary wokeness had profound effects: Trayvon Martin, the teen shot and killed in a confrontation with neighborhood watch coordinator George Zimmerman, was portrayed in the legacy media as an innocent kid (an image enabled by a years-old picture of a cherubic-looking youngster that the media ran obsessively). Yet Martin's character would not have been portrayed in the same light had it been known that he'd been caught at school with burglary tools and women's jewelry in the months before he was killed.[9]

The jewelry matched items that had been stolen from a local home, but police did not pursue the possible theft any further in an effort to reduce disciplinary infractions and suspensions of African Americans.

Under pressure to not suspend black students, the school resource officer wrote up the jewelry as "found items" and never submitted a police report.[10] The different departments, in a desire not to create yet another criminal record for a young African American male, helped paint a picture of Trayvon that was very different from the reality.

The full story of Martin's various brushes with serious school discipline, drug use, weapons flashing on social media, and other signs of incipient criminal behavior was nothing like the "sweet kid who was shot while going out for Skittles." Yet these details, though originally reported in the *Miami Herald*, were largely circulated only in the right-wing media ghetto.[11] The rest of America was in the dark. Martin eventually ended up on school suspension anyway for an unrelated offense, but he should likely have been headed for juvenile hall or adult prison (which, ironically, would have saved his life).

The Obama administration went out of its way to emphasize the importance of disparate impact in school discipline.[12] Because they effectively threatened schools' funding if students were disciplined at substantially different rates than their race's share of the population (ignoring the fact that some groups have objectively worse behavior in schools), white and Asian students became victims of violence in schools at increasing rates. Just as in the adult world, not punishing students who engage in violent and even criminal behavior makes life more dangerous for everyone.

In Florida alone, this resulted in two high-profile cases of violence. In addition to Martin, there was the even more tragic case of Nikolas Cruz, who shot and murdered seventeen kids at Marjorie Stoneman Douglas High School in one of the deadliest school shootings in American history.

Cruz, despite years of criminal behavior on school grounds and obvious signs of mental illness, was never reported to authorities because Broward County attempted to reduce such reports at least partially in the name of racial justice. Indeed, federal authorities used Broward's program, which dramatically reduced suspensions at the cost of not legally intervening in severe cases like Cruz's, as the model for a nationwide effort. According to the minutes of a teachers' group meeting held before the shooting and later publicly revealed, this created a "culture of leniency" in which a student's tenth serious infraction was often treated like his first.[13]

Had race-based "disparate impact" solutions not been used, Cruz likely would have been in jail and definitely would not have had legal access to a weapon. Yet under the disparate impact system, statistics on offenses were rigged and manipulated to make schools look better to federal bureaucrats. "The message out there is that the students are untouchable. Habitual negative behavior means nothing anymore," according to the notes from a teachers' group meeting that took place before the shooting.[14] Adding to the tragic absurdity, Cruz may not have been ethnically Hispanic at all. He was adopted by a Hispanic couple, and self-identified as Hispanic, but the ethnicity of his biological parents is unclear from public reports, and he belonged to a racist chat group in which he expressed violent anti-black, antisemitic, and anti-immigrant sentiments.[15]

The false picture of Trayvon Martin was a direct consequence of Obama administration policies, which threatened to punish schools that disciplined students at rates disproportionate to their population share using disparate impact analysis.[16] More than four hundred school districts representing over ten million students reached settlements with the Department of Education's Office for Civil Rights about their disciplinary procedures, in many cases at substantial cost to the school.[17] And certainly a very clear message was delivered: stop suspending black and Hispanic kids—causing many additional schools to change their disciplinary policies. But as suspensions went down, student reports of feeling less safe went up. Violence against (disproportionately white) teachers also increased.

Yet the administration was unapologetic: "Disparate impact is woven through all civil rights enforcement of this administration," said Russlynn H. Ali, Obama's head of the Education Department's Civil Rights Office, in a rare moment of candor.[18]

The disparate impact disciplinary strategy was a classic example of real "structural racism" at work—but structural racism in the opposite direction from the way it's presented in the media. (As a side note, we arguably should not call this "structural racism," since institutions are not people, do not hold beliefs, and thus cannot be racist. But the term "structural racism" is so woven into the lexicon that it is difficult to discuss these issues without referring to it.)

Ultimately, the Obama administration pushed policies that disproportionately put white students and teachers at risk in order to hide facts about the disciplinary records of black and Hispanic students, because Democrats were uncomfortable with the underlying demographics of school misbehavior. These policies put pressure on schools to not discipline kids like Trayvon Martin and Nikolas Cruz, who would reasonably have been expected to have a criminal record had policies been enforced in a race-neutral fashion. They led to not just numerous traumatized students at schools who were the victims of predators, but in some tragic cases, to dead bodies.

While the Trump administration ended Obama's disparate impact school disciplinary policies, the Biden administration was only too happy to bring them back.[19]

The racial disciplinary gap is not just anecdotal. While research is difficult to come by (partly because such politically incorrect topics are not favored in academia), it is possible to find data that can give us a sense of its scale. Disciplinary punishment for physical fighting is one of the better metrics for understanding school misbehavior rates because, somewhat like murder as a proxy for crime statistics, it is generally clear and uniformly measurable—and much less malleable and subject to administrative data massage than generalized "harassment" or "bullying." (Though even "fighting" is not a perfect metric—administrators under disciplinary quota pressures are more likely to look the other way after a few thrown punches than police are likely to cover up a murder.)

Even years after the Obama administration's strong-arming districts to reduce disciplinary disparities, from 2017 to 2019, in California schools, 3.7 percent of African Americans, 3.8 percent of Native Americans, and 2.1 percent of Hispanics were punished for fighting four or more times, compared to just 1.2 percent of whites and 1 percent of Asian Americans.[20] While this could be an indication of large amounts of intra-racial violence (which would be bad enough in and of itself), there are strong suggestions it is often interracial violence with disproportionately white victims.

Take affluent Santa Clara County, population almost two million. It's a county with very few African Americans, meaning that violence involving them would likely be primarily interracial. From

2017 to 2019, 28 percent of African American students were suspended for fighting, 7 percent four or more times, while 10 percent of Hispanic students were suspended for fighting. Just 0.9 percent of white students and 0.5 percent of Asian-American students had received such suspensions.[21]

That means the average African American student was *thirty times more likely to be suspended for fighting* than the average white student, while the average Hispanic student was eleven times more likely. While Santa Clara is something of an outlier, the data is grim elsewhere as well.

Among Asian Americans, the largest population within the Santa Clara County school districts at almost 38 percent, not a single student was punished more than once for physical fighting, and just 0.5 percent of white students were, as opposed to 16 percent of African American students and 8.9 percent of Hispanic students.[22] This is what schooling looks like in the heart of Silicon Valley, in one of America's most affluent communities.

## Anti-White Discrimination, SATs, and Class Ranks

Anti-white discrimination in academics and admissions is perhaps the most visible way in which anti-white policies are put in place and maintained in contemporary education.

Correctly anticipating an unfavorable Supreme Court ruling on affirmative action, education elites began to do everything they could to reduce objective performance measurements, largely under the cover of COVID (which made it more difficult to take standardized tests since these occur in a group setting). Some schools began moving to eliminate standardized tests entirely, first as a requirement and later even as an option, as happened in California. In situations where they weren't able to eliminate the test, the test itself was dumbed down, either through "range restriction," which scores more students at the highest end of the spectrum with little way to differentiate between them, or by eliminating more cognitively challenging elements of the test, as the SAT did when it eliminated its analogies section.[23]

Attacks on standardized tests (and grades and academic merit generally) have increased and are blatantly discriminatory against whites. They were originally intended to target whites, though on a per capita basis Asian students suffer from even more discrimination. Yet because of the vastly larger numbers of whites, far more of them overall are hurt.

One reason this doesn't cause much public outrage is that socially connected, overwhelmingly liberal whites from "elite" backgrounds are still often able to game the system, leaving average white students without connections to languish. A 2019 study found that 43 percent of white students at Harvard are legacies, athletes, or related to donors or staff—a number that was less than 16 percent for African Americans, Asian Americans, and Hispanics.[24] What's more, about three-quarters of these students would have been rejected without such qualifications.

"Removing preferences for athletes and legacies would significantly alter the racial distribution of admitted students, with the share of white admits falling and all other groups rising or remaining unchanged," according to the researchers' data analysis.[25]

But there are several problems with this assertion and its implications. While some athletic events (crew, fencing, and squash, for example) are merely back doorways to substantially privilege already affluent kids, others (such as football) attract and capture kids from up and down the economic spectrum.

Also, football or basketball player who is good enough to get an offer from Harvard, while not usually at the level of players admitted to, say SEC schools, is seriously talented and accomplished, and usually one of the top players in his state. The same is true in women's volleyball, basketball, and soccer. Sports are widely played throughout the nation, and competition is ferocious—to be recruitable by Harvard in a major sport is significantly more difficult than to have a high SAT score or be valedictorian of your high school class. Arguably, many of these would be considered "merit" admissions, assuming we are using a process that looks at a student's overall profile rather than solely academics.

Further, ending admissions favoritism to the children of truly major donors, while totally defensible, would have directly detrimental effects on the university, as these donors fund many university programs, including financial aid for low-income students.

The more interesting group collapsed into this analysis are the children of faculty and staff. In my own experience at Stanford, I saw far more faculty and staff kids admitted than would have seemed reasonable. While I did not have access to these students' transcripts, I have every reason to believe they received large admissions boosts that are difficult to justify. These are probably white students in great disproportion, but more crucially they are the children of white liberal elites. Normal whites need not apply. Overall, these preferences do not benefit "white students," but a very small share of disproportionately white and disproportionately liberal families.

In the recent Supreme Court suit, it is notable that *Students for Fair Admissions* was brought on behalf of Asian American students, rather than the far more numerous white students who were affected. These students may or may not suffer worse discrimination than whites. It's also notable that Columbia sociology professor Jennifer Lee, principal investigator of the largest national survey of Asian American students, claims that "all the research shows it's white Americans who would benefit the most"[26] from the ruling, which is a backhanded way of saying that white students are suffering the most discrimination under the current system. That Asian American students would be seen as a more appealing client to a Supreme Court with no Asian Americans but stocked with a majority of white conservatives is a very revealing window into our racial politics today.

An additional problem with the researchers' interpretation of their data is the "grades and test scores" approach tends to over-weight Asian Americans, as they do both substantially more test prep and homework than other groups. In fact, contrary to myths, even African American students are more likely to take SAT test prep than white students.[27]

This is a difficult balance for universities to find, as they want to reward performance and not just potential. But it seems likely that a pure grades-and-test-scores approach will tend to somewhat over-weight Asian American students, whose parents may have focused more on these areas. Overall, based on this data, a sensible, balanced, and comprehensive student evaluation would likely see a dramatic reduction in African American, Hispanic, and liberal politically-connected white students while boosting Asian Americans and polit-ically unconnected whites.

Furthermore, as African American Stanford economist Caroline Hoxby has documented, white rural students, and in particular, conservative white Christians, tend to be the most underrepresented demographic at these elite schools, making up the highest percent-age of qualified students who don't even bother to apply to such schools.[28] Yet reaching these students is not seen as an institutional priority for elite universities.

Not content with eliminating SATs, schools are racing to do away with class rankings in an attempt to disguise merit and jus-tify anti-white discrimination.[29] In general, the goal of the mod-ern educational establishment is to eliminate objective measurable standards by which they can evaluate students, in favor of inher-ently malleable and subjective standards that can be manipulated by diversity bureaucrats. With the downfall of affirmative action, this will become even more important. "The move toward more test-optional admissions has really prompted colleges and universities to think differently about their entire process," said one admissions officer.[30]

Test scores and grades are not a perfect proxy for long-term professional success, of course, nor are they a perfect measure of ability. The gap between school performance and life performance continues to be significant. In 2020, for example, among Fortune 500 CEOs, 92 percent were white while just 2.4 percent were Asian American.[31] Companies look for CEOs who can maximize shareholder value. They are also highly incentivized in the current political structure to promote minorities. If there were a proverbial $20 bill lying in the street in the form of more talented minority CEOs, it seems likely many of them would pick it up. (In this context, it is worth noting that the CEOs of some of America's most powerful technology companies, such as Microsoft, Alphabet, and Nvidia are Asian Americans.)

Not only do white students have an admissions disadvantage, but that extends to financial aid as well. Whites can expect less money than similarly situated minority students since black, Hispanic, and Native American students are eligible for many scholarships whites are not (though it remains to be seen how these may be subject to legal challenges in the wake of the *Students for Fair Admissions* decision).

Finally, whites are almost never eligible for help at schools they are underrepresented in. About a quarter of California high school seniors are white, but just 19 percent of students admitted to the University of California system are white (even though whites on average have substantially better academic qualifications than Hispanics, the largest group in the UC system).[32] Yet this will never be seen as a problem, nor have there been significant efforts to recruit whites to schools in which they are badly underrepresented.

If a tree falls in the forest and a diversity bureaucrat doesn't hear it, does it make a sound? By contrast, in the twenty-five years since California outlawed affirmative action at state universities, the state spent $500 million to boost "diversity"[33] in enrollment in the UC system, focusing on African American and Hispanic students. Little surprise that the UC university system has eliminated the SAT from even *optional* consideration in admissions.[34]

## DEI Bureaucracies and "Paper-Only" Minorities

Anti-white discrimination at American universities is sustained by enormous bureaucracies. A Heritage Foundation survey found an average of forty-five diversity employees at sixty-five top universities that are in the top-level "Power Five" athletic conferences. And this is almost certainly a substantial underestimate of the real number, as many DEI employees may simply not have the word "diversity" in their titles.[35]

At universities that presumably were more comprehensive with their listings, like the University of Michigan, 163 DEI employees were listed. Each one of these employees takes resources away from teaching students and is dedicated to discriminating against whites and Asian Americans, whose parents disproportionately pay their salaries. Eliminating these diversity bureaucrats at a school such as the University of Michigan would pay for hundreds and possibly even more than 1,000 full-tuition scholarships for deserving students regardless of race each year.[36]

One revealing anecdote of thousands: I was having lunch with a friendly acquaintance who, parenthetically (in a factual, non-obnoxious way), mentioned that he had two children attending highly prestigious universities. I expressed my appreciation for that accomplishment and said he must have really done a great job raising them.

After some more talking, he suddenly got a sheepish expression on his face and mentioned to me that his kids had a "secret weapon." Their mom was Hispanic, and they had "leaned into that" hard on their applications. Now this guy was about as white as white could be, and his kids were not disadvantaged in any way. As a principled conservative, he was slightly apologetic about having used this to his advantage, but I could hardly blame him. He understood that running away from whiteness (at least on paper) was the best way to get ahead.

We live in a society of anti-white privilege.

Compare this to many decades ago, when actual "white privilege" existed. My friend's kids, with their mixed "Castizo" ancestry, would have undoubtedly tried to "pass" for white. The legendary baseball player Ted Williams was half Mexican American, a fact known to almost no one when he played. Williams, the epitome of a middle-American icon, embraced a white identity. "If I had my mother's name, there is no doubt I would have run into problems in those days, [considering] the prejudices people had in Southern California," he said.[37] Williams did not even publicly disclose his Mexican American heritage until a parenthetical remark in his 1970 autobiography.

With the desperate demand for white racists far outstripping the meager supply available in modern academia, it is unsurprising that rich rewards are available for those who will invent some where none exist. A highly paid and highly regarded African American criminology professor at Florida State University resigned in disgrace after being credibly accused of faking data to exaggerate structural racism against African Americans. At least six of his papers were retracted.[38]

## Affirmative Action in College Admissions

Before the Supreme Court decision in *Students for Fair Admissions*, it was easy to overlook the level of discrimination in university admissions enabled by affirmative action. It was also easy to overlook how strongly public opinion leaned against this kind of discrimination.

Sixty-three percent of Americans in 2022 said universities should disregard race in college admissions.[39] Forty-nine percent of registered voters in a large Reuters-Ipsos poll that same year felt affirmative action and similar policies at universities discriminated against white people versus just 38 percent who disagreed. Seventy-one percent agreed that college admissions should be based solely on merit, and 41 percent strongly agreed versus just 5 percent who strongly disagreed.[40]

At the University of North Carolina, one of two schools involved in the *Students for Fair Admissions* cases, there was a staggering 176-point gap between the SAT scores of admitted African American students and admitted white students.[41] (The Asian American–black gap was even larger, at 235 points, but again, it affected a smaller number of students.) For context, that is the difference in SAT scores between the average at Harvard and the average at Stony Brook or Ohio State.

Nor is this just a question of white socioeconomic privilege. A 2006 study from the *Journal of Blacks in Higher Education* found that white students from families in the lowest family income bracket outscored the average black student by a whopping 130 points and outscored blacks from the highest income bracket by seventeen points. Among those who scored over 700 on each section of the SAT, arguably the minimum amount to be viable for a merit admission to one of the top twenty-five or so schools, whites outnumbered blacks more than 47–1.[42]

Yet at Harvard, white admissions for the class of 2026 outnumbered blacks by only about 2.5–1, a number that would be closer to 2–1 if "politically connected" students of all races were removed.[43]

Even those whites who are not legacies or athletes tend to be from elite private schools or wealthy public schools. Typical American whites are almost absent. "To date, I haven't met a single middle-class white student who was admitted through the standard admissions process," wrote one middle-class white student at the University of Chicago.[44]

In Michigan, a 2022 study that required virtually all high school seniors in the state to take the SAT painted an even starker picture. ZERO percent of the almost 10,000 African American high school seniors in Michigan scored over 1400 on the test (which is lower than the average SAT score for University of Michigan admits). This suggests an absolute maximum of 49 African American students who scored at that level, with a median assumption of twenty-four. One percent of Hispanics scored at that rate for a total of 75 out of 7,500 or so. One percent of 1,200+ Native Americans did—give or take 12. Twenty-five percent of 4,200 Asian Americans did (approximately 1,050). And approximately 4 percent of 62,300 whites did, or approximately 2,500.[45]

This suggests that based on standardized test scores (which are again highly predictive of academic performance in college), approximately 121 total blacks, Hispanics, and Native Americans scored highly enough to be competitive for the University of Michigan (average SAT score 1435) while 2,500 whites did.[46] Yet in 2021, these groups made up about 13.5 percent of the University of Michigan student body, a bit more than a quarter of the number of white students, suggesting these groups were represented more than five times what would have been expected as a function of their grades and test scores.[47] No wonder the University of Michigan needs 163 DEI staff.

Nationally, 7 percent of whites scored over 1400 on their SATs compared to 23 percent of Asian Americans. Given that the number of whites who graduated high school each year is almost eight times larger than the number of Asian-American high school graduates, even with the existing score differentials, the number of "elite" (1400+) white scorers would be about 2.3–2.4 times the number of Asian Americans.[48] Now compare that to the numbers at elite Ivies, which is substantially less than the ratio of their actual population at those schools.

At Stanford, the class of 2026 was even more extreme. Significantly more Asian Americans (29 percent) than white students (22 percent) were enrolled. Black student numbers were much lower than at Harvard (7 percent), though still substantially overrepresented on a merit basis, while Hispanic numbers were 17 percent. Keep in mind this is dramatically higher than the more than 2–1 ratio of white to Hispanic high school graduates nationwide.[49] And that doesn't even begin to consider the vastly superior academic profiles on average of these white students, or the fact that the whites who are admitted are likely to be rich, liberal, and connected. If you're a middle-class, high-achieving white student, you are out of luck.

Nor are test scores the only method by which colleges and high schools are penalizing white students. In Clark County (Las Vegas), Nevada, America's fifth largest school system, students are allowed to retake tests. There is no punishment for late assignments. Zeroes are no longer allowed—the worst grade a student can receive is 50 percent, even if he or she does no work. All of this has been done with the explicit intention of benefitting "underrepresented minorities," which, though they hope you won't draw this logical implication, means punishing white and Asian students.[50]

It's not just in Nevada. Dozens of school districts in Iowa, California, Virginia, and other states have jumped on the "equitable grading" bandwagon. Yet teachers who have experience with equitable grading say it leads to students' gaming the system while failing to learn accountability. Nonetheless, Joe Feldman, the leading proponent of equitable grading, has worked with school districts in New York, Los Angeles, and Chicago, America's three largest cities.[51]

Amid all this discrimination, even some privileged whites are finally waking up. At the tony Brentwood school in the Los Angeles area (tuition $40,000+ per year), parents were outraged after almost no white students from the class of 2026 got into elite U.C. schools. Note that affirmative action is already formally banned at these schools, yet they've still spent millions of dollars on work-arounds. Brentwood had recently been involved in a CRT-related uproar, being attacked for white privilege and having racially segregated dialogue sessions as part of the curriculum.

One former prep-school administrator explained, "The joke is that these [schools] are engines for sustaining and strengthening the plutocracy. These schools lecturing about equity and justice is like listening to Swiss bankers and asset managers lecturing the world about tax transparency."[52]

These schools may soon perhaps achieve their diversity nirvana, as the number of whites in the system (built into the world's most prestigious schools with decades and decades of white philanthropy and tax dollars) finally approaches zero. We shouldn't assume the favorable Supreme Court ruling, or the outlawing of affirmative action generally, will solve these problems. A look at California, where affirmative action has been banned for years, is telling. California has developed extensive proxies for race that have either not been challenged successfully in court or have not been challenged at all. African American and Hispanic students, law or no law, are being enrolled at numbers far higher than a pure merit-based approach would suggest.

From 1997 to 2022, in the twenty-five years after Prop 209 passed, which banned affirmative action in state schools, the percentage of African Americans and Latinos enrolled in UCs grew to 44 percent. Whites were just 18.6 percent of UC student admits for the class of 2026. That's substantially lower than their percentage of the state youth population, and certainly far lower than their share of qualified attendees, as California's remaining whites are disproportionately well-off and from highly educated families.[53] California has spent more than $500 million to boost "diversity" among students in the twenty-five years since it banned affirmative action.[54]

Nor is such racial meddling the sole province of deep blue states. Texas, with its "top 10" policy, which granted admission to the top 10 percent of students from all its high schools to the top public universities in the state, also games the system against whites and in favor of Hispanics.[55] By rewarding the "best" students, no matter how terrible their schools might be, blacks and Hispanics attending very low-achieving schools will benefit at the expense of better-qualified whites. With Hispanics surpassing whites in 2022 as the largest demographic group in Texas, this type of discrimination will only increase.

Anti-white discrimination also manifests itself in scholarships. Tucker Carlson cited as a particular offender Florida State University, one of many universities that has scholarships that effectively bar white people from applying.[56] Of course, as Chris Rufo and others point out, the thousands of scholarships from universities nation-wide almost certainly violate the Civil Rights Act—but until recently nobody had done anything about it. And countless scholarships advertise white exclusion as a feature rather than a bug.[57]

Fortunately, in the wake of the Supreme Court decision striking down affirmative action in college admissions, other states, such as Wisconsin, are now having public interest right-wing law firms jump into the fray alleging racial discrimination and Civil Rights Act vio-lations for minority-exclusive scholarships.[58]

In July 2023, as soon as the Supreme Court's decision came down, Missouri's GOP attorney general ordered colleges to adopt race-blind standards, and the University of Missouri immediately ended $16 million in race-based scholarships.[59] But few other states have followed suit. And the federal gravy train for race-based scholarships and services continues. If a school is designated as a "Hispanic Serving Institution" (meaning it has a student body that is more than 25 percent Hispanic), it's eligible for more than $350 million in targeted annual funding each year, whereas in the last two years alone, the Biden administration delivered $5.8 billion in funding to historically black colleges and universities, despite the generally poor academic track records of most of these universities and their graduates.[60]

The new "academic" elite has arrived, and despite the Supreme Court's ruling, there are going to be a lot fewer white faces in it.

## CHAPTER 6

# The Erasure of History

*"Who controls the past controls the future. Who controls the present controls the past."*
—George Orwell, *1984*

*"The only thing we learn from history is that we learn nothing from history."*
—Georg Hegel, *Lectures on the Philosophy of History*

With our schools in dire shape, it is hardly surprising that we're having a tough time transmitting our history to the next generation of Americans. This failure takes place both in the classroom, as we will discuss, but also in the erasure of the physical environment itself. Simply put, with increasing frequency, monuments to America's past are being torn down.

That past is now seen by many in our educational and political establishments as scandalous. Nobody is safe, from the (obvious) Confederates to the once-revered Abraham Lincoln, Teddy Roosevelt, and Christopher Columbus. The common thread uniting all these villains is that they are white men.

But, of course, not all monuments are coming down. Some are going up. Perhaps the ultimate expression of the Left's desire to humiliate white Americans, while bestowing esteem upon the most deranged people imaginable, is their dedication of monuments to people such as Marsha P. Johnson (born Malcolm Michaels Jr.), a violent, mentally ill, transgender sex worker. One of these monuments, in a deeply symbolic move, was originally supposed to replace a statue dedicated to Columbus.

That monument, still in the planning stages as of publication, is set to be built in Johnson's hometown of Elizabeth, New Jersey. A petition in favor of the statue collected more than 165,000 signatures before the city announced it would be built—though ultimately they decided on a different location, "saving" Columbus, at least for now.[1] Columbus, of course, "discovered" America, as his voyages led to the age of European settlement in the Americas and the birth of the society we know today.

His birthday is still a national holiday, despite the continuous howls of the Left to change it to "Indigenous People's Day," a holiday first born at a United Nations Conference in 1977 and first celebrated in the United States in far-left Berkeley, California, in 1992. As Trump noted at a 2020 rally, "Sadly, in recent years, radical activists have sought to undermine Christopher Columbus's legacy. . . . These extremists seek to replace discussion of his vast contributions with talk of failings, his discoveries with atrocities, and his achievements with transgressions."[2]

When people protest against Columbus, they protest against the creation of modern Western societies, which would have been impossible without his voyages. They thus protest against themselves. Like so many leftists, they're sawing off the civilizational limb they have heretofore been sitting on. And they do so in favor of people such as Johnson, whose significance is *anti-civilizational*. As I wrote about the gender cult in another context, "[T]he absurdity is the point. The deviance is the point. To have someone suffering from florid mental illness shaming and mocking normality *is the point*."

In 2020, Johnson had a fountain named for "her" in Manhattan, and subsequently the East River Park—a substantial seven-acre space in Williamsburg, Brooklyn—was also named for "her." Not content with that recognition, a group of transgender activists illegally installed a bust of Johnson in Christopher Street Park in New York City, across from the famous Stonewall Inn, the site of riots by patrons against a police raid that is seen as the birth of the modern gay rights movement. The bust, in a surprise only to those who do not understand leftist governance, was allowed to remain for at least a year and a half before going on exhibit at a prestigious city venue.[3] Imagine how long a statue of Columbus would be allowed to stay unauthorized in a New York City park.

And who was Marsha P. Johnson (born Malcolm Michaels),[4] you might ask?

He was a black drag queen who was evidently known within his circles for cultivating an unusual look and having a charismatic personality. Along with a few others, he briefly started a ramshackle group house to take in gay street kids. That's about it for redeeming virtues.

He was present at the Stonewall Riots, yet even assuming one found that praiseworthy, he was not one of the instigators. (As a side note, the original statues commemorating the Stonewall Riots, placed near the Stonewall Inn, were created by noted sculptor George Segal.[5] Segal's sculptures were usually white, a result of his use of plaster, a choice of material that would lead to Segal being attacked for racial exclusion. Black plaster matters, I guess.

Johnson described his life in New York City as having "been built around sex and gay liberation and being a drag queen," as well as engaging in prostitution. He founded the Street Transvestite Action Revolutionaries (STAR) and established a communal house where twenty of them, including some young street gays Johnson took in, lived, and presumably turned tricks. "Some overdosed, some were stabbed by johns," noted one account of the house. Of course, as

Johnson never paid rent, the place was a dangerous dive that lacked electricity.[6]

By his own account, during his "career" in street prostitution (during which he acquired HIV and no doubt spread it to many of his customers), he had several attempts made on his life, with at least eight nervous breakdowns and more than one hundred arrests. Not content to live on the margins (to put it politely) of mainstream society, he was banned from several gay clubs for his violent outbursts. One acquaintance in the local gay community called Marsha a "bully underneath that soft sweet manner."[7]

According to others who knew Johnson, he "become a very nasty, vicious man, looking for fights," and was described as schizophrenic.[8] He regularly picked fights with police and was frequently cited for violently assisting arrests. He would sometimes walk the streets naked before being hospitalized for mental breakdowns.[9]

What can we say about a society that elevates a man with virtually no redeeming virtues to a place of honor while denigrating Columbus, Washington, and others who created this country? We can say it is institutionally racist against whites and intrinsically depraved—two phenomena that are hardly uncorrelated.

## Erasing the Founders

No longer taught their own history, Americans cannot expect to keep their nation built on that history. This erasure was, of course, a very intentional project of the Left that was pursued over several decades. We no longer even have the words to define what we have lost, and into this intellectual void, the Left has inserted anti-white propaganda, falsely presenting America's history as a simple morality tale of evil white explorers and innocent, non-white victims.

The story of Johnson's statue is just one of the more extreme examples of the erasure of important figures in American history and their replacement with something more sinister. 1776 was a long time ago, and the Founders had inappropriately right-wing views on race and immigration by the standards of 2024.

In particular, the Founders viewed as critical the importance of America being a unified polity rather than a "multicultural" one. As John Jay wrote in *Federalist* #2, "With equal pleasure I have as often taken notice that Providence has been pleased to give this one connected country to one united people—a people descended from the same ancestors, speaking the same language, professing the same religion, attached to the same principles of government, very similar in their manners and customs."[10]

At the time, that was considered common sense. No less than George Washington said that immigrants "by an intermixture with our people, they, or their descendants, get assimilated to our customs, measures, laws; in a word soon become one people."[11] Yet in today's multicultural America, this is considered a racist heresy.

Given this history, it is perhaps unsurprising that the Founding Fathers are themselves under attack in their own homes, as we see with Presidents Washington, Jefferson, and Madison.

At Montpelier, James Madison's home, slavery and racism take center stage, while Madison's roles as the father of the Constitution and one of the pivotal early presidents are treated as a sideshow. During a 2022 tour, there were no American flags and no displays devoted to any of his accomplishments. Instead, a large donation from leftist billionaire and Carlyle Group co-founder David Rubenstein ensured the core presentations were about slavery and racial conflicts.[12]

One unhappy visitor who toured the new Montpelier called it "a one-hour critical race theory experience disguised as a tour."[13]

Even the children's gift shop at Montpelier had books by Ibram X. Kendi, including politically correct tomes like *Antiracist Baby* (how many serious works of American history it had were unclear).

Some are fighting back against this tendentious reading of history at Montpelier. That includes, hearteningly, a descendant of one of the slaves who lived on Madison's plantation and who accused the board of directors of trying to transform Montpelier into "a black history and black rights organization that could care less about James Madison and his legacy."[14]

"There were hundreds of thousands of slave owners. . . . But not hundreds of thousands who wrote the Constitution," said board member Mary Alexander, who is descended from Paul Jennings, a slave at Montpelier.[15] Sadly, this sensible approach, one that understands men and women as products of their times and chooses to focus on what was extraordinary about them, has fallen far out of fashion.

Things are scarcely better at Monticello, Thomas Jefferson's plantation, which he not only called home but designed.

Jeffrey Tucker, a writer and a visitor to Monticello, described how on his guided tour, "they were just debunking his history, his reputation, putting him down, demoralizing everybody on my tour."[16]

According to Tucker, the house looked like a "rummage sale" with contemporary paintings on the walls. Tour guides mocked Jefferson, calling his reputation "wildly overblown."[17]

Tucker's experience was echoed by online reviews left by other visitors to Monticello: "The tour guides play 'besmirchment derby,' never missing a chance to defame this brilliant, complex man," wrote one reviewer.[18]

In honor of the new Juneteenth holiday, a bleak contemporary painting of a faceless slave now greets visitors when they enter the main mansion at Monticello. The figure represents "the faceless lives of all who served in bondage, witnessing but never recognized," according to a display at the site.

According to a profile in the *New York Post*, "grievance has become the predominant theme at Monticello, from the ticket booth in the visitors center—decorated with a contemporary painting of Jefferson's weeping slaves—to its final gift shop display."[19]

Civil rights exhortations line the exhibits, while one store on the grounds has five books on Jefferson's slaves and just one on Jefferson.

There is a trigger warning before an exhibit on Sally Hemmings, Jefferson's alleged mixed-race slave mistress.

The board of directors is stacked with Democratic Party donors, including those such as Melody Barnes (board chair at the time of this writing and a former aide to Barack Obama), who seem unduly focused on Jefferson as a slaveowner rather than his pivotal role in America's Founding.[20]

Again, the point is not that we should airbrush the Founders—slavery is a part of many of their legacies. The point is that their involvement with slavery needs to be contextualized into the time and society in which they lived and weighed against their accomplishments that ultimately bought and preserved liberty for so many.

The denigration of our Founders has also moved online.

The left-wing website Anti-Racism Daily promises that visitors can "learn how the Declaration of Independence was motivated by slavery and attacks on Indigenous communities" and that "no cartoon villain portrait of America's enemies can whitewash the horror of a continental Indigenous genocide."[21]

According to the same site, praising Founders like Washington and Jefferson means "disregarding the crimes against humanity that they executed in their pursuit of the nation." Indeed, America appears to be worse than the Soviet Union on a bad day: "There are now more people under 'correctional supervision' in America than were in the Gulag Archipelago under Stalin."[22]

Such views are not only the province of a few cranks on the web. America's own National Archives says that the celebration and valorization of the Founding Fathers is an example of "structural racism."[23]

An official task force report from the National Archives criticizes the Rotunda of the Capitol because it "lauds wealthy white men in the nation's founding while marginalizing BIPOC [black, Indigenous, and other people of color], women, and other communities."[24] Never mind that white men, for better or for worse, were essentially the whole political community that created the Rotunda.

We can't have history if that history doesn't invent important contributions from every group. Equity trumps all.

The report suggests using "trigger warnings" to "forewarn audiences of content [at the National Archives] that may cause intense physiological and psychological symptoms."[25] We now need warnings before we can appreciate, or even study, our own history.

The Founders have been instrumentally misused for years, increasingly erased from history even as their words are praised. President Obama had quotes embroidered on his office rug in the White House that were, though he was likely unaware of it, examples of white erasure.

Obama was fond of citing Martin Luther King Jr. who said the "arc of the moral universe is long, but it bends toward justice." But little known to most (including, perhaps, Obama) is that King's quote is a paraphrase of an 1853 quote by the Reverend Theodore Parker, an abolitionist minister. Parker's quote as King would use it appeared almost verbatim in a book in 1918, though it is significant that neither Obama nor MLK cited Parker as the source.[26]

Parker's pedigree goes back to an exalted place in America's Founding: his grandfather, Colonel John Parker, captained the militia at Lexington in 1775, the first action of the American Revolution. His rifles, donated by his grandson, until recently hung in the Massachusetts state capitol. The original famous statue of the Lexington Minuteman at the battlefield of Lexington was based on Parker. Those words on Obama's rug were the words of America's Founders and their descendants—yet Obama appropriated them in a racialized frame to a version of "justice," justice that invariably meant injustice for white Americans.

## Tearing Down Our Monuments

As is clear from the story of Marsha Johnson, the most ominous trend of anti-white racism and the celebration of degeneracy in our society is the alteration of public and historical spaces. Most people don't read very many history books or visit many historical sites, but they will examine our built environments to obtain informal clues about what is to be celebrated.

The program to erase our history began predictably with the Confederate monuments since those were the easiest targets politically. After all, the Confederates supported slavery and fought on the losing side of a war in which hundreds of thousands of Americans were killed. Outside of the South, they are not seen as particularly sympathetic figures. Yet perceptive conservatives understood that the erasure of our history that started with the Confederate monuments would not stop there.

Crucially, most of these monuments were never particularly controversial in past years. The statues attempted to emphasize the martial heroism of the forefathers of those who had constructed them, which is not diminished even if the cause they fought for was less than worthy (and make no mistake, while slavery is generally viewed by historians as the preeminent cause of the Civil War, many fought for what they saw as their country regardless of their views on slavery as an institution[27]).

Yet the monuments' relatively uncontroversial status would soon change. In 2015, in the early days of the Great Awokening, a total of five Confederate monuments had been removed. By 2020, more than 140 had. Protesters used the murder of black churchgoers by white supremacist Dylan Roof in South Carolina, and the violence that was perpetrated during the Charlottesville Unite the Right Rally in 2017, as rallying cries.[28]

When Trump was bold enough to correctly say that bad people on both sides of the protests were to blame for the violence in Charlottesville, but added that there were "very fine people on both sides" of the issue of Lee's statue removal, the uniparty establishment howled with rage. Yet contrary to the incessant lies in the media, Trump at the time condemned "KKK, neo-Nazis, white supremacists, and other hate groups that are repugnant to everything we hold dear as Americans."[29] But because he also condemned Antifa, which took the lead in some of the violence in Charlottesville, his remarks were considered beyond the pale by all formulators of approved opinion.

Revealingly, Joe Biden said he entered the 2024 presidential race because of Charlottesville. Biden called Susan Bro, the mother of Heather Heyer, the woman who was killed after being intentionally struck by a car driven by white supremacist James Fields, on the day he launched his campaign. This call was remarkable given how busy campaign launches usually are. In giving it such a high profile, he reified the actions of a lone extremist who was condemned even by his fellow extremists. Biden claimed that Trump's "both sides" comment was the moment "I knew I had to run,"[30] suggesting he was either misinformed or a habitual liar—knowing Biden, it was probably both. (Did he really think Trump was suggesting neo-Nazis were "very fine people"?)

The groups that gathered in Charlottesville could not have been a more marginal movement. That Biden and the media turned a few hundred young Tiki Torch–waving misfits into a powerful force that supposedly threatened racial harmony in America was a remarkable feat of political prestidigitation. This is a skill the Left excels at, and it resulted in the removal of dozens of Confederate monuments. The death of George Floyd would later serve as a rallying point for the tearing down of over ninety more Confederate monuments.

Notably, these monuments were often removed by what was effectively state-sanctioned mob rule,[31] as those who tore them down without any legal authorization were either never punished or were punished so lightly that the message was clearly sent that they had *carte blanche* to act as they wished.

Of course, it's entirely fair to debate which historical figures we should honor or how we continue to honor them—not every monument ever constructed should always be left standing. But there should be a strong presumption toward keeping monuments in all but the most egregious cases, and adding additional monuments and context where necessary.

In fact, this has been done by far less "advanced" and "mature" democracies than America's. When I lived in India, I visited Lucknow, the site of the Sepoy "mutiny" of 1857 that was put down by the British and subsequently memorialized with statues and monuments to the British and Indian defenders of British rule. The Indian government, which has declared this revolt the first Indian independence movement, did not tear down the edifices but rather placed plaques by them acknowledging the "mutineers" as Indian independence heroes. It was very affecting, and it did not erase what had happened there, nor how the British had attempted to commemorate it. But it did add a contemporary context in line with the sympathies of a proud and independent Indian nation. Despite being colonized by a white nation, India appeared less institutionally anti-white than contemporary America.

Yale University, surprisingly, came up with a reasonably thoughtful standard for renaming buildings and removing monuments, which took into account the "principal legacy" of the person being honored, his contributions to the institution celebrating him, whether the initial naming had been heavily contested, and whether it currently played a principal role in the life of the institution.[32] But while these standards in a vacuum were reasonable, it is ludicrous to expect in 2024 that such debates are taking place in good faith. If anyone today had the temerity to tear down a George Floyd monument, he would soon be looking at the inside of a prison cell, possibly for years, on "hate crimes" charges. Meanwhile, statues of white Founding Fathers are torn down with almost no repercussions for the vandals.

Meanwhile, other regime-affiliated organizations have less thoughtful standards for what monuments should stay or go. As documented by my Claremont Institute colleague Ken Masugi, the *Washington Post* declared, "When the 118th Congress is sworn in on Jan. 3, its members will walk the halls of a building whose paintings and statues pay homage to 141 enslavers."

"Are the subjects recalled in art because they owned slaves?" Masugi reasonably asks. "Moreover, why isn't the signing of the Declaration, the subject of the first painting interpreted in the article, presented as an anti-slavery painting? After all, slavery was legal in all the colonies; after independence, the New England and mid-Atlantic states prohibited it."[33]

"Consider as well the Kentucky 'enslaver' John Marshall Harlan, who served in the Union army and afterward became the 'Great Dissenter' on the Supreme Court,[34] writing dissenting opinions expanding the scope of the Reconstruction Amendments, including the 'color-blind Constitution' dissent of *Plessy v. Ferguson*,"[35] Masugi writes. "There are few better examples of 'enslavers' who transformed themselves into republican citizens, championing equal protection under the law."

In Chapel Hill, North Carolina, the Silent Sam monument of a nameless Confederate soldier that had stood on the University of North Carolina campus for decades suddenly became, in the 2010s, the subject of a heated political debate. Its removal was never authorized, and in fact was forbidden by North Carolina law, but it was torn down by a "guerilla action" in 2018, and while the university administration pretended to be outraged, it was merely a show for those gullible enough to believe that the rule of law was still important. "It was all smiles and joy and dancing and jubilation, to be honest," wrote one participant in the mob action.[36] Those involved were given slaps on the wrist if they were punished at all.

On her way out, the UNC chancellor, now politically unaccountable, ordered the pedestal of the statue removed as well,[37] while attempts to give the statue to the Sons of Confederate Veterans were met with outrage.[38] Simply put, the Left owns the streets, they can tear down whatever monuments they wish, and the Right is afraid to challenge them (given the treatment of right-wingers in many left-wing jurisdictions, this fear is understandable).

Perhaps the most symbolic action in the monument wars was the decision of Charlottesville, Virginia, to donate a statue of Robert E. Lee (the defense of which had been the centerpiece of the infamous Charlottesville "Unite the Right" rally) to an African American–focused nonprofit that would melt it down to create a new and politically correct piece of public art. The activity around the removal of the Lee statue showed the seamless interaction between NGOs, the government, and the universities to achieve their political objectives.

The group that wanted to melt down the statue is headed by the chair of the Jefferson School African American Heritage Center and, among others, two professors at the University of Virginia. Its website referred to the statue as "a singular source of harm to the Charlottesville community." The Lee statue was removed from the park in July 2021.

The nonprofit group Swords into Ploughshares said they would build "a new work of art that will reflect racial justice and inclusion," and this was carried out, as leftist activities so often are, by a combination of wealthy out-of-state foundations and the government itself. The principal funding for Swords into Ploughshares was provided by Virginia Humanities, an arm of the National Endowment for the Humanities and an institute at the University of Virginia, funded by a variety of left-wing funders and the Open Society Foundations (the famous George Soros–run group).[39] Who removed the statue of Lee? Not popular sentiment, but our government bureaucracy working hand-in-hand with Soros. Before Richmond agreed to remove its own Lee statue from Monument Avenue in 2021, a mob attempted to destroy it.

Birmingham tore down a Lee statue in a park named for him—as did Jacksonville. The locations of these statues have been mapped out in detail for wannabe vandals by the anti-white Southern Poverty Law Center, which is largely funded by wealthy coastal elites.

As we've seen, what starts with Confederate statues rarely stops there. Sure enough, statues of Thomas Jefferson have been toppled. Statues of George Washington have been toppled. San Francisco's woke school board even proposed, in the midst of closing everything during the pandemic, to rename several schools, including those named after the Founders and Democrat Senator Dianne Feinstein (!). This was too much even for San Francisco's crazy voters, who promptly recalled the board members in question.[40]

In Portland, on the eve of Juneteenth (of course), protesters tore down a statue of George Washington on private property after having draped it with the American flag and lit the flag on fire. Previously they'd torn down local statues of Jefferson and those commemorating the white pioneers who'd first settled in Oregon.[41] The administration at the University of Oregon, where the pioneer statues were toppled, gave in to the vandals, and the statues were never replaced.[42]

Similarly, statues of Christopher Columbus are being taken down everywhere.[43] Such removals have been enthusiastically endorsed by the Left. The tearing down of the Christopher Columbus statue in front of the Minnesota State Capitol during the George Floyd riots was strongly supported by 36 percent of Minnesotans who identified themselves as liberal or very liberal, and viewed as "unfortunate but necessary" by an additional 21 percent of liberals. Among those classifying themselves as "very liberal," those who thought it was "entirely justified" outnumbered those who thought it was unjustified four to one.[44] As of 2023, the statue remains in storage.

## Native Americans and the 1619 Project

A similar story could be told about white relationships with Native Americans. Native Americans were not naïve or foolish: they largely did not want to share the lands they lived on—or even nearby lands they did not live on. They agreed to cooperate strategically with white settlers at times when they thought it served their interests.

Most Native American tribes sided with the British during the American Revolution, which further diminished their status, in post-independence America,[45] as they suffered the fate that losers of wars from time immemorial have suffered.

Unbelievably cruel massacres were the hallmark of both sides of the Native American versus white American conflicts. Fatalities among early white settlers were catastrophic, starting with the likely wholesale massacre by Native Americans of the "lost colony" in North Carolina, the first attempt at a permanent English settlement in America.[46] Eighty to 90 percent of the original settlers at Jamestown died, primarily due to starvation or disease, but many at the hands of Native Americans, a number that would dramatically increase after a 1622 massacre by Native Chieftain Powhatan.[47] Even obscure incidents such as the massacre of hundreds of European settlers near Bath, North Carolina, in 1711 as part of the Tuscarora War, left a lasting impression on colonists' minds.[48]

Contra the myths of either glorious conquest or unthinking genocide, the reality of those early white Americans was more mundane. Just like the native tribes, the Europeans were interested in conquest, settlement, territory, and wealth—they just had better technology and disease resistance, and a more advanced political organization.

Anyone who thinks whites in America had some kind of monopoly on atrocities should check out the story of the Erie people (for whom Erie County, New York, and Lake Erie are named) or any of the other tribes that were wiped out by other natives who desired their resources and territory. The Erie were eradicated by various Iroquois tribes through warfare, though a few survivors were presumably absorbed by the Iroquois. There were many things Native Americans learned from whites (and vice versa), but neither party needed instruction in brutal warfare.

Yet the myth of the "peaceful" Native American has proliferated thanks to decades of anti-white teachings in schools and programs in the media. In 2023, a survey of three thousand Americans found that more than 71 percent of Generation Z respondents believed that "Prior to the arrival of European settlers, Native American tribes lived in peace and harmony," with 18 percent "strongly agreeing" and another 23 percent agreeing (the remainder "somewhat agreed"). Older generations were better informed, but many had still absorbed anti-white myths. Eight percent of Boomers strongly agreed with this statement, and another 13 percent agreed, with 20 percent partially agreeing.[49]

## Erasing America

The ultimate goal of all of this leftist revisionism is *Erasing America*, which is the title of a 2018 book devoted to the contemporary Left's all-out assault on history. This erasure is particularly important to the ruling class because America's history and demography are far too white for their political purposes. "Today's students can readily identify Sacajawea and Harriet Tubman, but can often barely discuss Washington or Jefferson—except as slave owners," wrote one 1990s curriculum review. The National Education Association (the leading teachers union) discussed teaching Sept. 11 in the context of historical instances of "American intolerance."[50] A mathematics journal accused meritocratic math courses of "functioning as a tool of whiteness."[51]

One of the continual complaints of leftist historians, exemplified in books such as Howard Zinn's *People's History of the United States* (1980), is that the teaching of American history focuses too much on the story of whites. (This is, of course, laughable to anyone who has recently set foot in a high school history classroom.) But if the teaching of American history has traditionally been very focused on whites, it's because America itself had been so white. Examining the 1960 Census, the last before the Hart-Celler Immigration Act was passed, it's striking how overwhelmingly white most states were.[52] It's not white supremacy to say that whites were largely responsible for the development of modern America through the mid-twentieth century—it's just math. The numerical impact of other groups was relatively trivial.

Outside of the South, the most economically and socially marginal region of the country for most of our contemporary history, there were relatively few non-whites in most of America until quite recently. Southern states made up less than a quarter of the U.S. population in 1960, and their GDP made up approximately 16 percent of the national total. Not a single one ranked in the top half of states by per capita income. Meanwhile, twenty-one of the fifty U.S. states were more than 95 percent white, according to 1960 Census statistics. Fourteen states were at least 98 percent white.

The 2020 Census, fifty-five years after Hart-Celler, shows a vastly different country. The whitest state in America in 2020 was Maine, at 90.2 percent. Thirty-three states were whiter than that in 1960. Today, seven states, including California and Texas, by far the two most populous, are majority-minority. Again, one doesn't need a conspiracy theory or a desire to "erase" other people to observe that the vast majority of the modern United States prior to Hart-Celler was built by whites any more than to suggest this will no longer be true in America's future. Yes, there were African American agricultural laborers in the South and Chinese Americans who built railroads in the West, and Hispanic ranchers and cowboys in the Southwest, and we should tell their stories—but that doesn't change the fundamentals of America's demographic history.

Of even greater note, the 1960 Census was itself taken toward the tail end of the Great Migration, the enormous movement of more than six million African Americans from the South to other regions between 1910 and 1970. Whereas once more than 90 percent of African Americans had lived in the South, almost half lived outside the South just sixty years later.[53]

Before the great migration, these numbers were even more dramatically skewed. In the 1910 census, every state in New England was 98-plus percent white, and thirty states of the then forty-eight were more than 95 percent white. Almost every state that was less than 90 percent white was in the South or its immediate border regions. Four of the five most populated states and eleven of the thirteen most populated were more than 95 percent white.[54] Minority populations (overwhelmingly African American) were almost exclusively concentrated in economically backward areas. The notion that somehow the exploitation of black labor was necessary for the United States to thrive, a popular claim among revisionist historians and a narrative well-nigh ubiquitous on the pro-reparations Left, ignores that after a war that devastated the Southern economy, the overwhelmingly white North and Midwest led the drive that saw America become the world's largest economy by around 1890.

For example, in 1900, New York, by far the most important state with the most important city in America, which had recently become the largest economy in the world, was 98 percent white. Over the next century, New York's population would increase by about 2.5 times, but its African-American population would increase by about 40 times. At the beginning of the Great Migration, African Americans made up less than 2 percent of the population of every region except for the South, where they made up approximately 30 percent of the population (blacks were well less than 1 percent of the American West).[55] Out of twenty-three major cities outside the South, African Americans made up even just one-tenth of the population in only three in 1900.[56]

And contrary to the myth of America's supposed origins in slavery pushed by the 1619 project, from 1610 to 1680, pre-independence America's extraordinarily difficult founding years when the population of settlers grew from 350 to more than 150,000, the white population of the colonies was never less than 95 percent. In 1900, people who were not white or black (including Hispanics) were just 1 percent of the population.[57]

America's successes were what brought us from a tiny outpost of civilization to the world's pre-eminent superpower in the course of a bit more than 300 years. And these were by and large the successes of European-descended Americans. This isn't a statement of white supremacy—it's just one of basic history and demography.

We should not pretend that a great replacement and a great historical erasure have not happened. Even if one thinks that, on balance, a more diverse America is a better America, this remains true. The point of rewriting our history and tearing down our monuments is to occlude the record of what came before—to make us live in an eternal now, where the historical consensus is controlled by a diversity-obsessed regime.

# CHAPTER 7

# Immigration: When the Walls Come Tumbling Down

*"The one absolutely certain way of bringing this nation to ruin, or preventing all possibility of its continuing as a nation at all, would be to permit it to become a tangle of squabbling nationalities."*

—Theodore Roosevelt

*"It's very easy, as we all know, to be very tolerant of minorities until they become majorities and you find yourself a minority. It's easy to say, 'Oh yes, these lovely people—I love the way they wear such interesting costumes.' That's fine until someday you find that they're actually telling you what to do, and that they've actually taken over the town council, and what you thought was your home isn't."*

—Sir David Attenborough

While history tells the story of America's past, no subject is as central to America's future, and no subject gets to the heart of the racism of our current anti-white regime, more than immigration policy. As a result, few subjects are as riddled with taboos in their public discussion. What will happen when the ethnic composition of large parts of America is transformed in ways America's European founders never could have foreseen? And in the interim, what will happen to whites as they continue to lose political power amid their shrinking proportion of the population, as anti-white rhetoric and actions accelerate?[1]

Whether or not you believe that "demography is destiny," these fundamental demographic questions cannot simply be papered over with happy talk. The reality is that the white population, and thus the white voting share of the population, is rapidly diminishing. The fact that whites are under such a sustained attack with a current white voting supermajority does not inspire confidence in how society is likely to treat whites when they are a much-diminished minority.

There is a T-shirt that's popular in "Indian country" and on some left-wing college campuses. It comes in several versions, but the most popular has several Native Americans in traditional dress hoisting rifles while looking sternly at the camera.

"Homeland Security: Fighting Illegal Immigration Since 1492," it reads below. Another version with the same picture says, "We should have built a wall."[2]

I chuckled the first time I saw one of these shirts. It's a clever slogan on its own terms that makes the point that Native Americans, of course, were here when the first white settlers arrived. But upon further thought, I realized the statement it made was profound—it just cut in the opposite direction of the way it was intended.

First, there are the cultural ironies. The rifles the natives hoisted were, of course, not a Native American invention, but a very valued item obtained in trade with whites, a product of European civilization. Ditto the camera that took their picture—and any number of other associated items. The effect would be similar to a T-shirt with whites planting corn telling Native Americans to "get their own crops to plant."

But more profoundly, while Native Americans have arguably benefitted from joining the most globe-spanning power that has ever existed, they also paid a heavy price. Today, there are almost 10 million self-identified Native Americans in the United States, as well as millions of other white-identified Americans with at least some Native American ancestry.[3] But Native Americans learned, much to their regret, the consequences of the failure to protect their border, their language, and their culture. Their failure to do so should cause whites to redouble their efforts not to make the same mistake.

Indeed, in some important ways, the current treatment of whites in America has parallels to the treatment of Native Americans. Of course, whites haven't suffered the level of population or cultural loss that Native Americans did—yet. But while there were crimes committed on both sides of the white/Native American struggle, some of the early treatment of Native Americans, though we now see it as at least in part misguided, was a genuine attempt at acting for their benefit.

The first successful permanent settlement in the United States, Jamestown, had as one of its principal goals the Christianizing of the Native Americans, a task which most Bible-believing Christians would endorse to this day, despite the many failures and tragedies that occurred along the way. Reservations, while the subject of numerous broken promises and policy failures, were a way to give the tribes sovereignty and autonomy over some territory. The recent Supreme Court decision to hand over political jurisdiction over much of Eastern Oklahoma to the Cherokee (though narrowed in a subsequent decision) suggests these rights are still taken seriously.[4]

Given the tribes' often brutal treatment of each other and their treatment of white captives, it is difficult to argue that, had Native Americans triumphed, whites would have been better treated than natives were under a white-dominant regime.

## The Wide-Open Gates

For as long as there have been political communities, immigration—ultimately who is allowed to join a political community—has been a central concern. It was certainly a lively debate in the days of ancient Rome, which many have argued fell in large part thanks to poorly controlled immigration.

Distinguished English historian Peter Heather of King's College in London has argued for the centrality of immigration in causing the fall of the Roman Empire.[5] This interpretation was echoed by former British prime minister Boris Johnson: "When the Roman Empire fell," Johnson remarked on a 2021 trip to Rome, "it was largely as a result of uncontrolled immigration. The empire could no longer control its borders, people came in from the east, all over the place, and we went into a Dark Ages."[6] Romans had not always been so lax about immigration. At the peak of Roman power, immigration was only offered to conquered peoples. And even then, most were barred from settling in the Italian heartland.

As another writer pointed out, it was the Roman Empire's saving of thousands and thousands (some say upward of two hundred thousand) of Goth tribal refugees fleeing from the Huns in 376 that led to Rome's sack less than a century later. After a variety of mutually broken promises between the two sides, the Goths turned on their Roman rescuers at the Battle of Adrianople in 378, a massacre of Romans that saw the deaths of more than thirty thousand and would eventually lead to the fall of the Western Roman Empire.[7]

While few would suggest that today's immigrants have plans to militarily besiege America, it does not take a leap of the imagination to extend the analogy to our own times. Like Rome, we have lost our cultural confidence and moorings, which dramatically increases our risk of being overrun, both literally and metaphorically, by newcomers.

As the Christian conservative writer Rod Dreher wrote pointedly of the essential question facing the West, "The massive migration of barbarians into the Roman Empire, in the 4th through 6th centuries, changed European civilization permanently. They caused the fall of the Western Roman Empire, and centuries later, the rise of a new civilization there, based on the descendants of old Roman stock and Christianized Germanic tribes. Will the latter-day descendants of those Europeans be able to hold back the 'barbarian invasions' from Africa [by far the largest source of coming global population growth] in the 21st century? Or will they have to do as the Romans did and absorb the strangers, and, over centuries, create a new civilization?"[8] One can argue that the latter strategy is the correct one, both practically and morally. But either way, one cannot deny it is a choice.

Today, white people in America and throughout the West are facing the prospect of permanent minority status in countries founded by their ancestors. American (and increasingly European) immigration policies are not copied anywhere else in the world. China tightly controls its borders, letting in only a few thousand legal immigrants per year.[9] In Japan, despite having the world's most rapidly aging population and a shrinking workforce, just 2 percent of its population are immigrants, mostly from ethnically and culturally similar Asian countries.[10] Immigrants make up less than 1 percent of Mexico's population.[11] Yet increasingly whites find themselves self-ghettoized in America and Europe, with the new leaders of the "coalition of the ascendant" using the institutions and sociopolitical mechanisms developed from European traditions in the West to seize political power at the expense of Americans of European origin.[12]

We are told that America is a "nation of immigrants," itself a fascinating piece of propaganda that originates in 1950s ethnic group pressure.[13] America did not always conceive of itself this way. In its origins, as we have discussed, it was not a nation of immigrants but a nation of settlers.[14] Yet the historically inaccurate "nation of immigrants" concept has come to define much of our contemporary immigration policy.

The original British settlers in North America did not come to join an existing society but to create a new one. In doing so, they took on tremendous risks—almost 90 percent perished in some of the earliest settlements.[15] Half of the passengers on the *Mayflower* did not survive the first winter in New England.[16] In the modern world, where even a single death can sometimes make headlines, it is difficult to conceive of the bravery and faith that it took to settle the American colonies. It was anything but simple "immigration," much less the illegal immigration of today in which those who come are housed, fed, transported to the interior of the country, and given mobile phones and social services, all courtesy of the American taxpayer.[17]

Even more than 150 years after the first European settlements in the American colonies, as the new nation declared its independence, Americans were very much settlers on the frontier of Western civilization. Just 40,000 people lived in Philadelphia, our largest city, out of a colonial population of 2.5 million confined largely to the Eastern Seaboard. By comparison, the population of London at that time likely exceeded 850,000. Large numbers of Americans, meanwhile, lived on the frontiers of the frontier, tradesmen in small towns or isolated farmers, always at risk of disease, injury, and native attacks.

When the Founders wrote of "securing the blessings of liberty to ourselves and our posterity" in the preamble to the Constitution, their words had a specific meaning, and it was intended for a specific people. America was not simply a "proposition" nation (and if it were, it would be hard today to explain what that proposition is). When Alexis de Tocqueville, the most famous observer of early American customs, wrote his famous *Democracy in America* in 1835 based on his travels here, he did not mention the words "immigrant" or "immigration" once.

In 1830, after well more than two hundred years of European settlement (we are closer to Tocqueville's time than he is to the time of the first European arrival in America), the immigrant population of the United States was less than 2 percent of the overall population.[18] In fact, Tocqueville was skeptical of America's ability to assimilate its existing African-descended population and saw assimilation as key for Native Americans to succeed in European-American society.[19] (In the latter case, he was not necessarily wrong—the vast majority of self-identified Native Americans today have some European ancestry, and many who consider themselves white have some Native American ancestry. Most famously, many of the aristocratic "first families" of Virginia are descended from the Native American Pocahontas, the daughter of an important chieftain.[20])

Even through the end of the Civil War, the majority of immigrants arriving in America were English speakers from Great Britain and Ireland. And even as late as the early 1890s, more than two-thirds of American immigration was from Britain, Ireland, Scandinavia, and Germany. Before 1881, a period encompassing approximately two-thirds of our history, Northwest Europe provided 86 percent of American immigrants.[21]

Americans of European descent (which is to say virtually the entirety of the American political community) were becoming one people. As British playwright Israel Zangwill wrote in *The Melting Pot*, "America is God's Crucible, the great Melting-Pot where all the races of Europe are melting and reforming. . . . Germans and Frenchmen, Irishmen and Englishmen, Jews and Russians—into the Crucible with you all! God is making the American."[22] President Theodore Roosevelt, a champion of American national identity and a critic of hyphenated Americans (that is, anything less than a pure identification as an American) loved *The Melting Pot*, later writing to Zangwill, "That particular play I shall always count among the very strong and real influences upon my thought and my life."[23]

One reason we did not need a federal immigration system until the first immigration facility was established in New York in 1855 is that many immigrants were just joining their co-ethnics, who had a similar cultural background. It is not a coincidence that the first major immigration restriction laws in America were established in 1882, just as the sources of immigration were shifting.[24]

Still, unhappiness over immigration had begun with the initial surge in immigrants during the 1830s (though immigration opponents worried about volume, not "race"). The Know Nothing party in the 1840s and 1850s was the original anti-immigrant political force in America; its influence was sufficient to capture more than 20 percent of seats in the U.S. House of Representatives in 1854 and run former president Millard Fillmore as its presidential candidate in 1856, when he took more than 21 percent of the vote.[25] Their influence waned only during the Civil War.

We arguably became a "nation of immigrants" for the first time in the 1880s, as the Census Bureau in 1890 announced the closing of the frontier (although it is interesting to note that even during this time, the overwhelming majority of the western half of the United States, and most of Florida and Texas, were less densely populated than any American state today except Alaska).[26] And what continued throughout the western United States could still have been seen as settlement rather than immigration.

Three years later, Frederick Jackson Turner, at the time America's pre-eminent historian, would deliver his famous speech at the Columbian Exposition in Chicago, declaring, "The frontier is gone, and with its going, it has closed the first period of American history."[27] In response to this unprecedented wave of immigration in the late nineteenth and early twentieth centuries, America passed the Johnson-Reed Act of 1924, which, for the forty years it was in effect, shut the immigration window tighter than ever before. When John F. Kennedy made his argument for the United States being a "nation of immigrants"[28] and introduced that phrase into our lexicon, it had only been true for maybe forty or so of the previous 350 years. And it was particularly untrue in 1958 when he argued it[29]—our immigrant population was then at one of its lowest points in history—but politics was politics, and so the phrase remained.

The nature of modern immigration and the backgrounds of modern immigrants are also very different from early America. Early immigrants were overwhelmingly self-sufficient yeoman farmers or skilled laborers, with meaningful minorities of commercial and professional immigrants. But laborers and servants, who made up just over 20 percent of immigrants from 1820 to 1846, would from the end of the Civil War throughout the rest of the nineteenth century constitute the predominant group—this was what our first era of mass immigration brought us.[30] Meanwhile, from the 1920s into the 1960s, an era of immigration restriction, unskilled immigration plummeted, constituting just one-third of total immigration.[31]

The Northwestern Europeans who largely characterized America's first three hundred years of immigration took us from being a tiny strip of settlements and then colonies hugging the Eastern Seaboard to the world's largest economy.

In time, border security would strengthen as more groups from more backgrounds wanted to take part in America's success. The Texas Rangers were deployed to the border as early as 1904. The Naturalization Act of 1906 required immigrants to be able to speak English to become citizens (a requirement still in place today, though often ignored). That the United States began changing its open-border policies in the late nineteenth and early twentieth centuries can be seen as a reaction to (1) the ethnic mix of immigrants, which, as noted above, began to depart sharply from that of existing citizens; (2) the velocity of immigration, which accelerated in relation to the size of the population; and, some decades later, (3) the birth of the welfare state, which made it much easier for immigrants to stay.

During earlier eras of immigration, without a welfare state to prop them up, one in three immigrants returned to their native countries, ensuring those who would be long-term burdens would not stay.[32] Further, unlike most of today's immigrants, they were not given benefits (many of these benefits explicitly racially focused) upon arrival. The notion that an African or Latino immigrant could arrive here illegally and receive legal preferences in employment, education, and a host of other areas would have struck Americans of earlier generations as insane. Had we not been brainwashed by immigration rhetoric, it might strike us as insane as well.

Immigration has long been a force that pulls the country leftward and ultimately leads to anti-white attitudes. This is not due to some defect in the character of individual immigrants or ethnic groups, but the very nature of immigration itself. For example, while most of them today are on the Right, white immigrants from Southern and Eastern Europe fundamentally moved the country leftward in the twentieth century. Simply put, we could not have had the Hart-Celler immigration act in the 1960s without the votes of ethnic immigrants (particularly immigrant Catholics and Jews).[33] (Some scholars have suggested immigrants import their political preferences from their home countries, most of which are to the left on many policies relative to America.[34])

One recent study found that U.S. counties that received large numbers of immigrants between 1900 and 1930 were more liberal today than otherwise similar counties that did not, even when controlling for a host of other factors.[35] In 1952, long removed from their initial immigration, more than three times as many Catholics were Democrats than Republicans. Even today, white Catholics are more liberal than white Protestants. This was not, at least in the main, due to any inherent characteristic of Catholics or Southern Europeans, but simply a natural reaction to the very real social and economic interests of the immigrants who had arrived here in large numbers.

As the writer Helen Andrews noted in the *American Conservative*, "The closer we look at the New Deal, the more we see just how deeply entangled immigration is with the growth of the welfare state, in ways that go beyond demographics." She notes that this immigration brought us both mass political patronage (epitomized by New York's Tammany Hall) and Progressivism, a redoubt of liberal old-stock whites whose paternalism was an outgrowth of immigration policy that brought in immigrants who required "social services."[36]

As immigration accelerated, Franklin Roosevelt soon realized the power dynamics in American life had shifted. He told the disproportionately native-born Americans who opposed his policies at a 1936 rally that they were "already aliens to the spirit of American democracy. . . . Let them emigrate and try their lot under some foreign flag in which they have more confidence."[37] Such sentiments are a precursor to the Great Replacement ideology we have today.

In more recent years, as the differences between old-stock Americans and new Americans have become increasingly visible (a Pakistani or indigenous Peruvian immigrant is visibly not of the white majority culture in a way that a Dutch immigrant might have been), the demographic replacement of white Americans and its political effects have become more obvious.

As the *New York Times* observed, congressmen who challenged the 2020 election were most likely to come from districts with both falling white populations and poorer, less educated white Americans for whom the Great Replacement is just the latest step in their disenfranchisement and dispossession.[38] Nonetheless, the *Times* used this reality to mount a vicious attack on white conservatives. How did the replacement of their demographics and culture become something they were supposed to joyfully accept? Certainly, no one else in the world (outside of the historically white nations of Europe) has been told they must celebrate their replacement.

In this age of diversity and inclusion, it is worth exploring in addition to the census data we have already discussed just how overwhelmingly white the early American political community was. To suggest otherwise is an erasure of history. Virtually all of the even modest Latin-American immigration to the United States before the Mexican-American War in 1848 was into states and territories on the border. There were only 25,000 Hispanics living in the historic core of the United States outside of states bordering Mexico, out of a population of approximately 24 million. That's a bit more than 0.1 percent of the population, 240 years after the first European settlement. Another 85,000 were incorporated into the United States after the Mexican-American War. The Chinese American population, which made up the vast majority of early Asian Americans, was just 4,000 in 1840 and in 1940 was just 106,000, also less than 0.1 percent of the U.S. population.[39]

Meanwhile, the first Indian to gain U.S. citizenship did so only in 1909, and he was a "white" Parsi (that is, an Indian of Persian descent).[40] Fewer than 50,000 Indians total immigrated to the United States before 1965. Today, there are well over six million South Asians living in America.[41] There were just 130,000 African immigrants in the United States as late as 1980.[42]

Now, of course, to say such immigration is new is not the same as to say it is bad. There are perfectly reasonable arguments to be made in favor of this new immigration. And there are strong arguments that not strictly maintaining the previous ethnic status quo was advantageous for America. But those arguments must be made, not just assumed.

What is clear is that the post-1965 immigration boom, rather than serving as a continuation of longstanding American policy, was a spectacular repudiation of that policy. Over the last six decades, America's government has created a new American people. Democrats, who have not won the white vote since 1964, simply elected another people and attacked any white person who complained as a racist.[43]

Given the enormous changes it would engender, it was inevitable that Democrat leaders would lie about the Hart-Celler immigration bill before putting it forward in 1965. "This bill that we will sign today is not a revolutionary bill," President Johnson said. "It does not affect the lives of millions. It will not reshape the structure of our daily lives."[44]

Democratic Senator Ted Kennedy claimed, "The bill will not flood our cities with immigrants. It will not upset the ethnic mix of our society. It will not relax the standards of admission. It will not cause American workers to lose their jobs."[45] None of this turned out to be true. A more accurate assessment was given by North Carolina Senator Sam Ervin, who argued it was not possible to design an immigration policy that did not discriminate, so why not discriminate on behalf of those who had made the country? The American Legion said, "It is in the best interest of our country to maintain the present makeup of our cultural and social structure." A Harris poll in May of 1965 showed that by a 58–24 percent margin, Americans opposed loosening immigration laws.[46]

But who cares what the American people—in particular white Americans—thought?

To be fair, even many of the bill's proponents professed to be surprised by how radical it proved in practice, how its "family reunification" provisions, intended to help white ethnics, led to chain migration, particularly from Mexico.

As immigration policy quickly took on a dramatically different character than had been promised, the Left, unsurprisingly, shifted rhetorical tactics. In 1968, just a few years after the bill's passage, the *New York Times* reported that "the extent of the change" in immigration because of the new law had surprised nearly everyone, but that it was unlikely to be modified because "congressmen don't want to look like racists."[47] Even in the late 1960s, the Left's racial blackmail tactics were working.

Illegal immigration didn't begin *en masse* until the 1970s, and its history is even more fraught. We are constantly told that illegal aliens do not commit more crimes than natives—another carefully chosen anti-white statement. Many whites are not concerned with whether illegal aliens commit more crimes than current legal residents; they're concerned with whether they commit more crimes than their own communities of white Americans—which they most certainly do. The fact that there are non-white populations in the United States that commit even more crimes and thus raise the average should not convince whites that immigration makes them safer.

By the 1990s, even moderate New Democrat rhetoric on immigration was changing. As President Clinton said in a 1998 address at Portland State,

> Today, largely because of immigration, there is no majority race in Hawaii or Houston, or New York City. Within five years, there will be no majority race in our largest state, California. In a little more than 50 years, there will be *no majority race* in the United States [my emphasis]. . . . . [These immigrants] are energizing our culture and broadening our vision of the world. They are renewing our most basic values and reminding us all of what it truly means to be American.[48]

Sounds kind of like . . . a great replacement. Did the supermajority of white Americans ask for this? Nobody cared.

Nonetheless, the Left has reinterpreted immigration history to attack America. Leftist scholar Roxanne Dunbar-Ortiz recently wrote a popular book called *Not a Nation of Immigrants: Settler Colonialism, White Supremacy, and a History of Erasure and Exclusion*. And while Dunbar-Ortiz is right to define European arrivals to the United States as settlers, not immigrants, the rest of her history is faulty. From the beginning, the settlers worked in conjunction with some Native American groups and in opposition to others, depending on where their strategic goals lay. The Wampanoag allied with the Pilgrims, not out of some airy-fairy bloodless humanitarianism, but because they hoped to use the alliance to stave off the highly aggressive and violent Narragansett and Iroquois tribes.

In contrast to the sometimes cooperative relationship between Pilgrims and native tribes, Native Americans themselves often completely exterminated each other.

## The Political History and Consequences of Immigration

Immigration has had many political consequences for America. The Democrats have used their polarization of African American voters, in concert with mass immigration, to do something remarkable: they have achieved electoral pre-eminence while consistently losing the votes of the supermajority ethnicity. (This supermajority has ranged from an 89 percent white electorate in Jimmy Carter's victory in 1976 to a 67 percent white electorate in the 2020 victory of Joe Biden.)[49] Over this time, the Democrats have won six presidential elections and the popular vote in two additional elections without once winning the vote of white voters.[50] There is no other modern multiracial democracy of which I am aware where a party has achieved electoral success while perennially losing the votes of the supermajority ethnicity.

The mass growth of illegal immigration has created another problem: the representation of illegal immigrants in our Census—they are counted just like everyone else—has led to the creation of so-called "rotten boroughs" (a term originally used to describe very small constituencies in England that elected members to Parliament and that were eliminated in the Reform Act of 1832). These unequal districts amount to a modern three-fifths compromise in which the citizens of states and districts with large numbers of illegal aliens and other non-citizens are given disproportionate political power relative to those in districts with more citizens. While the Supreme Court theoretically established a "one person one vote" rule in *Baker v. Carr*, which set the stage for forcing states to create congressional districts with equal populations in the name of fairness, somehow the Court (and the media) has not considered the unequal representation from illegal aliens to be a problem.[51]

In contrast, our Founding Fathers were very aware of how critical the immigration debate was to the future of the nation. In the 1790 debate on naturalization in the House of Representatives, James Madison said, "When we are considering the advantages that may result from an easy mode of naturalization, we ought also to consider the cautions necessary to guard against abuses... [The purpose of immigration is] not merely to swell the catalogue of people. No, sir, it is to increase the wealth and strength of the community; and those who acquire the rights of citizenship, without adding to the strength or wealth of the community are not the people we are in want of."[52]

Pennsylvania Representative James Hartley said, "The policy of the old nations of Europe has drawn a line between citizens and aliens: that policy has existed to our knowledge ever since the foundation of the Roman Empire; experience has proved its propriety, or we should have found some nation deviating from a regulation inimical to its welfare."[53]

Alexander Hamilton, despite himself being an immigrant, was no fan of open borders and understood in particular the dangers of a multiethnic nation: "The United States have already felt the evils of incorporating a large number of foreigners into their national mass; it has served very much to divide the community and to distract our councils, by promoting in different classes different predilections in favor of particular foreign nations, and antipathies against others. It has been often likely to compromise the interests of our own country in favor of another."[54]

And no less than George Washington was clear on what was required of an immigrant to become an American: "By an intermixture with our people, they, or their descendants, get assimilated to our customs, measures, laws; in a word, soon become one people."[55]

In the context of America, an immigration policy properly considered should mean integration into American society, history, and traditions. Today, we have lost this emphasis on integration and, in fact, many immigrants, explicitly or implicitly, have declared war on

America's historically European-centered identity. Certainly, immigration has been pushed by the Left with the explicit goal of reducing the status of white Americans.

The political scientist and former national security official Michael Anton coined the term "celebration parallax" to describe an increasingly common feature of contemporary political life: "The same fact pattern is either true and glorious or false and scurrilous depending on who states it." As Anton notes, on no subject is the celebration parallax so closely observed as on mass immigration.[56]

This is true because immigration is so directly implicated in the demographic replacement of whites as the predominant racial group in America. Non-Hispanic whites accounted for 58 percent of Americans in 2020, down from 64 percent in 2010.[57] In 1960, the last census before Hart-Celler, whites made up 85.5 percent of the population while 10.5 percent were African American.[58] Of the Latino population, 48 percent had lived in America for more than three generations.[59] The total population of non-Hispanic non-whites was just 1.6 million, about 0.9 percent of the total.[60]

Sixty years later, the rate and volume of change are staggering. As of the 2020 census, there are 62.1 million Hispanics, 24 million Asian Americans, and 1.7 million Pacific Islanders in America.[61] There are even 4.6 million black immigrants (43 percent from Africa),[62] a number about half that of the total number of immigrants in America in 1960.[63]

Overall, we have more than 45 million immigrants in America (88 million if you also count the children of immigrants),[64] up from just eight million or so in 1960.[65] Of note, the number of immigrants from Europe and Canada has declined by almost 25 percent during that same period—almost all the rest come from areas where immigration had previously been minimal or nonexistent.[66] Indeed, since 1990, the Diversity Visa program welcomes fifty-five thousand immigrants each year from countries that are chosen precisely for their lack of connection with historical immigration patterns to the

United States.[67] Some entrants on this visa have committed terrorist activities.[68] Yet the Democrats have staunchly opposed eliminating the program, even when this number of visas was offset by an equal increase of visas in other categories.[69] Filling America with people with little or no ties to the historic American nation is an article of liberal ideology.

The result: among America's children, less than half are non-Hispanic white.[70] Within approximately two decades, America as a whole is projected to become majority-minority.[71] The Great Replacement isn't a conspiracy theory; it is, as 2024 GOP presidential candidate Vivek Ramaswamy observed, "just the basic immigration policy of the Democrats."[72]

Even as an Indian American, Ramaswamy's comments created a stir. Yet when whites (especially conservative whites) talk about the incredibly rapid demographic transformation of the country that's taken place over just a few decades, and express concern over the place of their own culture, history, and status in society, or when they note that diverse societies are much more likely to suffer from inter-ethnic violence as well as a lack of social cohesion (a fact documented by Harvard sociologist Robert Putnam among many others[73]), they are invariably attacked as racist. Diversity is our strength. Any other answer will land you in the gulag, comrade.

It has been a consistent finding of social science research that multiethnic societies suffer from low social trust and that low social trust does not just occur between ethnic groups (which might be expected) but even within ethnic groups (that is, in a multiethnic society, Asian Americans trust even other Asian Americans less).[74] Furthermore, high levels of diversity have been shown to be damaging to trust among neighbors—those who actually get to know each other—rather than a simple case of ethnic balkanization built out of self-interest or fear of an "other" who is unknown to you.[75]

When whites mention the fact that, as they are being replaced, their cultural and historical symbols are often challenged or even eliminated outright (witness the defacement of monuments to Washington, Jefferson, and even Lincoln during the Black Lives Matter riots in 2020), they are called bigots, white nationalists, and worse. When the Left celebrates this same demographic transformation, it is expected and welcome, part of America's continued march toward a brighter, happier, and more diverse future.

Go to the websites of left-wing "civil rights" organizations such as the Southern Poverty Law Center (SPLC) and the Anti-Defamation League (ADL), and you will see the Great Replacement dismissed as a "far-right conspiracy theory."[76] Even Wikipedia defines it as a "white nationalist, far-right conspiracy theory."[77] Yet a *New York Times* columnist can write a column about increased immigration titled "We Can Replace Them" while another can celebrate "the browning of America, the shrinking of the white population and the explosion of the nonwhite," and nobody bats an eye.[78] This is the celebration parallax defined.

NPR, which has received billions of dollars in federal funding, can suggest that replacement is a crazed fantasy as opposed to an empirical reality.[79]

Yet MSNBC's Joy Reid can tweet that she is "giddy" watching "all the bitter old white guys," while *National Journal*'s Ron Brownstein, elated about Obama's winning more than 80 percent of the minority vote while losing whites in his initial run for the presidency, can tout the "coalition of the ascendant."[80] Meanwhile, everyone from the Brookings Institution to CNN celebrates "the vanishing white American" that will "doom the GOP."[81]

As conservative columnist Pedro Gonzalez noted, "Biden himself said that a 'constant' and 'unrelenting' stream of immigration would reduce Americans of 'white European stock' to an 'absolute minority,' and that this was a source of our strength.'"[82]

Yet those who express concerns over how these future hyper-diverse Americans are supposed to get along with each other, or who wonder what culture, history, and traditions we are supposed to share in common, are accused of wishing for something terrible for the country. Meanwhile, those who extol America as a "proposition nation" (that is to say, one devoted to a particular set of ideas rather than a particular people) seem fuzzy on exactly what propositions we are mutually supposed to accept. Looking around at the increasing conflict-prone nature of America, it's difficult to see any propositions we can agree on at all.

To critique our current immigration policies is not to suggest that some sort of naïve and doomed racial purity standard is the way forward for America. It's to suggest that a dramatic slowdown of immigration followed by aggressive assimilation is the best way for a variety of groups to come together into a unified majority culture. This is the only realistic pathway for America to become "one people" again, as our Founders intended us to be.

As the geneticist and popular science writer Razib Khan writes of the modern Hungarians, who bear only a faint genetic resemblance to the Central Asian Magyar conquerors who swept through their country a thousand years ago and gave Hungary much of its cultural identity, "Despite the extinction of their genes, the Magyars live on in posterity. . . . Genetically, the Magyars are but a ghost, but culturally they remain with us, vibrant and vigorous, the most numerous and assertive of the Uralic people. . . . Sometimes language, myth, and legend live on long after flesh and blood have been washed away."[83]

White Americans are numerous enough that their flesh and blood will not be "washed away." But given where we are, the best plausible outcome might be that we become a nation of white and multi-racial Americans who nonetheless still admire the Founders as both our spiritual and, in many cases, literal ancestors.

# CHAPTER 8

# That's Entertainment?

*"Nobody knows anything."*
—William Goldman, screenwriter of *The Princess Bride*
and *All the President's Men*, speaking about Hollywood

*"I have done no harm. But I remember now I am in this
earthly world, where to do harm is often laudable, to do
good sometime accounted dangerous folly."*
—Lady Macduff in William Shakespeare's *Macbeth*

The entertainment that a society produces says a lot about it. Not for nothing has Hollywood been referred to as "the dream factory," for the movies and TV shows we produce, the albums of music we release, all tell us a great deal about who we are as a country, our hopes and goals and desires.

And there is nothing that says those dreams must be ethical or that aesthetically interesting art may not repulse us morally. D. W. Griffith's 1915 film *Birth of a Nation* was technically groundbreaking and, at the time of its release, the highest-grossing film ever—and on those terms was widely hailed as one of the greatest films of all time.[1] Yet its embrace of the Confederate "lost cause" and crude caricatures of African Americans caused many to condemn it even upon its release, and far more to do so later. (For many years, the Lifetime Achievement Award for film direction from the Directors Guild of America was named after Griffith in recognition of his multiple innovations in the art of film directing—before it was replaced in 1999 in a move the National Society of Film Critics saw as a "depressing example of political correctness."[2])

In another context, German director Leni Riefenstahl's films, in particular *Triumph of the Will* and *Olympia*, were praised for their startling technical achievements but equally excoriated as effective propaganda for the Nazis. Nonetheless, *The Economist* called Riefenstahl the "Greatest Female Filmmaker of the 20th century." As the legendary (and left-wing) critic Roger Ebert would write about both films, "*The Birth of a Nation* is not a bad film because it argues for evil. Like Riefenstahl's *Triumph of the Will*, it is a great film that argues for evil. To understand how it does so is to learn a great deal about film, and even something about evil."[3] While advocacy of good or evil can't be so easily teased out of today's film, this wisdom can teach us a great deal about the anti-white elements of the cinematic world.

Look at the American Film Institute polls celebrating the greatest stars of the first one hundred years of filmed entertainment's existence, and the top names roll out as icons of the American dream. Humphrey Bogart, Marlon Brando, Clark Gable, and Gary Cooper are among the top men, while Audrey Hepburn, Marilyn Monroe, Elizabeth Taylor, and Grace Kelly take top billing among the women.[4] All are icons of American masculinity and femininity, respectively, even today.

Of course, these images did not fully reflect reality. Behind the sheen of the all-American movie star was an often different and pained reality. And the stories of ethnic minorities were often marginalized from Hollywood's mythmaking (though given the relatively small number of non-African American minorities in America at the time, it is surprising how many well-known minority actors there were even in Hollywood's earliest days).

Hollywood indeed tended to ignore certain American stories and elevate certain others in the service of mythmaking. But overall, even in its early days, Hollywood was far more "progressive" than America as a whole, championing the rights of various groups disfavored by the larger society long before it was fashionable among the general public. And while those who work there have always held a range of views, Hollywood has long been famously left-wing and even far-left-wing. Not for nothing did Ronald Reagan get his political start warring against communists in Hollywood.

While at one point the Hollywood dream may have presented a version of white America tinted with rose-colored glasses, by now the situation has long since been reversed. Hollywood's dream factory has been explicitly co-opted in the service of anti-whiteness.

As one book on Hollywood history showed in attempting to statistically quantify the portrayal of minorities in film, by the mid-1960s, just as the civil rights revolution was getting underway, minorities were already portrayed more positively than whites in Hollywood films.[5] This, of course, does not mean there were no stereotypes of minorities, demeaning and otherwise, or that white heroes were not likely to get top billing—unsurprising given that the American ticket-buying public was overwhelmingly white in those days. But overall, when you saw a minority character on screen, the depiction was far more likely to be positive than negative.

These pro-minority (and, by contrast, anti-white) biases remain in films more than sixty years later, but the gap between reality and representation has widened dramatically. According to a quantitative analysis of prominent films, the percentage of minorities committing crimes on screen was equal to that of whites (in reality, the crime numbers for minorities are much higher) and minorities who did commit crimes were portrayed much more positively than whites who did not commit crimes. Minorities, and particularly African

Americans, were far more likely to be offered roles as police officers and soldiers, and less likely to be portrayed as criminals, than was warranted by real-life numbers.[6] Since the 1960s, a period encompassing most of the lives of the vast majority of Americans, Native Americans have been consistently portrayed more positively in film than whites, shown in particular as caring for the environment versus whites who often wanted to despoil it.

But if white people have long been out of favor in Hollywood, what has been in favor is the so-called "Magical Negro." It's a term that was popularized by African American film director Spike Lee in 2001, though its origins as a phenomenon can be seen in films as early as 1958's *The Defiant Ones*.[7] The "Magical Negro" would often have special powers and insights that were not available to the film's white characters. Another source describes him as a character "whose purpose in the plot was to help the protagonist get out of trouble, to help the protagonist realize his own faults and overcome them."[8] Think of many characters that Morgan Freeman has played, from Red in *The Shawshank Redemption* to Lucius Fox in the *Batman* franchise.

Meanwhile, even the biggest stars are not immune from being told to toe the racially correct line. When Tom Hanks called attention to the Tulsa race massacre—an early twentieth-century race riot of complex origins that has come to increasing prominence, and increasing exaggeration, in recent years in service of left-wing political agendas—he was called out by critics for not doing enough. He needed to be "anti-racist," not just non-racist.[9]

## The Color Casting Revolution

According to the Annenberg Inclusion Initiative, a study of "inequality in 1,300 popular films" done by the Annenberg School of Communication and Journalism at the University of Southern California, white characters are no more likely to have speaking parts in today's films than their percentage of the population.[10] Blacks are somewhat overrepresented while Asians are significantly overrepresented. Hispanics appear to be substantially underrepresented, but some Hispanics (many of whom are phenotypically white) are likely coded as white by those doing the analysis, both overestimating the white celluloid presence and underestimating the Hispanic one. Seventy-one percent of casting directors are white women and the overwhelming majority of them are liberal. Eighty-seven percent of directors are white.[11]

Of course, even when these studies come to honest conclusions, they still carry a liberal bias. The Annenberg study suggests that films that did not have minorities failed to include them because they were being "erased" or "were missing."[12] So if you do an eighteenth-century period drama set in England without an Asian character, you've "erased" Asians. If white people don't erase their own history—for example, if Marie Antoinette and Queen Elizabeth I aren't portrayed by minorities—they are seen as systemically racist.

Yet the race of these characters is a matter of historical fact. If minority writers and directors (or white writers and directors!) want to tell stories with predominantly minority characters, they can write those stories. And many are doing just that. Nobody is stopping them. Tyler Perry's "Madea" series isn't getting distribution deals because it is critically beloved but because it resonates with its overwhelmingly African American audience and makes money. As they say in Hollywood, it's not "show friends," it's "show business."

Yet this "color-conscious" casting only ever goes only one way. Anne Boleyn or Cleopatra can be black, but the idea of a white person playing a minority character is largely forbidden today. And even back in those supposedly more racist times, white actors playing these roles often did so because of a shortage of minority actors. Further, those who do not cast enough minorities often face pressure and scorn. Acclaimed directors such as Richard Linklater and Tim Burton have been attacked for making films that are "too white"—but Spike Lee is rarely criticized (nor should he be) for making films that are too black.[13]

Perhaps nowhere is this caste system casting more pervasive than at the Oscars. The Oscars have always been left-wing—think of Marlon Brando sending "Sacheen Littlefeather," a fake Native American not exposed as such until after her death, to read a protest speech as he refused the best actor award in the 1970s.[14] But in an effort to diversify, the Academy of Motion Picture Arts and Sciences has engaged in blatant tokenism.

The terrified Academy now requires pictures to meet two of four standards to be eligible for an Oscar. These standards include centering stories on LGBTQ or racial minorities, having a certain number of minorities among cast members, having various senior crew members be minorities (including numerical quotas), and having the financing and senior marketing and distribution executives be racial minorities.[15]

As actor Dean Cain, a multiethnic actor most famous for playing Superman in TV's *Lois and Clark*, tweeted about the rule, "How about we judge on this criteria—which film was the BEST PICTURE? (also, when do we start handing out participation Oscars?)"[16]

To benefit minorities, anti-white discrimination in Hollywood has become more explicit—but woe unto those who point this out. When a black film industry professional issued an explicit call to hire black film editors, he was met with pushback from successful white film editor Nathan Lee Bush, who described the ad as "anti-white racism."[17] Bush wrote, "Look what we're asked to tolerate. The people openly and proudly practicing racism are the ones calling everyone racist to shut them down, and anyone who dares to speak up is canceled, their livelihood and dreams." This simple common sense caused some of the top companies Bush worked with to pull their business, ultimately forcing him to apologize.[18]

The new woke casting is having the desired effect. "A revolution is underway," according to an article in the *Daily Mail*. "White actors are being fired. Edicts from studio bosses make it clear that only minorities—racial and sexual—can be given jobs."[19]

This extends to the writers' room, where storylines for shows are written. As one industry source recounted, "Every white male writer in Hollywood has stories of being snubbed, but only recently have I heard of white men being paid—against WGA [Writers Guild of America] rules—to take their names off projects; to eschew credits for higher payouts, so others can take credit for their work."[20] Modern times in Hollywood increasingly resemble the days of the communist blacklist, when writers affiliated with the Communist Party had to ghostwrite their material. But instead of the blacklist, we now have the whitelist—writers penalized for the crime of being white.

The choice to hire minorities over whites is being made at the most senior levels of the entertainment conglomerates. "Directors normally have a say about who is in their project. Not anymore. It's all about 'BIPOC hiring'. And it's coming directly from the heads of the studios who know their jobs are on the line," wrote one Academy Award nominee who wished to remain anonymous.[21]

"You could argue that it's a good thing," said another prominent insider, "that this swinging of the pendulum so far the other way is only fair after years of white privilege. But at what cost? Surely it is best for everyone if people are hired on the basis of talent and ability? I can tell you, we are hiring people based purely on their ethnicity, gender, and social-media profiles."[22] All true—except for the idea that Hollywood was once a bastion of white privilege. The data shows that hasn't been the case for a long time.

## Anti-White Ideology in Contemporary Film

"I don't see myself casting a white dude as the lead in my movie," the African American director and actor Jordan Peele said. "Not that I don't like white dudes. But I've seen that movie before."[23]

Now, of course, Jordan Peele should feel free to cast whomever he wants in his movies. He seems to be a talented filmmaker. But can you imagine a white director saying, "I don't see myself casting a black dude as the lead in my movie?" The anti-white racism and black privilege are so obvious that they don't even need to be stated.

Little wonder that Peele's movie *Get Out*, adored by critics (and to be fair, popular with audiences as well), was not attacked for its anti-white racism, except among a few, largely conservative sources.

Armond White, the gay, conservative, African American film critic at *National Review*, wrote a brilliant review of *Get Out*. White delves into the heavily anti-white core of the movie, linking it explicitly to the anti-white leaders of our cultural milieu.

"What was it, exactly, that the *all-media screening* [my emphasis] audience at the new movie *Get Out* was cheering for when the black protagonist killed an entire family of white folks one by one?" he asks. White is quick to connect Peele's broader ideology in the film to contemporary political trends: "Pushing buttons that alarm blacks yet charm white liberals, Peele manipulates the Trayvon Martin myth the same way Obama himself did when he pandered by saying, 'Trayvon Martin could have been my son.'"[24]

*Get Out* centers on a cult that extracts the energy (both physical and mental) of black men to give greater power to whites. This is not exactly Ralph Ellison–level subtle social commentary on the issue of race. White understands the unpleasant political agenda that informs these movies and their popularity: "Just as Obama did, Peele exploits racial discomfort, irresponsibly playing racial grief and racist relief off against each other, subjecting imagination and identification to political sway."[25]

Or, as another (approving) African American reviewer put it, "So, go ahead and call Peele's movie 'anti-white.' Frankly, it is. . . . *Get Out* is anti-white because it exposes the hypocrisy of even the nicest white folks."[26]

And this sin, according to the reviewer, deserves no salvation. "White supremacy, anti-blackness, and racism is so meticulously ingrained into our culture that it's now more of a runaway train filled with generations of passengers who no longer know what a brake looks like."[27]

Explicitly ethnonationalist fare is celebrated in Hollywood as long as it is not white ethnonationalist. Conservative commentator and former actor Michael Knowles noted this about the Africa-themed superhero movie *Wakanda Forever*, after some of the film's fans suggested whites shouldn't show up during its first week in theaters.[28]

"Because there is a constant celebration of black creativity, the real vibranium, by white people who claim it for themselves without credit in service of agendas that erase us or do us harm," wrote one black contributor to Andscape, a black-focused website owned by ESPN, thus revealing both her racism and historical illiteracy.[29] These anti-white bigots, of course, don't care that the Black Panther character who is central to Wakanda in the films was not invented by African Americans, but by two Jewish comic artists decades ago.

In any case, such commentary barely registered. The audience for *Black Panther* was 65 percent non-white and 37 percent black on opening weekend.[30] Parenthetically, it is worth noting that the notion of a high-tech Afrocentric paradise untouched by whites is beyond historically illiterate—and sits in stark contrast to the low levels of technological development usually seen in African communities *not* touched by colonialism. Whatever its other merits and demerits, it was colonialism that brought modern technology to Africa.

Little wonder that conservative activists attempted in their sphere to capitalize on *Black Panther*'s racial double standards.[31]

As conservative commentator Ben Shapiro noted (in an overall laudatory review of the film), "The contrast between victimized black people (Killmonger) and gloriously successful black people who are successful because no white person has ever interfered in their lives (T'Challa) is obvious." It's also entirely fictional, a cathartic "blame whitey" for the problems of black America. In this way, it is, somewhat ironically, a modern update and reversal of *Birth of a Nation* (*Birth of Wakanda?*). Or, as Shapiro notes, "One of the premises of the film is that if Killmonger had been brought back to Wakanda and grown up in this utopia, he wouldn't have become Malcolm X. It was America that made him into Malcolm X rather than an ally to T'Challa."[32]

Not coincidentally, the far right took note of *Black Panther*'s racial double standards. A meme, "*Black Panther* is alt-right," pointed out that Wakanda was anti-immigration, anti-diversity, and anti-refugee, as well as pro-wall and ethno-nationalist. It correctly skewered the idea that *Black Panther*'s values are allowed for blacks but not whites.[33]

Those surprised by *Black Panther*'s anti-white ideological stance should not be. Director Ryan Coogler made his directorial debut with the propaganda film *Fruitvale Station*, a seminal documentary of the early Great Awokening released in 2013. It celebrated African American small-time hoodlum Oscar Grant, who, resisting arrest while intoxicated on a BART train in Oakland in 2009, was fatally shot by an officer who accidentally mistook his Taser for his gun and would be imprisoned for eleven months as a result.[34]

The officer was lucky. While his name became the subject of unjustified infamy, juries in liberal locales in those days were not so insane as to imprison a white officer on a clearly spurious murder charge. After the jury verdict, there were many days of riots and lawlessness that became a precursor to the Black Lives Matter movement.[35] Grant's father, who had been in prison since before Grant was born, also filed suit to try to get in on the monetary damages.[36] Yet Coogler's movie turned the Grant saga into a parable of society's alleged systemic racism against blacks.

As one critic asked of *Black Panther*, "Is black superiority better than white superiority?"[37] In a savage review in *National Review*,

Armond White exposed *Black Panther*'s real agenda: "For race-focused naïfs, Wakanda is the Afro-futurist fount of Millennial black intelligence, scientific advancement, and political sovereignty." White added that "Hollywood repeats Black Lives Matter's Marxist effort to destroy the family unit by appealing to the divide-and-conquer yearnings of black feminism."[38]

The *Black Panther* films were the furthest thing possible from marginal. *Black Panther* ranked sixth overall at the all-time U.S. domestic box office as of 2023, and *Wakanda Forever* ranked twenty-fifth.[39] Combined, they had a cultural reach that could only be dreamed of by any writer.

## Madison Avenue's Racial Myths

Anti-white animus isn't just confined to the silver screen. Racial mythmaking is also present in modern commercials, which, in service of an ideological agenda, consistently show higher levels of interracial relationships and friendships than exist in real life.[40]

A 2019 study of interracial relationships in TV advertisements found they occurred at almost twice the level as were present off-screen.[41] Or, as another scholar commented on interracial interactions in commercials, "The lens through which people learn about other races is absolutely through TV, not through human interaction and contact," adding, "Here, we're getting a lens of racial interaction that is far afield from reality."[42] Reality can be bent in ways both subtle and obvious. As Morgan State University professor Jason Johnson, who has studied multiracial advertising, noted, 70 percent of interracial commercials show a white man and a black woman,[43] whereas in reality, black men are more than twice as likely as black women to be in an interracial marriage.[44]

Scholars have consistently pointed out that this is done to push multiculturalism and diversity ideology while selling more products to those who already value those things. One might reasonably ask, what's the harm? Commercials, of course, have always presented an ideal, one that is more beautiful and harmonious than real life. But when this false image is pushed for the sake of a social and political agenda, and not just because it's popular with audiences (interestingly, minorities tend to prefer to see white actors in commercials, rather than members of other minority groups), it is fair to ask questions.[45]

Portrayals of whites in the commercial world are disproportionately negative. As *The Cranky Creative*, an advertising industry blog, puts it, "White people (60-plus percent of the population) are seeing themselves erased and replaced by people of color who look, talk, and act just like them," while minorities have representation but not authentic cultural representation (that is, minorities who are represented tend to have the same interests, and affects, as whites). Meanwhile, actual white males "are the bungling idiots of the ad world, just as they've been for years and will continue to be for as long as the culture deems them toxic."[46] Or, as another advertising site put it, "The go-to ad joke is—still — the white male moron."[47] There's even a popular Twitter account, "White Men Are Stupid in Commercials" (@stupidwhiteads), dedicated to the negative portrayals of whites in television ads.[48]

The point is that commercials do not simply reflect the culture; they drive perceptions and changes in the culture, and in a particularly anti-white way.

## Narrow-Minded Broadway

While this chapter focuses primarily on Hollywood, anti-white rhetoric can be found throughout the entertainment industry. The show *Hamilton*, the biggest Broadway sensation in modern times, with a box office of well over $1 billion, is perhaps the most interesting example of anti-whiteness in the entertainment world.[49] *Hamilton*'s anti-whiteness is in some ways a transitional Obama-era product, as in not fully woke, seeming to uphold the accomplishments of white Americans who fought in the American Revolution while glorifying Alexander Hamilton, a conservative white male Founding Father. Composer Lin-Manuel Miranda wrote *Hamilton* between 2008 and 2015, with the great majority of it completed before the Great Awakening got going in earnest.[50]

*Hamilton* is undeniably an impressive accomplishment artistically, and on one level it is a presumably sincere homage to the Founding Fathers. While some of them come in for rough treatment (for example, Thomas Jefferson), others fare better, particularly George Washington and, of course, Hamilton himself. In the context of the current year, a portrait of the Founding as a heroic act and the Founders as historic if flawed figures is ultimately praiseworthy.

*Hamilton*'s casting is explicitly color-conscious (most of the principal cast of the original Broadway production was played by African Americans, with the exception of Puerto Rican-American Lin-Manuel Miranda's Hamilton and Hamilton's wife, Eliza, played by Philippa Soo, an Asian American). This casting can be seen to give ownership of these heroic revolutionary roles, and of the Founding itself, to all Americans. Further, in situating them within a hip-hop context, the rebel Americans seem more, well, rebellious. As far as it goes, that is arguably a praiseworthy monument to national integration.

Yet dig beneath the kumbaya surface, and a more disquieting picture emerges. The one notable character in *Hamilton* played by a white actor is the villain, King George III, portrayed with a foppish, gay insouciance by Jonathan Groff.[51] That is to say the main enemy—the one person who is *not* in any way a part of the American story but rather a figure of mockery—is white. One suspects this is no mere accident of casting.

Further, the casting of blacks as white revolutionaries is an act of historical erasure—and an erasure of truth. It was enough to confuse some of my younger children when they first heard about *Hamilton*. The Founders were, in fact, white men, and it is possible to acknowledge this without denying the universality of their message or the ability of Americans of all racial backgrounds to embrace the Founding today. In this, *Hamilton* is similar to the removal of monuments in America—a replacement of history. A truly multiracial *Hamilton* cast might be seen as an act of artistic daring or a statement that color does not matter. But by casting minorities, overwhelmingly African American, for almost every part except for that of the most notable, uncomplicated villain, an unsettling message is being relayed.

This message is very much aimed at the young. "My two White teenagers have memorized nearly every word of the musical, and they are not unique among their peers," says one anthropologist. She calls the cast "strikingly racially diverse actors," but they are not really that—except in the modern sense in which "diverse" simply means "less white."[52] While the casting director says the musical had "no specific racial breakdown" and Miranda claimed in a 2013 interview that he only wanted the best rappers regardless of race, the 2016 casting call encouraged "non-white" actors to audition for lead roles.[53] Color-blind casting, as the article seems to suggest, was when minorities had less power—now that they have more power, color-conscious casting cements it.

According to one writer, the biggest applause line in *Hamilton* is when Hamilton turns to Lafayette and says "Immigrants—We get the job done" (ignoring, of course, that these were both white immigrants of European origin—and Lafayette would eventually return to the country from which he came). It was no coincidence that the Hispanic Federation launched the "Immigrants—We Get the Job Done Coalition," supported by Miranda and involving several prominent organizations advocating for (mostly illegal) immigrants. The politics of our modern artistic works are rarely far beneath the surface.[54]

Indeed, when Charter Cable was dealing with its own racial discrimination lawsuit, it suggested (implying such a situation would be terrible) that accepting its opponents' position would require the casting of white actors in *Hamilton*.[55] Charter thus asserted that it had a First Amendment right to consider race in determining what shows to carry.[56]

But even so-called color-blind casting also serves to marginalize white stories and erase white history. Today, we expect to see minority actors in spaces that, using historical accuracy, would have been white, but we would never expect to see a white actor playing a clearly minority character.

One African American actress complained that a reviewer focused on her race amid her casting of Eliza Doolittle in Lerner and Loewe's classic musical *My Fair Lady*.[57] One can sympathize with her complaint, but the real problem is that her casting has an element of absurdity—the entire story of *My Fair Lady* centers on Eliza's being a cockney, lower-class, white woman from a very specific time and place in England.

Now, one could easily imagine *My Fair Lady* being updated in plot and style to encompass a role that would work for a black actress (this has been done quite successfully in shows such as *The Wiz*, a highly successful musical based on *The Wizard of Oz* with an all-black cast). Such an adaptation would focus on race rather than social class as a point of entry for high society (as *My Fair Lady* itself was an updating of George Bernard Shaw's play *Pygmalion*). But the way it stands as written, Eliza Doolittle is ultimately a role that makes the most sense in the hands of a white actress. Obviously, a casting director can put whomever he or she wants in that role, but it's a heavy lift to ask the audience to ignore the historical anachronisms, and we could hardly imagine such a strongly culturally situated black character being played by a white actress today.

## Music and Literature

Anti-whiteness in entertainment and culture goes far beyond Hollywood, Broadway, and Madison Avenue. Even such staples of high culture as classical music and literature have suffered, as Heather Mac Donald documents in her outstanding book *When Race Trumps Merit*.

As Mac Donald notes, the League of American Orchestras in 2020 released a *mea culpa* for its alleged discrimination against black musicians. The Seattle Opera said that it would "continue to prioritize" antiracism while apologizing for causing harm.[58] The head of the Juilliard's music theory division called for the field's "whiteness" to be remedied.[59] The head reviewer at the *New York Times*, in an explicit call to discriminate against white and Asian musicians, called for the end of blind auditions.[60]

Other organizations called for mandatory racial quotas in orchestras and substantial percentages of orchestra budgets to be used to address "systemic racism."

The Scottish Opera was attacked and issued a groveling apology for allowing white opera singers to have the roles of Mao and Zhou Enlai in *Nixon in China*. As Mac Donald notes, the fact that they had a black performer in the role of Nixon gave them no protection from the mob.[61]

Things are scarcely better in literature. White male authors are heavily discriminated against by literary tastemakers. The 2023 National Book Awards longlist was dominated by what commentator Shelyuang Peng referred to as "marginalized group torture porn,"[62] with books about whites watching blacks fight to the death for entertainment, the cruelty of Indian boarding schools, and the eviction of mixed-race islanders from an area in Maine.

This was merely a continuation of a long-standing trend that I documented in a 2017 article in *National Review* in which the awards obsessed over race. Of the previous year's winners, all four had focused on "confront[ing] the US's racist past (and present)."[63]

Unsurprisingly, white male authors sometimes attempt to take on minority identities to get published. In 2015, white poet Michael Derrick Hudson wrote a poem that was rejected forty times under his name before he decided to attempt to publish it under the name Yi-Fen Chou. After a few more rejections, it was published and then selected for that year's edition of the prestigious *Best American Poetry* anthology edited by prominent Native American writer Sherman Alexie.

When Hudson revealed his true identity, Alexie, after wrestling extensively with the decision, decided to keep the poem. "I am quite aware that I am also committing an injustice against poets of color, and against Chinese and Asian poets in particular," Alexie wrote. "But I believe I would have committed a larger injustice by dumping the poem. I think I would have cast doubt on every poem I have chosen for BAP. It would have implied that I chose poems based only on identity."[64] Alexie's decision was brutally criticized by writers, particularly Asian Americans, who wanted him to do just that.

## Anti-Whiteness in Contemporary Pop Culture

In his article "The End of White America?," published to great fanfare in *The Atlantic* in 2009 in the wake of Obama's election, Pulitzer Prize–winning writer and academic Hua Hsu said the rise of hip-hop "has bred an unprecedented cultural confidence in its black originators. Whiteness is no longer a threat, or an ideal: it's kitsch to be appropriated." Hsu pointed out that shows such as *The Colbert Report* and *The Office* existed to make fun of the "clueless white male."[65] One can think of countless other movies and TV shows that do the same. The hapless white guy is so omnipresent that he's almost a cliché. He has been, so to speak, normalized.

"Pop culture today rallies around an ethic of multicultural inclusion that seems to value every identity—except whiteness," Hsu wrote frankly.[66] "It's become harder for the blond-haired, blue-eyed commercial actor," remarks Rochelle Newman-Carrasco of the Hispanic marketing firm Enlace. "You read casting notices, and they like to cast people with brown hair because they could be Hispanic. The language of casting notices is pretty shocking because it's so specific: 'Brown hair, brown eyes, could look Hispanic.'"[67]

"I think white people feel like they're under siege right now—like it's not okay to be white right now, especially if you're a white male," according to Bill Imada of the IW Group, a multicultural marketing and communications agency. "I always tell the white men in the room, 'We need you,'" Imada said. "We cannot talk about diversity and inclusion and engagement without you at the table. It's okay to be white!"[68]

Understandably, whites in Hollywood may not believe it is okay to be white. In fact, as we will see later it's not even okay to use the phrase "it's okay to be white," unless you are not white yourself.

Hsu understood that even in 2009, whiteness was a burden, not a benefit. "If white America is indeed 'losing control,' and if the future will belong to people who can successfully navigate a post-racial, multicultural landscape—then it's no surprise that many white Americans are eager to divest themselves of their whiteness entirely," Hsu wrote, predicting this would happen not just across the cultural landscape but in politics as well.[69]

Understanding the anti-white cultural zeitgeist, a site called *Stuff White People Like* burst into popularity in the late aughts by mocking things that young, fashionable, middle- and upper-class white people appreciated. "I get it: as a straight white male, I'm the worst thing on Earth," *Stuff White People Like*'s founder Christian Lander told Hsu.[70]

"Like, I'm aware of all the horrible crimes that my demographic has done in the world," Lander says. "And there's a bunch of white people who are desperate—*desperate*—to say, 'You know what? My skin's white, but I'm not one of the white people who's destroying the world.'" Rarely has the psychology of so many of today's elite self-hating whites been stated so succinctly.[71]

"As a white person, you're just desperate to find something else to grab onto," Lander says. "You're jealous! Pretty much every white person I grew up with wished they'd grown up in, you know, an ethnic home that gave them a second language."[72]

Matt Wray, a sociologist at Temple University and a fan of Lander's work, sees Lander's and similar white-mocking media as products of a racial/cultural identity crisis among whites: "They don't care about socioeconomics; they care about culture. And to be white is to be culturally broke. The classic thing white students say when you ask them to talk about who they are is, 'I don't have a culture.'" Consider the vast levels of anti-white propaganda that were necessary to convince the heirs of the Western tradition, the cultural ground on which America was built, that they do not have a culture.[73]

"The best defense is to be constantly pulling the rug out from underneath yourself," Wray notes. "Beat people to the punch. You're forced as a white person into a sense of ironic detachment. Irony is what fuels a lot of white subcultures."[74]

Meanwhile, as victims of a cultural assault from all sides, blue-collar whites have retreated into their own form of identity politics. Hsu cites late-2000s examples such as Jeff Foxworthy, Kid Rock, and the Blue-Collar Comedy Tour, as well as the continued growth of NASCAR and country music. He correctly flags Ross Perot, Pat Buchanan, and Sarah Palin as having tapped into this identity, which in many ways reached its apotheosis in the figure of Donald Trump, who was as much an entertainer (think *The Apprentice*) as he was a businessman.

Hsu sees these cultural cues as a form of racial pride, a desperate attempt for the now-hopelessly outnumbered working-class white minority, increasingly and overtly disdained by its fast-growing multicultural replacement, to reclaim the mantle of the "real America."

Turn on the TV or watch a movie, and you'll understand. In few areas is the Great Replacement as visible as in our pop culture.

Yet Hsu sees a multicultural mashup as the great American future. "This moment was not the end of white America; it was not the end of anything. It was a bridge, and we crossed it," he writes.[75]

The problem is, for many white Americans, the bridge Hsu describes is a bridge to nowhere.

# CHAPTER 9

# The Unbearable Whiteness of the Green Movement

*"All there is to thinking is seeing something noticeable which makes you see something you weren't noticing which makes you see something that isn't even visible."*
—Norman Maclean, *A River Runs Through It and Other Stories*

*"God bless America. Let's save some of it."*
—Edward Abbey, environmentalist and writer

The statement hit my desk early that morning as I prepared for my day's work as deputy assistant secretary of the Interior in the Trump administration.

"Hiring Jeremy Carl, an avowed white nationalist, to run major portions of the Interior Department is the culmination of a long and intentional process that started early in the Trump administration," said Congressman Raúl Grijalva, then chair of the House Natural Resources Committee.[1]

While structural racism against whites has long been one subject I've cared about (there is a reason I wrote this book), I have never even remotely advocated for white nationalism, which would be completely destructive of the fabric of American society. I'm determined to see justice applied equally to white Americans precisely because I believe this is the only way America can succeed as a multiethnic country. Yet in response to a newspaper hit piece, the predictable jackals were out in force.

I was appalled by Grijalva's invective, and seriously considered taking legal action against him, but unfortunately for me, Article 1, Section 6, of the Constitution gives racial arsonists like Grijalva latitude to make outrageous statements when done in the context of their official duties. This is, for example, how Congresswoman Ayanna Pressley was able to tweet without any evidence that Kyle Rittenhouse was a "white supremacist domestic terrorist."[2] Her tweet has since been viewed by millions of people, and she's never had to apologize or take it down.

Most of my career has not been spent writing about racial issues. In fact, I've done the majority of my work in the fields of environmental and energy policy, where I came face to face with once-proud environmental groups that had become obsessed with anti-white racism to the detriment of their mission. I experienced this firsthand when these groups hysterically attacked me after I joined the Trump administration.

Of course, like many anti-white racists, in assailing me for standing up for unjustly accused and slandered white Americans, Grijalva was merely projecting his own racism, which has gone largely unchallenged during his more than two decades in Congress, including his time chairing the House Natural Resources Committee.[3]

Grijalva started his career in politics writing for a radical Chicano political journal with the slogan "*Mi raza primero*," which translates to "My race first."[4] He led protests (some of which turned violent) in Tucson and involved himself in the radical MEChA movement, whose motto at the time translated to "For the race, everything, outside the race, nothing."[5] He was "so militant that he alienated some members of Tucson's Mexican-American community," in the words of one profile.[6] These are the sorts of people whom the Democrats elect to Congress today.

Not to be outdone, a senior official at the Sierra Club, America's oldest and arguably most prestigious environmental group, said that "racism has no place on our public lands, and it has no place atop the Department of the Interior."[7] Certainly a statement that I would heartily agree with, but also bizarre given that I had once been a member of the Sierra Club and had never advanced any race-based environmental policies.

## Anti-White Environmental NGOs

The hysteria that greeted my nomination to the Trump administration was indicative of how much performative anti-white racism has become a core part of the modern environmental movement, even to the point of working against actual environmental interests.

Ironically, as most of those denouncing me would have known if they'd glanced at my background, despite being solidly on the GOP's right wing in the vast majority of policy areas, I was probably one of the most "dovish" people in Trump's Department of the Interior on environmental issues, having once worked briefly for a major center-left environmental group and having published widely on environmental issues with prominent bipartisan co-authors. But none of that mattered to them. They were obsessed with my forthright and unsparing critiques of left-wing racial hysteria.

Experiences like mine hint at a dramatic shift in the topics environmental groups will even address. Discussing issues such as how illegal immigration leads to environmental damage at the border is largely verboten in the contemporary environmental movement.[8]

Of course, to some degree, they are just compensating. Environmental groups have long had a fraught relationship with the multicultural Left. Their membership and leadership have historically been very disproportionately white, even by the standards of what was once an extremely white country.[9] To compensate for this "failing" in a dramatically diversifying America, they needed to double down on anti-white racism to ensure their continued political viability. And that is just what many of them have done.

One political problem for environmental groups is that a lot of people who care for the environment are historically against mass immigration, since they understand that ultimately a more crowded country puts more pressure on its natural resources.[10] In 1998, 60 percent of the Sierra Club membership voted to take a neutral position on immigration issues.[11] This was fairly shocking for a group that even at the time was down-the-line liberal on virtually every other political issue.

But this neutrality represented a step to the left for the Club. In 1969, the Sierra Club's board of directors had called for population stabilization, and in the late 1970s the Club lobbied Congress to study the effects of immigration on the environment.[12]

In 2003, the Club elected, by member petition (that is, against the wishes of its professional leadership), two anti-immigration candidates to its board.[13] In 2004, several other impressive petition candidates came forward, including Democratic former Colorado governor Dick Lamm and Frank Morris, former head of the Congressional Black Caucus Foundation. In response, the board took the unprecedented step of attaching an "urgent election notice" warning voters about "white-supremacist groups" trying to influence the election.[14] Using this scare tactic, they were able to defeat the insurgent candidates.[15]

By the late 2010s, though, a change in leadership meant that the Club, America's most prominent environmental organization, was regularly using its Twitter account to attack Donald Trump over the border wall and immigration policy, subjects that were related tangentially (at best) to the environment.[16] In part, this turn has been to placate big donors, some of whom threatened to withhold funds if the Club didn't take an open borders stance.[17] And in part, it was to show that the Club was now a proud member of the intersectional Left, environment be damned.[18] I still think of my wife's Republican grandmother, who supported the Club because she believed it was first and foremost about protecting wild spaces. Nobody paying attention to the Club's activities would ever make that mistake today.

The Club has rarely missed an opportunity in recent years to bolster its standing with the intersectional Left. In 2020, the Sierra Club's then–executive director Michael Brune issued numerous statements concerning the police killings of George Floyd, Breonna Taylor, and others.[19]

According to Brune, blacks in America were in constant danger. "They deserve to be safe sitting in their own vehicles, as George Floyd was before he was pinned to the ground and murdered by police. They deserve to be safe relaxing in their own homes, as Breonna Taylor was doing when officers fired more than 20 rounds into her kitchen and living room," Brune wrote.[20] These are, to put it mildly, extraordinarily tendentious readings of the cases involved.

Brune also claimed that "the companies that have profited from fossil fuels and accelerated the climate crisis are the same ones who have benefited from environmental injustice, colonialism, and racism." He told Club members, "Ask your local park administrator what they're doing to protect people of color," as if people of color were somehow under regular assault at America's national parks.[21]

But perhaps the most remarkable aspect of the Club's self–great replacement is that it recently "canceled" its legendary founder John Muir, which is roughly the equivalent of America canceling, well, George Washington (come to think of it, perhaps that's not so remarkable).

In a post on the Sierra Club's blog in July 2020, at the height of the George Floyd protests, entitled not so subtly "Pulling Down our Monuments," Brune wrote, "We must also take this moment to reexamine our past and our substantial role in perpetuating white supremacy."[22] He attacked Muir for some of his friendships with other early leading conservationists, who, like many progressives in the late nineteenth and early twentieth centuries, also dabbled in eugenics and scientific racism.[23]

This was, needless to say, an egregious example of presentism, judging those of the past by the standards of today. While Muir made certain comments that today would be seen as racist, he was also by the standards of his time a racial progressive (though his views about the environment, rather than race, should be at the center of his legacy).

The Sierra Club's apologetic blog post soon descended into Stalinist show-trial levels of self-parody.

"For all the harms the Sierra Club has caused, and continues to cause, to Black people, Indigenous people, and other people of color, I am deeply sorry. I know that apologies are empty unless accompanied by a commitment to change. . . . I invite you to hold me and other Sierra Club leaders, staff, and volunteers accountable whenever we don't live up to our commitment to becoming an actively anti-racist organization," Brune wrote.[24]

He announced a new plan (of dubious legality) to have a majority-minority leadership team making top-level organizational decisions for the club going forward.

Future blog posts were equally hair-raising, including one supporting reparations that announced that "justice for Black people in this country is never guaranteed—it is an afterthought and sometimes, not a thought at all. . . . While systematic discrimination and racism terrorize Black communities, the same systems also openly endorse extraction, degrade our humanity and create sacrifice zones in the name of profit and big business."[25]

The post goes on to claim that "Black liberation is essential to solving the global climate crisis, and that liberation is impossible without reparations." I am not making that up—they actually wrote that.

Needless to say, in addition to being politically radical, the post is also scientifically illiterate. I am sure that China and India, which together contribute nearly 40 percent (and rapidly rising)[26] of the world's emissions, would be fascinated to know that whites paying slavery reparations to blacks in a country that contributes just 12 percent (and falling)[27] of global emissions is somehow the *sine qua non* of successful global climate policy. Completely unrelated to reparations, the United States could take its $CO_2$ emissions to zero and it would have only a modest long-term effect on the global emissions trajectory.[28] But who needs facts when you are engaging in anti-white polemic?

In another post, the Club noted, "Thankfully, the Trump administration's white supremacist politics are not only unpopular and under fire from the courts. They're also facing mass opposition in the military, across the economy, and in the streets, where thousands of Black people and their allies have demanded an end to police brutality and racist criminal justice systems."[29]

All well and good. The Club's leadership and officials are clearly members of the anti-white Left in good standing. However, challenging the Sierra Club's new commitment is the fact that the Club is a heavily volunteer-led organization, and the volunteers are disproportionately white retirees who are still committed to traditional environmental issues rather than often fuzzy and politically abused concepts like "environmental justice"—let alone slavery reparations.

The story does have a beautiful ending, however. If you guessed that all of the self-flagellating anti-white rhetoric wasn't enough to save white man Brune's job, give yourself a pat on the back. In 2021, he resigned, according to a report by The Intercept, "amid upheaval around race, gender, and abuses."[30] There were accounts from numerous ethnic minority staff members decrying the racism of Club members.[31]

Brune couldn't even find a scrap of dignity on his way out. Instead, he attacked his own membership, which had fought countless

environmental battles, devoted literally millions of hours to the pres-
ervation of the natural environment, and built and maintained trails
and backcountry cabins: "The Sierra Club is a nearly 130-year old,
white legacy organization that is in the middle of a transformation to
become more equitable and just," he told The Intercept.[32]

Later, in November 2022, we found out exactly what this transition looked like. The Club hired former NAACP head Benjamin
Jealous as executive director, someone with modest environmental
credentials but a record chock-full of civil rights activism.[33]

Of course, the dedication to anti-white wokeness did not
always produce the desired results. Shortly into his tenure, Jealous
announced the Club was running a $40 million annualized deficit (a
massive amount for a group with a $167 million budget),[34] and that
there would be layoffs.[35] To be fair to Jealous, he actually seems, in
the process of budget cutting, to have curbed some of his predeces-
sor's worst ideological excesses, laying off the entire "equity team,"
among other steps, while Aaron Mair, who had previously served
as the Club's first black board chair, criticized Brune's "ahistorical"
criticism of Muir.[36]

I have spent a lot of time on the Sierra Club because it is arguably
the largest and best-known of the American environmental organizations and certainly the most influential among the grassroots.
But its problems are emblematic of environmental groups in general.
Throughout the environmental movement, staff, boards, funders,
and members of green groups are overwhelmingly white, a fact that
causes no end of distress to the hapless liberals who run and staff
them.[37] This trend is even more extreme for environmentally focused
foundations—virtually all money for environmental causes comes
from either white individuals or foundations run by whites.

Liberal white environmentalists even attack other liberal white
environmentalists for caring about climate change. One memorable
piece appeared in *Scientific American*, the oldest continuously published magazine in the United States and America's most prestigious

popular science journal (though its prestige has been hit in recent years by its invariable elevation of leftism over actual science).[38] The fact that it reads more like a Tumblr post than an article at a prestigious science news organization is an indication of where we are in 2024.

"I have been struck by the fact that those responding to the concept of climate anxiety are overwhelmingly white," wrote the author. "Indeed, these climate anxiety circles are even whiter than the environmental circles I've been in for decades."[39]

Having identified the phenomenon, she was quick to attribute it not to the unique mental instability of white liberals (which I'll explore elsewhere in this book) but as a marker of racial privilege.

"Is climate anxiety a form of white fragility or even *racial* anxiety? Put another way, is climate anxiety just code for white people wishing to hold onto their way of life or get 'back to normal,' to the comforts of their privilege?" the author asks.[40]

Whatever it is, you can be sure white people are to blame: "The white response to climate change is literally suffocating to people of color. . . . We can't fight climate change with more racism. Climate anxiety must be directed toward addressing the ways that racism manifests as environmental trauma and vice versa—how environmentalism manifests as racialized violence," the author writes. Again, this appeared in *Scientific American*, America's most prestigious popular science magazine.

In an article attacking white environmentalism on GreenBiz, a popular business-oriented environmentalist website, one author quotes an activist who argues that environmentalism is so white because some members of the Latino community view environmental problems as less urgent than issues such as immigration. "Immigration is #1, with people being detained," she says. "How can you tell your students to care about the environment when they are afraid that their parents won't be home?"[41]

Such groups are damned if they do and damned if they don't. The same article quotes an activist who attacks green groups that do diversify. "They bring in that one Latinx person, that one Indigenous person, that one person of color, and they think that's enough. They think that one perspective speaks for all of the community."[42]

Others celebrated the browning of the environmental movement, regardless of whether those being added would actually make it stronger.[43]

Some of the newer environmental activists, according to a piece in *National Geographic*, were inspired by the blood libel created around the death of Michael Brown (who, according to a report from the Obama Justice Department, was justifiably killed by a police officer whom Brown lunged at after committing a strong-arm robbery).[44] Activist misinformation about his shooting, amplified by left-wing politicians, led to an orgy of rioting in Ferguson, Missouri in 2014.

Said one black environmental activist about Brown's case, "The more I learned about the incident, and when I began to study environmental injustice, I started thinking about intersectional theory and how it could also be applied to the environmental movement."[45] Armed with this anti-white myth (though having little environmental background), she went on to work for the National Park Service and Patagonia, and will doubtless, if she chooses, continue to rise in the new environmental movement, which cares more about showing that it is sufficiently brown than that it is sufficiently green.

According to *National Geographic*, these activists "are leveraging opportunities to lessen threats for Black and brown people in those spaces doing activities that white people take for granted."[46]

What threats?

I'm sure that in a country as big as ours, some issues exist, but in my extensive personal experience on public lands, I've never seen any threats to people of color on account of their race—I've hardly seen threats to anyone at all.

Another piece in *National Geographic* attacked white Americans because less than 2 percent of national park visitors are black, which is somehow the fault of whites.[47] Never mind that visits to national parks and other public lands are, if planned carefully, just about the least expensive and therefore most accessible vacations one can plan. Everyone involved in outdoor recreation knows people who have lived on or near National Parks for weeks and even months at a time on a shoestring budget.

"The great outdoors in the U.S. has never truly been a welcoming place for people of color," intones the author.[48] But why? Visitors to national parks tend to be extremely polite when compared to virtually any other venue I've been to (certainly, as a parent, I can say that behavior at national parks is better than at, for example, amusement parks). This is true even at parks like Yellowstone, near my home in Montana, where visitors are often mocked for being clueless and getting too close to dangerous geysers and wild animals—but not for their race. Our national parks were ordered desegregated in 1945,[49] and while that did not happen all at once, the park system has been open to all for many, many decades.

## The Government Role

These accusations of environmental racism against whites do not occur in a vacuum: they have received political sanction from very high places. As he prepared to leave office, Barack Obama advanced a presidential memorandum to public land agencies called "Promoting Diversity and Inclusion in Our National Parks, National Forests, and Other Public Lands and Waters."[50] The memo ensured that the National Park Service would train for "unconscious bias" and "diversity and inclusion," including mandatory training for senior leaders, while making it clear that leaders would be promoted based on their championing of diversity and inclusion rather than, say, how well they stewarded parks resources.[51]

Sure enough, national parks have responded to these incentives. In Glacier National Park in Montana, I personally encountered one egregious example. A signboard near the wilderness entrance in a remote section of the park, twenty-seven miles down a gravel road, had several articles posted on it. The first was about a federal Indian boarding school initiative announced by Deb Haaland, the Department of the Interior's first Native American secretary (the schools, once seen as progressive, are now attacked for cultural erasure—doubtless calls for reparations are soon to come). Another article celebrated the transfer of the National Bison Range lands to local tribes. A third article celebrated the brand-new federal holiday of Juneteenth (which 60 percent of Americans knew little to nothing about when it was created).[52] Fourth was an article about disability history, fifth was about efforts to consult with native Hawaiians to discuss possible changes to the Native American Graves Protection and Repatriation Act, and sixth was an article celebrating Latino Conservation Week. This was in addition to two other articles lauding disability activism and the pro-transgender "Progress Pride" flag.[53]

Secretary Haaland was also busy in her early days in power, renaming more than 650 places that had "squaw" in the name, a term activists have described in recent years as derogatory toward Native American women, though the preponderance of the historical evidence suggests it was merely a neutral descriptive word derived from local native (primarily Algonquin) languages.[54] Of course, woke capital was not far behind. Squaw Valley resort in Lake Tahoe, the site of the 1960 Olympics, was renamed "Palisades Tahoe" in 2021.[55]

While individually most of the articles posted on the signboard were not objectionable, in totality they sent a different message. As I wrote elsewhere, "Literally the entire message board was devoted to one form or another of minority activism, whether for Hispanics, African Americans, Hawaiians, Native Americans, LGBT, or the disabled. Any notion that the Department of the Interior had a core mission to serve the entire American people was lost completely."[56]

There was nothing on the board about trail conditions, recent bear sightings, or other items that might be of more interest to remote area hikers than political correctness. Meanwhile, the park's ability to serve environmental needs has been crippled in recent decades. Hard-to-obtain permits, which sell out in minutes, are needed to visit virtually every area of the park. The Going-to-the-Sun Road, the park's main attraction, was open more often sixty years ago, when the park had one-fifth of its current visitors, than it is today. There was more lodging in the park in the 1940s (when visitation was one-tenth of its current rate) than there is in 2024. Yet park officials, busy attacking the various sins of whites, have done nothing to expand access to the park for all visitors.[57] As in so many other areas of government, the more they yell about anti-whiteness, the more they hope you won't notice their gross incompetence.

## Whiteness and Climate Policy

Anti-white animus is also visible in much of mainstream climate policy, particularly international climate policy, which has morphed into simply another way of taking money from historically white countries (the United States, Europe, Australia) and spending it in non-white countries (China, India, various African nations).

In many cases, the "help" we are providing with our wallets hardly makes things better for the recipient countries. President Biden recently agreed to help pay South Africa more than $8 billion[58] to shut down its coal plants and replace them with alternative energy—despite South Africa already suffering from an unprecedentedly unreliable power grid (a result of their aggressive affirmative action regime at the state power company, once the envy of Africa, that placed unqualified people in positions of authority due merely to their not being white).[59]

Climate change is the big new pot of money for the anti-white Left. The ACLU calls climate change "a racial justice issue,"[60] while the BBC informs us that "climate change is inherently racist" and points out that poor African American areas of the United States were hit by hurricanes Katrina and Harvey, which were clearly very racist storms. "There is a stark divide between who has caused climate change and who is suffering its effects," the article says, blaming white people for bringing modern industrial technology to the world.[61]

Would the BBC staff ever dream of saying, "There is a stark divide between who invented electricity generation, the automobile, and the airplane and who is benefitting from its effects"? They would never in a million years dream of doing so. Yet while white people do not get credit for the enormous number of innovations that inventors and entrepreneurs of European descent have brought into this world, they are unhesitatingly blamed for dubious possible climate effects that are second- and third-order consequences of these inventions and for which many white scientists and engineers (among others) are working diligently to provide solutions.

Complaints go beyond evil white people causing climate change to African voices not being represented at climate summits. "Racism and white supremacy have long excluded African voices from environmental policy," according to the BBC.[62] Even if we were to grant that this was true, Africans are doubtless represented in numbers far in excess of their global emissions profile. (China alone produces nearly one-third of global emissions,[63] while all of Africa produced 3.9 percent of emissions in 2021, largely a consequence of its far less-developed economies.[64])

But if you guessed that American- and European-driven industrial progress, which led to an unprecedented renaissance of global affluence, was just a colonialist monstrosity, then give yourself a cookie. According to one anthropologist quoted by the BBC, "The nations of the Global North have effectively colonised the atmospheric commons. They've enriched themselves as a result, but with devastating consequences for the rest of the world and for all of life on Earth."[65] Setting aside the dubious factuality of this statement, this anthropologist would never admit that the West has also generated the majority of the world's technology (and is developing and funding most of the tech that may eventually allow us to affordably address climate change).

Not coincidentally echoing the arguments of U.S. slavery reparations advocates, a leading United Nations official said that we cannot address climate without also addressing Systemic racism, colonialism, and slavery. In a broad report, the official documented "the racist colonial foundations of the ecological crisis, transnational environmental racism, and climate injustice, as well as racially discriminatory environmental and climate-related human rights violations."[66]

Well, how convenient. Get ready to open up that pocketbook, Uncle Sam.

Of course, exploding population is never considered a contributor to climate change, since that would reflect less well on non-European peoples.[67] As they say in the business world, what gets measured gets managed.

## Environmental Injustice

Perhaps most indicative of the elite anti-white axis of activism among environmentalists is the environmental justice movement. In an interview with Yale's Environment 360, Elizabeth Yeampierre argued that the fight against climate change and the fight against racial injustice are part of the same struggle: "Climate change is the result of a legacy of extraction, of colonialism, of slavery." She added, "The idea of killing black people or indigenous people, all of that has a long, long history that is centered on capitalism and the extraction of our land and our labor in this country."[68]

I am sure the communist countries, which used resources far less efficiently and emitted more pollution (in overwhelmingly white countries in Eastern Europe, for example), would be interested to learn this. But blaming white people and capitalism for their problems is simply a reflex reaction for these activists. And they can rely on the most prestigious forums to parrot their nonsense.

Another small problem with Yeampierre's statement is that it appears not to be true. A recent study of the state of Mississippi (a place where you would expect to find environmental racism if it existed as a major problem) concluded that "no positive association exists between heavy black population and large amounts of air pollution in the state of Mississippi. If anything, the tables and graphs show less pollution in counties with higher black representation."[69]

There are a variety of reasons for this, the authors hypothesize, including highly black areas having less economic activity (indeed, Mississippi pollution is borne more by lower- and middle-class whites, who are, of course, implicitly blamed for being racist in the environmental justice pollution narrative).[70]

None of this is to suggest there is no correlation between pollution and economic class. The richest areas anywhere are unlikely to have highly polluting industrial projects, and if such projects were to be improbably relocated to such areas, those areas would be unlikely to stay rich because the rich people would relocate. But this doesn't constitute a racist conspiracy. Rich people of whatever race will always live in more desirable areas. The takeaway from the Mississippi study is that middle- and working-class whites tend to be the predominant group living near polluted areas (often because they work at the companies doing the polluting).

This study meshes with my experiences fieldwork in and near India's remote East Central tribal belt. In the truly impoverished areas where I spent time, the environment was more or less pristine because there was no industrialization bringing its attendant jobs and the pollution that accompanied them. It was in the middle-class, more industrialized areas that you saw pollution—and also much greater affluence and economic opportunity.

The pollution observed in the developing world today is there for the same reason that London was so polluted during the Industrial Revolution. The "dark Satanic Mills" that William Blake referenced in his poetry teemed with people because industrial urbanism, even with its attendant pollution, was far preferable to rural starvation for huge numbers of Englishmen. And then, as now, racism had nothing to do with it. The difference now is that with modern technologies, we can produce things much more cleanly, and with international NGOs ready to pounce, extreme pollution usually comes to public attention.

Yet blaming pollution on racism serves an instrumental purpose. It justifies the transfer of massive amounts of money from historically white countries to non-historically white ones. Climate change is also leveraged to demand more open borders through dubious studies about "climate refugees."[71] Environmental justice thus serves as racial blackmail in a green wrapper. The Biden administration and the EU have agreed to create a "climate reparations" fund, which could be worth hundreds of billions of dollars.[72]

Overall, the trajectory is clear. Given the choice between creating bipartisan alliances to promote a clean environment and racially abusing whites, most environmental groups and advocates will choose to slander whites every time. They will manufacture whatever evidence they need to support their theories. On everything from the formation of environmental groups to national parks to climate policy, they are more devoted to making the environmental movement, and America, less white than to making the planet more green.

# CHAPTER 10

# Big Business, Big Tech, and Big Discrimination

*"If they can get you asking the wrong questions, they don't have to worry about answers."*
—Thomas Pynchon, *Gravity's Rainbow*[1]

*"It was terribly dangerous to let your thoughts wander when you were in any public place or within range of a telescreen. The smallest thing could give you away."*[2]
—George Orwell, *1984*

Entertainment and technology increasingly sit atop the commanding heights in America's economy. It is little surprise, therefore, that the anti-white attitudes and policies that dominate the entertainment arena are echoed by our business and technology leaders.

In June 2020, as Black Lives Matter protests raged across the country, billionaire Jamie Dimon, the longtime CEO of JPMorgan Chase and widely considered the world's most powerful banker, took a knee while masked up for COVID in his first public appearance since undergoing heart surgery a few months prior. Dimon, visiting a bank branch in Mount Kisco, New York, was surrounded by an impressively multiethnic group of employees.[3] His kneeling was widely interpreted as protesting the death of George Floyd and supporting the Black Lives Matter movement (though officially Chase neither confirmed nor denied this).

A year earlier. after allegations of discrimination had rocked JPMorgan Chase, Dimon had sprung into action. He declared, "We have done some great work on diversity and inclusion, but it's not enough. We must be absolutely relentless on doing more."[4]

Now Dimon was doubling down.

"Let us be clear—we are watching, listening and want every single one of you to know we are committed to fighting against racism and discrimination wherever and however it exists," he wrote in an earlier memo to his staff.[5]

And that racism was, of course, a systemic problem that, according to Dimon's memo, "highlights the inequities black and other diverse communities have and continue to face every day,"[6] an assertion for which, needless to say, no evidence was provided.

By kneeling in seeming support of BLM, Dimon signaled that even one of the world's most powerful businessmen is largely a captive of the anti-white regime. And while the woke might still love to rail against big business, that's no coincidence.

## American Business Embraces Race

The business world has not traditionally been known for being at the forefront of social justice warfare. The conservative businessman who doesn't want to rock the boat is a well-worn cliché. In its purest form, the ideology of business is simply the ideology of the marketplace—the customer is always right, even when he's wrong. The average business shies away from controversy and loathes anything that brings negative media attention.

Yet with the Left in almost complete control of our media and social institutions, businesses are under intense pressure to conform to the latest trends. This has come in particular with the growth of technology companies—six of the top eight U.S. companies by market cap are in tech, and those make up approximately one-fourth of America's total S&P 500 value.[7] As the engine of American business, situated in the famously left-wing San Francisco Bay Area, Big Tech has had a profound effect on business's stances on socio-political issues. They have created so-called "woke capital," and woke capital is, at its core, anti-white capital.

Yet the trend has also spilled outside of tech, as demonstrated by Dimon's actions. The growth of an "elite" class of workers disproportionately likely to have gone to "elite" left-wing schools has infected the most powerful businesses from banking to technology consulting.

"Capitalists will compete for the contract to sell us the rope with which we will hang them," is a quote often attributed to Lenin. This is a good commentary on the anti-white discrimination in the modern business world.

Even iconic American companies are not immune. In 2020, McDonald's released a one-minute commercial listing blacks allegedly unjustly killed by police or whites (including widely discredited "victims" like Michael Brown and Trayvon Martin).[8] They suggested, like Dimon, that these were victims of "systemic oppression" and violence because of their race. Starbucks likewise shut down all of its stores (more than eight thousand) for a day of "racial bias training" after two black men loitering in a store refused to leave when repeatedly asked to do so by the manager, leading to their arrest.[9] Coca-Cola launched diversity trainings to get its employees to be "less white."[10]

The momentum and money behind these decisions only snowballed. The fifty largest companies in America pledged a staggering $50 billion to so-called "racial justice" organizations in the wake of the George Floyd–BLM riots. Eight of these companies (Apple, Microsoft, Amazon, Google, Oracle, Coca-Cola, PepsiCo, and

Qualcomm) gave directly to Black Lives Matter and its affiliates. Banks, enabled by new federal programs, gifted hundreds of billions of loans to black and Hispanic communities, taking money away from potential white borrowers.[11] Overall, my colleagues at the Claremont Institute documented almost $100 billion in donations to Black Lives Matter and related organizations by American corporations.[12]

The system itself is rigged. As one article noted, "The big banks are expected by law to meet the credit needs of underserved communities, and regulators consider their record of doing so when evaluating applications for mergers, acquisitions and branch openings."[13] In other words, if you are a bank and want to grow your business, you'd better be making enough otherwise uneconomic loans to politically preferred minority groups. Federal civil rights law permits banks to create Special Purpose Credit Programs, which allow increased lending to so-called "disadvantaged groups" (read "racial minorities") if their standard lending practices result in racial disparities.[14]

Perhaps the ultimate recent example of this was a 2023 Biden administration decision that added special charges for home loans of creditworthy borrowers to subsidize the loans of borrowers with poor credit. While positioned as an initiative to help those with poor credit, it was functionally a racial wealth transfer, with white borrowers (and, to a lesser degree, Asians) subsidizing blacks and Hispanics.[15] The Biden administration understood perfectly well the racial element of what they were doing—but by adding an economic fig leaf, the predominant racial element was obscured.

Meanwhile, the Business Roundtable, "which represents the CEOs of more than 200" of America's most important companies, claimed at the height of the BLM riots that it had dedicated 20 percent of its entire advocacy budget not to core business issues but to "police reform." This would eventually culminate in the First Step Act of "criminal justice reform" sponsored by President Trump.[16]

The growth of corporate diversity, inclusion, and equity has been tremendous in recent years. Just in the wake of the George Floyd protests, from May to September of 2020, DEI postings grew a staggering 123 percent. While they have since come back to earth as the Right has pushed back, the ideological substructure of these programs still exists in corporate America. "An October 2020 survey conducted by Fortune and Deloitte revealed that 96% of CEOs agree[d] that DEI [was] a personal strategic priority for them."[17]

## Civil Rights Law Brings Business to Heel

The growth of DEI training is deeply entwined with the growth of civil rights law. Early forms of "corporate training" arose during the 1960s and 1970s in response to lawsuits that were bolstered by official affirmative action policies and civil rights legislation, programs that were eventually shown to be ineffective and, in many cases, counterproductive at reducing workplace bias.[18]

Yet the Left continues to push the envelope. California attempted to enforce formal "diversity quotas" on corporate boards before they were struck down by the courts.[19] In response to George Floyd, corporate board appointments for African Americans skyrocketed. "We conservatively estimate that the acceleration of the racial justice movement has thus far led to a 120% increase in the number of black directors appointed in the post-Floyd era," according to the authors of one study.[20] The message has been delivered: violence and threats from minorities work to get valuable concessions from whites.

Numerous companies are engaging in race-based hiring in presumed violation of federal law, confident that with the DOJ's anti-white interpretation of these laws, they will not face consequences. For example, companies such as Boeing and Adidas "promised to increase their hiring of people of color by certain percentages," a fairly clear proxy for numerical quotas that would be illegal under civil rights law. United Airlines declared they wanted half of the five thousand pilots they would train in their flight schools to be women or people of color by 2030.[21] Most passengers would prefer they focus on training pilots who will fly airplanes effectively regardless of race, but then most passengers aren't corporate diversity bureaucrats.

On the other hand, who can blame them when councilmen in major cities like Denver are arguing publicly that white-owned businesses should be taxed extra with the revenue redistributed to black-owned businesses?[22]

The end result of this is clear. According to a Bloomberg analysis, a staggering 94 percent of the workforce increase in 2021 among eighty-eight S&P 100 companies (a total of over three hundred thousand jobs) went to ethnic minorities. Just 6 percent of the increase went to whites. This took place in both junior and senior roles at more than double the rate that it had in the pre–George Floyd era. David Larcker, director of the Corporate Governance Research Initiative at Stanford University, called these "astounding percentages," but for white workers, they were astoundingly grim.[23]

There are some signs of pushback and a sense that, even for the establishment Left, some of this anti-white discrimination may have gone too far. The white Starbucks manager fired amid her company's racial panic was later awarded $25 million for wrongful termination by a jury in June of 2023. She had been punished as the regional manager of the store where the incident took place, while no action had been taken against the actual store manager, who was black.[24]

Yet for all of this anti-white discrimination in the business world, nowhere is the prejudice more pervasive than in Big Tech.

## The Uncanny Anti-Whiteness of Silicon Valley

In one sense, Big Tech seems like a strange place to talk about anti-white discrimination.

While Asians and Asian Americans are increasingly finding success at American technology companies, it's still a field that has historically been dominated by whites and in particular white men. Silicon Valley, arguably the greatest innovation engine the world has ever seen, was built first by Hewlett and Packard in their Palo Alto garage in the 1930s. That innovation continued with the "Traitorous Eight" engineers who founded Fairchild Semiconductor and are considered the founding fathers of the Valley—all white men, many of them conservative.

The success of white guys in Silicon Valley has continued to this day. As I wrote in the *American Conservative*, "Looking at successful 'unicorn' startups, among those that achieve more than $1 billion market value as private companies [as of 2021], 77 percent of the founders were white. And, as a recently compiled list of the 40 best (highest-return) venture capital investments of all time showed, of the 43 U.S.-based founders, 39 were white men."[25]

Unsurprisingly, given that industry success is often considered an essential prerequisite for becoming a venture capitalist, venture capital is dominated by white men. As of 2021, 72 percent of startups backed by VCs had white CEOs.[26] Sixty-eight percent of the top 100 venture capitalists in 2018 were white (and most of the rest were Asian, with both African Americans and Hispanics badly underrepresented).[27]

These (largely) white men have built an industry that is the envy of the entire world. I lived for many years in Silicon Valley, and we were constantly inundated with visitors from other countries hoping to capture our magic. Even today, the rate of unicorn startups—privately owned startups that make it to a valuation of $1 billion or more—in America dwarfs its rivals, not just in absolute numbers but even per capita. The United States was barely edged out on a per capita basis by the tiny nations of Israel and Singapore, while the closest country of substantial size, the United Kingdom, was only about one-third as likely to see unicorn startups. China was less than one-sixteenth as likely per capita, India one-fortieth, and Japan one-forty-second. (Indeed, on a per capita basis, both India and Japan were outperformed by Mexico.[28])

Yet despite these numbers, the push for diversity, equity, and inclusion in tech is omnipresent. Of course, the over-representation of whites (and to an even greater degree Asian Americans) in America's technology world would be a problem if these companies were making poor products or delivering poor financial returns— but there is no indication this is the case. On the contrary, the financial returns for Silicon Valley venture capitalists have been extraordinary, and American tech companies dominate the global marketplace.[29]

Nonetheless, the usual grifters are howling for change. A sociology professor at San Jose State, Scott Myers-Lipton, who is affiliated with the school's Human Rights Institute, developed a so-called "pain index," "White Supremacy and Income/Wealth Inequality in Santa Clara County," while California state assemblyman Ash Kalra praised the report's inclusion of white supremacy as a driving ideology in Silicon Valley.[30] Imagine looking at a place rapidly being taken over by affluent Asian Americans as whites fled and thinking white supremacy was the main problem.

Professor Myers-Lipton said the index shows that not just policing, but all major institutions both public and private need "transformational change" in Silicon Valley. "What this report shows is that the entire playing field, that is the whole system, is tilted to advantage whites over Blacks, Asians, Latinos, and Native Americans," Myers-Lipton said. "It is a call to every one of us in Santa Clara County [the county at the heart of Silicon Valley] to examine our policies, our attitudes, our culture, to ensure that Black lives matter, and to develop specific plans to end white supremacy in the institutions that we are connected to."[31]

"The Silicon Valley Pain Index shows that white supremacy is operating in most all of the institutions and systems in Santa Clara County, whether it be in the criminal justice system, the economy, education, healthcare, or housing," Myers-Lipton said.

Myers-Lipton's claims were then topped by *The Guardian*, which claimed without evidence that "In Silicon Valley, Young White Males Are Stealing the Future from Everyone Else."[32]

But move to the next generation, and whites are now badly underrepresented in Silicon Valley. An estimated 57 percent of the Valley's technical workforce is Asian or Asian American. Asian Americans and Asians are far, far over-represented among both the technology mainstream and elite as compared to their percentage of the U.S. population (around 7 percent). So when critics say that Silicon Valley companies are not diverse enough, what they really mean is (1) Asian Americans do not count as diverse and (2) we need fewer white people in tech![33] (It is almost taken for granted that "more diversity" means "fewer white people," even in situations, as with Silicon Valley engineering positions, where white people are currently badly underrepresented.)

Of course, Big Tech, even more than most big business, is careful to cover its tracks, with many major companies publishing "diversity reports"[34] that they hope will be studiously ignored by the press while throwing money at racial activists to buy them off.

But the true dedication of some tech leaders to woke ideology became evident in the wake of George Floyd's death. Mark Zuckerberg of Meta promptly gave $10 million to African American groups, Jack Dorsey of Twitter gave $3 million to a group run by Colin Kaepernick, Amazon pledged $10 million to "social justice and black communities," Google gave $12 million to "civil rights" groups, and Apple and Microsoft also gave millions away to far-left activists.[35]

Cisco's CEO tweeted "#BlackLivesMatter" while announcing a donation to the radical Equal Justice Initiative and Color of Change among other groups. YouTube donated $1 million to the Center for Policing Equity. WeWork (soon to become one of the all-time great failed attempted IPOs)[36] announced that it would give $2 million in grants to WeWork businesses that were African-American owned.[37]

Aaron Levie, the CEO of Box.com, announced a $500,000 gift lionizing people like Breonna Taylor, an accessory to crime who was killed when police fired on her drug dealer boyfriend during a home raid.[38]

The most prestigious venture capital firms, Sequoia Capital and Kleiner Perkins, also announced donations, part of a staggering total of more than $97 billion given to Black Lives Matter and affiliated organizations as documented by my Claremont colleagues at the Center for the American Way of Life.[39]

Apple CEO Tim Cook pronounced that his company's strength was its diversity. "This is a moment when many people may want nothing more than a return to normalcy, or to a status quo that is only comfortable if we avert our gaze from injustice," he said. "As difficult as it may be to admit, that desire is itself a sign of privilege. George Floyd's death is shocking and tragic proof that we must aim far higher than a 'normal' future and build one that lives up to the highest ideals of equality and justice."[40] This is utter nonsense, but it played well in the media.

Twitter (pre-Elon), in response to the death of Floyd, "swapped" out "its standard logo for a black and white version" and added a #BlackLivesMatter hashtag to its official account's bio.[41]

Amazon posted the following message on Twitter: "The inequitable and brutal treatment of Black people in our country must stop. Together we stand in solidarity with the Black community—our employees, customers, and partners—in the fight against systematic racism and injustice." This bore no resemblance to reality, in which qualified African Americans were already offered every advantage. But I'm sure it felt good in the moment.

Future Amazon CEO Andy Jassy added a *cri de coeur* on his account: "*What* will it take for us to refuse to accept these unjust killings of black people? How many people must die, how many generations must endure, how much eyewitness video is required?"[42]

## Employment Policy

Most of the white supremacy rhetoric around Silicon Valley relies almost exclusively on Asian erasure, which I documented at the beginning of the book. For all of the success of whites in Silicon Valley, in recent years, Asian Americans have become far more successful on a population-proportional basis. The inherent hostility to whites and the blindness to the success of other non-white groups in tech leads to amazing sentences like this one that appeared in an article from Axios: "Asians make up the majority of Silicon Valley's tech workforce at roughly 57%, according to MarketWatch. Yet they're vastly underrepresented at the leadership level: 27% at Apple, 40% at Google, and 25% at Facebook."[43]

In other words, Asian Americans are absurdly overrepresented relative to their population among workers in the most prestigious and sought-after businesses in America. But because on a population basis, they are only four times overrepresented in leadership at Apple, six times at Google, and three and a half times at Facebook, they are clearly suffering from white supremacy as opposed to being even more absurdly overrepresented in technical fields (and this couldn't have anything to do with language/cultural barriers, soft leadership skills, or anything else other than the crushing virulent white racism of the KKK Kleagles who run the Valley).

Interestingly, it has been documented that the higher up one rises in the tech ecosystem, the more the achievement gap between Indian Americans and those from elsewhere in Asia grows. This is not because those other groups are lazy and stupid and Indians are awesome, nor is it because some white power structure loves Indian Americans but hates Chinese. It's presumably because of the smaller linguistic and cultural barriers that Indian Americans must overcome to succeed here. Virtually every Indian who arrives in America comes speaking fluent English, and most (if they are not American-born themselves) have trained in Indian universities under the British/American model. The CEOs of Alphabet, Microsoft, IBM, and Adobe, and the former CEO of Twitter, come from just this relatively small community.

This erasing of Asian-American success, because it proves inconvenient to the anti-white narrative, is a necessary aspect of our modern racial discourse. The Bay Area Equity Atlas, funded by wealthy left-wing foundations, has an extensive analysis of areas of concentrated white wealth as well as areas of concentrated Hispanic, Asian, and black poverty, but does not list areas of concentrated Asian wealth, despite Asian Americans being the second largest population group in the Bay Area and often living in wealthy enclaves.[44] Those questions that don't get asked, don't get answered.

## Big Tech's Anti-White Censorship

It's not just in hiring. Anti-white censorship is a core element of the tech products we all use. This was why it was such an earthshaking change when Musk took over Twitter, and why it was fought so ferociously.

The way this works is clear. In the wake of the January 6 episode at the Capitol, the influential technology magazine *Wired* referred to the alternative social network Parler as a "neo-Nazi haven,"[45] whereas in reality, it was a haven for conservatives and Trump supporters (who, like most conservatives, are disproportionately white). An alternative to censored Twitter was seeing incredible growth until it was banned from app stores amid thinly sourced claims it was used to plan the "insurrection." Ultimately, Amazon Web Services yanked its hosting, killing a service that had 15 million users and was rapidly growing. Parler was offline for over a month, effectively killing its momentum. The company referred to the actions of Amazon, Google, and Apple as "a coordinated attack by the tech giants to kill competition in the marketplace."[46]

The attack on Parler was just an extreme example of the tactics used to deplatform Trump supporters, the racial valence of which was hard to miss. As a January 2021 article in *Wired* magazine put it, "online disinformation, particularly about election fraud, fell by an incredible 73 percent in the week after Twitter's suspension of Trump's social media account. Online forums for Trump supporters are now fractured and weakened."[47] This was all part of the plan. "Online disinformation" is something the Left will always get to define.

Wrote one black activist in *Wired* in arguing for the continued censorship of white voices, "When Black activists and other protected classes are silenced on Facebook, Twitter, and other social platforms for talking about or organizing against racism [note: does this ever really happen at any scale?] that's censorship. But when an oppressed minority seeks equality and justice, and freedom from the harm and violence brought on by the systematically privileged speech of others, that's not censorship, that's accountability."[48] Shutting down "white supremacy" (that is, unwoke speech) is just accountability. Also note the use of "protected classes" and consider who qualifies as an unprotected class.

Soon to come in the *Wired* writer's assertions was blood libel against whites: "With Black and indigenous women killed in America more than any other race, the confluence of digital and real-world racial and gendered violence is undeniable, at least by those who directly experience it."[49] The strong implication is that whites are largely responsible for the killing of black and indigenous women, which is not only not true but not even close to being true, at least on a proportional basis. The overwhelming majority of black women are killed by other blacks, mostly black men.[50]

The activists' endgame is clear. In a museum-quality example of Orwellian doublespeak, the *Wired* writer demanded that social media companies distribute "First Amendment rights and protections more equally." Which, of course, involves "disavow[ing] the myth of race neutrality" in favor of "equity" policies. The Left wants white people who espouse conservative views to be shut down online, and the scary thing is they've been incredibly successful. (This is why Elon Musk's purchase of Twitter was so consequential, as it opened up a free speech forum for everyone—but most notably conservative whites, who are the group most often denied speech rights on other platforms.)

The end goal of such censorship is inevitably political deplatforming. With non-white, overwhelmingly liberal employees playing a larger role each day at tech companies, it's little surprise that political discrimination against conservatives online is increasing. The number of conservative accounts that have been banned is enormous, with most of them belonging to white conservatives. One piece complaining about Elon Musk cataloged twenty-one accounts that he'd placed in line for reinstatement, seventeen of which had white owners.[51] *The Guardian* had a similar list, showing all nine reinstated accounts were for whites.[52]

Again—with only the rarest exceptions, like Louis Farrakhan who has publicly defamed Jews for decades[53]—black nationalists and Chicano nationalists are extremely unlikely to be banned from Twitter. I don't agree with the political agendas of many of those who have been banned and even more rarely with their manners. But in America, we protect free speech rights, *especially* of those we disagree with. There is no codicil to the First Amendment that says white people have a lesser right to free speech.

Protesters who attended the infamous Charlottesville "Unite the Right" rally were also targeted for de-banking and removal from Airbnb—an unprecedented tactic. This would never have even been considered for Antifa members or those involved in violent Black Lives Matter riots. Many of the most popular right-wing personalities, almost exclusively white, have been permanently banned from social media, and not just Twitter. Pro-Trump activist Laura Loomer, who took 44 percent against an incumbent in a congressional primary, was banned from Twitter, Facebook, Instagram, Venmo, PayPal, Uber, Lyft, Uber Eats, and her local bank.[54] Loomer is undoubtedly a very, very difficult personality, but if we're using that standard, many, many politicians would not be on social media either.

Even the technology itself is biased. Those who search on Google for certain subjects deemed politically incorrect will not have auto-suggestions made for them, while other relevant searches are buried by the algorithm, particularly those that involve race in a way the Left doesn't like. One investigator documented that for right-wing takes on police violence in a breaking news story, Google will tell users to "come back later" when there is more reliable information on the topic. But when searching for left-wing sources on the same breaking news story, no such warnings existed.[55]

This, of course, is not an accident, but the result of woke engineers working hand-in-glove with activist NGOs to tilt the direction of the approved racial narrative.

"Today's hateful Google search might become tomorrow's hate crime," said Jonathan Greenblatt, CEO of the Jewish activist organization the Anti-Defamation League (ADL), upon the release of its report "White Supremacy Search Trends in the United States."[56] But, of course, what is hateful? You can be sure the way the ADL defines hate is as anything that offends the far Left's sensibilities on race. The ADL's study naturally looked only at "white supremacy." The idea that non-Jewish white people could be the subject of hateful content on the internet did not even occur to them. Again, what gets measured gets managed.

Anti-white racism in South Africa has similarly been disappeared, despite anti-white discrimination being explicitly a part of present-day South Africa just as anti-black discrimination was under Apartheid. A speech by a leader of the Afrikaner rights organization AfriForum to the South African Human Rights Commission was classified by Google as "dangerous and derogatory" content and hidden from searchers.[57]

Little surprise, then, that internal corporate documents at Google revealed by anti-CRT crusader Chris Rufo asserted that America is a "system of white supremacy," while discussing intersectionality, systemic racism, and alleged "white privilege."[58] Even less surprise that Kamau Bobb, the former head of diversity at Google, was reassigned (not fired) after blog posts emerged in which he said Jews had "an insatiable appetite for war and killing." Google's global inclusion director held a staff meeting with radical critical race theorist and anti-white activist Ibram Kendi, while Google's diversity, equity, and inclusion lead referred to "Make America Great Again" and "Columbus Day" as "expressions" of "covert white supremacy." Even mainstream conservative writer and media personality Ben Shapiro was identified as "a foundation of 'white supremacy.'"

When Ben Shapiro is a foundation of white supremacy, anti-whiteness has taken over your business. And that's exactly what's happened with Big Tech.

## No Tech Jobs for White Men

Bias has also seeped into Silicon Valley's employment policies. After he was fired for sharing a pro-diversity memo that nonetheless attempted to address controversial but defensible reasons why women may be underrepresented in tech, Google engineer James Damore sued his company for discriminating against white conservative men.[59] His lawsuit was one of multiple contending Google discriminates against white males, which, as of this writing, are still working their way through the court system.

Damore noted in his lawsuit that Alphabet, the parent company of Google, "goes to extreme—and illegal—lengths to encourage hiring managers to take protected categories such as race and/or gender into consideration as determinative hiring factors, to the detriment of Caucasian and male employees and potential employees."[60] Among the names publicly released, a corporate "blacklist" of people barred from visiting the campus were all white men. After public inquiries, Alphabet shut down the ability of regular employees to see this list.[61]

Getting far less publicity, even though it's even more damaging, is a lawsuit by Arne Wilberg. Wilberg, a former Google and YouTube recruiter, claimed he was fired for refusing to discriminate against white and Asian men in his hiring practices.[62] Given that as a recruiter he would have had intimate knowledge of the details of Google's hiring practices, this is a damning indictment indeed.

According to Wilberg, "recruiters were given quotas" and "told to cancel interviews with white and Asian male job candidates," and then "to 'purge' applications that weren't" from women or so-called underrepresented minorities. "When he complained about these practices to Google's human resources department, the recruiters reacted by deleting emails that referenced [their] quota system."

To some degree, this can be traced back to government policy. "Companies that are government contractors, like Google, are obligated to seek out, recruit, and bring in women and minorities," said Gary Siniscalco, an employment lawyer familiar with the case, pointing to the centrality of civil rights laws in such discrimination.[63] Yet from its public statements, Google seems to think it is great to discriminate against whites (and, in particular, white men).

Why is it fine to discriminate against white candidates? Would Google ever allow a similar process to reduce the number of Hispanic or Indian employees? To even ask the question is to acknowledge how absurd it is. Until recently, there hadn't been a single white starting cornerback in the NFL in nineteen years. Should NFL teams give preferences to white cornerbacks? Different groups can achieve differently in all sorts of fields for reasons other than discrimination. But if you suggest that any factor other than discrimination could be important, particularly if you are white, you will be banished into outer darkness.

This is not limited to tech. A survey of one thousand hiring managers revealed that one in six was requested not to hire white men (to be clear, this is illegal), with another 14 percent discouraged from hiring white women. Most hiring managers in a recent survey believe their companies discriminate against whites in hiring and that a failure to bring in sufficiently "diverse" hires will put their jobs in danger. A quarter of hiring managers surveyed *strongly* believe their company practices reverse discrimination. Just 22 percent of hiring managers said they *almost* never had been told not to hire candidates unless they were diverse enough, while 17 percent said it happened *very often.*[64] And this is just what they admit to! Hiring managers are part of the HR industrial complex, the most liberal part of the corporate world. If this is what they are willing to acknowledge, be sure the truth is far worse.

Another survey showed a broader trend of hiring managers discriminating against white men. One of the most blatant examples was when the tech company Twilio announced it would do a round of layoffs through an "Anti-Racist/Anti-Oppression lens," a virtual certainty that more white workers would be sacked than would have been justified by business concerns.[65]

"As you all know, we are committed to becoming an Anti-Racist/Anti-Oppression company. Layoffs like this can have a more pronounced impact on marginalized communities, so we were particularly focused on ensuring our layoffs—while a business necessity today—were carried out through an Anti-Racist/Anti-Oppression lens," Twilio's CEO said.[66] To be clear, this means white people, regardless of ability, will be the first out the door. As best I can determine, this CEO suffered no legal penalties.

Admittedly there have been other complaints that minority workers have been systematically discriminated against during tech layoffs. Netflix was criticized in a report for disproportionately laying off "BIPOC" and other "oppressed" groups. "Minorities are vulnerable in the recent tech layoffs because they were disproportionately hired into positions viewed as less vital to the business success," wrote one commentator.[67]

The solution for this is for more people in these groups to develop skills to be hired into positions that are vital for business success. They are not "seen" as less vital—on average, they "are" less vital. Another interpretation, equally valid for this data, would be that companies hire less qualified but optically necessary non-Asian minority employees (at a cost to opportunities for similarly situated white workers) only to have to jettison them during leaner times when essential highly skilled workers are actually needed to run the business.

## The H-1B Scam

The H-1B employment visa, which allows companies to employ high-skilled foreign workers in specialty occupations, is also used in the tech industry to discriminate against whites. A significant percentage of fired workers replaced by H-1Bs are white, whereas virtually all H-1Bs are non-white—mostly from India. If whites were a "protected class," it would be easy to prove a governmental discrimination case against them.

Thus does the H-1B serve the interests of Big Tech companies in replacing senior developers (often white) with compliant, immobile foreign workers (since visas are tied to specific employers) for a fraction of the cost.

As Dr. Ron Hira, a professor at Howard University and a critic of H-1Bs, has observed, the H-1B system transfers wealth from employees to employers. "Guest-worker programs are supposed to fill domestic labor shortages. The H-1B program does not fill shortages," he said.[68] H-1Bs hold approximately 13 percent of tech engineering jobs and one-third of those are specifically given to outsourcing companies from India like Wipro and Infosys.[69] Many studies have found that H-1Bs lower earnings and can displace workers.[70] *Politico* went so far as to call Silicon Valley a "den of spies" because of the potential for espionage from bringing so many foreign employees into such a sensitive economic sector.[71]

For those who say the racial element of this is just coincidental, it is notable that U.S. Tech Workers, an advocacy group that protects the rights of American technology workers and opposes H-1Bs, has been attacked by the odious Southern Poverty Law Center for its ties to the supposed "hate group" the Federation for American Immigration Reform (FAIR) as well as the Center for Immigration Studies, both entirely mainstream, Washington, D.C.–based policy organizations.[72]

Of course, this enormous influx of foreign workers into Silicon Valley did not just affect the tech companies. It affected the Valley as a whole, which became half foreign-born and overwhelmingly from Asia, after being overwhelmingly white American in previous years. (Silicon Valley was 94 percent white and 82 percent white non-Hispanic in 1970.[73]) This unsurprisingly has led to white flight from Silicon Valley, as real estate prices have soared with massive population growth from immigration and inadequate homebuilding.

The H-1B influx has thus destroyed not only corporate wages, not only white tech workers, but a Silicon Valley community that had been nurtured over decades.

## White Demographic Displacement from Silicon Valley

The white flight from Silicon Valley, despite its affluence, shows the limits of the purely economic approach to national progress taken by some in the GOP establishment. Whites ultimately left this land of unlimited professional opportunity *en masse* because mass immigration transformed it into a place many no longer recognized as traditionally American.

While it has not received as much publicity as white flight from less affluent areas its scale is just as striking. In 1970, Santa Clara County, at the heart of Silicon Valley, was more than 94 percent white with 1.03 million whites out of a total population of 1.064 million. By 1990, shortly before the internet boom, the population was just 69 percent white, having grown by almost 50 percent to 1.5 million in just twenty years (but still having a small net gain in whites).[74] By the 2020 census, Santa Clara County had almost doubled from its 1970 population to 1.89 million. But the number of non-Hispanic whites had fallen to just 544,000, and they were disproportionately much older.[75]

In 2021, just 21 percent of births in Santa Clara County were to non-Hispanic white mothers.[76] With approximately one-quarter of marriages in the county being interracial,[77] it is reasonable to think that the number of white children born in Santa Clara County is today just 16 percent of kids there. This again from an extremely affluent corner of America, one that was overwhelmingly white a half-century previously. The whites who left Silicon Valley weren't racist. But cultural alienation was more important to these people than even the best economic opportunity.

Incredibly, while this center of innovation once enriched millions, whites fled the area and are now represented at just a fraction of their population numbers from fifty years prior, even as the Valley as a whole continues to grow. (It should be noted there was a substantial influx of Hispanics into Silicon Valley at the same time.)

One has to go back to the 1950 census, when it had just 290,000 people total, to find fewer non-Hispanic whites in Santa Clara County than are there today.[78] Similarly, in next door San Mateo County (population 737,000),[79] you also have to go back to 1950, when the county had just 235,000 total residents,[80] to find fewer non-Hispanic white residents than today's 275,000.[81] Whites in these areas have almost gone the way of whites in Detroit, but rather than being driven out by poverty and violence, they've been driven out by the high cost of living (thanks to a liberal failure to build sufficient housing) and cultural displacement.

Overall, just 23 percent of California children are white non-Hispanics,[82] while an estimated 54 percent of California voters in 2022 were white non-Hispanics.[83] Meanwhile, almost 60 percent of California senior citizens are white, but among non-senior citizens, the number is approximately 31 percent.[84] California in many ways is the future of America.

Silicon Valley shows that even with the outstanding economic opportunity created by highly skilled immigration, culture matters, and demographic replacement is more important than economic opportunity. And this future is the best-case scenario for white Americans under Biden and the Democrats' open borders regime. Or, to quote the science fiction writer William Gibson, "The future is already here. It's just not very evenly distributed."

# CHAPTER 11

# Unhealthy Disrespect

*"Aegrescit medend" (The cure is worse than the disease)*
—Virgil, *The Aeneid*, Book XII, 46

*"If you haven't got your health, you haven't got anything."*
—Count Rugen to Prince Humperdinck
in *The Princess Bride*

It is not an exaggeration to say that anti-white discrimination in America has become a matter of life and death.

Healthcare may not be a "right" in the way the Left conceives of it, but it is something that everyone values and something that, at least at a basic level, we would like to provide to all Americans. Which is why it is increasingly disturbing to see it being taken away from white Americans on account of their race.

From hospitals to medical schools, health "equity" is invariably the buzzword of the day, and as in other areas, that "equity" is merely a byword for racial discrimination.

We can see this in the organs of our state bureaucracy in charge of determining health outcomes. The website for the Centers for Disease Control and Prevention states,

Across the country, people in some racial and ethnic minority groups experience higher rates of poor health and disease for a range of health conditions, including diabetes, hypertension, obesity, asthma, heart disease, cancer, and preterm birth, when compared to their white counterparts. For example, the average life expectancy among black or African American people in the United States is four years lower than that of white people. These disparities sometimes persist even when accounting for other demographic and socioeconomic factors, such as age or income.[1]

This is an accurate statement so far as it goes—but the CDC is silent on the health outcomes of groups such as Asian Americans that are better than whites.[2] If institutional racism and "historic disparities" rather than behavioral and social differences were the reasons for these gaps, then Asian Americans, who have suffered discrimination and often arrived here with very little in the way of resources, would be worse off than whites.

Again, as in many other areas, Asian Americans are cynically erased in order to slander whites. They must be made invisible and ignored in any cross-racial analysis because to make them visible would be to expose the complete intellectual bankruptcy of the claim that most of these differences in health outcomes are a result of white supremacy.

According to the CDC's page on "health equity," racism "shapes social and economic factors that put some people from racial and ethnic minority groups at increased risk for negative mental health outcomes and health-related behaviors, as well as chronic and toxic stress or inflammation. Racism prevents millions of people from attaining their highest level of health, and consequently, affects the health of our nation."[3] Again, the evidence this is caused by "racism" rather than other economic and social disparities is not presented. And, of course, Asian Americans are erased from the analysis.

This formulation of America's health problems is increasingly part of the standard narrative. The *New England Journal of Medicine* touts its "commitment to understanding and combating racism as a public health and human rights crisis,"[4] while *Health Affairs* is implementing a strategy to "dismantle racism and increase racial equity."[5] Brigham and Women's Hospital in Boston (one of America's most prestigious) wants to pilot the delivery of "preferential care based on race,"[6] while the Biden administration is giving better Medicare reimbursement rates to hospitals that implement "anti-racism" plans, which, stripped of their airy rhetoric, involve discriminating against white Americans.[7] And, of course, numerous "racial equity" nonprofits will be there to get their own piece of the grift.

## Health Research

The CDC's statement reflects a trend that is seen throughout American medicine. As an article in STAT, an online health news site, puts it, "Health equity research is now in vogue. Journals are clamoring for it, the media is covering it, and the National Institutes of Health, after publicly apologizing for giving the field short shrift, recently announced it would unleash nearly $100 million for research on the topic."[8] The NIH had previously said it would tackle DEI issues, appointing diversity and inclusion officers at every one of its centers.[9]

What could go wrong? Less than 2 percent of NIH investigators are black. Yet 19 percent of senior investigators are Asian American and 22 percent of overall investigators are Asian American.[10] So Asian Americans are dramatically overrepresented in comparison to their population in the NIH (and given current trends, those numbers are sure to increase). Is this a problem? Certainly, you will never hear the journal editors who cry about "systemic racism" say so.

Even when white researchers decide to look critically at supposed health inequities from a sympathetic perspective, they are attacked.

The *Journal of the American Medical Association (JAMA)* published a paper on health disparities in medicine that was assailed for not having enough Hispanic and African American authors. According to an account of the dispute, "A *JAMA* spokesperson said its editors do not consider the demographics of authors in selecting research papers, but critics say that neutral stance perpetuates long-standing inequities rather than addressing them."[11] In other words, not being racist in your selection of authors perpetuates racism. You can be sure that in the future, *JAMA* and other journals won't make that mistake. Meanwhile, white researchers, especially newer researchers in the field, were attacked as "health equity tourists,"[12] suggesting it was somehow wrong for new, talented scholars to take an interest in the field. One might expect them to be accused of academic gentrification.

We are already seeing the effects of this toxic atmosphere. According to an account in STAT, Christopher Bennett, an emergency room physician and assistant professor at Stanford, committed the sin of being a senior author of a paper on health equity with a subject similar to a previous paper by an African American author, Elle Lett. He did cite her earlier research but did not ask her to collaborate with him, nor did he "find a Black co-author whose career could have benefited from being on such a publication," according to STAT.[13]

According to Lett, "For this [research] to be ethical and just, it requires you to redistribute some of your privilege and benefit." Leaving aside the question of whether there was any privilege and benefit to be redistributed, this is, shall we say, a rather novel theory of how scholarship works. Lett said, "The reality is my highest-cited publication will be silenced by his," which is really only true if his work was a substantial improvement on Lett's. And if Lett's paper was cited by Bennett, she is credited and thus hardly silenced. You can be assured that many academics would love to be "silenced" by being cited by a Stanford professor for their academic work.[14]

If you want to write about the (alleged) plight of blacks in academic medicine but you are white, it is not all right. "It is troubling that a white man, who has had every privilege conferred on him, is writing a paper about the plight of Black academics," said Lett. "He is extracting from our pain for his career advancement."[15] Again, this is not how any scholarly discipline should work.

But, of course, Lett understood how the real hierarchies of power and privilege work in modern academia. Predictably, Bennett later offered a groveling apology: "It was not my goal to be either colonial or extractive. Regardless of the intent, it is clear that a mistake was made on my part by not utilizing the opportunity and ensuring that a work on diversity included a diverse author byline. For this, I am sorry."[16] This response is beyond parody. A white researcher looking into a health issue that impacts minorities is now "colonial." And he must distribute extensive credit (beyond mere citation) to minority researchers (whether or not those researchers provide value to his project) in order to exist in modern scientific academia.

Are you trusting the science yet?

Critics claim there is racial discrimination in academic research funding from the major government research institutes (for example, the National Institutes of Health). Yet funding rates for minority researchers are scarcely different than for white researchers, and when taking into account the seniority of researchers (whites are older on average and therefore more likely to be senior researchers and get funded), the disparities would seem to disappear.[17] Given that we already know that underrepresented minority researchers with lesser qualifications are advantaged in academic admissions, hiring, and promotions, it seems extraordinarily unlikely they are being discriminated against at this stage of our development.

(It's worth noting that most of the people tripping over themselves to decry the "structural racism" of academic medicine are absolutely opposed to race-blind grant application evaluations.)

The article that brought Lett's attack to light was funded by the Commonwealth Fund,[18] founded (of course) by a wealthy white woman a century ago and now used to fund numerous articles attacking white people.[19] This is the modern face of white privilege.

Nor was this simply a one-off.

Robin Evans-Agnew, a nursing professor, dared to co-author a paper on "reproductive justice" (an inherently left-wing framing of a subject that means anything but justice for the baby in question) with other white nursing professors. When she was attacked by an African American critic, the editor who published her piece apologized before genuflecting, "To say that I'm not aware this is a terrible, racist country with terrible racist problems isn't true."[20]

So if I don't think America is a terrible, racist country (yes, as this book clearly shows, America is systemically racist against white people, but I would still not go so far as to call it a terrible country), then I shouldn't be publishing scientific articles?

In explaining why she had published such a piece of unforgivable whiteness, the journal editor said she'd only sent the article to one minority reviewer out of a total of three (only 33 percent minority representation!). She commented that she knew minority researchers were overloaded. "They're asked a lot to review. They're asked to be a spokesperson for oppression. They're asked to be on every committee." Sounds like those minorities are favored in our system rather than oppressed.[21]

Evans-Agnew also knew the drill, saying white researchers must be aware of their "white colonial perspective and white colonial biases." "I leave my white fragility at the doorstep," she said. "This is work I have to do."[22]

"The issue has erupted in many academic fields. #CiteBlackWomen has become a hashtag, and a social movement," according to STAT.[23] How about #CiteGoodScholars, regardless of their race?

Unsurprisingly, these attitudes have had broad ramifications. One researcher said we should avoid "unsubstantiated claims that black people are somehow biologically distinct from other racial groups."[24] "When science claims poor health outcomes in Black folks are genetic, that pathologizes blackness," according to Rhea Boyd, a pediatrician who wrote an article in the journal *Health Affairs* demanding a new standard for publishing on "Racial Health Inequities." "Racism is, perhaps, America's earliest tradition," the article opens, leaving little doubt as to where the author's sympathies lie.[25]

While, of course, researchers should not cavalierly impute to race health outcomes what could be better explained by other social factors, Sickle Cell disease, Tay-Sachs, and many other syndromes and maladies that appear almost exclusively or in great disproportion in certain racial and ethnic populations would like to have a talk with Dr. Boyd. But I guess that's just white man's medicine.[26]

Meanwhile, health equity research is exploding. "Health equity researchers say they are getting besieged by offers from white teams who have never worked in health equity to either pick their brains or collaborate on grants," writes the editor of one journal.[27] Because, as anyone who has worked in academia knows, people begging you to work on papers with them is a sure sign of oppression.

Another researcher, an anthropology professor at the University of Florida who focuses on "the health effects of racism," said people need to "make sure they cite, partner with, and support scholars of color." Again, the demand is to cite and collaborate with researchers based on their skin color rather than the quality of their work. The essayist goes on to describe "well-meaning white people" as an oxymoron.[28]

This goes to the top of the medical community and speaks to who is allowed to discuss these issues. For example, when a podcast on structural racism was presented by the American Medical Association, it turned into such a fiasco that the podcast hosts were eventually put on leave since they seemed too skeptical of the idea that many individual physicians were racist.[29]

Much of America's medical history has also been distorted in the service of anti-white racial animus. While I do not deny that racism has been a factor in historic healthcare disparities, even some of the most notoriously racist elements of that history turn out to be more complicated when viewed in greater detail and context.

Perhaps the most famous moral outrage in modern medicine centers on the Tuskegee Syphilis Study that began almost one hundred years ago and ended more than fifty years ago. The study is infamous because its African American participants were not informed of their syphilis diagnosis, and they were not treated once treatments were available. Yet this study was done with the full collaboration of officials at the famous Tuskegee Institute, a historically black college. It is clear that, by the standards of today's medicine, there were serious medical and informed consent violations, but it is far from clear that those were due primarily to racial animus. The damage of the Tuskegee experiment would seem now to be far exceeded by the damage caused by those citing the experiment to feed anti-white racial paranoia while making African Americans unduly skeptical of modern medical care.[30]

While the Tuskegee Syphilis Study would never be considered appropriate today, neither was it a plot to get African Americans, as an article in the *Lancet Infectious Diseases*, the world's leading infectious disease journal, noted in 2005 (back when such thoughtcrimes could be spoken freely by those who had not gotten the memo)[31]. It was hardly unusual in the era of the Tuskegee study that groups were experimented on with informed consent policies that would horrify us today. "The Tuskegee study has become the archetype of unethical research and racism in medicine," the authors acknowledge, but those who viewed the study purely in terms of racism were "merely invoking one set of conspiracy beliefs to explain another."[32]

Though President Bill Clinton publicly apologized for the study in 1997, according to the *Lancet*, "It is debatable whether the study was racist." The article went on to accuse its critics of presentism, pointing out that Tuskegee had its origins in a study begun by the Rosenwald Fund, which was run by a wealthy liberal and specifically created to advance the interests of African Americans, supporting countless black artists and intellectuals. "Black health-care professionals were involved at all stages of the study," according to the *Lancet* piece. Even as late as 1969, the mostly black Macon County medical society was assisting with the study.[33]

In other words, while the study itself was damaging, its origins were not clearly racist, and the racist mythology around them has allowed them to appear so, in the service of modern political arguments. The *Lancet* paper argues persuasively that there was nothing in the initial design of the experiment that was inappropriate by the standards of the time, though by its twentieth anniversary, that was no longer true.[34] Yet the constant drumbeat of the Tuskegee Syphilis Study has been used to attack medicine and white physicians as racist and to both excuse and exacerbate black vaccine hesitancy and public health problems within the African American community.

Even those who blame racism for the Tuskegee experiment acknowledge that, after a great deal of study, black hesitancy to participate in medical studies is not even primarily a result of Tuskegee itself.[35] It seems the real lesson of the Tuskegee experiment is as much about the use and abuse of racial politics to score points in medicine as it is about medical racism.

## Racial Disparities in Health Treatment

The deceptive narratives surrounding health and race affect treatments just as much as studies.

Much of the alleged disparity between white and minority outcomes in health is a product of either misleading analysis or misleading rhetoric. For example, the notion that systemic medical racism is leading to an epidemic of black maternal mortality is not supported by the available evidence.[36]

Another important area where we see the abuse of racial rhetoric is around heart disease. More Americans die of heart disease than any other illness, so treating it effectively is critical.[37] The American Heart Association guidelines define race as "a social construct not rooted in biology"[38]—but this is simply wrong, and frighteningly so.

It would be more accurate to write about race as a social construct that *is* generally rooted to some degree in biology. In many cases, physicians can treat people more accurately based on their self-identified race, though obviously, the effectiveness of this treatment will vary in accordance with many factors, including how heterogeneous the effects are in certain racial groups.

It would usually be more accurate to treat people by sequencing their whole genome, but analysis at that level is not always immediately available. More importantly, when attempting to reach individual social and ethnic groups with health-related messages, you are invariably reaching out to cultural groups—not targeting messages to people who might have a particular mutation, which would be wildly impractical.

To cite one example from a field that should interest the American Heart Association, Indian Americans, the wealthiest major ethnic group in the country, along with their other South Asian counterparts, develop heart disease four times as frequently as the general population and may develop it up to a decade earlier in life than members of other ethnic groups. While some of this may be attributable to social or dietary factors, it appears to be largely a function of different genetics in at least some parts of the South Asian population.[39]

In 2018, though this had been known for some time, the American Heart Association finally issued guidelines recommending doctors treat South Asians differently when considering prescribing statins, drugs that are protective against heart attacks.[40] To the extent it was "racist" to wait so long to acknowledge this fact, it was not due to indifference but a fear of being politically incorrect and acknowledging racial differences in disease proneness. Yet that sort of "racism" saves lives.

But the public health community is not on board with life-saving approaches such as this. Witness a fact sheet from the American Public Health Association (APHA), the umbrella group for public health practitioners in America. The APHA, which is notoriously politically radical, was busy during COVID recommending severe restrictions—often in the face of incomplete or even contradictory evidence.[41] APHA defines racial equity as being achieved "when racial identity no longer predicts how a person fares in many aspects of life."[42] So according to the APHA, when we've achieved pure race communism, we'll know we've reached a public health nirvana. Any racial disparities between groups are inherently explained by racism. Science!

As we see, the real meaning of medical equity is anti-white discrimination (and, to some degree, anti-Asian discrimination, but Asian Americans are not the ones being targeted nor are they the vast majority of those affected).

At times, the absurdity of the public health community's equity language spills over into sheer destructiveness. In several states, including some run by Republican governors, initially scarce COVID vaccines were distributed according to a racial preference regime. (I realize that people have a wide variety of views on the effectiveness of COVID vaccination, but public health authorities at the time considered them a highly desirable and potentially life-saving medical intervention.) In Vermont, perhaps the most egregious example, "BIPOC" [Black, Indigenous, and People of Color] residents of *any age* were eligible for COVID-19 vaccines before white Americans, many of whom were older and thus at much higher risk.[43]

To the extent this approach could have had any medical justification, it would require acknowledging that race is a concept with biological validity, which much of the medical establishment refuses to do—or at least will only do reluctantly when it serves a broader political interest. The rest of the time, it is the emperor's new healthcare, and white Americans are required to say how great it is.

What are those "extenuating circumstances"? Well, it seems they will happily bend the rules about the biological roots of race if they can be used to disadvantage white people. For example, there is reasonable evidence that, as with many other diseases, Native Americans are more susceptible than whites to dying from COVID even when a variety of other risk factors are controlled for.[44] But acknowledging this would also mean, to be intellectually consistent, acknowledging that, *on average*, Native American biology may differ in some important ways from the biology of whites. (Which should be uncontroversial—Native Americans' lack of immunity to many European diseases was an essential factor in the white settlers' conquest of the Americas.) A 2016 paper in the prestigious journal *Science* documented how the genetics of some Native American populations were changed by exposure to European diseases.[45]

But in weighing the costs and benefits of a racially administered vaccine, one must weigh the size of a public health benefit versus the social cohesion costs of racially stratifying access to life-saving treatments based on ancestry. Ideally, if such standards were used at all, they would have been to make sure that, say, Hispanics who were sixty-plus years of age received the same priority as whites who were seventy-plus years of age, based on a similar risk profile at those ages.

But even this strategy is, appropriately, controversial. Speaking hypothetically, if a white forty-year-old was somehow shown to have an equivalent COVID risk profile to a black seventy-year-old, can we really imagine that we would let the white younger person go first? Further, the white/Hispanic risk comparisons elide the fact that Hispanics on average may have engaged in behaviors that, all things being equal, put them at higher risk.[46] In such cases where a personal choice in behaviors stratifies risk factors, how should priority be weighted? These are serious questions of medical ethics, questions that rarely surfaced when whites were put lower in the vaccine priority.

But the practical reality of COVID-19 vaccine prioritization was even worse than that. In some states, a black person twenty-five years of age could have received priority over a white person sixty years of age, despite the latter having an overwhelmingly higher risk of COVID-19 mortality.[47] Overall, it seems like racially stratifying potentially life-saving medical treatments for COVID or any other disease is a can of worms that is dangerous to open.

The medical benefit, except in extreme cases of racial disparity of disease susceptibility, would not seem to be worth the risk to social cohesion. But because the "losers" in the case of COVID vaccinations were white, opposition to a racially stratified vaccination program was publicly muted. While the COVID vaccine's effectiveness is a subject of controversy that goes well beyond the scope of this book, if we accept the medical consensus opinion, it seems likely that no small number of whites died because they were told to go to the back of the bus when it came time to prioritize who would get COVID vaccines.[48]

## Race and Health Economics

The question of who pays for healthcare also has an increasingly anti-white dimension. Through Medicaid, a government program that covers healthcare for those who can't afford it, white taxpayers pay disproportionately for the care of non-whites. According to recent numbers, just 38 percent of Medicaid recipients were white versus 58 percent of the overall population, and there are 89.5 million people on Medicaid.[49]

Net Medicaid spending was $867 billion in 2022, representing a massive racial subsidy.[50] Obamacare is another "private" health subsidy, estimated by the non-partisan Congressional Budget Office to total $1.1 trillion over the next decade.[51] From 2010 to 2015, those gaining insurance through Obamacare spending were just 43 percent non-Hispanic white,[52] which might help explain the white animus to Obamacare: it's yet another government healthcare program disproportionately paid for by whites and disproportionately benefitting minorities.[53] (Again, to state the insultingly obvious, none of this implies there are not millions of whites who receive Obamacare benefits and numerous minority taxpayers paying a high tax burden. It is to say that on average these programs have highly unequal racial incidence in terms of who pays and who benefits from them—and this racial incidence can, on average, explain both the politics and illuminate anti-white discrimination in ways that are not necessarily overt.)

The Medicare population is, unsurprisingly, like older Americans themselves, disproportionately white: 76 percent in 2019—on par with the percentage of white Americans in that age bracket.[54] But as the minority population ages, one would expect this to come into alignment with the overall population. Yet no such trend is evident for Medicaid.

These economic disparities of payment are, of course, rarely emphasized in the healthcare literature, in which one can find endless shirt-rending excoriations of racial disparities in healthcare spending (much of which is simply a function of the older average age of whites). Such literature is far more reluctant to forthrightly discuss who, in general, funds government healthcare (whites) and who benefits from it (not whites).

## Medical Education

Being white is increasingly a barrier to entering the medical profession at all. Most visibly, this takes place with respect to the MCAT, the standard medical school admissions test, which is under pressure from activists. While Asian Americans are arguably the biggest losers in de-emphasizing this test on a percentage basis, because of the much larger numbers of whites who score well on the MCAT (a function of their substantially larger population), many more whites are affected overall.[55]

Which is exactly what they deserve, according to some critics. "The MCAT is steeped in a history of racism and white supremacy," wrote a physician and journalist at *Slate* (this despite the fact that the American Medical Association found that the MCAT was more predictive of medical school success than college GPA[56]). "Medical schools have a choice. They can embrace what has always been—a test and admissions system steeped in racism that endangers us all—or they can change."[57]

White students, we are told, attend wealthier colleges with more expensive curricula and can take lots of test prep. MCAT critics, of course, push for a more "holistic" (that is to say, not objective) set of criteria for medical school admissions, which invariably tilt the scales against whites. Never mind that the last American medical school class prior to this book being published was only 48 percent white (with Asians being dramatically overrepresented).[58] That 48 percent is too much for equity advocates. (Strangely, you will find much more complaining about "white supremacy" in medical school admissions than you will about the dramatic Asian-American over-representation.) Consistently here, as elsewhere, the "diversity" that advocates are hoping to achieve is simply a polite way of saying, "Fewer whites."

The MCAT was devised by Abraham Flexner, hailed as the father of modern American medical education, who would go on to found the legendary Institute for Advanced Study at Princeton (where Einstein would eventually ply his trade). Flexner's program for improvement in medical school quality made him a titan in the field—but today he's just another racist white man. Until very recently, the Association of American Medical Colleges named its award for distinguished service to education after Flexner, only to remove it for alleged racism and sexism in 2020. Flexner was banished for demanding excellence in medical schools, which led to the decertification of historically black medical schools that could not meet the objective standards he'd set. The renaming of the award was done, according to the AAMC, "[a]s part of its commitment to becoming an anti-racist, diverse, equitable, and inclusive organization."[59]

The momentum is on the side of the test abolishers. First, the pressure on affirmative action means that all objective standards (of which tests are the most prominent) will be under pressure. The head of diversity and equity at Yale Medical School proposed abolishing the MCAT in 2018.[60] And around two dozen medical schools no longer require the MCAT for all students.[61]

Given the importance of the MCAT and the huge racial disparity in test scores, it is unsurprising that racial preferences in medical school admissions are dramatic. An MCAT/GPA profile that would see 56 percent of African Americans and 31 percent of Hispanics admitted to medical school would see just 8 percent of whites and 6 percent of Asian Americans admitted.[62] An academic profile that would see 81 percent of African Americans and 60 percent of Hispanics admitted admits just 29 percent of whites and 21 percent of Asian Americans.[63] Despite this enormous thumb on the scale, the AMA is officially against removing affirmative action from medical schools.[64]

Once in the door, students can count on anti-whiteness in their medical school curriculum. After students in 2019 complained about race being cited during classroom discussions, Boston University School of Medicine unveiled a new Orwellian "educators guide" to reinforce the appropriate groupthink. "Providing an education that is focused on health equity and actively antiracist is essential," wrote medical school officials. "Many of the programs will target young people before they even reach college with the intention of cultivating a more multicultural group interested in postgraduate medical education," according to one source.[65] In other words, whites need not apply.

This is not an attack on culturally competent medicine. It's important for medical professionals to understand patients' different backgrounds and perspectives so they can provide high-quality care. But there is a large difference between being culturally competent and just being anti-white, and current medical schools are busy erasing that distinction.

As the *Wall Street Journal* wrote in an editorial: "Healthcare is being infected by the radical ideology that has corrupted education and public safety. But while critical race theory and crime waves have been in the news, the public is largely unaware of medicine's turn toward division and discrimination." The editorial continued, "Health disparities do exist among racial groups, but physician bias isn't the cause."[66]

Medical academia, which should be focused on both advancing basic innovations in medical science and coming up with appropriate healthcare policy frameworks, has fallen into an appalling state. One researcher says the "most commonly cited studies are shoddily designed, ignore such critical factors as pre-existing conditions, or reach predetermined and sensationalized conclusions that aren't supported by reported results. These papers in turn are used to source even more shoddy research."[67]

As an additional example of how far the rot has spread, many medical students are now forced to take the widely discredited implicit association test, which claims to detect "hidden" racism, with some states even requiring it for a medical or nursing license.[68]

Overall, the environment of American healthcare is like the environment of so much else in America today. As the essayist Ralph Waldo Emerson said of the visit of someone disreputable, "The louder he spoke of his honor, the faster we counted our spoons."[69] In a similar way, the louder the Left speaks of systemic racism in healthcare, the faster we should count the ways that our current healthcare system is being rigged against white Americans.

## CHAPTER 12

# Not Everyone Who Says, "Lord, Lord"

*"Not everyone who says to me, 'Lord, Lord,' will enter the kingdom of heaven, but only the one who does the will of my Father who is in heaven. Many will say to me on that day, 'Lord, Lord, did we not prophesy in your name and in your name drive out demons and in your name perform many miracles?' Then I will tell them plainly, 'I never knew you. Away from me, you evildoers!'"*

—Matthew 7:21–23 (NIV)

*"There is a self-hatred in the West that can be considered only as something pathological. The West attempts in a praiseworthy manner to open itself completely to the comprehension of external values, but it no longer loves itself; it now only sees what is despicable and destructive in its own history, while it is no longer able to perceive what is great and pure there."*

—Pope Benedict XVI

O ur last two subject matter chapters will focus on religion and the military. These are institutions that have generally managed to maintain significant respect in America, even in an era of declining social trust. But as we will see, even these have increasingly fallen prey to anti-white attitudes and behaviors.

Religion is fundamental to the lives of many Americans, and for many of us, it forms a basic core of our social structure. But regardless of what religion one follows—assuming one belongs to a religion at all—all of them are invariably touched by the world and its failings.

Given this reality, it is unsurprising that modern American religious institutions, which once struggled with anti-minority racism, have become a source of anti-white ideology, with some Christian denominations particularly hard-hit. Some critics see this failing as endemic to Christianity itself (an argument made by Nietzsche, who criticized Christianity's "slave morality"),[1] but Christianity's compassion for the downtrodden, as evidenced most profoundly in the story of Christ's perfect sacrifice, cannot in and of itself explain much of what we are seeing today.

While this chapter will focus especially, though not exclusively, on the Christian church, as this is still the dominant institution in American religious life, we can find these problems in synagogues, mosques, and other religious institutions as well. As an actively engaged Christian of Jewish descent, I have witnessed the problems of anti-whiteness in a variety of religious environments.

That anti-white sentiment would find a home in the church is unsurprising. The church is reflective of a fallen world, and the church has on many occasions in the past failed on racial issues. At previous times in history, American churches defended slavery, segregation, the burning of "witches," and any number of other practices that Americans today abhor.

The problem of anti-whiteness is most acute, and indeed absurd to the point of parody, in so-called "mainline" Protestant denominations led by the so-called "seven sisters": the Episcopal Church, the Evangelical Lutheran Church of America, the Presbyterian Church

(USA), the United Church of Christ (UCC), the United Methodist Church, the Disciples of Christ, and the American Baptist Church. These institutions, which once defined mainstream Protestantism in America, have collapsed about as quickly as is possible for once-durable churches to collapse.

The number of self-described evangelical Protestants is now twice or more the number of mainline Protestants. And that gap is widening, as membership in the leading mainline Protestant churches has dropped by a staggering two thirds in less than forty years.[2] When all the church has to offer is left-wing "social justice," including a healthy dose of anti-white sentiment, rather than the gospel, it is hardly surprising that it struggles to maintain the interest of parishioners.

The UCC, perhaps the most liberal of these denominations and one that has lost a staggering 70 percent of its membership in the last forty years, is now down to approximately 770,000 official members (the number of active members being far smaller).[3] Unsurprisingly, the UCC's website is chock-full of information about racism.[4]

"Very few Christian churches are leading bold and courageous conversations, engaging in direct social activism, and participating in civil disobedience as a way to bring attention to and disrupt racist systems and structures," the UCC webpage informs visitors. According to the UCC, God disapproves of "Inhumane social confinement due to mass incarceration and surveillance of communities of color," "Deportation and the separation of families from immigrant communities," "Police brutality and militarized tactics and abuses resulting in the murder of people of color," and "supporting White Christian supremacy over and against non-Christian faith communities."[5]

Again, this sort of rhetoric is largely indistinguishable from what one might find on an Antifa or BLM website, or frankly the website of any secular left-wing organization. Though the fact that the UCC proclaims that Christianity might not be superior to other religions is a strange note for a Christian church.

In 2021, at its General Synod, the UCC declared racism (meaning white racism only) to be a "public health crisis," a resolution that passed with a North Korean–level 96 percent of the vote.[6] The UCC declared itself an "anti-racist church" in 2003, clearly far ahead of the wokeness trend.[7]

What has been the result of all this anti-racism and anti-white invective?

Sixty-two percent of UCC churches are essentially zombie churches, with an average of less than fifty worship attendees every Sunday—and that was before the COVID pandemic reduced attendance even further.[8] Many of them stay alive because have substantial endowments from previous generations of faithful Christians that keep the lights on. Yet almost all of those faithful Christians would be rolling over in their graves to see what has become of their denomination.

Without this money, these churches could never sustain themselves as viable entities. Another 26 percent of UCC churches have 51–100 attendees—hardly what most would call flourishing.[9] Just 4.7 percent of UCC congregations have even 150 or more attendees on average each Sunday, again down nearly 75 percent from the 17 percent answering to that description in 2005.[10] While the Gospel is not a popularity contest, the speed of the woke church's collapse indicates its fundamental failure to shepherd its flock.

If you guessed that, despite its radical racial politics, the membership of the UCC is whiter than a marshmallow-covered snowman doing lines of cocaine, give yourself a pat on the back. As of 2023, the UCC's demographics are 83.5 percent white, 4.9 percent African American, and just 0.4 percent Hispanic.[11] As it turns out, substituting anti-white wokeness for the Gospel doesn't appeal to white congregants—and it doesn't appeal to minority congregants either.

The Presbyterian Church (USA) is another example of the same phenomenon. Once one of the largest religious denominations in America, it has only a bit more than 1.1 million members today, having lost nearly 20 percent of its membership in just five years and nearly 70 percent from its peak in the 1960s.[12]

More than 20 percent of PC (USA) churches have fewer than twenty-five members and another 22 percent have fewer than fifty members, while 23 percent have fewer than 100 members (note that this is membership, not average Sunday attendance, which is much lower).

Needless to say, PC (USA) is 88 percent white, just 4 percent black, and 1.6 percent Hispanic. Just 25 percent of members are under the age of forty and just 42 percent are under fifty-five. Youth baptisms in 2022, the most recent year statistics were available, numbered just over 7,700. By contrast, as recently as 2006, PC (USA) had 30,500 youth baptisms.[13]

As PC (USA) has fallen, it's embraced any number of fashionable leftist causes. In 2022, its "international engagement committee" declared Israel to be "an Apartheid state," in what was considered by major Jewish organizations to be an antisemitic statement.[14] But its antisemitism also has roots in anti-whiteness.

Yet despite their cratering membership, in a "special report on racial justice ministries," they invite us to "learn within community settings the impact of 500+ years of structural racism resulting in government policies, institutional acts of injustice, and individual acts of harm and violence toward communities of predominately African, Asian and Pacific Islander, Latinx, and/or Native descent."[15]

During the COVID pandemic, a PC (USA) Zoom webinar on Juneteenth had almost two thousand participants while one on Ahmaud Arbery (a young black man killed by two white men in Georgia in disputed circumstances) had almost fifteen hundred.[16] All this in a religious denomination that can't get even fifty people in half of its congregations. Yet PC (USA) is happy to tell us that facilitator trainings for "sacred conversations to end racism" went from nine to thirty-four between 2019 and 2020.[17] It's clear that anti-whiteness is the main object of worship in these congregations—not God. And it's equally clear that radical anti-whiteness is driving away congregants.

At this point, the typical mainline denomination is only able to keep its biblical exodus from becoming a biblical flood by deceiving many of its remaining congregants about what their denominations stand for.

"There's a caricature by some conservatives that typical mainline congregations focus on social justice and wokery," writes the influential religion website *Juicy Ecumenism*. "In fact, the average local mainline church remains mostly traditional in worship and includes conservatives and liberals. . . . The political activism is usually confined to mostly out-of-sight national or regional denominational structures. Congregations are typically old and almost entirely white."[18] They also prevent a mass exodus through stiff exit fees. Churches that are more interested in the Gospel than the gospel of anti-whiteness must pay an extortionate amount to leave PC (USA), with one megachurch in Silicon Valley with over four thousand members recently paying almost $9 million to exit.[19]

Anti-white animus has infected the entire mainline Protestant establishment. The National Council of Churches, the classic umbrella group for "mainline" Protestantism, which claims to speak for more than 40 million congregants (though that may be substantially inflated), spoke out in 2022 in favor of reparations for slavery.[20] (It should be pointed out that, historically African American churches make up a significant, though by no means decisive, percentage of the NCC's active membership.) While the Council has always been left of center, it has increasingly embraced radical political causes well outside the Christian mainstream.

At one recent conference, Christian Brooks, PC(USA)'s Office of Public Witness's representative for domestic issues, gave the party line about the "difference between equality and equity." Regarding the latter concept, Brooks defined it as "giving people the resources they need to have so they have opportunities to achieve equal outcomes as their counterparts."[21] Stripped of its fancy rhetoric, this is just racial communism wearing ministerial robes. Again, everyone can get woke nonsense in the secular world, so why would they go to church for it?

The Episcopal Church, formerly the religious standard bearer for the American establishment, also saw a collapse in its churches to a median Sunday attendance of just twenty-one during COVID before "recovering" into the forties. Ninety percent of Episcopal congregations draw fewer than 100 people each Sunday.[22]

Why are people staying away in droves? Well, in October of 2022, Episcopal Council of Deputies president Julia Harris proclaimed, "We are finally beginning the truth-telling around racism and white supremacy in our beloved church."[23] It's not clear who they are telling this truth to, because there is nobody in the pews.

The modern mainline church has largely done away with the Gospel and made believers worship its anti-white skin suit.

In the nineteenth and twentieth centuries, the mainline Protestant leadership sometimes embraced racism against minorities over the Gospel when it was fashionable to do so. Now they embrace anti-white racism over the Gospel because it's fashionable to do so. No wonder these churches have crumbled.

## Anti-Whiteness in the Evangelical Church

At some level, critiquing the institutional leadership of mainline Protestantism for anti-white racism is like shooting fish in a barrel. While there are still some strong believers even at these churches, many of those involved, from the pastors to the parishioners, are really, when pressed, not interested in defending the core doctrines of historic Christianity.

Yet even evangelical denominations, which are far more serious about worship and theology, are increasingly infected with unbiblical anti-white sentiment.

James 2:1 (NIV) says, "My brothers and sisters, believers in our glorious Lord Jesus Christ must not show favoritism," but some evangelicals, often in the name of outreach, consistently show such favoritism to people from non-white racial backgrounds.

At places like the Gospel Coalition, *Christianity Today*, and the Ethics and Religious Liberty Commission, stalwarts of modern popular evangelicalism (often referred to derisively as Big Eva by their critics in the evangelical community[24]), Critical Race Theory has a significant presence. A tweet by Brett McCracken, a senior editor at the Gospel Coalition, is instructive. He calls on white Christian leaders to "Listen to and defer to nonwhite & nonwestern Christian leaders."[25] While, of course, Christian leaders of all types should listen with sympathy and understanding to the perspectives of other Christians, they should only defer to Scripture. And that applies to non-white Christians as much as white ones.

As we have noted earlier, the race hate hoax around Michael Brown in Ferguson, Missouri, was dismissed even by Obama's radical Justice Department.[26] That Brown's mother should appear onstage at the 2016 Democrat convention was unsurprising.[27] But that Christian leaders like Jemar Tisby, a prominent evangelical who briefly worked with Ibram X. Kendi, were still invoking Brown's name five years later is surprising and dismaying.[28] In a distressing sign, Tisby won a 2022 ECPA Christian Book Award for his book *How to Fight Racism* from the most prestigious group in Christian publishing.[29] A Gospel Coalition Conference, MLK50, also had a poet pay tribute to Michael Brown.[30] Matt Chander, executive director of the prominent Acts 29 network, said of his churches that "If we find an Anglo 8 and an African American 7, what do you want? I said I want the African American 7."[31] This sort of favoritism is foreign to the Gospel.

But the average evangelical church parishioner is much more skeptical of anti-white rhetoric, and fortunately, there are worthy leaders in the church speaking out against the current madness.

Reverend Voddie Baucham's book *Fault Lines: The Social Justice Movement and Evangelicalism's Looming Catastrophe* is the single best exposition I have seen on the growth of wokeness in the church, and I will use Baucham's wisdom as the jumping-off point for the rest of my discussion of evangelicalism.

The evangelical church has a significant advantage over most mainline churches in that it still takes God, Jesus, and the promise of salvation seriously. Because it is less willing to conform immediately to the demands of the world, there is certainly hope that it will be able to resist the current secular trends toward an anti-white stance. But such an outcome is by no means assured.

Baucham, who has been in the thick of these battles for more than two decades, is unsparing in his critique. He makes clear the seriousness of the situation right at the beginning of his book, surveying the secular and religious aspects of America and declaring, "The United States is on the brink of a race war, if not a complete cultural meltdown."[32]

Baucham's perspective is unique in that he came up through the church originally as a young pastor supporting the core tenets of CRT (he amusingly recounts arriving at seminary as a twenty-two-year-old-scholarship student wearing a shirt with pictures of Elijah Muhammad, Malcolm X, and MLK on it[33]) before over many years moving to his current, far more sound, theological position.

Importantly, in eviscerating CRT (which he refers to as critical social justice), Baucham does not deny the anti-black racism in the history of American Christianity and particularly of his own denomination, the Southern Baptist Convention. He just doesn't want to add to it by pushing anti-white racism. Baucham describes being actively discouraged by black pastors from preaching in majority-white churches and says those who told him that racial reconciliation work was important were all white. He describes being attacked for "robbing the black church" when he chose to speak to predominantly white congregations.[34]

Baucham is a particularly trenchant critic of the Black Lives Matter movement from a Christian perspective. "The facts on Black Lives Matter are not in dispute: The organization is Marxist, revolutionary, misandrist, pro-LGBTQIA+, pro-abortion and anti-family with roots in the occult. It is unacceptable for Christians to partner with, celebrate, identify with, or promote this organization. And that includes being bullied or pressured into using the phrase 'black lives matter,' a test that far too many evangelicals have already failed," Baucham writes.[35]

Baucham, currently working in Zambia as dean of the divinity school at African Christian University, is very interested in real justice—including racial justice. But as he notes, "real justice requires Truth." He quotes Leviticus (19:15), "You shall not be partial to the poor, nor honor the person of the mighty."[36]

Baucham is quick to excoriate the fashionable Christian nonsense surrounding George Floyd, mentioning Tony Timpa (discussed earlier in this book), who died a few years earlier in an almost identical manner to Floyd but was ignored by the Christian community "because he was white and did not advance the right narrative."[37] He further points out that the unbiblical "Black Lives Matter is founded on bearing false witness," pointing to its origins in the wake of the Trayvon Martin and Michael Brown cases—cases in which evidence was manufactured to support anti-white conspiracy theories while blameless whites were punished.[38]

One of Baucham's most trenchant insights is that what he calls "wokeness," a superset of anti-white racism, is a fundamentally *religious* phenomenon, and one incompatible with the Gospel. Baucham is deeply steeped in both theology and apologetics and is uniquely qualified to understand the fundamentally religious nature of wokeness. His discussion of woke theology is outstanding and is summarized below.

- Cosmology: CRT
- Original Sin: Racism

- Law: Antiracism
- Gospel: Racial Reconciliation
- Martyrs: Saints Trayvon Martin, Mike Brown, Breonna Taylor, etc.
- Priests: Oppressed minorities
- Means of Atonement: Reparations
- New Birth: Wokeness
- Liturgy: Lament
- Canon: Critical Social Justice, social science
- Theologians: Robin DiAngelo, Ibram X. Kendi, etc.
- Catechism: "Say their names"

For each of these Christian elements, CRT substitutes anti-whiteness for Gospel truth. Baucham calls this Ethnic Gnosticism, playing on Gnosticism, an ancient Christian heresy whose adherents claimed to have a special knowledge of divinity, except in this case, the special knowledge arises due to the adherents' ethnicity.

He is also quick to see the fundamental ways in which the anti-white elements of the evangelical church are fundamentally at odds with the Gospel. As he notes, the woke anti-white racist church offers no soteriology (means of salvation) but rather "perpetual penance in an effort to battle an incurable disease (racism)."[39] It would be hard to be more at odds with the fundamental message of the Gospel, which offers continued salvation through belief in Christ.

Baucham notes that "whiteness" is as central to this theology as Genesis 1:1 is to Christianity, and in explaining how fundamental it has become for some evangelicals, recounts an "evangelical" Facebook group that called on white evangelicals not to "Whitesplain" to their non-white colleagues.

This type of thinking recently infected Baucham's own denomination, the Southern Baptist Convention, the largest Protestant denomination in America. In 2020, Matthew Hall, the provost of

Southern Baptist Theological Seminary, said in an interview: "I am a racist. . . . I am going to struggle with racism and white supremacy until the day I die and get my glorified body and a completely renewed and sanctified mind because I am immersed in a culture where I benefit from racism all the time."[40]

This statement is not, at least as a general statement, factual about white people, and it is certainly not biblical. If Hall was truly a racist, rather than simply a virtue-signaler, he was spectacularly unqualified to be the provost of the Southern Baptist Theological Seminary. Perhaps realizing this himself, he subsequently moved on to Biola University, where he currently serves as provost.[41]

Hall, perhaps under fire for these and similar remarks, has since made it clear that he rejects Critical Race Theory, but it is very hard to square that rejection with remarks such as this one.[42] The Southern Baptist Convention eventually considerably moderated its stance on Critical Race Theory, but the subject is still a contentious one in the denomination to this day.[43]

As Baucham notes in his discussion of Hall, the doctrine he espouses mirrors the Calvinist doctrine of total depravity (Romans 5:12) but falls into heresy by implying this depravity is only something characteristic to those with certain skin colors. Or, as Baucham puts it beautifully, universal guilt and sin "is not the state of white men, it is the state of *all* men"—racial guilt, in this context, is strictly unbiblical.[44]

As Baucham observes, the new original sin also happens to be an unpardonable sin. The bad news, from a Christian perspective, is that man is guilty of far worse than being racist. The good news is that through faith in Jesus, he can be redeemed from this sin. Or, as the late Pastor Tim Keller put it so aptly, "The gospel is this: We are more sinful and flawed in ourselves than we ever dared believe, yet at the very same time we are more loved and accepted in Jesus Christ than we ever dared hope."[45] This truth applies to *all* men and women regardless of skin color.

Attacking Ibram X. Kendi's demand for proportionality in outcomes as a standard of "equity," Baucham pronounces it "neither biblical, nor reasonable, nor achievable."[46]

He understands the fundamentally un-Christian nature of these attacks on the Church and white Christians, noting that "antiracists have abandoned the gospel, since, in their view, there is no good news of grace. There is only law."[47] If one only applies the "law," like Kendi, everyone falls short and everyone is responsible for the sins of themselves and their ancestors. This introduces a never-ending cavalcade of sin from which we can never extract ourselves. Any serious Christian understands that grace through Jesus redeems us from this problem.

As Baucham points out, another problem with pro-CRT "Christians" is that CRT is at overt war with Christians, with one major CRT text classing Christianity with "other forms of oppression that stand in the way of social justice."[48] Baucham addresses this powerfully, pointing out that racism is *necessarily* from the perspective of Christianity a "sin of the human heart."[49] It cannot be structural, as structures are unable to repent.

This is a rather subtle point and one that goes beyond the scope of this book, where I speak of structural anti-white racism simply because I'm paralleling the terminology of our opponents for the sake of simplicity. But again, racism is a sin, and structures cannot repent—only people can. It would be more accurate to say that the current system is anti-white in terms of its discriminatory patterns.

## Catholicism and Critical Race Theory

It is not just Protestants who have embraced anti-whiteness as a substitute for the Gospel.

The Catholic Church, while not in as dire straits as mainline Protestantism, finds itself in a similar position to the evangelicals.

This is partly due to the changing demographics of American Catholicism. The growing Hispanic Catholic population means that the Church increasingly equates with racism any sort of attempt for the United States to have a border.

*U.S. Catholic Magazine* recently published an article on why it was important to portray Saint Augustine as black (Augustine, a North African of Berber origins, was almost assuredly not "black") because it "decenters whiteness." It refers to a new painting at Villanova, a prominent Catholic university, that seeks to make its school "anti-racist" by showing Augustine as essentially a black man.[50]

Talks at Catholic universities such as "Anti-Racism, the Catholic Church and the Sin of White Supremacy" are widespread. In Catholicism, the anti-white movement is led by Catholics such as Tina Pratt, the president of a diversity consulting firm who "is a sociologist specializing in systemic racism in the Catholic Church and how that racism impacts African American Catholic identity."[51]

The Catholic Archdiocese of Washington came up with an entire anti-racism initiative in the wake of the Kenosha riots. And at the subsequent Conference of Catholic Bishops, Sheldon Fabre, then the chairman of the conference, demanded "racial justice" while a talk by Catholic intellectuals discussed combating "racism and white privilege."[52] Amazingly, despite the enormous numbers of Catholic immigrants from Mexico and other parts of Latin America who have arrived in the last few decades, Catholic Mass attendance has plummeted by half since 1970 with a fairly linear rate of decay.[53] (Some of the few congregations seeing growth are generally more conservative ones where the Traditional Latin Mass is offered.[54])

The *National Catholic Reporter*, a "progressive" Catholic publication, put out an "anti-racism reading list,"[55] while the liberal Jesuit magazine *America* said white Americans needed to put "white fragility" behind them and become "anti-racist." "I am exhausted by white fragility," claimed the author, who had been a campus pastor and part of officially "anti-racist" activities within the church. "White fragility tended to control the agenda and frame the narrative to meet white sensibilities." In contrast, "I believe that the cruel, brutal, immoral and monstrous havoc caused by white supremacist ideology needs to be presented with full intensity, without pulling punches." The author went on to cite and recommend Critical Race Theory stalwarts such as Kendi, DiAngelo, and Peggy McIntosh.[56]

While, of course, there are many strong Catholics in America who reject such thinking, it is clear that anti-white theology and ideology have burrowed their way into the Catholic Church in America.

## The Historically Black Church

While I have not particularly focused on it here, the historically black church has seen many of its most prominent leaders infected by anti-white sentiment, from the Reverend Jesse Jackson calling New York "HymieTown" (an antisemitic slur) and constantly shaking down white businesses,[57] to the endless provocations of the race-hustling tax fraud Reverend Al Sharpton (who visited the White House dozens of times under Barack Obama),[58] to Obama's former pastor Jeremiah Wright shouting "God damn America" from the pulpit while regularly excoriating whites.[59] Obama was so close to Wright that he titled his 2006 book *The Audacity of Hope* after one of Wright's sermons—before ultimately distancing himself after Wright's racism and other controversial comments came to light.[60]

And this is to say nothing of the Nation of Islam and its leader, Louis Farrakhan, who has regularly been given a place of honor in American life (witness President Clinton sharing the dais with him at Aretha Franklin's funeral).[61] The same radical racial essentialism can be seen in endless YouTube clips of preachers extolling the confirmation of Ketanji Brown Jackson to the Supreme Court.[62]

## Waiting for a (Non-White) Messiah

Christians are not the only Americans suffering from a plague of anti-whiteness. Though American Jews remain 92 percent white (this is likely an underestimation as 4 percent are classified as Hispanic, a large number of whom are ethnically Jewish immigrants from Spanish-speaking countries[63]) and have historically had little interest in reaching out to minority (or other) converts, they are happy to play with anti-whiteness to boost their left-wing bona fides.

At the same conference where the Presbyterian Church (USA) was apostatizing, David Harris, the longtime CEO of the American Jewish Committee, regarded widely as the "Dean of American Jewish Organizations," according to the *New York Times*, argued in favor of reparations for slavery by appealing to the Jewish tradition. He said the concept of *teshuvah*, as explained by the medieval rabbi and philosopher Maimonides, suggests that "victims of a crime . . . can be made whole by financial repayment for the damages that were done."[64]

Harris added that "black people cannot have racial equity now or moving forward without reparations. It has to be the foundation."[65] Of course, it would have been reasonable to pay reparations to those who were actually enslaved but those people died long ago (even the last child of a known American slave has passed). In the meantime, their descendants have been disproportionately the beneficiaries of government handouts and legal favoritism for almost six decades, regardless of how well-situated they were in contemporary America. Much as some might like it to, the victimhood spigot doesn't gush forever.

The Religious Action Center (RAC), the political and legislative outreach arm of Reform Judaism, a group that represents approximately 55 percent of Jewish religious adherents who identify with a denomination, has also been getting on the anti-white bandwagon.[66]

"Despite the abolishment of slavery in 1865, systemic oppression, police violence, and racial discrimination against Black Americans and people of color continues today," says the Religious Action Center's website, while announcing another website intended to combat "voter suppression."[67]

"To affirm that Black Lives Matter is to recognize that we are a racially diverse Reform Jewish Movement, and that our diversity is a source of our strength," it adds elsewhere.[68] Again, this is a laughable interpretation of a community that has survived and thrived for thousands of years on the basis of ethnic tribalism and remains remarkably mono-ethnic (at least in the United States). Reform Judaism's relationship to serious biblical Judaism is similar to mainline Protestantism's relationship to serious biblical Christianity—which is to say, one effectively parodies the other. But it is notable because, unlike the mainline church, Reform Judaism still claims the majority of Jewish denominational adherents—and therefore its pronouncements matter.

In public speeches, RAC members are quick to identify the original Native lands where Americans now live.[69] Elsewhere, the RAC has referred to "the racial reckoning rooted in 400 years of oppression and dehumanization that emerged during the tragic events of summer 2020"[70]—and be assured they aren't talking about the Black Lives Matter riots. Helpfully, the site also features a "Colorblind/ Microaggression Resource."[71]

The most important prayer on Jewish high holidays is the *Al Cheit* (a confession of sins). Yet the Reform movement's blog suggests an *Al Cheit* focused on illegal immigrants to whom Jews should atone for "enduring and perpetrating violence and extortion," "for putting people in danger," and "for using human beings as political stunts," among other sins.[72]

According to that same blog, Jews of Asian descent are evidently under siege. After a shooting spree in Atlanta that saw a gunman claim lives at Asian massage parlors, a blogger approvingly described his mother as not wanting him to go out alone—evidently worried the next white maniac would jump out from behind a tree.[73] Other than playing into stereotypes about neurotic Jewish mothers, it's hard to see how this particular blogger had serious concerns that needed to be addressed.

Yet that didn't stop this particular Jew of color from pushing an even larger indictment of America's racism: "We [Asian Americans] have also been reduced to a convenient exemplar for purposes of the model minority myth and used as a cudgel to browbeat our Black, Latinx, and Indigenous partners. The model minority myth helps prop up white supremacy, with the goal of dividing people who might otherwise be allies."[74] The message is clear: there is no alliance to be had with the overwhelming majority of the author's religious brethren who are white. Because those very white people tend to think highly of Asian Americans, it makes it difficult for Asian Americans to participate in the struggle against white people.

Another post on the same blog refers to supposed "state-sanctioned racist violence" in America. While urging readers to "join in the efforts to combat racist systems, including this nation's policing,"[75] it notes that "this includes the modern-day lynching of Ahmaud Arbery"[76] while referring to the self-defense killing of Trayvon Martin as a "vigilante attack on Black Americans."[77]

The Reform Jewish movement's healthcare policy lead confessed she was ashamed that she did not immediately understand that George Floyd's plight was more important than her work. "This framing, however, was wrong, a product of my own privilege. The truth is that COVID-19 and police violence are both public health emergencies, linked by more than 400 years of systemic racism. Racism itself is a health crisis, and these events are just two important symptoms of it."[78]

Nor are such problems limited to Judaism's official institutions. In the wake of George Floyd's death, sixty-one Los Angeles–area rabbis and cantors, mostly representing wealthy Jewish communities that generally segregate themselves at great expense from the minority underclass, published an open letter declaring, "We are a country that is rooted in institutional racism" and "Black people are being killed in our streets."[79]

Even the more right-wing Orthodox Jewish world is not exempt from the anti-white madness. A former editor-in-chief of the newspaper at Yeshiva University, the flagship school for Orthodox Judaism in America, wrote in the wake of the George Floyd riots, "I have never excused the racism which infects the Hasidic community, and I've spent much of my life fighting it. . . . This racism is part of why I left the Hasidic community." The writer threw down a challenge to Orthodoxy: "Now is your chance to prove you can be anti-racist. . . . Systemic racism runs deep in America and it runs deep in Orthodox communities. The very foundations of Orthodoxy must be shaken for racial equality to be assured."[80]

In other words, the entire foundations of an ancient religious tradition must be shaken to conform to focus on "systemic racism" and an anti-white racial agenda.

Nothing could better sum up the current religious moment in America.

## CHAPTER 13

# Apocalypse Now:
# The Anti-White Military

*"The enemy is within the gates; it is with our own luxury,
our own folly, our own criminality that we have to contend."*
—Cicero

*"The truth of the matter is that you always know the right
thing to do. The hard part is doing it."*
—Norman Schwarzkopf, U.S. Commanding General
in the Persian Gulf War

The U.S. military has served as a model for America's shared values and integration. Pick a movie from the World War II era and you'll inevitably find soldiers from different backgrounds—one Italian, one Irish, one old-line Yankee, one Southerner, one New Yorker—all coming together in the service of the American cause as they fight the bad guys (usually actual Nazis, as opposed to the "Nazis" cosplaying Antifa claims to struggle against).

Millions of soldiers of every race and religion have served in every war since the American Revolution. The 442nd Infantry Regiment in World War II, composed almost entirely of Japanese American soldiers, remains the most decorated in American military history, having performed great works of heroism on the battlefield even as many of their relatives were interned back in the States.

Like most institutions in society, the armed forces were segregated for most of their history and often failed to live up to their professed ideals, but they were formally desegregated in 1948—long before most of society—and every unit was desegregated by 1954. The armed forces offered opportunities to people from a variety of racial and ethnic backgrounds well before this was true of society as a whole.[1]

It's no accident, given this history, that the military has often been lauded as a national model for integration. Significant numbers of conservative minority politicians have military backgrounds, which makes sense as our military, while traditionally apolitical (as the very popular General MacArthur found out when he challenged President Truman's leadership and was fired), has historically had a membership that leans right. Military towns are the most integrated places in the United States.[2] In 1940, long before any African American had a leading place in American political life, Benjamin O. Davis Sr. became a Brigadier General in the U.S. Army. (His son, General Benjamin O. Davis Jr., who would command the famous Tuskegee Airmen in World War II, would later serve as an Air Force General.)

As Wallace Terry, a black journalist with *Time* magazine, observed, "In his famous 1963 speech at the Lincoln Memorial [Martin Luther King Jr.] said he had a dream that one day the sons of former slaves and sons of slave owners would sit at the same table. That dream came true in only one place, the front lines of Vietnam."[3] While Terry would later offer a more pessimistic assessment in the wake of the assassination of MLK, it remains beyond dispute that the military has led America in promoting racial cooperation toward a common goal.[4]

Of course, even the "good old days" were not always so good. Even going back to the 1960s, white servicemen were often the victims of criminal violence by black servicemen, though such incidents were often hushed up for reasons of morale. And as in the civilian world, interracial violence rarely went the other way. For example, "a mob of thirty to forty black and Puerto Rican Marines" beat to death a white corporal named Edward Bankston in 1969.[5]

Yet overall, the situation in the military, while far from perfect, was historically still far better than in the civilian world. Today, unfortunately, the armed forces have since gone beyond cohesion, and even beyond color consciousness, and into the cult of anti-whiteness.

At some level, the origins of this are longstanding. For example, contrary to the incessant portrayals of the military drafting poor black kids to fight a white man's war, 87 percent of Americans who were killed in Vietnam were Caucasian, while just 12.5 percent were African American, with blacks making up slightly less than their share of those who were draft age.[6]

The idea that blacks disproportionately served as cannon fodder has been described as one of the myths of the Vietnam War.[7] Yet relentless propaganda from Hollywood and the media has convinced many that this was so. (Blacks were more likely to be drafted and somewhat more likely to serve in combat units, but this was largely due to the same socio-economic circumstances that applied equally to poor whites.[8]) Regardless, they were not disproportionately more likely to be killed than white soldiers.[9]

One recent Hollywood effort, Spike Lee's *Da 5 Bloods*, opens with former Black Panther leader Bobby Seale saying, "In the Civil War, 186,000 black men fought in the military service, and we were promised freedom and we didn't get it. . . . In the Second World War, 850,000 black men fought, and we were promised freedom and we didn't get it. . . . Now, here we go with the Vietnam War, and we still ain't getting nothing but racist police brutality, et cetera."[10]

In more recent wars, the level of white casualties has become even more disproportionate, even as our missions have become less and less about protecting middle America. One report on early casualties in the Iraq and Afghanistan wars "appears to support the contention that service in the military reserves is most attractive to young men living in low- or medium-income families in rural communities."[11] This is a group that is substantially more likely to be white—the Scotch-Irish core that has served on the front lines of so many American wars.

In the wars in Iraq and Afghanistan, a 2005 report found that whites made up 67 percent of active duty and reserve forces and 71 percent of fatalities, with African Americans 17 percent of the force and 9 percent of fatalities and Hispanics 9 percent of the force and 10 percent of the fatalities.[12] With white non-Hispanics roughly 56 percent of the military-age population during the war, whites are significantly over-represented in both the military and the "tip of the spear" doing the military's most dangerous work, while non-whites, contributing 44 percent of the military-age population but just 29 percent of the fatalities, are underrepresented.[13]

In the military's most dangerous and important jobs, the special forces, roughly 80 percent of the officers were white during the Iraq and Afghanistan conflicts.[14] Just 2 percent of Navy SEALs are black. Green Berets were more than 85 percent white, while just 1 percent of Marine special operators were black as of 2015.[15] This is not a result of discrimination. People are selected for these positions by grueling objective trials. To the degree they are racially imbalanced, it reflects both the choices made by soldiers of different races as to which units they wish to serve in and the differential performance on required tasks between individuals of different races.

Meanwhile, as white soldiers were more likely to fight and die on the front lines of the War on Terror, senior Defense Department officials were making disparaging comments about whites. "I am exhausted by 99% of the white men in education and 95% of the white women," wrote Kelisa Wing, then the Defense Department's chief diversity and inclusion officer for education, in comments that surfaced in 2023 that she made before her appointment.[16]

Wing commented, "[T]his lady actually had the CAUdacity to say that black people can be racist too . . . I had to stop the session and give Karen the BUSINESS."[17]

Get it? "CAUdacity." "Karen." This is where we are as a nation, even in our armed forces.

Don't worry, though, Wing made her comments only in her capacity as a "private" individual, so it's okay. Can you imagine that sort of excuse working for a white person in 2024?

When confronted about her remarks, Wing replied, "I did not make disparaging comments against white people. I would never categorize an entire group of people to disparage them. I'm speaking now as a private individual, about my private free speech from July of 2020." Elsewhere, Wing called herself a "woke administrator" and recommended a series of books on "racial justice," including books on defunding the police and white privilege.

Soldiers were forced to do a "stand down" on racism during the Black Lives Matter protests, focusing their training on marginal white supremacist groups (white supremacy in America always being something where, at least in recent decades, the demand exceeds the supply), while ignoring large and often violent anti-white groups like Black Lives Matter and Antifa.[18] "It caused service members to otherize one another, it impaired group cohesion. And interesting to me, is that I've heard those sentiments most frequently from units that are majority-minority," said Representative Matt Gaetz about the military's "stand down."[19] This, of course, is unsurprising to anyone familiar with military culture, which depends on teamwork. Anything that divides the team is deeply detrimental to the mission.

## Anti-White Racism and Challenges to Cohesion

Unfortunately, the challenges to cohesion are coming ever more frequently.

Will Thibeau, director of the Military Project at the Center for the American Way of Life at the Claremont Institute and a former Army Ranger with multiple combat deployments, has documented the downsides of diversity ideology in the military. In a 2023 congressional testimony to the House Armed Services Committee, Thibeau noted, "Diversity advocates will have you simultaneously believe a diverse military is the cornerstone of our national security, all the while minimizing any effect diversity considerations have in practical application for men and women in uniform."

He referred to this focus on demographic characteristics as "toxic," noting that "Senior military leaders and elected representatives often insist that, to receive inspiration and motivation, a soldier must see a leader who looks like him to strive for excellence."

Such an approach has consequences. According to Thibeau, "History is littered with examples of militaries whose consideration of political ideology precipitated a collapse in military professionalism, all of which served as a precursor to the collapse of their respective nations. America should not wait to find out if we can outrun the drumbeat of such history."[20]

This is not just rhetoric, but firmly backed by facts: in July 2021, Senator Tom Cotton released an extensive list of examples of anti-white racism and the use of Critical Race Theory in the armed forces. Cotton documented soldiers who said they were required on several occasions to watch videos declaring the importance of systemic racism. A reserve battalion leader documented having to discuss police brutality and white privilege (this complaint came from a Hispanic soldier) as well as how the military was systemically racist. One of the officers doing the training turned out to be a former staffer from the Democratic National Committee.[21]

Another noted that an equal opportunity officer had said, "[A]ll you whites need to [shut] the hell up and listen to your black counterparts," while decrying the military as systemically racist. Others attended training sessions where CRT author Ibram X. Kendi's work was assigned along with "White Privilege: Unpacking the Invisible Knapsack," a foundational essay of Critical Race Theory.

Another, a self-described "brown-skinned" immigrant from a "third world" country, complained how officers (most of whom had grown up in modest circumstances) confessed their white privilege, which the immigrant did not feel existed. Even more damningly, another soldier complained of a fifty-foot-long and fifteen-foot-high Black Lives Matter flag that was hung for weeks from a military barracks in an active combat zone.[22] Soldiers should not have to risk their lives underneath a banner that celebrates violent riots while condemning some of them for racism.

Unsurprisingly the woke military has increasingly had trouble meeting its recruitment standards, leading to pressure from Congress and a lowering of those standards.[23] Of course, it is whites, in particular working-class whites, who are disproportionately being asked to pay the toll for our military adventurism. The question is how many more of our soldiers will be willing to die in futile attempts to bring lesbian feminism to places like Afghanistan when they are being attacked as racists by the institution they serve.

No wonder that, given its increasing focus on diversity at the expense of excellence, the military has found itself historically weak, no longer able to fight multiple wars simultaneously.[24] Meanwhile, our Chinese adversary, which does not trouble itself with diversity and wokeness, grows stronger by the day. It deploys the world's largest navy, with shipbuilding capabilities far beyond America's and a rapidly growing nuclear stockpile. It is developing hypersonic missiles. The People's Liberation Army is the world's largest.[25]

Liberal congressmen back home are only too happy to saddle our military with handy new regulations that require the Pentagon to revise command climate surveys of troops to include questions on whether they had noticed any "extremist activity" in the workplace."[26] An official report from the Defense Department states that "a lot of latitude for interpreting what constitutes extremist activity will be left up to the local commanders who know their service members well and have their fingers on the pulse of what is going on in their units."[27] In other words, this is ripe for abuse.

It's also a sure dog whistle, as it rewards rooting out such activity and places a particular target on white conservative men (wearing BLM merch around the base is fine).

Even under Trump, the military bureaucracy was out hunting the white supremacist extremist boogeyman. "Among DVEs [domestic violent extremists], racially and ethnically motivated violent extremists—specifically white supremacist extremists (WSEs)—will remain the most persistent and lethal threat in the Homeland," declared the official Homeland Security *Threat Assessment* in October 2020. Virtually every one of the relatively few white supremacist attacks in America in recent years has been a disturbed "lone wolf"—and none, to this author's knowledge, were organized efforts involving multiple members of the military.[28]

Meanwhile, there have been multiple notable Islamist domestic attacks from within the military, most notably the Fort Hood massacre, in which Nidal Hassan killed thirteen of his fellow soldiers and wounded more than thirty. Despite writing to the then-head of the Islamic State requesting citizenship in 2014 (five years after the massacre), he was not charged with terrorism, proof that such charges are often political.[29]

The Fort Hood massacre showed how much the army was already worshipping diversity at the cost of cohesion—and common sense. In the wake of the killings, Army Chief of Staff George Casey, channeling Dan Quayle after the Los Angeles riots, said, "Our diversity not only in our Army, but in our country, is a strength. And as horrific as this tragedy was, if our diversity becomes a casualty, I think that's worse."[30] To sacrifice diversity was now literally worse than the mass fratricidal murder of American soldiers.

Meanwhile, highly organized Antifa and BLM groups carry out racist riots that kill people and cause property damage, often targeting whites and white-owned businesses, yet are never listed as a national security threat. Does the military think that the billions of dollars in riot damage and numerous fatalities caused by BLM are a threat to the homeland? It doesn't seem so, judging by their actions.

After the death of George Floyd, every single member of the Joint Chiefs of Staff spoke out about racism. Rather than showing concern over the rioters who were at that moment wreaking havoc in the streets, today's military validated their grievances. First to speak was Air Force Chief of Staff David Goldfein who said Floyd's death was a "national tragedy" and that "every American should be outraged" by the police's conduct.[31] Meanwhile, the chief master sergeant of the Air Force posted to Twitter a list of black men killed by police, including criminals like Michael Brown, while declaring "I am George Floyd."[32]

"I don't have all of the answers," the chief master sergeant claimed, "but I'm committed to seeing a better future for this nation. A future where Black men no longer suffer needlessly at the hands of White police officers, & Black airmen have the same chance to succeed as their White counterparts."[33] As we have shown elsewhere in the book, that future is already here—and in fact, it is white soldiers who are being denied equal opportunities as our readiness weakens in response to affirmative action. It is hard to imagine something worse for unit cohesion than asking white soldiers, those most likely to be at the "tip of the spear," to accept racial guilt for a problem that doesn't exist.

Meanwhile, the Confederate flag is off-limits on army bases. It was banned in 2020 in the wake of the George Floyd riots. According to a Military.com article reporting remarks by Marine Commandant General David Berger, "The Marine Corps is a combat organization, that can't afford breakdowns in trust or unit cohesion." According to Berger, "Things that divide us are not good."[34] Evidently, this need to protect military cohesion from supposedly offensive flags did not include the Pride flag, Black Lives Matter banners, or other tokens of pride for groups other than whites. The State Department even authorized BLM flags to be flown from our embassies.[35] The secretary of Veterans Affairs in 2023 approved the use of the Pride flag during Pride Month.[36]

Propagandized by the media and their superiors, military respondents in a recent survey saw white nationalism (a marginal force with few adherents and no electoral constituency) as just as much of a threat to America as radical Islam (against which we have fought multiple recent wars).[37] This rather remarkable statement was a testament to the power of propaganda.

## Disparate Racial Treatment and Fake Hate Crimes

The military is, in fact, fully devoted as a matter of course to enabling anti-white discrimination. When the *Students for Fair Admissions* case came before the Supreme Court, our military leadership panicked about having to recruit and promote based on actual merit rather than race.

Legal experts and military leaders said that in response, they would increase "recruitment of minority applicants" (meaning they would discriminate against white applicants by recruiting them less), "prioritize class rank" (again to discriminate against white and Asian applicants, though Asians make up just 4.4 percent of the military[38]—so it is primarily white applicants who will be affected) in favor of underrepresented minorities who do well at poor schools, and, most importantly, demand national security exemptions to do non-merit promotion. There was no suggestion anywhere in the amicus brief former military leaders filed before the Supreme Court that racial discrimination is fundamentally wrong.[39] This from one of the allegedly "conservative" institutions in our society today.

Numerous top former military leaders, including twenty-two four-star generals and four former chairs of the Joint Chiefs of Staff, asked the Supreme Court to preserve anti-white discrimination through affirmative action. It should be noted that a rebellion of six hundred veterans formed a group called "Veterans for Fairness and Merit." It included many retired generals, including twelve four-stars and twenty-five three-stars, though revealingly in its amicus brief opposing affirmative action, eighteen of those generals, including a four-star, requested anonymity.[40]

It was an indication of where the cultural and social power lay. Imagine being powerful enough to command forces in battle at the highest level, but not powerful enough to publicly oppose anti-white discrimination.

As Students for Fair Admissions, the group that successfully fought racial quotas at the Supreme Court, argued, "Department of Defense (DOD) surrogates speciously have argued to the Supreme Court that the DOD's use of racial preferences in service academy admissions is 'mission critical' and 'indispensable to' national security. That strategy was contrived only because of the legal framework courts must use when examining practices that otherwise violate the Constitution. Evidence must clearly prove a 'compelling state interest' sufficiently strong to justify the drastic measure of suspending the constitutional provision that prohibits such practices." As they note, these would not just be for academy admissions but assignments and promotions as well.[41] The military brass is doing everything it can to bake anti-white discrimination into its standard procedures.

In addition to the structural elements outlined above, there have been several more idiosyncratic incidents of anti-white discrimination in the military.

In 2021, the Navy's Task Force One Navy released a report that found that racial disparities existed in the military justice system (just as they do in every American justice system due to the substantially differential rates of offending by race—though in the military these disparities are lowered by the use of what are effectively IQ tests and other screens that tend to weed out criminals before they enlist).[42]

In 2017, the Air Force Academy got in a dudgeon after racist graffiti was found outside the dorm of five black cadet candidates at their preparatory academy. A speech from the superintendent decrying racism accumulated over a million views on YouTube. "So many young black men are getting killed, and there is no justice for them," wrote the mother of one of the cadets affected. It was later discovered that the graffiti was written by one of the black students, who was attempting to avoid trouble for other misconduct. While the cadet in question was said to be "no longer enrolled at the school," there was no indication that any other punishment was given, a common outcome when "hate crimes" are discovered to be fake.[43]

Yet the fact that it was all built on a lie didn't matter to the media or military, since the blood libel had served an instrumental purpose, as military leaders acknowledged. "No matter its origins, the incident sparked a national discussion on racism and the academy's swift and public response." Lieutenant General Jay Silveria, the superintendent of the Air Force Academy, "was widely praised for his strong speech, with some suggesting he run for high office after he leaves the service," according to an account in Colorado Springs's *The Gazette*.[44] The system thus rewards those who react hysterically to fake hate crime incidents, while the perpetrators go unpunished and those leaders who fail to participate in the ideological mania are not rewarded. Young military leaders can see what the incentives are.

The Air Force Academy incident was hardly an isolated one. In 2019, a group of West Point cadets were accused of making a "white power" hand gesture during a televised Army-Navy football game. While the gesture was widely condemned as racist, it later emerged that the cadets were playing a game in which they tried to sneak a hand sign into the background of TV shots—there was nothing racist about their intent. Nonetheless, there was a media frenzy and the teens were extensively attacked before ultimately being exonerated.[45]

And the new leadership of the military figures to make things worse. Air Force general C. Q. Brown, selected by Biden to be the

242   The Unprotected Class

chairman of the Joint Chiefs, installed "a system of racial and gender quotas for the Air Force officer corps". Scott Cain, another Air Force general, viewed the implementation of DEI as his top accomplishment. And yet another Air Force general, Elizabeth Alredge, expressed concerns about "whiteness" in American institutions.[46]

## Fighting Back against Military Anti-Whiteness

Encouragingly, some military figures and veterans' groups, driven by the patriotism that has always motivated the volunteer military, are beginning to speak out.

The Center for Military Readiness (CMR) has warned that a woke military will weaken the special forces, pointing out that while SOCOM's (Special Operations Command) Diversity and Inclusion Strategic Plan says on twelve occasions that diversity and inclusion are a strategic imperative, it never bothers to explain why this is the case. As it says in a serious understatement, "Lowered standards to meet diversity goals are inevitable, even though mission requirements will not change."[47] In other words—we have the same mission but will have less qualified people to carry it out.

As CMR points out, Critical Race Theory training programs "polarize and demoralize the troops." It observes about the prioritizing of diversity as an operational imperative that "attitudes are not free." Drawing from experience with integrating women into combat units, it notes that inevitably physical and mental fitness standards will be redefined and lowered to meet diversity imperatives.[48]

SOCOM's statement calls for "[i]dentify[ing] diversity gaps in SOF [special forces] career fields and us[ing] SOF key leadership positions to leverage resources to fill gaps by refining, maintaining and sustaining reliable databases and dashboards to continually monitor data and demographics." By ensuring that "accountability mechanisms" exist for diversity, commanders essentially know they won't be safe unless they abide by an anti-white quota system.[49] As a veteran friend of mine told me when he was trying to explain the psychology of several senior admirals we were working with on a project, "They throw those stars on a pile of shit, and see who jumps in after them." This is where the military is choosing to throw the stars today.

The special forces' plan to "integrate diversity and inclusion principles within operational planning and mission execution" means ultimately that DEI will be driving mission execution. One can only imagine how that will go. We have a difficult enough time winning wars even when excellence is supposed to be driving mission execution. The Pentagon's plan also clearly calls for outside "affinity groups" to be incorporated into the DEI mission, an invitation for almost limitless meddling in Americans' security by destructive NGOs.[50]

These diversity mandates are increasingly at the very core of the military structure. In February 2023, President Biden dramatically ratcheted up diversity and inclusion requirements in the military, building on three previous executive orders. As the CMR wrote, "[W]ith a stroke of his pen Biden established a powerful new Diversity Industrial Complex designed to continue racial discrimination, no matter what the Supreme Court says." New "Equity Action Teams" are being deployed throughout the federal government to make it stop. That will take a "whole-of-government approach to racial equity." It will dramatically expand the corps of "chief diversity officers," who will then have to approve all new promotions.[51]

In discussing who this is meant to help, the executive order lists a panoply of groups, from indigenous people to persons with disabilities. But as CMR notes, absent from the list are "healthy white males who are young or middle age, financially secure, Christian, and English language proficient."[52] This group formed the backbone of our military when America actually won wars. Now they are an afterthought at best and actively discriminated against at worst.

As Representative Mike Waltz and Major General Patrick Brady wrote in a *Wall Street Journal* op-ed about Biden's efforts,

"Selflessness, which has been vital to the warrior ethos for generations, requires subordination of self and subgroup identity and the ability to regard teammates' racial and ethnic differences as inconsequential.[53] In the Army and Marines, sayings such as 'We're all green' or 'We all bleed red' were part of training that transformed millions of diverse civilians into warfighters." Now, as the authors point out, Air Force Academy cadets are being taught that color-blindness is offensive, a direct contravention of this tradition.[54]

To their credit, Senator Marco Rubio and Representative Chip Roy have introduced legislation to abolish the Pentagon's chief diversity officers and other diversity bureaucrats,[55] but under President Biden, the chances of it ever becoming law are slim to nonexistent. Passing a law explicitly preventing this sort of diversity bureaucracy within the military would be an excellent priority for the next GOP administration.

Meanwhile, the military establishment is pushing back on attempts to curb its anti-white policies with a "see no evil, hear no evil" approach. "I personally find it offensive that we are accusing the United States military—our general officers, our commissioned and non-commissioned officers—of being, quote, 'woke' or something else because we're studying some theories that are out there," said General Mark Milley, chair of the Joint Chiefs under both President Trump and President Biden. "I want to understand white rage. And I'm white," he added.[56] The notion of a generalized white rage exists solely in Milley's head, which may impede his search for understanding. Arguably, white Americans *should* be enraged by the level of discrimination they are experiencing in Milley's military—but white rage is ultimately pretty scarce on the ground. It is hard to win a war when you are fighting the wrong enemy.

CHAPTER 14

# The End Game:
# Reparations and Expropriation

*"I don't feel responsible for the sins of my father and grand-father, I feel responsible for what the situation is today for sins of my own generation[,] and I'll be damned if I feel responsible to pay for what happened 300 years ago."*
—Senator Joe Biden, 1975[1]

*"I was never more hated than when I tried to be honest. Or when, even as just now I've tried to articulate exactly what I felt to be the truth. No one was satisfied—not even I."*
—Ralph Ellison, *Invisible Man*

In previous chapters, I have documented how anti-whiteness manifests itself in many different areas of American society. These areas are often treated as unconnected, but they are part of a larger overall pattern, driven by the same broad forces.

What I will now attempt to do is to sketch out, more explicitly, a theory of *why*. Major political and social phenomena do not spring up fully armored and ready for battle, like Athena from Zeus's head. They have powerful motivations that drive them and gestate for years

245

before they can come into being—they also have powerful interests that they serve. This chapter will attempt to elucidate those interests and explore the long-term goals of those who are pushing them.

The author is not in possession of a functioning crystal ball. The hypotheses that follow are just that—declarations of informed opinion, not declarations of fact, though I believe my contentions are well supported by the evidence I have laid out.

My central contention is that many of the fundamental trends I have outlined serve a common ideological purpose. That purpose is to create an intellectual and cultural environment to justify the expropriation of land, property, and other wealth from whites while instituting a permanent regime of anti-white employment and legal discrimination. If this sounds alarmist or implausible, let me assure you that it is already ongoing. In many cases, it is still on the margins of our popular politics, but like so many other leftist political movements of the twentieth and twenty-first centuries, what was marginal will soon become mainstream.

This is not to suggest that direct expropriation is the conscious strategy of most participants in these movements. Like every good political strategy, anti-whiteness has an exoteric and esoteric meaning—there is an "inner party," a limited group that understands what the end game is, even if, at times, they may not even express it to themselves, and a far larger, more diverse, and less sophisticated "outer party" that simply thinks that in attacking "white privilege" they are fighting for "justice."

Different anti-white political actors are working in their own fields to obtain benefits and status at the expense of whites. These individuals and groups are not engaged in an active conspiracy—there is no "Protocols of the Elders of Anti-Whiteness." But there is a conscious effort by those in the political system to delegitimize whites and to retell the American story in a way that makes whites the villains to justify expropriating the vast wealth and prosperity produced by whites on behalf of the new American people.

The social phenomenon of expropriation is, of course, not unique to American whites. The forced expropriations of the Chinese in Indonesia, Jews in Nazi Germany, Tutsis in Rwanda, and Indians in Uganda are just a few of the many recent historical examples where this has occurred. I do not suggest that violence on the scale that we witnessed in these countries is the likely outcome in the United States. (For one thing, even in a white-minority America, white numbers will be much larger and there will be no one dominant group to oppress them.) On the other hand, for those who have eyes to see it, a great deal of interracial violence of which whites are disproportionately and increasingly victimized has an overt or scarcely hidden undertone of racial revenge.

I first became sensitized to these issues while living in India and observing that country's caste and religious politics, which had the same motivations as America's identity politics but with entirely different groups involved. In India, caste, tribe, and religion, rather than race, were used as the excuses for official legalized discrimination, but other than that the paradigms were virtually identical. As a popular saying in India went: "You don't cast your vote, you vote your caste." At least in India, there was genuine and significant ongoing discrimination to be remedied. Thomas Sowell's book *Affirmative Action Around the World*, which I first read while resident in India two decades ago, provided valuable empirical and theoretical grounding for my work.

Sadly, there is a long tradition worldwide of financially and socially successful but politically less powerful groups being expropriated by politically more powerful but financially and socially less successful groups. Multiethnic democracies in which political power is determined by the number of people you can get out to vote, and in which most citizens are members of clearly definable groups, are particularly at risk. And this is not a remote long-term risk but a contemporary and immediate one.

According to the Census Bureau, by 2045, whites will be a minority in America, and that minority will be disproportionately older and less active in society. Already, the median age for white Americans is 43.7, compared to 37.5 for Asian Americans, 34.6 for African Americans, 29.8 for Hispanics, and 20.9 for multiracial Americans.[2]

For now, appeals to expropriation are usually indirect. But over time, these appeals will become more direct and in need of less justification as the political power of white Americans continues to decline. If we do not push back aggressively, the logic of Ibram X. Kendi, already a beloved establishment figure despite his anti-white radicalism, will increasingly rule the day.

In 2019, Kendi called for an anti-racist constitutional amendment. One of the core principles guiding the amendment would be that "Racial inequity is evidence of racist policy."[3] In other words, if there are unequal outcomes between groups, the culprit is racism. This book has attempted to forthrightly refute this statement in an American context. Different outcomes between groups can, of course, be caused by racism, but they can also be caused by some mix of differing interests, cultures, abilities, and proclivities. This is true of any society and for any definable group of people.

But if we accept Kendi's logic, if the culprit can only be racism (and in this case, white racism), then there must logically be redress. Needless to say, this is both radical and radically wrong. But we would be fools to think this is not where the Left is headed.

According to Kendi, "The amendment would make unconstitutional racial inequity over a certain threshold, as well as racist ideas by public officials." America must "establish and permanently fund the Department of Anti-racism (DOA) comprised of formally trained experts on racism and no political appointees. The DOA would be responsible for preclearing all local, state, and federal public policies to ensure they won't yield racial inequity, monitor those policies, investigate private racist policies when racial inequity surfaces, and monitor public officials for expressions of racist ideas."[4]

It is important to note that while these ideas are themselves entirely pieces of racist crankery, Kendi himself is a member of the establishment in good standing. He was selected as one of *Time* magazine's 100 most important people in the world in 2020. He has taught at Harvard, became the youngest-ever winner of the National Book Award, won Guggenheim and MacArthur Fellowships, and wrote five *New York Times* number-one bestsellers.[5] Despite the seemingly embarrassing struggles of his anti-racism institute at Boston University, where he appears to have wasted millions of dollars, he has far more power and status than almost any of us who think he is dangerous.[6]

Kendi's work is particularly valuable for us because it underscores in its purest, most reduced form how "anti-racist" is simply a euphemism for "anti-white."

## Reparations[7]

African Americans like Kendi currently sit at the forefront of anti-white racial demands, though as we will see later, they are merely the first and most aggressive in line.

While Kendi's amendment might sound absurd, reparations also sounded absurd when Ta-Nehisi Coates proposed them in 2014 in an article in *The Atlantic*, and a decade later they are increasingly close to reality.[8] It is not a coincidence that the initial push for reparations came not from former slave states (which have large black populations but are generally run by largely white GOP majorities) but from states and localities where whites have reduced political power or where those whites who are present are on the far left. Evanston, Illinois (near Chicago, home of Northwestern University), implemented one of the first reparations plans, followed by proposals from San Francisco and the state of California.[9]

This expropriation will continue over a matter of decades and will use the government and America's public institutions, largely built and paid for by several generations of white Americans, as its engine. Universities, built over centuries with hundreds of billions of dollars in donations from white and often conservative donors, have already been captured and turned into engines of racial wealth and status redistribution and anti-white ideology. The value of American university endowments alone is rapidly approaching $1 trillion.[10] Many of these wealth transfers will be disguised as benefits for the poor and disadvantaged, though their racial component will be implicit, and, at times, explicit.

While most of the arguments for reparations are made in bad faith, it is still important to refute them.

Of course, one might begin by noting that the Civil War caused the deaths of 750,000 Americans[11] (the equivalent on a population basis of seven million Americans today, almost one thousand times more than were killed in Afghanistan and Iraq) of whom almost 95 percent were white.[12] One might consider these deaths alone a fairly substantial payment of any debt incurred. Among fighting-age men in the Confederacy, deaths may have been as high as one in five, with countless others wounded and often permanently disabled—again, hardly a trivial payment.

With a similar number wounded or missing, possibly 40 percent of young Southern men were either killed or significantly wounded in the Civil War along with the almost complete destruction of the Southern economy and the personal fortunes of the vast majority of slaveowners. This was followed by more than a decade of military occupation.[13]

Since then, trillions of dollars of "reparations" have been paid in the name of welfare programs, set-asides, quotas, affirmative action, and other programs that have gone on for more than sixty years, much of which has gone to people (African immigrants, Latinos, etc.) who are not even distantly descended from those harmed. Black immigrants and their descendants now represent almost one-fifth (and rapidly rising) of the U.S. black population.[14]

Vice President Kamala Harris is one of these, descended from a Jamaican immigrant who was a professor of economics at Stanford.[15] President Obama was descended from an African immigrant who repatriated to Kenya after earning a degree at Harvard.[16] More than half of young adults in Africa want to emigrate, with the United States being the dream destination.[17] Someone clearly forgot to tell all these immigrants—and those who are desperate to cross the border every day—that the United States is a hellhole of systemic racism that discriminates against them.

Nonetheless, the reparations train moves on. California's and specifically San Francisco's efforts are exemplars of how intellectually vacuous the arguments for reparations are. Keep in mind these are states and cities that never enslaved anyone. And that slavery ended more than 160 years ago, several lifetimes before anyone living today. There are no children of former American slaves living today. Even the last grandchildren of former slaves are passing from the scene.[18]

Even if one were to accept the disingenuous arguments for reparations, the fact is that those directly harmed by slavery are no longer with us. Ironically, the last known living child of an American born into slavery spoke of his father's love and appreciation for his country. "We could never talk negatively about America in front of my father. . . . He did not have much but he really, really loved America. Isn't that funny?"[19] It is only funny if you lack the historical perspective that this wise gentleman clearly had.

But, of course, logic and a sense of perspective have nothing to do with reparations. Never mind that African Americans are the wealthiest African-descended people in the entire world by far, and they are infinitely wealthier and better off on average than the Africans whose ancestors were largely responsible for selling their ancestors into slavery. And they are infinitely better off than they would have been had their ancestors been sold into slavery in the Arab world or the Caribbean, where conditions were far more brutal than they were in America.

Black Californians should get $350,000 each, said the reparations committee there, while San Francisco has suggested providing up to $5 million and a host of other benefits.[20] And these are just the opening bids.

The right loves to mock San Francisco, but pretending that what happens in San Francisco stays in San Francisco is pure wishcasting. Despite dysfunction and emigration, the greater Bay Area has enormous cultural, financial, and technological clout in our current era. For decades now, San Francisco movements that once seemed marginal have been entering and then becoming the mainstream.

The first legal same-sex marriage was performed under the administration of then–San Francisco mayor Gavin Newsom in 2004. In 2015, the Supreme Court in *Obergefell v. Hodges* made it mandatory nationwide. It took just eleven years to go from "crazy thing only people in San Francisco do" to "constitutionally mandated throughout the country."

"America must admit its sin," Reverend Amos Brown, an influential African American San Francisco pastor, told Fox News.[21] But we cannot atone for another's sin—Brown's biblical logic is that of the enslavers who suggested African Americans deserved to be subjugated because of the Curse of Ham.

The broader philosophical claims of reparations are equally absurd. Collectively, the United States does not owe anyone anything just because they have a certain skin color or because of the experience of their ancestors.

Again, we have the experience of Jews and Asian Americans as illustrative examples—both groups have experienced undeniable discrimination in the historical United States, yet both groups are among the most successful in America. Jews today make up approximately one-third of the four hundred richest Americans despite being just 2 percent of the population.[22] Asian Americans have the highest income of any ethnic group.[23] Are we going to hand Jewish billionaires and Asian technology executives reparations?

As seen, by many measures, the African American population is already very successful. As a recent article in the German news service *Deutsche Welle* put it, "America is home to the biggest group of wealthy, highly successful Black people in the world."[24] It also has a large middle class, one that, depending on the definition, constitutes anywhere from one-third to two-thirds of the African American population. While African Americans have been the victims of some of America's greatest crimes and failures, they have also reaped (and continue to reap) enormous benefits of living here, benefits far greater than they would have had if their ancestors had never left Africa. White Americans should point that out assertively and without apology whenever the reparations grifters make their claims.

History is inherently messy, and the attempt to divide it between perpetrator groups and victim groups is intellectually incoherent and dishonest. It's also politically explosive. What Thomas Sowell calls the "quest for cosmic justice" invariably, as he notes, causes greater injustice.[25]

## Reparations beyond Black and White

Calls for black reparations for slavery are just the edge of the anti-white expropriation racket. Just as "medical" marijuana opened the door to mass decriminalization and legalization, black reparations will open the door to massive multi-trillion-dollar payments to any group that can seize the holy grail of victimhood—payments that will, implicitly or explicitly, come from the white "perpetrator" class.

"This is madness," said the *National Review* editorial board, quite accurately, of early reparations attempts.[26]

Or, as my Claremont Institute colleague and longtime Californian Steve Hayward said in a recent interview, "This is an invitation to open ethnic conflict in the country."[27]

But attempting to make sense of reparations in the context of logic and facts misses the point. The current quest for reparations is a pure racial shakedown.

We aren't going to win this fight by nibbling around the edges, by compromising, or by saying that groups deserve reparations for this but not that. We must pull up root and branch the entire concept of mass racial reparations. Otherwise what will follow will be an attempt at racial extortion on an almost unimaginable scale, one far more likely to lead to inter-ethnic violence and a collapse of American society than to a voluntary wealth transfer on a scale unseen in human history.

America needs to decide: Does it want mass inter-racial score-settling or does it want something resembling a functioning multi-ethnic democracy? How we deal with demands for reparations will determine what future lies before us.

## Land Acknowledgments and Land Expropriation

If white Americans are gullible enough, or politically weak enough, to fall for this, they can be sure every discernable minority or "marginalized" group from left-handed lesbians to transgender Native Americans will be next in line. Asian Americans (the Chinese Exclusion Act, limitations on citizenship) will step up. Hispanics (Operation Wetback, the Mexican-American War) will have even more claims. The entire white population will become a lower caste with "liabilities" in the trillions. These are more likely to be taken from communal American assets than individual white people per se, because when acting through large government programs and policies, it is easier to hide what is really being done. But functionally the net result will be similar, with some trade-off in expropriation efficiency being an acceptable compromise to at least provide a fig leaf of respectability for what is going on.

Some of this can be done through the tax code. Another likely method will be the "return" of "stolen" lands, whether to "indigenous communities" or to Mexican Americans for whom "the border crossed them."

The Supreme Court has already shown some appetite for this with the left-wing bloc plus Justice Neil Gorsuch effectively handing over eastern Oklahoma to the Cherokee, before walking it back to a significant degree when Justice Amy Barrett joined the court and the full implications of their logic became clear.[28] Look for reservations to be expanded and relocated to more attractive and financially lucrative lands while payments are made for "broken treaties." More stolen Mexican "land grants" will be discovered for which payment to Latinos or ceding of lands to their "rightful" Latino owners is required.

The ideological predispositions for this can be seen in the birth and growth of so-called "land acknowledgments"—a practice that began among left-wing Canadians and that has exploded in popularity within American universities and governments. It is customary in many spaces now to use "a carefully crafted public statement to express a commitment to the past history, current reality and future relationship between the institution, Indigenous Peoples/Nations and the land."[29] On my state humanities board in Montana, where at least it can be said we have a substantial Native American population, we do a land acknowledgment before every meeting. This was an official federally chartered group.

Such "land acknowledgments" quickly devolve into laughable intellectual incoherence. Multiple lands were claimed by multiple tribes in warfare over countless generations. Many tribes were exterminated entirely by groups claiming their land. But "we'd like to honor the Chippewa, who drove the Sioux out of their ancestral lands into new lands where they could massacre the Pawnee, Omaha, and Kiowa" just doesn't sound as touchy-feely as anti-white leftists would like it to be.[30]

In reality, there was no moral difference between the Native American tribal conquest of these lands and the white American conquest of them. Conquest is not the special province of any one ethnic group, and as long as there have been peoples they have tried to conquer each other.

Land acknowledgments are a subtle re-creating of history that attempts to ideologically justify expropriation by putting excessive value on the land itself rather than on its development, which was overwhelmingly accomplished by white Americans. This is true in countless places, including major cities that were established in swamps or other previously unproductive areas.

For example, the land in Montana where I live is often spectacularly beautiful but also raw, spare, and unforgiving. It has, for this reason, long been thinly, and at many times and places only seasonally, populated. In eastern Montana, most homesteads during the early twentieth century failed, because even on hundreds of acres it was difficult to make enough money to sustain a family at a basic level.[31] This led to the massive depopulation of eastern Montana over the ensuing decades, a process chronicled in Jonathan Raban's book *Bad Land.*

Implying the value is the "land" in a land acknowledgment commits historical erasure of the white pioneers who struggled to build settlements against incredible odds (and native attacks) and failed well into the twentieth century. It ignores the difficulties faced by pioneers and the government to carve a modern society (the kind that all of us live in) out of thinly settled land that was largely wilderness.

Montana became a valuable part of America because of these (overwhelmingly white) settlers, who built farmsteads, ranches, and roads, strung electric wires over inhospitable territory, and survived brutally cold winters where temperatures regularly hit thirty below zero and sometimes dipped even lower. While certainly we should teach native history and acknowledge native accomplishments, "land acknowledgments" before official events erase the true history of Montana's (and America's) development and implicitly apologize for its existence. Land acknowledgment is an intellectual precursor to expropriation and needs to be treated as such.

Those angrily demanding land acknowledgments are sitting in their natural gas–heated homes, watching television, and driving internal combustion cars over paved roads, all largely developed by white Americans or their European "cousins." Such demands for redress merely need to serve the grubby ideological or financial interests of those making them.

Yet such claims are gaining momentum: "Indigenous people across the US want their land back—and the movement is gaining momentum," proclaimed CNN in a 2020 article.[32] A tribe that wasn't even recognized by politically correct federal bureaucrats until 2007 can claim descent from the Native Americans who met the *Mayflower* and darned if they don't want all of their lands back. In 2015, that tribe was given a small reservation on which they were sovereign, touching off a fight to claim and then disestablish the reservation, with Senator Elizabeth Warren pushing for its continued establishment and the Trump administration arguing that its establishment was invalid. In reality, much of the question of the reservation's legitimacy had little to do with history and everything to do with modern partisan politics and, in particular, the desire of the tribe to establish a lucrative casino business.[33]

Others demand reparations for land allegedly stolen from ancestors, often based on highly contestable claims. A 2020 article describes Mexican Americans as also seeking their "stolen" lands.[34] This claim is based on their opinion that land agreements were not honored (largely because the terms of those agreements were not agreed to by the U.S. Senate, which ratifies treaties).

"We come from Spanish communities that came over, [and from] Native American communities as well," Archuleta said. "So we really are sort of mestizo. We're mixed . . . We're a land-based people. Half of our soul was here before Columbus ever hit the sand."[35]

She seemed less eager to acknowledge that the Spanish land grants her family received were merely expropriating the natives. "Losing their land" in many cases simply means the families sold the land—not because they were legally expropriated, but because they, like anyone who sells land, needed or wanted the money for other things.

Yet legislation is being pushed in Congress to give a "federal definition of traditional uses on federal lands for land grant communities. . . . Access to fuelwood, for example, to heat your home. Access to pasture to graze livestock [a huge economic value]. And it would also require that the federal agencies work with land grant communities and consult with them."[36] In other words, this is a shakedown for land they sold and don't own. Expect to see much more of this in the future.

Other Mexicans are attempting to file suit to nullify the Treaty of Guadalupe Hidalgo, which ended the Mexican-American War.[37] The most important figure on the Mexican left wants to bring the case before the International Court of Justice and has proposed reparations and indemnification.[38]

The goal is to create ambiguity. The United States isn't handing California and the Southwest back to Mexico, but that doesn't mean reparations couldn't be paid. Those of Mexican descent living on lands ceded by the treaty have benefited greatly from living as Americans, rather than under the corrupt government of Mexico. The Mexican-American War was controversial at the time, even in America, but that is an event to be studied and learned from, not a source for contemporary shakedowns. Again, the false implicit premise is that somehow, had this area remained in Mexico, Mexico would have done great things with it—a premise belied by the state of Mexico today.

After a litany of complaints, noted Mexican historian Enrique Krauze, writing at the *New York Times*, of course, announced that "the best and most just reparation would be American immigration reform that could open the road to citizenship for the descendants of those Mexicans who suffered the unjust loss of half their territory."[39] Game, set, and match to the con men and woe to anyone dumb or weak enough to believe them.

The final destination is a world in which whites have been stripped of political power and resources, which are then redistributed to non-whites using both "legal" and "democratic" processes. Again, this is already underway, but its speed and scale will dramatically increase as white political power diminishes. That the expropriators may not succeed is only true to the extent that whites can politically organize themselves and sympathetic non-white allies to oppose the state-sanctioned theft of their wealth and assets. White Americans already pay billions each year to subsidize our cross-border invasion and cultural erasure. If we don't fight harder, we will soon be subsidizing our own expropriation.

# CHAPTER 15

# Finding Our Way Home

*"Hope is not the conviction that things will turn out well—but the certainty that something makes sense, regardless of how it turns out."*
—Václav Havel, *Disturbing the Peace*

*"You must never confuse faith that you will prevail in the end—which you can never afford to lose—with the discipline to confront the most brutal facts of your current reality, whatever they might be."*
—Admiral James Stockdale on the seven and a half years he spent as a Vietnam POW

In 2017, seemingly out of nowhere, signs began appearing initially around college towns but later in other locales, too. Simple and unadorned, they read, IT'S OKAY TO BE WHITE in all capital letters with no additional information. The phrase seemed innocuous enough. In fact, it was identical to one spoken by a minority executive quoted in our entertainment chapter, who was encouraging whites to feel like they were still welcome in our multicultural wonderland. But, of course, the signs were hardly viewed as harmless by the establishment.

It turns out the slogan was the creation of the /pol/ (politically incorrect) channel of the trollish 4chan internet message board. The creator(s) were trying to provoke, to create a dissonance between a seemingly harmless message and the anger that it would stoke in our anti-white public culture—anger that would expose that "leftists and journalists hate white people," according to the poster who generated the idea.[1]

Mission accomplished.

The posters appeared at Harvard, Princeton, and many other prestigious universities, where they were invariably removed by campus officials, who condemned them as "divisive" and "racist."[2] They were also condemned in the *Washington Post, Newsweek,* by the Anti-Defamation League, and across other organs of elite opinion.[3]

In Saskatchewan, the University of Regina president declared angrily, "These signs have no place in our university."

"If, indeed, these tactics are meant to silence our work in diversity and inclusion, please know we shall not be deterred. We will continue to engage our campus in critical discussions and work together to enact real change," pronounced the University of Utah's DEI office.

Meanwhile, Tucker Carlson, quite reasonably, asked on his show, "Okay so what's the correct position? That it's not okay to be white?"[4] This was the entire point. Because we live in a political climate that is hostile to white people, the notion that it could be okay to be white—that whiteness is not something worthy of being condemned—is viewed by many elites as a hostile statement. The signs exposed that reality in brilliant fashion.

Yet encouragingly, normal Americans do not share our elites' fanatical anti-white animus. In a February 2023 poll conducted by the respected pollster Rasmussen Reports, 72 percent of people agreed that it was "okay to be white." Among black respondents,

53 percent agreed while 26 percent disagreed, and majorities of Democrats, Republicans, and unaffiliated voters "strongly agreed."[5]

Savvier leftists, like the leader of Washington State University's DEI office, agreed too: "Sure, it's OK to be white. It's OK to be African American. It's OK to be Latino."[6]

I couldn't have said it better myself.

The question this book asks, and attempts to answer, is why so many American elites seem to passionately disagree with that statement, and in this final chapter, we'll explore what we should do about that.

While it is clearly not as immediately dire, in twenty-first-century America, the position of whites to some degree has come to resemble the position of Native Americans back when whites were asserting their dominance on the North American continent. It is known that Native Americans, the victims of the original "Great Replacement" in America, have a long history of so-called "deaths of despair" (alcohol, drugs, suicide). The reasons for this are both contested and complex, and it is not the purpose of this book to definitively discuss them. But while there is a dispute among scholars as to whether Native Americans tend to have a higher genetic susceptibility to substance abuse, most scholars and observers would attribute at least some of their difficulties to the emotional trauma of their defeat and displacement.[7]

In our first chapter, I discussed the work of the economist Angus Deaton and his wife and fellow economist Anne Case in documenting the huge rise of "deaths of despair" among middle-aged white Americans. Pre-COVID, such rises were not observed among minority groups (in fact, deaths of despair fell).[8]

Deaton notes, "Globalization and automation are experienced in similar ways by other rich countries. Yet in other rich countries, you don't see deaths of despair on anything like the same scale. So, we've always been looking at a peculiarly American culprit."[9]

Raphael Lemkin, the Polish Jewish lawyer who invented the term *genocide* and drafted the original United Nations Convention on Genocide, was the first to develop the concept of cultural genocide.

For Lemkin, key components of cultural genocide included the mass distribution of intoxicants, re-education of children, forced relocations, and the destruction of important cultural symbols.[10]

Certainly, we see all of this in our current cultural context with white Americans. We have the re-education of children (the curriculum wars, Critical Race Theory), the destruction of cultural symbols (the tearing down of statues, denigrating the Founding Fathers and other central figures of American history), and even what are effectively forced relocations ("white flight" to the suburbs as crime increased in the cities). The notion of "white genocide" has generally been associated with the far-right fringes of American political debate—yet according to Lemkin's typology, slow-motion "cultural genocide" would seem a fair description of what's currently happening to white Americans.

Yet whites are often not fully aware of the extent of the transformations happening around them. The average white American in a metropolitan area lives in a neighborhood that is 71 percent white, though metropolitan areas as a whole are just 55 percent white.[11] In rural areas, whites, who make up 78 percent of the total rural population, tend to live in even more uniformly white areas.[12] And even those of us in the thick of multicultural America can convince ourselves that things aren't really that bad—right? We have diverse friend groups and enjoy lots of great ethnic food. Yet as this book has shown, these superficial positives mask a far more disquieting reality.

I did not write this book so the reader would resign himself to defeat or lash out at fellow Americans of different races or ethnicities. There is hope, not just for white Americans but for all Americans. America has faced stiffer challenges than the ones we face today and has prevailed. This hope could take any number of forms, from a cultural and governmental course correction led by a decisive, focused, and energetic conservative president to some sort of radical federalism that would allow those of us who wish to escape the Left's increasing racial tyranny to exercise much greater sovereignty at the state and local levels.

These challenges are addressable, and all groups in America, not just white Americans, stand to gain from addressing them.

Many people of all racial backgrounds understand the danger of our current situation, still believe in the vision articulated by America's Founders, and want to fight for equal rights for Americans regardless of the color of their skin. Anyone who has been involved in this struggle knows countless minorities who have stood by the side of whites in recent years as they have demanded equal treatment under the law as promised in the Constitution.

Some of the prominence of non-white champions of our cause occurs because, as we live in a systematically anti-white environment, whites such as this author who advocate for their legitimate interests will be falsely labeled as white nationalists and the like, thus raising the social and professional costs of speaking out to a level that most find unacceptably high. This has become increasingly true even for minority advocates of equal treatment for whites. You'll sometimes hear the Left and the media (but I repeat myself) refer to Asian white supremacists, Hispanic white supremacists, and even black white supremacists.

The good news is that the hysterical charges are no longer deterring people from speaking out. The environment is *vastly* freer than it was just a few years ago. It has even improved notably while I have been writing this book. To speak of anti-white racism is no longer universally taboo.

But even those not inclined to fight for equal rights in the name of justice can be convinced to do so out of self-interest. Smart people of all backgrounds understand that the America built largely by Europeans and their descendants over several hundred years is the golden goose, and that to kill the golden goose in the name of obtaining a few additional short-term eggs is an unwise strategy. A civil conflict of some sort caused by a fundamental refusal to stop discriminating against white Americans serves nobody's interests.

To avoid dire consequences, there are several steps we can take.

Some of these steps are more general, and some are more specific. I will lay out a number that fall under each category below.

Some passionate advocates may find these proposals insufficient. They may reasonably ask why white Americans should compromise at all on issues of identity and culture when they have been the victims of full-scale discrimination and replacement for decades now.

Yet whether or not they acknowledge it even to themselves, the "solutions" these advocates usually desire or propose would ultimately involve force or violence. This would cause far more problems than it solves and would be immoral by harming well-meaning fellow Americans. Those wishing to dabble in such "solutions" deny the reality that America is now a multiethnic country. They are not interested in the messy give-and-take of politics, which invariably involves painful compromises, but in something else entirely.

The goal of my work is not to arrive at some version of Sowell's "cosmic justice" for white people, which we will never obtain, but to acknowledge the realities we are faced with and to set off on a path that leaves ALL Americans better off than we are today.

In that spirit, I offer some general and some specific strategies and solutions that I believe could rescue America from its current racial quagmire.

## General

### (1) "Whiteshift" America's Ethnicity
The term whiteshifting comes from political scientist and race and ethnicity scholar Eric Kaufmann (himself multiracial: white,

Hispanic, and Asian) who posits in his 2019 book *Whiteshift* that many minorities, particularly multiracial minorities in a future multiethnic America, will come to embrace a white identity. This sort of "multiracial whiteness" could be a very positive development for American solidarity over the long run. It would create a new American ethnicity that would incorporate people from a variety of different ethnic and racial backgrounds who identify themselves with the culture, legacy, and interests of America's historic majority.

The census remains one of the most powerful vectors of anti-white civil rights law. The Biden administration is desperate to "racialize" the Hispanic ethnicity as well as to create a new category of Arab and North African Americans (who are currently treated as white and therefore denied special benefits).[13] The Democrats' long-term goal is to create ever more categories of people with a stake in the anti-white civil rights regime. They have accomplished this in the past by changing the wording of census questions while running circles around their GOP opposition.[14]

Our goal must not just be to stop the momentum but to roll it back. There have been some heroes on the right side of this debate, such as Mike Gonzalez of the Heritage Foundation, who did incredible work defeating the Democrats' attempts to create ever more racial categories in the 2020 census.[15] But more vigilance is needed to stop further Democrat meddling in 2030.

Our current racial and ethnic categories were not handed down to Moses on Mount Sinai or even given law in the Constitution. "Hispanic" as a census category dates back only to the 1980 census.

By changing the wording of census questions, liberal bureaucrats ensured that 53 percent fewer Hispanics identified themselves as "White Alone" between the 2010 and 2020 censuses, even as the number of overall Hispanics increased substantially.[16]

It would be best to eliminate the "Hispanic" census category entirely, changing it to "native Spanish speaker," "born in a

Spanish-speaking country," or something else that would more clearly capture a culturally distinct population rather than attempt to "racialize" a nonracial category. This was closer to the census category that existed before 1980.

But solutions must go beyond the census, which is more of an indicator than a benchmark for benefits. As several scholars have observed, much anti-white discrimination is driven by existing civil rights law. Therefore, making more people eligible for benefits under civil rights law means that things will be worse for whites. Instead, we should create incentives for more of America's multiracial population to identify with the historic majority.

Already, 27 percent of Hispanic newlyweds are marrying whites.[17] Over time, as global Hispanic population growth diminishes (total fertility rates in most countries in Latin America are now well below replacement—Brazil was just 1.6 and Mexico 1.8 in 2022[18]), there will likely be less Hispanic immigration to America. The increasingly Americanized Hispanic population figures to intermarry even more frequently with non-Hispanic whites, creating what will effectively be a large number of multiethnic Hispanic-white Americans who can be encouraged to identify with the majority culture. With Hispanics set to make up one quarter of the population by 2060, simply encouraging much of this group to recast itself as part of America's historic white majority by taking away its legal incentives not to do so could arguably be the best "one simple trick" for defeating anti-white racism and creating a bedrock for a new majority culture and American ethnicity.[19]

Even today, self-identified Hispanic Americans have at least two-thirds European ancestry, about 3.5 times what they have from any other source.[20] This is why so many already identify as white. With continued intermarriage between non-Hispanic whites and white Hispanics, we would expect that to increase over time. The only reason, over the long term, to categorize many Hispanics as something *other* than white is the legacy of racist "one drop of blood" rules that imply anyone with identifiable African or Native ancestry cannot identify as white.[21]

"Whiteshifting" this population would also contribute to national cohesion and unify an American history that did include a substantial Spanish and Mexican component in our three most populous states (Texas, Florida, and California) and throughout much of the rest of the Southwest. There is historical precedent for this approach. While initially many were treated as outsiders, the integration of Southern Europeans into a white "American" identity happened quite quickly (over the course of a few generations) because the system did not incentivize them through affirmative action and other benefits to embrace a non-white identity or through continuing mass immigration to build eternal ethnic enclaves walled off from the majority American culture.

The same basic principles outlined above apply to other ethnicities, particularly America's rapidly growing Eurasian population, and we should similarly encourage them to identify with the historical American majority—but Hispanics would seem to be the simplest and largest opportunity.

**(2) Recruit Asian Americans as Allies and Hold Them Accountable**
While many of the policies and procedures discussed in this book directly target whites, others do so only incidentally, because they are designed to help groups in society that, on average, have not historically prospered as much as whites in America. In those cases, such policies also usually end up hurting Asian Americans, often even more severely than whites on a per capita basis. This represents a tremendous opportunity for an alliance between whites and Asian Americans.

Asian Americans, for a variety of reasons, primarily cultural, remain fully ensconced in the left-wing coalition (Biden won them in 2020, 63–31 percent, while the smaller and more conservative group that voted in the 2022 midterms still went Democrat, 58–40 percent).[22] While individual Asian American voters' views are mixed, Asian American community groups tend to actively support far-left anti-white organizations, as was seen with the Black Lives Matter and #StopAsianHate movements.[23]

White Americans need to increase outreach to Asian Americans while at the same time holding accountable community groups and politicians within the Asian-American community that push anti-white racism. There are various reasons why many Asian Americans are not comfortable in today's conservative coalition, but the level of discrimination against them on the Left is becoming untenable. There is a huge opportunity to bring them into a merit-focused coalition with whites, with whom Asian Americans have a large commonality of interests.

### (3) Hold Black Political Leaders and White "Progressives" Accountable for Anti-White Policies and Rhetoric

A perceptive reader cannot have missed how much of anti-whiteness in America is attributed to, or benefits, the black community. This is largely because of America's history with slavery and the racial guilt that afflicts many whites as a result. But this perspective insults African Americans and helps nobody (it is also increasingly at odds with reality as a rapidly growing percentage of African Americans are the descendants of modern immigrants from Africa).[24]

In an American context, slavery and Jim Crow were unique evils, but American slavery was far from unique from a global perspective. Until it was first disestablished in the West, slavery was an almost ubiquitous feature of societies from time immemorial, and it remains stubbornly persistent in Africa and the Middle East in particular. Furthermore, slavery was abolished almost 160 years ago and Jim Crow almost 60 years ago, replaced by programs to help African Americans.

Contra Ibram X. Kendi, the level of lawlessness, anti-white racism, and anti-social behavior against whites (and others) from blacks can no longer be waved away, nor can its failures simply be blamed on racism. It is time to respect the African American community enough to hold individual African Americans responsible for their own behavior, rather than inaccurately attributing all difficulties and failures in the African American community as resulting from "white supremacy" or "the legacy of slavery and Jim Crow."

Of equal concern is what to do about white "progressives," the most powerful and most uniquely toxic group in American society. White progressives have, in almost unprecedented fashion, developed an outgroup preference (that is to say, in survey data, they show they prefer other ethnic groups to their own, at least in theory). While sympathy for other groups is healthy, ethnic self-hatred is toxic. As Manhattan Institute scholar Zach Goldberg has documented extensively in his empirical research, no other American ethnic group, regardless of ideology, has anything even remotely resembling the self-hating attitude of liberal whites.[25]

Progressive whites occupy the commanding heights of culture and in many ways are the straw that stirs the anti-white drink. They must be confronted, exposed, and shamed, and their dangerous moral imperialism put down. Their moral mania (often a substitute for the Christianity or Judaism they have left behind) has made them, without question, the most destructive group in American life. No real solution to our racial problems is possible until they either reject their current anti-white animus or are removed from their positions of power and authority.

### (4) Speak Out and Create a Preference Cascade against Anti-White Discrimination

Studies have shown for years that white people (correctly) perceive anti-white racism to be a larger and more severe problem than anti-black racism or other forms of anti-minority racism. Yet shamed by the Left's moral imperialism, too many whites are afraid to say this publicly. Or, to quote a paper written by professors at Harvard and Tufts, "Whites See Racism as a Zero-Sum Game That They Are Now Losing."[26] In part this is due to perceived practical consequences, but it's still a self-fulfilling prophecy. When one person speaks the truth, it becomes easier for others to do so.

As the popular anonymous Twitter poster @FischerKing wrote, "The United States won't be in a position to right the ship until white people can say all the things that minorities can say without personal consequences. GOP creates surrogates to say what whites can't say without ruining their lives and that tells you everything."[27]

I experienced this phenomenon even in the context of writing this book—a number of people, many of them knowledgeable about the subject, thought it was a great idea, but told me it would be better if a non-white person wrote it. Somehow a white person advancing arguments that white people should be treated fairly was seen as unseemly. It's an understandable political instinct for anyone who has been involved in American politics in recent decades, but ultimately it's an attitude we need to eliminate.

This tendency shows the level of self-defeating behavior we have even on the activist Right. The poet Robert Frost wrote, "The liberal man is too broadminded to take his own side in a quarrel." Perhaps the same could be said of most white political activists and politicians today—except substitute "cowardly" for broadminded. The notion that to speak the truth about anti-white discrimination requires an ethnic minority to do so is an ideology of defeat. That has to change, and this book, I hope, can be a small part of that change. We have nothing to apologize for in opposing the racist civilization-wreckers we are fighting against.

## (5) Engage in Civil Disobedience

There is probably no solution to this problem that doesn't at some level involve putting bodies in the streets. This is something that is not in the cultural DNA of many middle-class whites, and it needs to be done carefully. The tactics that work for the anti-white Left

will not work for us. The treatment of January 6 versus the Black
Lives Matter rioters shows this clearly to anyone paying attention.
Yet as Frederick Douglass wrote, "Power concedes nothing without
a demand. It never did and it never will. Find out just what any people will quietly submit to and you have found out the exact measure
of injustice and wrong which will be imposed upon them."[28] The
notion that we will receive just and equal treatment solely due to the
moral strength of our arguments, or even our electoral strength at
the ballot box, is farcical. We will receive just and equal treatment,
and a full vindication of our natural rights under the Constitution,
when those who refuse to give it to us begin to understand there is a
price to be paid for not doing so.

There are practical challenges to this. In blue cities especially,
those who publicly advocate for just treatment for whites will receive
no sympathy and be instantly blamed for any criminal behavior that
happens around them. If they are attacked by Antifa, for example, or BLM, they are more likely to be treated as the perpetrator
rather than the victim. Nonetheless, they need to emerge, carefully
and responsibly, in areas where they can make a graceful show of
strength. Ultimately, people need to show they are willing to sacrifice—to "put their bodies upon the gears," as Mario Savio famously
said during Berkeley's Free Speech Movement—to disrupt the current plans of our opponents. "No justice, no peace" applies to white
people as well.

## (6) Boycott Anti-White Racism in Hollywood and Madison Avenue

We need to become more aggressive about boycotting anti-white
Hollywood companies and encourage the emergence of alternative talent ecosystems. While globalization will inevitably lead to
a more multicultural cast of Hollywood heroes, there is no reason
to accept the current practice of inevitably featuring the great
white villain or pathetic white buffoon. It only takes a few effective boycotts (witness Bud Light[29]) to change corporate behavior.

Similarly, anti-white commercials, film, and TV should not go unchallenged.

The noted political scientist Timur Kuran developed a concept called preference falsification, the misrepresenting of one's actual preferences or beliefs under real or perceived public pressures. Many whites understand that we currently suffer under a regime of anti-white racism but are deterred from saying so because of preference falsification. When private opinion and public opinion diverge, a shock to the system can create what Kuran called a preference cascade, in which many are suddenly empowered to reveal their actual views. I hope this book, as well as the actions of other ordinary Americans, will help create just such a shock to the system. There is no reason that we should apologize for demanding equal treatment under the law.[30]

## Specific Policy Actions

### (1) Implement Net-Zero Immigration

Perhaps nothing would do more for American unity than the introduction of net-zero or even net-negative immigration. This is not a fantasy, but a proposal embraced by many elected congressmen and thought leaders on the Right. Note: Net-zero immigration does not mean zero total immigration. Like a great business that wants to hire the best employees, there should always be room in the United States for a limited number of foreigners with truly extraordinary skills who can add to our economy and culture. But with at least 45 million immigrants and countless more children of immigrants, it is long past time to halt mass immigration so America can recohere a national identity. This also means that for each legal immigrant we let in, we should be deporting at least one illegal immigrant.

It was no coincidence that the heyday for a unified American identity—the time so often shown in cheesy Americana commercials, a time of high fertility and marriage rates across all groups along with low divorce rates and rising living standards—occurred in the 1950s, at the end of an extended period of very low immigration.

With a population of more than 335 million, the United States is not running out of people. Nor does having an endless procession of new immigrants seem necessary for America to flourish. While we should accept immigrants from everywhere, we should unashamedly prioritize migration based on skill and from countries with which we have historical ties (primarily, though not exclusively, countries in Europe).

Overall, our immigration policy should be dictated by what journalist and commentator Steve Sailer has referred to as "citizenism," prioritizing what is best for Americans and our needs over the interests of foreigners. As Sailer wrote in *The American Conservative* in 2006, "Citizenism is patriotism understood not as shouting that America is the best but as wanting the best for Americans."[31] This—considering our fellow citizens as "ourselves and our posterity" and acting unashamedly in their interests—offers a strong ethical basis for a future multiethnic America.

## (2) Embrace Lawfare against the Anti-White Establishment

We need to build and nurture a massive lawfare operation to fight anti-white discrimination the same way that the Left's civil rights legal regime has done. What makes our current cultural moment so frustrating is that so much of what is going on is often patently illegal under existing laws. Blatantly anti-white discrimination goes unchallenged because of a feeling of futility, a worry over being called racist, or an expectation that this is just "how things should be."

Fortunately, a backlash is emerging. Groups such as America First Legal, arguably the most effective organization to come out of the Trump administration, openly advertise for clients (in particular white or Asian clients ignored by "civil rights" groups) who have been discriminated against because of their race.[32]

America First Legal has filed lawsuits against the Biden administration and other groups. As mentioned earlier, a Starbucks manager was recently awarded $25 million for being discriminated against because she was white.[33] A group of teachers in Philadelphia won $3 million for the same reason.[34]

### (3) Eliminate Affirmative Action Everywhere

The recent Supreme Court ruling on affirmative action (that is, racial discrimination) in universities, though only the beginning of a long struggle, is nonetheless a watershed, as it explicitly rules against race-based discrimination as contrary to the equal protection clause of the Fourteenth Amendment.[35]

This gives us terrain on which to fight. Our affirmative action regime is all about incentives. If we give people incentives to identify as minorities, they will do so and use that energy to organize in ways that discriminate against white Americans. If we give them no incentives to identify as minorities, they are likely to want to identify with the white American majority that has historically shaped our country's culture.

The Supreme Court has helped us here—but as Winston Churchill said in another context: "This is not the end. It is not even the beginning of the end. But it is, perhaps, the end of the beginning."[36]

### (4) Enact Wholesale Reform of Civil Rights Laws

This change is arguably the most necessary yet could be among the most challenging to bring about. Overall, our long-term goal must be to repeal those parts of the so-called "Constitution of 1964" (the civil rights legal and bureaucratic framework) that are incompatible with the human freedoms guaranteed to all Americans in our original Constitution. The government must still ensure equal treatment for all Americans in the public sphere (based on equal laws, not equal outcomes), but freedom of choice and association must be returned to the private sphere—or we don't have a private sphere at all.

That task is a daunting one. The Left has done an incredible job of making "civil rights" a synonym for virtue. Thankfully not every major policy change requires a legislative fix. Eliminating "disparate impact" and other harmful provisions from civil rights enforcement (many of which were never intended in the original statutes), as well as repealing civil rights executive orders on affirmative action, would be a good starting point. Changing the burden of proof for discrimination to be found in certain situations would be another promising move. While doing this without passing new laws would be challenging, there is no doubt that some of it can be accomplished under existing legal authorities.

Of course, doing things through executive authority can also be undone through executive authority, but that misses the larger point.

Even if the formal legality of these executive orders is something of a "bouncing ball" depending on whether you have a Democratic or Republican administration, putting these orders in place shifts these issues from being politically settled to being politically contested. Over the long term, that will prove highly beneficial. Furthermore, it will have the downstream effect of making some corporations not comply with anti-white regulations except when absolutely necessary and could bring new allies from the business community (heretofore silent) into play on our side of the fight.

### (5) Eliminate DEI Bureaucracies

As with civil rights laws, the existence of diversity bureaucracies is how the Left bakes in its conditions for victory. Yet they can be undone. Florida and Texas have removed DEI bureaucracies from their university systems, and eighteen other states have taken action against them.[37] While legal challenges are inevitable and stringent follow-up will be necessary because university environments tend to be particularly sympathetic to DEI, these are still powerful tools that can strengthen our side while weakening those whose jobs are to discriminate against us. The simple knowledge that their positions are contested will remove some of their power and decrease the attractiveness of these positions for potential applicants.

By exposing these positions as political and immoral, such policies will dramatically reduce their ability to cause harm. Honest people should be ashamed to work in DEI—like the stigma that was attached to working for cigarette companies decades ago. "Florida's farmers and waitresses and truck drivers should not be subsidizing a permanent bureaucracy of left-wing activists who hate them and hate their values," said Chris Rufo of the Manhattan Institute, which wrote Florida's model legislation to eliminate DEI.[38]

## (6) Strengthen Law Enforcement

The freedom to be safe in one's person or possessions is perhaps the most cherished and fundamental of human freedoms. As whites are disproportionately the victims of crimes that have driven them out of their historic communities at great personal cost, we can strengthen the hand of police to maintain community safety through a presumption that police have the right to use deadly force. We can also bring criminal charges against police only in the most extreme instances of police negligence or malevolence.

We grant police a monopoly on force to keep our communities safe. The response to incompetent use of that monopoly should generally be the removal of a policeman from policing, not criminal charges against the law enforcement officer. Americans of good will recognize that even well-meaning officers, acting in the spur of the moment under enormous pressure, may sometimes make the wrong choice—at times with catastrophic consequences. That does not make them criminals. At the same time, actual police corruption, evidence tampering, or malevolent use of force must be punished severely. Strengthening the ability of the police to crack down on crime will benefit all communities, not just whites.

Eliminating affirmative action in police hiring, which makes it more likely that incompetent or malevolent officers will join the force, would be another important step. Public safety is too important to be put at the mercy of diversity bean counters.

Also, we could better and more comprehensively categorize statistics on race and crime to puncture left-wing myths that are often used to criticize the police—for example, what are the real numbers on racial violent crime from strangers (the type of crime most people care about)? If we don't ask the questions, we'll never find the answers. What gets measured gets managed. Much of the anti-white mythmaking on crime is a result of our not having all the information easily available that's needed to rebut these myths.

There are many other steps we could take to begin to reverse the course of anti-white discrimination in American society, but these would serve as a useful starting point.

◆ ◆ ◆

There is a story from the ancient pre-GPS days, of a man who was driving from somewhere in the Midwest to the wedding of a friend in New York City. At some point, he takes a wrong turn, followed by another wrong turn, followed by another, and eventually finds himself hopelessly lost, driving down a rutted dirt road. To his relief, he notices an old farmer dressed in a pair of blue jean overalls standing by the side of the road in front of a small, weather-beaten farmhouse.

Rolling down the window, the man asks the farmer how to get to New York City. The farmer pauses, his brow furrowed, his wrinkled face seemingly lost in thought, until he looks directly at the driver and says, "Well . . . I wouldn't start here!"

The farmer disappears into his farmhouse and comes out with a dusty old map, from which he is able to point the driver to his current location, and shows him how to get from the farmhouse to the nearest county road. This county road, the farmer assures him, will take him to a state highway, which will connect with the interstate that will deliver him, at last, to Gotham.

The farmer's instructions are relevant as we look to extract ourselves from the racial thicket we are in. America has taken many wrong turns, and we are now lost, traveling on a bumpy road far from our destination, with badly worn tires, a cracked windshield, and perhaps not a lot of gas left in the tank. Given the choice, we wouldn't start here—but here we are, and we must do the best we can to get to our destination.

Your author, at best, is like that farmer—I cannot point us directly to where we need to go but I can at least hope to give a map of the terrain and direct us back to larger and more promising roads that eventually, with great care and foresight, will allow America find its way home.

That home is one of freedom and equality under the law, what James Madison was referring to when he discussed "equal laws protecting equal rights"—equal laws that he thought were "the best guarantee of loyalty, and love of country; as well as best calculated to cherish that mutual respect and good will among citizens."[39]

It is a destination that Americans are always seeking, and usually, after fits and starts and several wrong turns, we find ourselves arriving closer to it than many would have ever dared to dream.

# ACKNOWLEDGEMENTS

Having developed this book over a number of years, there are so many people worth thanking that it seems overwhelming. Whether they suggested an angle I hadn't considered, pointed me to a source of which I was not yet aware, or disagreed, even strenuously, with me in a way that sharpened my own thinking, I could not have written this book without the help of so many others.

First, my colleagues at the Claremont Institute, and in particular the Institute's president, Ryan Williams. While so many conservative "leaders" over the years have run and hidden from our toughest fights, Ryan has always encouraged Claremont's scholars to engage in the most important and controversial debates and has always had our backs when the inevitable storms came.

The phrase "if you're taking flak, you're over the target" very much describes Claremont today—it's why the *New York Times* recently called us a "nerve center of the American right."[40]

So many of our scholars and friends, including Michael Anton, Glenn Ellmers, Spencer Klavan, Ken Masugi, Scott Yenor, Seth Barron, Theo Wold, and Steve Hayward have contributed thoughts, ideas, and critiques, either personally or publicly, that have informed this text. In particular, I wish to commend Christopher Caldwell, whose outstanding book *The Age of Entitlement* spurred and sharpened my thinking about these issues. I also wish to thank the executive director of Claremont's Center for the American Way of Life, Arthur Milikh, who offered wise advice and counsel as I began this project and was kind enough to introduce me to the folks at Regnery.

My pastors and my friends in my church have provided me with spiritual nourishment during a difficult project while keeping the Gospel in mind. The commitment I finally made a few years ago to follow Jesus after many years of deliberation and prayer has had a profound effect on my politics and has taught me to value people first and foremost, not due to any utilitarian or materialist calculation but because they are made in the image of God. It also helped prepare me for the political storms that inevitably came. "If the world hates you, keep in mind that it hated me first" (John 15:18). This took off the pressure and helped me understand that I did not need to be a perfect person to advance an intellectually sound thesis. *Res ipsa loquitur*—the thing speaks for itself.

Many other friends, most known to me personally but a few only online, were valuable companions on this intellectual journey. Hillsdale's David Azerrad has written fearlessly about racial issues for some time and provides a model for serious scholarly engagement. The late Secretary of State George Shultz, with whom I worked closely for a decade, thought deeply about these issues and believed that governance as it relates to diversity was the great political challenge of the twenty-first century. I greatly benefitted from his wise counsel and experience for many years, and his perpetually optimistic spirit reminded me that in America, anything is possible. My friends Erielle Azerrad and Paul Gregory, whom I met during my time at Hoover, have proved a useful sounding board for many ideas.

Harmeet Dhillon of the Republican National Committee and Gail Heriot at the U.S. Commission on Civil Rights have been deeply enmeshed in these issues in both theoretical and practical ways, and I have benefitted from their writing and public remarks.

Twitter/X anons like Lafayette Lee, Benjamin Braddock, Fischer King, The Prudentialist, Indian Bronson, Lomez, and The Columbia Bugle constantly pushed the envelope with provocative ideas and commentary. Closer to home in Montana, my friends Aaron Flint (host of *Montana Talks*) and his wife Jessica have been stalwart sources of support. Jenna McKinney, Trish and Matt Schreiber, Roger and Ann Koopman, Kerri Seekins-Crowe, John and Ramona Baden, Jonathan Keeperman, Tom Burnett, Henry Kriegel, Emily Daniels, Paul Nachman, and Rob Sisson have been a few (among many) Montana policy friends who have been excellent sources of advice and support.

Among national conservative figures, my debts are too numerous to count. Heather Mac Donald, who has written bravely on these issues for years, was the first person I consulted when I set out to write the book. She was somewhat mystified by my worries about how to "position" the book and gave me the confidence to simply write what I believed and let the chips fall where they may.

Victor Davis Hanson, Mark Granza, Curtis Yarvin, Richard Hanania, Ann Coulter, Charles Haywood, Darren Beattie, Julie Kelly, Saurabh Sharma, Julie Ponzi, Daniel Horowitz, Auron MacIntyre, Raheem Kassam, Allum Bokhari, Zineb Riboua, Rod Dreher, Alex Kaschuta, Steve Sailer, Aaron Sibarium, Helen Roy, Mike Cernovich, Anthony Sabatini, Eric Kaufmann, Inez Stepman, Chris Rufo, Julie Ponzi, Will Chamberlain, Ying Ma, Matthew Peterson, and Nate Fischer have all provided helpful advice and/or inspiration.

Zach Goldberg's work on racial ingroup and outgroup preferences was a touchstone for this book. Mark Krikorian from the Center for Immigration Studies has always been helpful in adding to my knowledge of the pivotal and complex issues surrounding immigration. John Fonte, Pedro Gonzalez, Razib Khan, Reihan Salam, Stephen Cox, Michelle Malkin, Lanhee Chen, Noah Kotch, William Wolfe, Nate Hochman, Jakub Rehor, Naweed Tahmas, Avikk Ghose, and Dave Reaboi have all inspired me through interesting conversations.

At *National Review*, Rich Lowry broke me into the conservative publishing business many years back. Helen Andrews and Micah Meadowcroft gave me space to explore these ideas in the *American Conservative*. John O'Sullivan, the former editor of *National Review*, hosted me for two very productive visits at the Danube

Institute in Budapest. Sean Davis and Joy Pullman at The Federalist were always fearless about publishing even my more provocative work. Josh Hammer at *Newsweek* was always unfailingly encouraging. At Claremont, Charles Kesler of *The Claremont Review of Books* and James Poulos and his colleagues at the *American Mind* have generously provided a forum for my ideas.

Tom Spence, the publisher of Regnery, was unfailingly polite and patient and encouraging in taking on a new author in this space. Matt Purple, my editor at Regnery, was both patient and constructive in working with me, leaving the manuscript far better than he found it. Michael Baker, Kathleen Curran, and Joshua Monnington at Regnery did a superlative job of copy editing.

Elizabeth Kantor and Daniela Rapp at Skyhorse Publishing/ Regnery gracefully managed the publishing process upon transition.

Looming large among my intellectual debts is Thomas Sowell, long a giant in this field, whose works on race and affirmative action first got me thinking seriously about these issues in a cross-cultural context.

My parents and my sister have always encouraged me in my life and my work. They indirectly influenced me when I was growing up by providing strong examples of abhorring discrimination and injustice of any kind. My family's support has been a lifetime constant throughout many other changes.

Children make one look at the world through new eyes, and I have been fortunate to help raise five children of my own. While my children are still very much just beginning to develop their own worldviews, their existence certainly sharpened mine. They are the stakes I am playing for here—the "skin in the game" that makes this all worthwhile.

Most of all, I would like to thank my wife, who is not particularly political, but who nonetheless has stuck with me for twenty-four years, across several continents, multiple careers, and five children. Those who know writers and politicos know we are often a moody, depressing bunch and that consequently our care and feeding can be difficult. She has juggled her own challenging career, managed our household, and never wavered in either her extraordinary work ethic or her support of me, even if something I wrote might have caused her to lose a fair-weather friend or to experience some other difficulty.

With all of these thanks noted, and with apologies to many more people who have helped me whom I have failed to acknowledge, I cannot stress enough that the views expressed in this book are not in whole or in part to be attributed to any of the above individuals. They are mine alone.

# ENDNOTES

## Introduction

1  *Fentanyl Safety for First Responders* (North Carolina Department of
   Health and Human Services, 2017), 1, https://www.ncdhhs.gov
   /documents/fentanyl-information-1st-responders-final/download.

2  N'dea Yancey-Bragg and Tami Abdollah, "Jury Selection Begins in
   Derek Chauvin Trial. What Did the First Day Reveal about Legal
   Strategy, Human Perception?," *USA Today*, March 9, 2021, https:
   //www.yahoo.com/lifestyle/jury-selection-begins-derek-chauvin
   -021057908.html.

3  Tucker Carlson, "Everything the Media Didn't Tell You about the
   Death of George Floyd," Fox News, March 11, 2021, https://www
   .foxnews.com/opinion/tucker-carlson-george-floyd-death-what
   -media-didnt-tell-you.

4  Caroline Downey, "Al Sharpton Stands by His Handling of Tawana
   Brawley Rape Hoax," *National Review*, January 13, 2023, https:
   //www.nationalreview.com/news/al-sharpton-defends-stance-rejecting
   -grand-jury-hoax-ruling-in-1987-rape-case.

5  Jaclyn Reiss, "'Get Your Knee off Our Necks!' Watch the Al Sharpton
   Speech That Got Multiple Standing Ovations at George Floyd's
   Memorial," *Boston Globe*, June 4, 2020, https://www.bostonglobe
   .com/2020/06/04/nation/get-your-knee-off-our-necks-listen-al
   -sharpton-speech-that-got-multiple-standing-ovations-george-floyds-
   memorial.

6  Emily Shapiro and Whitney Lloyd, "$27 Million Settlement for
   George Floyd's Family Approved by Minneapolis City Council,"
   ABC News, March 12, 2021, https://abcnews.go.com/US/27-million
   -settlement-george-floyds-family-approved-minneapolis/story?id
   =76419755.

7  Alexi McCammond, "Biden Compares 'Tragic' Death of George Floyd
   to Eric Garner," Axios, May 27, 2020, https://www.axios.com/2020
   /05/27/joe-biden-george-floyd-minneapolis; John Verhovek and
   Molly Nagle, "Biden Addresses Nationwide Floyd Protests, Condemns
   Trump Church Photo Op in Philadelphia Speech," ABC News, June 2,
   2020, https://abcnews.go.com/Politics/biden-address-nationwide-floyd
   -protests-condemn-trump-church/story?id=71017544.

8  Andrew Mark Miller, "Private School Head Compares Parents
   Opposing 'Woke' Curriculum to Jan 6 Rioters," Fox News, July 29,

2021, https://www.foxnews.com/politics/private-school-head-parents
-jan-6.

9  Jeff Johnston, "'We're Demonizing White People for Being Born,'
Head of Elite School Agrees with Teacher He Let Go," Daily Citizen,
April 22, 2021, https://dailycitizen.focusonthefamily.com/were
-demonizing-white-people-for-being-born-head-of-elite-school-agrees
-with-teacher-he-let-go.

10  Henry Louis Gates Jr., "A Negro Way of Saying," *New York Times*,
April 21, 1985, https://www.nytimes.com/1985/04/21/books/a-negro
-way-of-saying.html.

11  William Shakespeare, *Julius Caesar*, Act I, Scene II, https://shake
speare.mit.edu/julius_caesar/julius_caesar.1.2.html.

**Chapter 1: The Lay of the Land**

1  "Return of the Whole Number of Persons within the Several Districts
of the United States" U.S. Census Burau, Washington D.C., 1790,
https://www2.census.gov/library/publications/decennial/1790/number
_of_persons/1790a-02.pdf. p.1.

2  Roger Green and Rick Becker, *Census Racial, Economic and
Population Trends 1790–2020* (New York: New York Department of
Labor, March 2021, 3 https://dol.ny.gov/system/files/documents
/2021/03/census-trends-in-tracking-ethnicity-1790–2010_0.pdf;
Michele Connolly and Bette Jacobs "Counting Indigenous American
Indians and Alaska Natives in the US census," *Statistical Journal of
the IAOS*, 2020, p. 201–2010, https://content.iospress.com/articles
/statistical-journal-of-the-iaos/sji200615.

3  Tejvan Pettinger, "Facts about the American Revolution," Biography
Online, February 21, 2017, https://www.biographyonline.net/facts
-american-revolution.

4  This is not to discount the considerable cultural variation even within
the British origin population, as discussed in books such as *Albion's
Seed* by David Hackett Fischer (Oxford University Press, New York,
1989).

5  Jeremy Carl, "A Nation of Settlers," The American Mind, September
1, 2022, https://americanmind.org/features/rule-not-by-lies/a-nation
-of-settlers.

6  Indeed, it is important to note that the first continuously inhabited
European settlement in what is now America is St. Augustine,
Florida, established by the Spanish in 1565. However, Florida did not
achieve statehood until 1845, and the Spanish contribution to early
American history, while not unnoticed or insignificant, was not one
of the earliest or most important streams of our country's cultural,
economic, or political history.

Santa Fe, New Mexico, was founded almost contemporaneously with Jamestown, and while New Mexico did not become a state until the twentieth century, a significant percentage of Hispanics in America in the mid-twentieth century were from old New Mexico, Texas, California, and Colorado families. People like Ken Salazar, a former Colorado senator and Joe Biden's ambassador to Mexico, trace their family roots back to these populations.

7  "Nationality Act of 1790," Immigration History, accessed November 8, 2023, https://immigrationhistory.org/item/1790-nationality-act.

8  Jacob Bennett, "White Privilege: A History of the Concept" (thesis, Georgia State University, 2012), 9, https://scholarworks.gsu.edu/cgi /viewcontent.cgi?article=1051&context=history_theses.

9  Justin McCarthy, "U.S. Approval of Interracial Marriage at New High of 94%," Gallup News, September 10, 2021, https://news.gallup .com/poll/354638/approval-interracial-marriage-new-high.aspx.

10 Jeffrey M. Jones, "New Low in U.S. See Progress for Black Civil Rights," Gallup News, September 9, 2020, https://news.gallup.com /poll/319388/new-low-progress-black-civil-rights.aspx.

11 *STAATUS INDEX 2023: Attitudes towards Asian Americans and Pacific Islanders* (The Asian American Foundation, 2023), 39, https: //staatus-index.s3.amazonaws.com/2023/STAATUS_Index_2023.pdf.

12 "Protected Class," Thomson Reuters Practical Law, accessed November 8, 2023, https://content.next.westlaw.com/practical-law /document/Ibb0a38daef0511e28578f7ccc38dcbee/Protected-Class ?viewType=FullText&transitionType=Default&contextData=(sc .Default)&firstPage=true.

13 "Race/Color Discrimination," U.S. Equal Employment Opportunity Commission, n.d., https://www.eeoc.gov/youth/racecolor-discrimination.

14 Derek Brown, "Quotes from Louis Farrakhan," *The Guardian*, July 31, 2001, https://www.theguardian.com/uk/2001/jul/31/race.world1; Vinson Cunningham, "The Politics of Race and the Photo That Might Have Derailed Obama," *New Yorker*, January 28, 2018, https://www .newyorker.com/culture/annals-of-appearances/the-politics-of-race -and-the-photo-that-might-have-derailed-obama; Valerie Richardson, "Bill Clinton Slammed for Sharing Stage with Louis Farrakhan at Aretha Franklin Funeral," Associated Press, September 2, 2018, https://apnews.com/article/entertainment-music-religion-bill-clinton -race-and-ethnicity-4f9bf2f93650939a093be8e189bd1e8c.

15 Rod Dreher, "The Left's Anti-White Racism," *American Conservative*, December 23, 2015, https://www.theamericanconservative.com/the -lefts-anti-white-racism.

16 Jordan Boyd, "In Racist Screed, NYT's 1619 Project Founder Calls 'White Race' 'Barbaric Devils,' 'Bloodsuckers,' Columbus 'No Different Than Hitler,'" The Federalist, June 25, 2022, https://the

federalist.com/2020/06/25/in-racist-screed-nyts-1619-project-founder
-calls-white-race-barbaric-devils-bloodsuckers-no-different-than-hitler.

17 See, for instance, Adam Serwer, "Why Conservatives Want to Cancel
the 1619 Project," *The Atlantic*, May 21, 2021, https://www
.theatlantic.com/ideas/archive/2021/05/why-conservatives-want-cancel
-1619-project/618952; Brian Stelter and Oliver Darcy, "1619 Project
Faces Renewed Criticism—This Time from within the *New York
Times*," CNN, October 12, 2020, https://www.cnn.com/2020/10/12
/media/new-york-times-1619-project-criticism/index.html.

18 Andrew Sullivan, "When Racism Is Fit to Print," *New York
Magazine*, August 3, 2018, https://nymag.com/intelligencer/2018/08
/sarah-jeong-new-york-times-anti-white-racism.html.

19 Ibram X. Kendi, "Ibram X. Kendi Defines What It Means to Be an
Antiracist," Penguin, June 9, 2020, https://www.penguin.co.uk
/articles/2020/06/ibram-x-kendi-definition-of-antiracist.

20 Robin DiAngelo, *White Fragility: Why It's So Hard for White People
to Talk about Racism* (New York: Beacon Press, 2018), 50.

21 Mohamad Moslimani, Luis Noe-Bustamante, and Sono Shah, "Facts
on Hispanics of Argentine Origin in the United States, 2021," Pew
Research Center, August 16, 2023, https://www.pewresearch.org
/hispanic/fact-sheet/us-hispanics-facts-on-argentine-origin-latinos.

22 "S0201|Selected Population Profile in the United States," United States
Census Bureau, accessed December 5, 2023, https://data.census.gov
/table?q=American+Community+Survey&t=-A0.

23 B. Joseph, "Why Nigerian Immigrants Are One of the Most
Successful Ethnic Group [*sic*] in the U.S.," Medium, July 2, 2018,
https://medium.com/@joecarleton/why-nigerian-immigrants-are-the-
most-successful-ethnic-group-in-the-u-s-23a7ea5a0832.

24 Anne Case and Angus Deaton, "Rising Morbidity and Mortality in
Midlife among White Non-Hispanic Americans in the 21st Century,"
PNAS, November 2, 2015, https://www.pnas.org/doi/10.1073/pnas
.1518393112.

25 "Births," March of Dimes, January 2022, https://www.marchofdimes.
org/peristats/data?reg=99&top=2&stop=4&lev=1&slev=1&obj=1.

26 Steve Sailer, "Flight from White," Taki's Magazine, May 15, 2019,
https://www.takimag.com/article/flight-from-white/#.XNupjf_WH70
.twitter.

27 "Table 4: Hispanic or Latino Origin by Race," Census.gov, accessed
November 9, 2023, https://www2.census.gov/programs-surveys
/decennial/2020/data/redistricting-supplementary-tables/redistricting
-supplementary-table-04.pdf.

28 Nicole Chavez and Harmeet Kaur, "Why the Jump in the Native
American Population May Be One of the Hardest to Explain," CNN,

August 19, 2021, https://www.cnn.com/2021/08/19/us/census-native
-americans-rise-population.

29 Circe Sturm, "How the Native American Population in the US
Increased 87% Says More about Whiteness Than about Demographics,"
The Conversation, December 15, 2021, https://theconversation.com
/how-the-native-american-population-in-the-us-increased-87-says-
more-about-whiteness-than-about-demographics-170920.

30 Kenneth Johnson, "New Census Reflects Growing U.S. Population
Diversity, with Children in the Forefront," University of New
Hampshire, October 6, 2021, https://carsey.unh.edu/publication
/new-census-reflects-growing-US-population-diversity.

31 Dudley L. Poston Jr., "3 Ways That the U.S. Population Will Change
over the Next Decade," PBS, January 2, 2020, https://www.pbs.org
/newshour/nation/3-ways-that-the-u-s-population-will-change-over
-the-next-decade.

32 Eric McGhee, Jennifer Paluch, and Vicki Hsieh, "California's
Children Offer a Window into a More Diverse Future," PPIC, January
11, 2022, https://www.ppic.org/blog/californias-children-offer-a
-window-into-a-more-diverse-future.

33 Eric Kaufmann, "Don't Take This Personally," *City Journal*, June 5,
2023, https://www.city-journal.org/article/the-wests-culture-of-therapeutic
-individualism. ·

**Chapter 2: Civil Wrongs**

1 "Executive Order 11246," Office of Federal Contract Compliance
Programs, n.d., https://www.dol.gov/agencies/ofccp/executive-order-11246
/regulations.

2 Dan Quayle, "Address to the Commonwealth Club of California,"
Dan Quayle website, May 19, 1992, http://www.vicepresidentdanquayle
.com/speeches_standingfirm_ccc_1.html.

3 Robert Lindsey, "White/Caucasian—," *New York Times*, April 3,
1977, https://www.nytimes.com/1977/04/03/archives/whitecaucasian
-and-rejected.html.

4 Julie Marquis, "Doctor Becomes Symbol in Affirmative Action
Debate," *Los Angeles Times*, September 2, 1997, https://www.latimes
.com/archives/la-xpm-1997-sep-02-mn-28080-story.html; Jon
Christian Ryter, "A New Look at Affirmative Action," johnchristian
ryter.com, 2003, https://www.jonchristianryter.com/Two_Cents
/030519.html; Douglas Martin, "Patrick Chavis, 50, Affirmative
Action Figure," *New York Times*, August 15, 2002, https://www
.nytimes.com/2002/08/15/us/patrick-chavis-50-affirmative-action
-figure.html.

5 Douglas Martin, "Patrick Chavis, 50, Affirmative Action Figure."

6   Richard Pearson, "Patrick Chavis Dies," *Washington Post*, August 12, 2002, https://www.washingtonpost.com/archive/local/2002/08/12 /patrick-chavis-dies/821232fc-42a4–495c-a65b-0625cd709b6a; Nicholas Lemann, "Taking Affirmative Action Apart," *New York Times*, June 11, 1995, https://www.nytimes.com/1995/06/11/magazine /taking-affirmative-action-apart.html.

7   Michelle Malkin, "The Life and Death of Patrick Chavis," Chron, August 9, 2002, https://www.chron.com/opinion/editorials/article /malkin-the-life-and-death-of-patrick-chavis-2105603.php.

8   Michael Powell and Ilana Marcus, "The Failed Affirmative Action Campaign That Shook Democrats," *New York Times*, June 11, 2023. https://www.nytimes.com/2023/06/11/us/supreme-court -affirmative-action.html

9   Christopher Caldwell, *The Age of Entitlement: America Since the Sixties* (New York: Simon & Schuster, 2020), 6.

10  Ibid., 5.

11  Ibid., 159.

12  Ibid., 11.

13  Ibid., 267.

14  Ibid., 276.

15  Ibid., 243.

16  Jeremy Carl, "Overturn *Griggs v. Duke Power*," *American Conservative*, August 15, 2022, *https*://www.theamericanconservative.com/overturn -griggs-v-duke-power.

17  "EEOC History: 1980–1989," U.S. Equal Employment Opportunity Commission, n.d., https://www.eeoc.gov/history/eeoc-history-1980–1989.

18  Adam Clymer, "Civil Rights Bill Is Passed by House," *New York Times*, November 8, 1991, https://www.nytimes.com/1991/11/08/us /civil-rights-bill-is-passed-by-house.html.

19  Roger Clegg, "Introduction: A Brief Legislative History of the Civil Rights Act of 1991," *Louisiana Law Review* 54, no. 6 (July 1994): 1463, https://digitalcommons.law.lsu.edu/cgi/viewcontent.cgi?article =5539&context=lalrev.

20  Gail L. Heriot, "Title VII Disparate Impact Liability Makes Virtually Everything Presumptively Illegal," *New York University Journal of Law and Liberty* 14, no. 1 (2020): https://www.nyujll.com/home /blog-post-seven-fzhxe

21  Ibid., 3.

22  Ibid., 169.

23  "Avoiding Adverse Impact in Employment Practices," SHRM, March 18, 2022, https://www.shrm.org/resourcesandtools/tools-and-samples /toolkits/pages/avoidingadverseimpact.aspx.

24  Arnett v. Kennedy, 416 U.S. 134, 231 (1974) (Marshall, J., dissenting).

25  Caldwell, *The Age of Entitlement*, 14.

26  "Rand Paul: I Support the Civil Rights Act," House.gov, April 10, 2013, https://lee.house.gov/news/articles/rand-paul-i-support-the-civil-rights-act.

27  Leo Strauss, "Why We Remain Jews: Can Jewish Faith and History Still Speak to Us?" in *Jewish Philosophy and the Crisis of Modernity: Essays and Lectures in Modern Jewish Thought* (New York: State University of New York Press, 1997), 315.

28  Alice Speri, "Progressive Group Roiled by Accusations Diversity Leader Misrepresented Her Ethnic Background," The Intercept, February 16, 2023, https://theintercept.com/2023/02/16/american-friends-service-committee-raquel-saraswati.

29  Richard Hanania, "Where Does 'Wokeness' Come From?," Quillette, September 22, 2023, https://quillette.com/2023/09/22/where-does-wokeness-come-from.

30  Richard Hanania, "Woke Institutions Is Just Civil Rights Law," Richard Hanania's Newsletter, June 1, 2021, https://www.richardhanania.com/p/woke-institutions-is-just-civil-rights.

31  Ibid.; Heather Mac Donald, "Undisciplined," *City Journal*, Summer 2022, https://www.city-journal.org/article/undisciplined.

32  Eugene Volokh, "What Speech Does 'Hostile Work Environment' Harassment Law Restrict?," UCLA.edu, n.d., https://www2.law.ucla.edu/Volokh/harassg.htm.

33  Hanania, "Woke Institutions Is Just Civil Rights Law."

34  Laura Meckler and Devlin Barrett, "Trump Administration Seeks to Undo Decades-Long Rules on Discrimination," *Washington Post*, January 5, 2021, https://www.washingtonpost.com/education/civil-rights-act-disparate-impact-discrimination/2021/01/05/4f57001a-4fc1-11eb-bda4-615aaefd0555_story.html.

35  "The Widening Racial Scoring Gap on Standardized Tests for Admission to Graduate School," *The Journal of Blacks in Higher Education*, 2006, https://www.jbhe.com/news_views/51_graduate_admissions_test.html.

36  Mark Moore, "Biden Judicial Nominee Charnelle Bjelkengren Stumped by Basic Constitution Questions," *New York Post*, https://nypost.com/2023/01/26/biden-judicial-nominee-stumped-by-questions-about-the-constitution.

37  Carrie Johnson, "President Biden Has Made Choosing Diverse Federal Judges a Priority," NPR, January 2, 2023, https://www.npr.org/2023/01/02/1146045412/biden-diverse-federal-judges-women-black-appeals-courts; Laura Litvan, "Biden Builds Judicial Legacy with Diversified Federal Courts," Bloomberg Law, December 27, 2022, https://news.bloomberglaw.com/us-law-week/biden-builds-judicial-legacy-with-diversified-federal-courts.

38 Maria Ramirez Uribe, "Tucker Carlson is wrong: Diversity makes the Biden administration more representative, not less," Poynter.Org, Feb 20, 2023. https://www.poynter.org/fact-checking/2023/biden-federal -judge-nominations-diversity-race-based/.

39 National Association for Law Placement, "2020 Report on Diversity in U.S. Law Firms," p.4, https://www.law.berkeley.edu/wp-content /uploads/2021/02/2020_NALP_Diversity_Report.pdf

40 Jacob Sullum, "Defending OSHA's Vaccine Mandate, Sonia Sotomayor Says 'I'm Not Sure I Understand the Distinction' between State and Federal Powers," *Reason*, January 10, 2022, https://reason .com/2022/01/10/defending-oshas-vaccine-mandate-sonia-sotomayor -says-im-not-sure-i-understand-the-distinction-between-state-and-federal -powers.

41 Carrie Campbell Severino, "A Landmark Victory for the Colorblind Constitution," *National Review*, June 20, 2023. https://www.national review.com/bench-memos/a-landmark-victory-for-the-colorblind -constitution/.
    Haley Strack, "Fact Check: Liberal Supreme Court Justices Rely on False Claims about Racism, Anti-Gay Bigotry to Bolster Dissents," *National Review*, June 30, 2023, https://www.nationalreview.com /news/fact-check-liberal-supreme-court-justices-rely-on-false-claims -about-racism-anti-gay-bigotry-to-bolster-dissents/.

42 Carrie Campbell Severino, "Nancy Abudu, Another Concession to the Far Left and to One of Its Most Disreputable Organizations," *National Review*, April 19, 2022, https://www.nationalreview.com /bench-memos/nancy-abudu-another-concession-to-the-far-left-and- to-one-of-its-most-disreputable-organizations.

43 "Senate GOP: Southern Poverty Lawyer a Poor Choice for Judge," Family Research Council, April 28, 2022, https://www.frc.org /updatearticle/20220428/splc-judge.

44 Senator Josh Hawley, "Senator Hawley Slams Biden's Radical Judicial Nominee for Not Condemning Violent Rhetoric," YouTube video, April 27, 2022, 5:57–6:17, https://www.youtube.com/watch?v =sZjcYWimsq0.

45 Rorie Solberg and Eric N. Waltenburg, "Trump and McConnell's Mostly White Male Judges Buck 30-Year Trend of Increasing Diversity on the Courts," The Conversation, October 8, 2020, https://the conversation.com/trump-and-mcconnells-mostly-white-male-judges- buck-30-year-trend-of-increasing-diversity-on-the-courts-146828.

46 Ibid.

## Chapter 3: Crime and Punishment

1 Meredith Deliso, "Officer Who Shot Jacob Blake Acted 'Within Policy,' Won't Face Discipline, Chief Says," ABC News, April 13,

2021, https://abcnews.go.com/US/officer-shot-jacob-blake-acted-policy-face-discipline/story?id=77053649.

2  Todd Richmond, "Feds Won't Seek Charges against Cop in Jacob Blake Shooting," Associated Press, October 10, 2021, https://apnews.com/article/us-news-us-department-of-justice-rusten-sheskey-jacob-blake-kenosha-4f8493dd0776ef6046e052a538cd1460.

3  Michael Ginsberg, "This Lawyer Regularly Makes False and Unfounded Claims about Deaths That Inspired Riots," The Daily Caller, April 27, 2021, https://dailycaller.com/2021/04/27/ben-crump-black-lives-matter-breonna-taylor-trayvon-martin-george-floyd.

4  Alexis McAdams, "Kenosha Unrest Damages More Than 100 Buildings, at Least 40 Destroyed, Alliance Says," ABC 7 Chicago, September 2, 2020, https://abc7chicago.com/kenosha-shooting-protest-looting-fires/6402998.

5  Michelle Voepel, "All Three WNBA Games Wednesday Postponed as Part of Protest of Jacob Blake Shooting," ESPN, April 26, 2020, https://www.espn.com/wnba/story/_/id/29748510/all-three-wnba-games-wednesday-postponed-part-protest-jacob-blake-shooting.

6  Katherine Rosenberg-Douglas, "Fledgling Militia Group Put Out Call to Arms in Kenosha and 5,000 people Responded. Now It's Banned from Facebook after Fatal Shootings during Protests.," *Chicago Tribune*, August 28, 2020, https://www.chicagotribune.com/news/breaking/ct-kenosha-wisconsin-militia-social-media-shooting-20200828-aenx5ropmrfmtca34ezqvhwe7e-story.html.

7  Arpan Rai, "Kyle Rittenhouse Tells Tucker Carlson He Wanted to Give First Aid to One of the Men He Shot but Was Chased Off," *Independent*, November 23, 2021, https://www.independent.co.uk/news/world/americas/tucker-carlson-kyle-rittenhouse-first-aid-b1962576.html.

8  Michael Ruiz, "Kyle Rittenhouse Trial: Who Are Joseph Rosenbaum, Anthony Huber, and Gaige Grosskreutz?," Fox News, November 17, 2021, https://www.foxnews.com/us/kyle-rittenhouse-trial-who-are-joseph-rosenbaum-anthony-huber-and-gaige-grosskreutz.

9  Jorge Fitz-Gibbon, "Sole Survivor of Kyle Rittenhouse Shootings Has Criminal Past: Report," *New York Post*, November 15, 2021, https://nypost.com/2021/11/15/sole-survivor-of-rittenhouse-shootings-has-criminal-past-report.

10  Dan MacGuill, "Did Joe Biden Call Kyle Rittenhouse a 'White Supremacist'?," Snopes, November 24, 2021, https://www.snopes.com/fact-check/kyle-rittenhouse-biden.

11  Ayanna Pressley (@AyannaPressley), "A 17 year old white supremacist domestic terrorist drove across state lines, armed with an AR 15. . . .," Twitter, August 26, 2023, 8:33 p.m., https://twitter.com/AyannaPressley/status/1298780540431224832.

12 Janine Anderson, "Breaking Down the Election Data," *Kenosha News*, December 21, 2017, https://kenoshanews.com/news/breaking-down -the-election-data/article_950b2bad-d093–53bd-b783-cffdf2526584 .html https://www.kenoshacounty.org/2095/Election-Results-for -1132020.

13 Averi Harper, "Kamala Harris Meets with Family of Jacob Blake in Wisconsin, Blake Joins by Phone," ABC News, September 7, 2020, https://abcnews.go.com/Politics/kamala-harris-meets-family-jacob -blake-wisconsin-blake/story?id=72863184.

14 Bret Lemoine, "Darrell Brooks Trial 'Really Hard' for Milwaukee Dancing Grannies," Fox 6 Milwaukee, October 27, 2022, https: //www.fox6now.com/news/darrell-brooks-trial-really-hard-milwaukee -dancing-grannies.

15 Kelly Sadler, "George Soros–Backed District Attorneys Are Ruining America," *Washington Times*, November 23, 2021, https://www .washingtontimes.com/news/2021/nov/23/george-soros-backed -district-attorneys-are-ruining; Melissa Caen, "Why Did San Franciscans Recall Their DA?," *Commonwealth*, June–July 2022, https://issuu.com/thecommonwealth/docs/the_commonwealth_june _july_2022/s/16065437.

16 Elijah Westbrook, "Biden Decries Buffalo Shooting as 'Domestic Terrorism,' Says 'White Supremacy Is a Poison," CBS News, May 17, 2022, https://www.cbsnews.com/newyork/live-updates/president -biden-to-visit-buffalo-today-following-deadly-mass-shooting-at -tops-supermarket.

17 Dana Kennedy, "'Not Fitting Their Narrative': Waukesha Feels Abandoned after Tragic Parade Attack," *New York Post*, December 14, 2021, https://nypost.com/2021/12/13/why-waukesha-parade -attack-doesnt-fit-media-narrative.

18 Adam B. Coleman, "Democrats' latest attempt to use a 'white supremacy' scare to crush their opposition," *New York Post*, January 18, 2023, https://nypost.com/2023/01/18/democrats-latest-attempt-to -use-a-white-supremacy-scare-to-crush-their-opposition/

19 Christina Zhao, "Bipartisan Senators Ask Outsiders to Stop Exploiting Deadly Parade for Political Purposes," *Newsweek*, November 27, 2021, https://www.newsweek.com/wisconsin-senators-ask-outsiders -stop-exploiting-deadly-parade-political-purposes-1653737.

20 Jason M. Breslow, Evan Wexler, and Robert Collins, "The Return of School Segregation in Eight Charts," PBS Frontline, July 15, 2014, https://www.pbs.org/wgbh/frontline/article/the-return-of-school -segregation-in-eight-charts.

21 Jason L. Riley, "Hate Crime Hoaxes Are More Common Than You Think," *Wall Street Journal*, June 25, 2019, https://www.wsj.com /articles/hate-crime-hoaxes-are-more-common-than-you-think-11561503352.

22  Gaurav Sood and Daniel Trielli, "The Face of Crime in Prime Time: Evidence from Law and Order" (working paper, SSRN, February 18, 2017), https://papers.ssrn.com/sol3/papers.cfm?abstract_id=2856766.

23  Tom Wolfe, *The Bonfire of the Vanities* (New York: Farrar Straus Giroux, 1987), 105.

24  Christian Watson, "Prosecutors Wield Way Too Much Power. And Their Misconduct Brings Far Too Few Consequences," *USA Today*, April 4, 2019, https://www.usatoday.com/story/opinion/policing /2019/04/04 /criminal-justice-prosecutors-misconduct-policing-the-usa/3336351002.

25  Larry Elder, "Derek Chauvin: The Great White Defendant," Townhall, April 22, 2021, https://townhall.com/columnists/larryelder /2021/04/22/derek-chauvin-the-great-white-defendant-n2588363.

26  "UK Teens Who Mocked George Floyd Death on Snapchat Have Been Arrested," Metro.co.uk, June 1, 2020, https://www.mirror.co.uk/news /uk-news/uk-teens-who-mocked-george-22122018.

27  "California Man Died Screaming 'I Can't Breathe' as Police Restrained Him, Video Shows," *The Guardian*, March 17, 2022, https://www.theguardian.com/us-news/2022/mar/17/california-man -george-floyd-police-death-new-video.

28  Erin Donaghue, "Disturbing Video Shows Dallas Officers Joking as They Restrain Man Who Died," CBS News, August 1, 2019, https: //www.cbsnews.com/news/tony-timpa-disturbing-video-shows-dallas- officers-joking-as-they-restrain-man-who-died; Cary Aspinwall, "A Death in Dallas, and a Family's Long Fight for Justice," The Marshall Project, October 7, 2023, https://www.themarshallproject.org /2023/10/07/texas-dallas-tony-timpa-police-accountability.

29  Matthew Clarke, "U.S. DOJ Statistics on Race and Ethnicity of Violent Crime Perpetrators," Prison Legal News, June 1, 2021, https://www.prisonlegalnews.org/news/2021/jun/1/us-doj-statistics -race-and-ethnicity-violent-crime-perpetrators.

30  Allen J. Beck, *Race and Ethnicity of Violent Crime Offenders and Arrestees, 2018* (Bureau of Justice Statistics, 2021), 5, https://bjs.ojp .gov/content/pub/pdf/revcoa18.pdf.

31  Margaret A. Zahn and Philip C. Sagi, "Stranger Homicides in Nine American Cities," *Journal of Criminal Law and Criminology* 78, no. 2 (Summer 1987): 388. https://scholarlycommons.law.northwestern .edu/cgi/viewcontent.cgi?article=6559&context=jclc.

32  "The 100,000; Understanding Inter-Racial Murder in the USA from 1968–2021 Crime Stats," Datahazard (Substack), March 22, 2023, https://datahazard.substack.com/p/interracial-murder.

33  Ibid.

34  ~~datahazard~~ (@fentasyl), "Crime doesn't get much more heinous than *Murdering the victim you just Sexually Assaulted. . . .,*"

Twitter, June 19, 2023, 4:11 p.m., https://twitter.com/fentasyl/status/1670886991515230209.

35  "No Escape: Male Rape in U.S. Prisons," HRW, n.d., https://www.hrw.org/reports/2001/prison/report2.html.

36  Ibid.

37  Kevin Medina and Brian Nguyen, "Acknowledged but Ignored: A Critical Race Theory Approach to the Prison Rape Elimination Act," *Queer Cats Journal of LGBTQ Studies* (2018): 65, https://escholarship.org/content/qt0kv784rc/qt0kv784rc.pdf?t=p5ofrh.

38  Ryan Shepard, "Black American Anxiety at All-Time High, Experts Say," ABC News, September 5, 2020, https://abcnews.go.com/US/black-american-anxiety-time-high-experts/story?id=72651176.

39  Eyewitness News (@ABC7NY), "Actor Rick Moranis identified as victim of random attack on the Upper West Side," Twitter, October 2, 2020, 11:09 a.m., https://twitter.com/ABC7NY/status/1312047025446432769.

40  "Police Added in Brooklyn Neighborhood amid 'Knockout Game' Attacks," NBC New York, November 20, 2013, https://www.nbcnewyork.com/news/local/knockout-game-polar-bearing-hate-crimes-punch-slap-video/2071591.

41  John Sexton, "Elon Musk: Check Out the Merch Closet at Twitter (Plus the Ferguson Tweet)," Hot Air, November 23, 2022, https://hotair.com/john-s-2/2022/11/23/elon-musk-check-out-the-merch-closet-at-twitter-plus-the-ferguson-tweet-n513182.

42  Zora Neale Hurston, "Letter to Katherine Tracy L'Engle, November 4, 1945," published in Carla Kaplan, *Zora Neale Hurston: A Life in Letters* (n.p.: Anchor, 2003). This riot (in 1935, not 1936) was considered by historians to be the first modern race riot, with violence directed at property rather than people and fights primarily between police and rioters, rather than racial groups. New York City District Attorney William Dodge accused communists of distributing literature to help spark the riots (a position supported by Hurston, who was present), while the official committee report of Mayor LaGuardia was shelved, presumably for political reasons.

43  Chris Francescani, "Zimmerman's Own Black Roots—& Drive to Aid the Poor," *New York Post*, April 26, 2012, https://nypost.com/2012/04/26/zimmermans-own-black-roots-drive-to-aid-the-poor.

44  Emma Tucker and Priya Krishnakumar, "Intentional Killings of Law Enforcement Officers Reach 20-Year High, FBI Says," CNN, January 13, 2022, https://www.cnn.com/2022/01/13/us/police-officers-line-of-duty-deaths/index.html.

45  Donald J. Trump, "Bring Back the Death Penalty! Bring Back Our Police!," *Daily News*, May 1, 1989, http://apps.frontline.org/clinton-trump-keys-to-their-characters/pdf/trump-newspaper.pdf.

46  Elizabeth A. Harris, "Linda Fairstein Attacks Her Portrayal in 'When They See Us,'" *New York Times*, June 11, 2019, https://www.nytimes .com/2019/06/11/arts/television/linda-fairstein-when-they-see-us.html.

47  "The Central Park Five: Crime, Coverage & Settlement," History. com, May 14, 2019, https://www.history.com/topics/1980s/central -park-five.

48  Ann Coulter, "Coulter: What You Won't Hear about 'Central Park 5,'" Clarion Ledger, April 23, 2014, https://www.clarionledger.com /story/news/2014/04/23/coulter-hear-central-park/8082301.

49  "Guilty—in Their Own Words," The Central Park Five Jogger Attackers, 2023, https://centralpark5joggerattackers.com.

50  Linda Fairstein, "Netflix's False Story of the Central Park Five," *Wall Street Journal*, June 10, 2019, https://www.wsj.com/articles/netflixs -false-story-of-the-central-park-five-11560207823.

51  Elizabeth A. Harris and Julia Jacobs, "Linda Fairstein Dropped by Her Publisher after TV Series on the Central Park 5," *New York Times*, June 7, 2019, https://www.nytimes.com/2019/06/07/arts/linda -fairstein-when-they-see-us.html.

52  Ann Coulter, "The Wilding of Linda Fairstein," Townhall, June 12, 2019, https://townhall.com/columnists/anncoulter/2019/06/12/the -wilding-of-linda-fairstein-n2548118.

53  Susan Welsh, Keren Schiffman, and Enjoli Francis, "'I So Wish the Case Hand't Been Settled': 1989 Central Park Jogger Believes More than 1 person Attacked Her," ABC News, May 23, 2019, https: //abcnews.go.com/US/case-settled-1989-central-park-jogger-believes -person/story?id=63077131.

54  Coulter, "Coulter: What You Won't Hear about 'Central Park 5.'"

55  Welsh, Schiffman, and Francis, " I So Wish the Case Hand't Been Settled.'"

56  Mishel Reja, "Trump's 'Chinese Virus' Tweet Helped Lead to Rise in Racist Anti-Asian Twitter Content: Study," ABC News, March 18, 2021, https://abcnews.go.com/Health/trumps-chinese-virus-tweet -helped-lead-rise-racist/story?id=76530148.

57  C. W. Nevius, "Dirty secret of black-on-Asian violence is out," SF Gate, March 2, 2021, https://www.sfgate.com/bayarea/nevius/article /Dirty-secret-of-black-on-Asian-violence-is-out-3265760.php.

58  Jeremy Carl, "The Truth About Asian Americans and Hate Crimes," American Greatness, February 28, 2021, https://amgreatness.com /2021/02/28/the-truth-about-asian-americans-and-hate-crimes.

59  Anne Anlin Cheng, "What This Wave of Anti-Asian Violence Reveals about America," *New York Times*, February 21, 2021, https://www .nytimes.com/2021/02/21/opinion/anti-asian-violence.html.

60 Li Zhou, "Asian American Communities Grapple with Whether Police Are the Right Answer to Recent Attacks," Vox, March 15, 2021, https://www.vox.com/22308407/attacks-asian-americans-police.

61 "Asian Organizations across the Bay Area Join Forces to Demand Action against Violence," Chinese for Affirmative Action," February 9, 2021, https://caasf.org/press-release/asian-organizations-across-the -bay-area-join-forces-to-demand-action-against-violence.

62 Tina Tchen (@TinaTchen), "The increase in racist attacks against Asian Americans - and Asian American women in particular—is absolutely unacceptable. White supremacy perpetuates this violence and has no place in our country.," Twitter, February 19, 2021, 3:48 p.m., https://twitter.com/TinaTchen/status/1362866662123442178.

63 "Chinese Refugee Given Leave to Stay in Columbus," *Newark Advocate*, March 22, 1956, https://www.newspapers.com/article /the-newark-advocate-peter-tchen-22-mar-1/15401822.

64 Levi Sumagaysay, "Asian-American Business Leaders Rally against Wave of Hatred: 'We Don't Deserve to Live in Fear in Our Own Country,'" Market Watch, April 6, 2021, https://www.marketwatch .com/story/asian-american-tech-leaders-rally-against-wave-of-hatred -we-dont-deserve-to-live-in-fear-in-our-own-country-11617740339.

65 "Athletes Denounce Atlanta Shootings, Condemn Anti-Asian Racism," Sportsnet, March 17, 2021, https://www.sportsnet.ca/more /article/athletes-denounce-atlanta-shootings-condemn-anti-asian-racism.

66 The Recount (@TheRecount), "'Racially motivated violence must be called out for exactly what it is. We must stop making excuses or rebranding it as economic anxiety or sexual addiction.'—Rep. Marilyn Strickland (D-WA)," Twitter, March 17, 2021, https://twitter .com/therecount/status/1372222252058619904?lang=en.

67 "Enough," *Wall Street Journal*, March 31, 2021, https://standwith asianamericans.com/wp-content/uploads/2023/01/swaa-wsj-pledge.pdf.

68 Ibid.

69 Evan Minsker, "YouTube Won't Pull YG's 'Meet the Flockers' amid Staff Outcry over Anti-Asian Lyrics," Pitchfork, March 30, 2021, https://pitchfork.com/news/youtube-wont-pull-ygs-meet-the-flockers -amid-staff-outcry-over-anti-asian-lyrics.

70 Jack Morse, "Jane Kim Wants YouTube to Remove 'Anti Asian-American' Music Video," SFist, September 28, 2016, https://sfist .com/2016/09/28/jane_kim_wants_youtube_to_remove_an.

71 Ibid.

72 Turning Point USA, "Rapper YG Tried To Ruin My Life," YouTube video, February 28, 2020, https://www.youtube.com/watch?v =6xoE5mic508.

73 Marianne Garvey and Stella Chan, "YG Arrested on Robbery Charges after Los Angeles Home Raid," CNN, January 25, 2020,

https://www.cnn.com/2020/01/24/entertainment/yg-arrested/index .html.

74  Melissa Chen (@MsMelChen), "Okay, I need to get this off my chest because it's been bothering me for a few months now. . .," Twitter, February 10, 2021, 2:16 p.m., https://twitter.com/MsMelChen /status/1359582082540863494.

75  Melissa Chen, "Thread by @MsMelChen on Thread Reader App," Thread Reader, February 10, 2021, https://threadreaderapp.com /thread/1359582082540863494.html.

76  "2020 FBI Hate Crimes Statistics," U.S. Department of Justice, updated April 4, 2023, https://www.justice.gov/crs/highlights/2020 -hate-crimes-statistics.

77  "'May Their Memories Always Be a Blessing': Jewish Community Comes Together after Gunman Is Convicted in Synagogue Massacre," *Pittsburgh Post-Gazette*, June 17, 2023, https://www.post -gazette.com/news/crime-courts/2023/06/16/pittsburgh-tree-of-live -synagogue-shooting-trial-verdict-robert-bowers/stories/202306160050.

78  Matt Talhelm, "Wilson Man Sentenced to Life in Prison for Shooting 5-Year-Old Neighbor in Head," WRAL News, December 29, 2022, https://www.wral.com/story/wilson-man-sentenced-to-life-in-prison -for-shooting-5-year-old-neighbor-in-head/20647970.

## Chapter 4: There Goes the Neighborhood

1  Devan Cole, "Michelle Obama: White people are 'still running' from minority communities," CNN, October 30, 2019, https://www.cnn .com/2019/10/30/politics/michelle-obama-white-flight/index.html.

2  Ibid.

3  Nicola Murphy, "Michelle Obama's $191k Childhood Home Is Nothing Like the White House," *Hello Magazine*, July 5, 2021, https://www.hellomagazine.com/homes/20210705116812/michelle -obama-childhood-home-inside-photos.

4  William Voegeli, "The Truth about White Flight," *City Journal*, Autumn 2020, https://www.city-journal.org/article/the-truth-about -white-flight.

5  "Most Dangerous Neighborhoods in Chicago," PropertyClub, July 9, 2023, https://propertyclub.nyc/article/most-dangerous-neighborhoods-in -chicago.

6  Voegeli, "The Truth about White Flight."

7  Ibid.

8  Ibid.

9  John Hogan, "Man Who Assaulted Rosa Parks in 1994 Faces Charges in Similar Grand Rapids Case," ABC 13, March 19, 2020, https: //www.wzzm13.com/article/news/crime/man-imprisoned-for-rosa

-parks-attack-charged-in-home-invasion/69–7f5ecd4a-8d19–4a26
–9da1–6bc430aa8348.

10  Voegeli, "The Truth about White Flight."

11  Shelley v. Kramer 334 US 1 (1948), https://www.oyez.org/cases/1940
    –1955/334us1.

12  Norris Vitchek as told to Alfred Balk, "Confessions of a Block-
    Buster," *Saturday Evening Post*, n.d., https://www.saturdayevening
    post.com/wp-content/uploads/satevepost/Confessions-of-a-Block
    -Buster.pdf.

13  Arnold H. Lubasch, "Editor Is Backed on Secret Source," *New York
    Times*, February 20, 1972, https://www.nytimes.com/1972/02/20
    /archives/editor-is-backed-on-secret-source-court-rules-he-need-not
    -say-who.html.

14  Leah Boustan, "The Culprits behind White Flight," *New York Times*,
    May 15, 2017, https://www.nytimes.com/2017/05/15/opinion/white
    -flight.html.

15  Kerner Commission, *Report of the National Advisory Commission
    on Civil Disorders*, 35, https://belonging.berkeley.edu/sites/default
    /files/kerner_commission_full_report.pdf?file=1&force=1.

16  Virginia Postrel, "The Consequences of the 1960's Race Riots Come
    Into View," *New York Times*, December 30, 2004, https://www
    .nytimes.com/2004/12/30/business/the-consequences-of-the-1960s
    -race-riots-come-into-view.html.

17  60 Minutes, "September 27, 1966: MLK—A Riot Is the Language of
    the Unheard," YouTube video, March 15, 2018. https://www.youtube
    .com/watch?v=_K0BWXjJv5s.

18  Kerner Commission, *Report of the National Advisory Commission
    on Civil Disorders*, 35, https://belonging.berkeley.edu/sites/default
    /files/kerner_commission_full_report.pdf?file=1&force=1.

19  Postrel, "The Consequences of the 1960's Race Riots Come Into
    View."

20  Kerner Commission, *Report of the National Advisory Commission
    on Civil Disorders*, 3.

21  David R. Francis, "How the 1960s' Riots Hurt African-Americans,"
    NBER, September 2004, https://www.nber.org/digest/sep04/how-1960s
    -riots-hurt-african-americans.

22  Ibid.

23  Meghan E. Hollis, *Homicide, Home Vacancies, and Population
    Change in Detroit* (Detroit: Michigan State University, 2017), 5, https:
    //ippsr.msu.edu/sites/default/files/MAPPR/Homicide_Vacancies
    _PopChange.pdf.

24  "City and Town Population Totals: 2020–2022," United States
    Census Bureau, last revised June 13, 2023, https://www.census.gov
    /data/tables/time-series/demo/popest/2020s-total-cities-and-towns.html.

25 Balk, "Confessions of a Block-Buster."

26 Ibid.

27 As cited in Whet Moser, "How White Housing Riots Shaped Chicago," Chicago Mag, April 29, 2015, https://www.chicagomag.com/city-life/april-2015/how-white-housing-riots-shaped-chicago.

28 Balk, "Confessions of a Block-Buster."

29 Ibid.

30 Renee Mattie, "Governor-Elect Seeks Repeal Of Rumford Open Housing Act," *Madera Tribune 75*, no. 133 (November 1966), https://cdnc.ucr.edu/?a=d&d=MT19661121.2.56&e=-------en--20--1--txt-txIN--------.

31 "Excerpts from Speech by Governor Ronald Reagan / California Real Estate Association Convention, Los Angeles, September 26, 1967" in *Reagan, Ronald: Gubernatorial Papers, 1966–74: Press Unit*, 103, https://www.reaganlibrary.gov/public/digitallibrary/gubernatorial/pressunit/p17/40–840-7408624-p17–007-2017.pdf.

32 Scott Cummnings, *Left Behind in Rosedale: Race Relations and the Collapse of Community Institutions*, Westview Press, Boulder, Colordado, 1998, 3, 13, 22.

33 Ibid., 37, 55.

34 Ibid., 67, 70.

35 Ibid., 85, 93.

36 Ibid., 98.

37 Ibid., 103, 162.

38 "QuickFacts: East St. Louis City, Illinois," United States Census Bureau, n.d., https://www.census.gov/quickfacts/fact/table/eaststlouiscityillinois/LND110210.

39 Kevin S. Held, "East St. Louis Tops List of 'Most Dangerous Cities in America,'" Fox 2 Now, May 8, 2018, https://fox2now.com/news/east-st-louis-tops-list-of-most-dangerous-cities-in-america.

40 U.S. Department of Commerce, *1970 Census of Population and Housing* (Springfield, Illinois: Bureau of the Census, 1970), https://www2.census.gov/prod2/decennial/documents/39204513p21ch1.pdf.

41 "Pacific Heights Residents," Niche.com, https://www.niche.com/places-to-live/n/pacific-heights-san-francisco-ca/residents/.

42 Eric Kaufmann, "Diversity for Thee but Not for Me," *City Journal*, May 4, 2023, https://www.city-journal.org/article/white-progressives-more-likely-to-flee-diverse-neighborhoods.

43 Eric Kaufmann (epkaufm), "1/ White progressives champion greater diversity but vote with their feet against it . . .," Twitter, April 7, 2023, 8:45 a.m., https://twitter.com/epkaufm/status/1644320529770323972.

44 David Sikkink and Michael O. Emerson, "School Choice and Racial Segregation in US Schools: The Role of Parents' Education," *Ethnic*

*and Racial Studies* 31, no. 2 (2008): 286, https://hechingerreport.org
/wp-content/uploads/2019/03/Sikkink-and-Emerson.pdf.

45  Rich Benjamin, *Searching for Whitopia: An Improbable Journey to
the Heart of White America* (New York: Hachette Books, 2009),
https://www.amazon.com/Searching-Whitopia-Improbable-Journey
-America/dp/1401322689/ref=sr_1_3?crid=194IRCTDSU0MB
&keywords=searching+for+whitopia&qid=1687022272
&sprefix=searching+for+whito%2Caps%2C626&sr=8-3;
"Searcing for Whitopia," Live-brary com https://livebrary.overdrive
.com/media/265942.

46  John McWhorter, "What's Missing from the Conversation about
Systemic Racism," *New York Times*, September 28, 2021, https:
//www.nytimes.com/2021/09/28/opinion/redlining-systemic-racism
.html.

47  Ibid.

48  Ibid.

49  Ibid.

50  "School Busing: Success or Failure?," *New York Times*, July 27, 2019,
https://www.nytimes.com/2019/07/27/opinion/letters/school-busing
-desegregation.html.

51  Ibid.

52  Astead W. Herndon and Sheryl Gay Stolberg, "How Joe Biden Became
the Democrats' Anti-Busing Crusader," *New York Times*, July 15,
2019, https://www.nytimes.com/2019/07/15/us/politics/biden-busing
.html.

53  "S.2937 - A bill to clarify the jurisdiction of certain courts with
respect to public schools.," 94th Congress, 1976–1976, https://www
.congress.gov/bill/94th-congress/senate-bill/2937/cosponsors?q=%7B
%22search%22%3A%5B%22S.2937%22%5D%7D&r=7&s=5.

54  Herndon and Stolberg, "How Joe Biden Became the Democrats' Anti-
Busing Crusader."

55  "Stop Gentrification" (video), Crenshaw Subway Coalition, n.d.,
https://www.crenshawsubway.org/gentrification.

56  Colin Kinniburgh, "How to Stop Gentrification," *New Republic*,
August 9, 2017, https://newrepublic.com/article/144260/stop
-gentrification.

57  Sandra Feder, "Stanford Professor's Study Finds Gentrification
Disproportionately Affects Minorities," Stanford.edu, December 1,
2020, https://news.stanford.edu/2020/12/01/gentrification
-disproportionately-affects-minorities.

58  Jacquelynn Kerubo, "What Gentrification Means for Black
Homeowners," *New York Times*, August 17, 2021, https://www
.nytimes.com/2021/08/17/realestate/black-homeowners-gentrification
.html.

59  Ibid.

60 Kerubo, "What Gentrification Means for Black Homeowners."

61 John Buntin, "The Myth of Gentrification," Slate, January 14, 2015, https://slate.com/news-and-politics/2015/01/the-gentrification-myth -its-rare-and-not-as-bad-for-the-poor-as-people-think.html.

62 Holly Otterbein, "The Death of Gentrification Guilt," *Philadelphia*, September 27, 2015, https://www.phillymag.com/citified/2015/09/27 /death-gentrification-guilt-le-bok-fin.

63 Office of the Press Secretary, "President Calls for Expanding Opportunities to Home Ownership" (press release), The White House, June 17, 2002, https://georgewbush-whitehouse.archives.gov/news /releases/2002/06/20020617–2.html.

64 Jo Becker, Sheryl Gay Stolberg, and Stephen Labaton, "Bush Drive for Home Ownership Fueled Housing Bubble," *New York Times*, December 21, 2008, https://www.nytimes.com/2008/12/21/business /worldbusiness/21iht-admin.4.18853088.html.

65 Ibid.

66 Kevin Drum, "Chart of the Day: Hispanics Got Hurt the Worst by the Housing Bubble," *Mother Jones*, January 16, 2014, https://www .motherjones.com/kevin-drum/2014/01/chart-day-hispanics-got -hurt-worst-housing-bubble/#disqus_thread.

67 Alan S. Kaplinsky, Barbara S. Mishkin, and Jeremy T. Rosenblum, "Obama Administration Announces $275 Billion-Plus Housing Bailout," casetext, February 19, 2009, https://casetext.com/analysis /obama-administration-announces-275-billion-plus-housing-bailout.

68 Carolina K. Reid, Debbie Bocian, Wei Li, Roberto G. Quercia, "Revisiting the subprime crisis: The dual mortgage market and mortgage defaults by race and ethnicity," *Journal of Urban Affairs* 39, no. 4 (2017): https://www.tandfonline.com/doi /abs/10.1080/07352166.2016.1255529?journalCode=ujua20.

69 Christopher Caldwell, *Age of Entitlement* (Simon & Schuster, 2020), 183.

70 Binyamin Appelbaum, "How Mortgage Fraud Made the Financial Crisis Worse," *New York Times*, February 12, 2015, https://www .nytimes.com/2015/02/13/upshot/how-mortgage-fraud-made-the -financial-crisis-worse.html.

71 Paul Kiel, "Bailed Out Bank Had Friends in High Places," ProRepublica, March 12, 2009, https://www.propublica.org/article /bailed-out-bank-had-friends-in-high-places-312.

72 Debbie Gruenstein Bocian, Wei Li, and Keith S. Ernst, *Foreclosures by Race and Ethnicity: The Demographics of a Crisis* (Raleigh, North Carolina: Center for Responsible Lending, 2010), https://sociology infocus.com/files/mortgage-lending/research-analysis/foreclosures -by-race-executive-summary.pdf.

73 U.S. Department of Housing and Urban Development, "Hud Announces New Proposed 'Affirmatively Furthering Fair housing' Rule, Taking a Major Step towards Rooting Out Longstanding Inequities in Housing and Fostering Inclusive Communities," news release no. 23–013, January 19, 2023, https://www.hud.gov/press/press_releases_media_advisories/hud_no_23_013.

74 Jeremy Carl, "The Senate Republicans' Latest Disgrace," *National Review*, May 19, 2016, https://www.nationalreview.com/corner/affh-disaster-senate-republicans-latest-disgrace.

75 Jeremy Carl, "The Obama Administration Thinks Hillary's Hometown Is Racist: Does Congress Agree?," *National Review*, May 18, 2016, https://www.nationalreview.com/2016/05/hud-rule-fair-housing-suburbs-zoning-westchester-county-mike-lee.

76 Robert VerBruggen, "Biden Takes On Local Zoning Laws," *National Review*, June 10, 2021, https://www.nationalreview.com/2021/06/biden-takes-on-local-zoning-laws.

77 Peter Kirsanow, "Letter to Secretary Carson re: AFFH," July 20, 2017, https://www.newamericancivilrightsproject.org/wp-content/uploads/2014/03/Letter-to-Secretary-Carson-re-AFFH-July-20–2017.pdf.

**Chapter 5: School Daze**

1 *Executive Order 1: Ending the Use of Inherently Divisive Concepts, Including Critical Race Theory, and Restoring Excellence in K-12 Public Education in the Commonwealth*, Virginia.gov., https://www.governor.virginia.gov/media/governorvirginiagov/governor-of-virginia/pdf/eo/EO-1-Ending-the-Use-of-Inherently-Divisive-Concepts.pdf.

2 Dominic Gustavo, "Yale University Hosted Speaker Who Shared Fantasies about Murdering White People," World Socialist Website, June 13, 2021, https://www.wsws.org/en/articles/2021/06/14/yale-j14.html.

3 Zach Goldberg and Eric Kaufmann, "Yes, Critical Race Theory Is Being Taught in Schools," *City Journal*, October 20, 2022, https://www.city-journal.org/article/yes-critical-race-theory-is-being-taught-in-schools.

4 Ibid.

5 Hannah Rubinton and Maggie Isaacson, "School District Expenditures and Race," *Economic Research*, February 16, 2022, https://research.stlouisfed.org/publications/economic-synopses/2022/02/16/school-district-expenditures-and-race.

6 R. Shep Melnick, "The Two Billion Dollar Judge," *Claremont Review of Books 9*, no. 2 (Spring 2009): https://claremontreviewofbooks.com/the-two-billion-dollar-judge.

7 Ibid.

8 "Kansas City Public Schools," U.S. News, 2021, https://www.usnews
.com/education/k12/missouri/districts/kansas-city-33–107736.

9 "Police Investigated Trayvon Martin over Jewelry," *Times Union*,
March 27, 2012, https://www.timesunion.com/news/article/Police
-investigated-Trayvon-Martin-over-jewelry-3439400.php.

10 Sundance, "M-DSPD Cover Up—The Curious Case of Trayvon
Martin's Backpack with Stolen Jewelry and Burglary Tool . . .," The
Last Refuge, May 1, 2013, https://theconservativetreehouse.com
/blog/2013/05/01/m-dspd-cover-up-the-curious-case-of-trayvon
-martins-backpack-with-stolen-jewelry-and-burglary-tool.

11 "Trayvon Suspended THREE Times for 'Drugs, Truancy, Graffiti and
Carrying Burglary Tool' and Did He Attack Bus Driver Too? New
Picture Emerges of Victim as Parents Claim It's All a Smear," *Daily
Mail*, March 26, 2012, https://www.dailymail.co.uk/news/article
-2120504/Trayvon-Martin-case-He-suspended-times-caught-burglary
-tool.html.

12 Lauren Camera, "Civil Rights Spat Takes Center Stage in Education,"
U.S. News, December 8, 2017, https://www.usnews.com/news/education
-news/articles/2017–12-08/civil-rights-spat-takes-center-stage-in-education.

13 Scott Travis, "School's Culture of Tolerance Lets Students Like Nikolas
Cruz Slide," *Sun Sentinel*, May 12, 2018, https://www.sun-sentinel
.com/2018/05/12/schools-culture-of-tolerance-lets-students-like-nikolas
-cruz-slide.

14 Ibid.

15 Paul P. Murphy, "Exclusive: Group chat messages show school shooter
obsessed with race, violence and guns," CNN.com, February 18,
2018, https://www.cnn.com/2018/02/16/us/exclusive-school-shooter
-instagram-group/index.html. Ian Schwartz, "Teacher: FL School
Shooter Had A Hispanic 'Pride' Issue, 'Didn't Like To Speak Spanish,'
RealClearPolitics.com, February 15, 2018, https://www
.realclearpolitics.com/video/2018/02/15/teacher_alicia_blondle
_florida_school_shooter_hispanic_pride_issue_didnt_like_speak
_spanish.html.

16 Mary Ann Zehr, "Obama Administration Targets 'Disparate Impact'
of Discipline," *Education Week*, October 7, 2010, https://www
.edweek.org/leadership/obama-administration-targets-disparate
-impact-of-discipline/2010/10.

17 Max Eden, "Safe and Orderly Schools: Updated Guidance on School
Discipline," Manhattan Institute, March 14, 2019, https://manhattan
.institute/article/safe-and-orderly-schools-updated-guidance-on-school
-discipline.

18 Zehr, "Obama Administration Targets 'Disparate Impact' of Discipline."

19 Will Flanders, "Biden Signals Return to Obama's Misguided School
Discipline Policies," RealClearEducation, October 18, 2021, https:

//www.realcleareducation.com/articles/2021/10/18/biden_signals
_return_to_obamas_misguided_school_discipline_policies_110651
.html.

20  "Physical Fighting at School, by Race/Ethnicity," Kids Data, n.d.,
https://www.kidsdata.org/topic/410/fight-at-school-race/table#fmt=55
7&loc=2,127,347,1763,331,348,336,171,321,345,357,332,324,369,
358,362,360,337,327,364,356,217,353,328,354,323,352,320,339,3
34,365,343,330,367,344,355,366,368,265,349,361,4,273,59,370,32
6,333,322,341,338,350,342,329,325,359,351,363,340,335&tf=134
&ch=7.

21  Ibid., https://www.kidsdata.org/topic/410/fight-at-school-race/table#fmt
=557&loc=127,347,1763,331,348,336,171,321,345,357,
332,324,369,358,362,360,337,327,364,356,217,353,328,354,323,35
2,320,339,334,365,343,330,367,344,355,366,368,265,349,361,4,
273,59,370,326,333,322,341,338,350,342,329,325,359,351,
363,340,335,2&tf=134&ch=,7&sortColumnId=0&sortType=asc.

22  Ibid.

23  Freddie deBoer, "Don't Blame SATs for American Inequality,"
Unherd, December 29, 2022, https://unherd.com/2022/12/dont-blame
-sats-for-american-inequality.

24  Daniella Silva, "Study on Harvard Finds 43 Percent of White Students
Are Legacy, Athletes, Related to Donors or Staff," NBC News,
September 30, 2019, https://www.nbcnews.com/news/us-news/study
-harvard-finds-43-percent-white-students-are-legacy-athletes
-n1060361.

25  Ibid.

26  "Asian-American Plaintiffs Are 'Pawns' in Affirmative Action Lawsuit,
Says Professor," CBC, September 3, 2018, https://www.cbc.ca/radio
/asithappens/as-it-happens-friday-edition-1.4731087/asian-american
-plaintiffs-are-pawns-in-affirmative-action-lawsuit-says-professor
-1.4808856.

27  Alex Tabarrok, "The SAT, Test Prep, Income and Race," Marginal
Revolution, March 11, 2014, https://marginalrevolution.com
/marginalrevolution/2014/03/the-sat-test-prep-income-and-race.html.

28  Ross Douthat, "Rural, Poor Whites Underrepresented at Elite
Colleges," *Seattle Times*, July 19, 2010, https://www.seattletimes
.com/opinion/rural-poor-whites-underrepresented-at-elite-colleges.

29  Sarah Wood, "Is High School Class Rank Still Important?," *U.S.
News*, December 14, 2022, https://www.usnews.com/education/k12
/articles/is-high-school-class-rank-still-important.

30  Ibid.

31  Richard L. Zweigenhaft, "Diversity among Fortune 500 CEOs
from 2000 to 2020: White Women, Hi-Tech South Asians, and
Economically Privileged Multilingual Immigrants from around the

World," USCS.edu, January 2021, https://whorulesamerica.ucsc.edu /diversity/diversity_update_2020.html.

32 Nami Sumida, "Who Is Actually Going to UC Schools amid Record Application Numbers?," *San Francisco Chronicle*, March 2, 2022, https://www.sfchronicle.com/bayarea/article/Record-number-of -Black-and-Hispanic-students-are-16969458.php.

33 Sharon Bernstein, "How U.C. Berkeley Tried to Buoy Enrollment of Black Students without Affirmative Action," Archive.ph, July 18, 2023, https://archive.ph/IaKbD.

34 Giulia McDonnell Nieto del Rio, "University of California Will No Longer Consider SAT and ACT Scores," *New York Times*, May 15, 2021, https://www.nytimes.com/2021/05/15/us/SAT-scores-uc -university-of-california.html.

35 Jay Greene and James Paul, "Diversity University: DEI Bloat in the Academy," The Heritage Foundation, July 27, 2021, https://www .heritage.org/education/report/diversity-university-dei-bloat-the-academy.

36 Author calculation from Ibid.

37 Alexandra Francisco, "What If Ted Williams Embraced His Mexican-American Heritage? Here's Under-Told [*sic*] Story," NESN, September 18, 2021, https://nesn.com/2021/09/what-if-ted-williams-embraced -his-mexican-american-heritage-heres-under-told-story.

38 C. G. Jones, "Black FSU professor resigns in disgrace amid allegations he faked data on commonality of racism, had 6 papers retracted," *Human Events*, April 12, 2023, https://humanevents.com/2023/04/12 /black-fsu-professor-resigns-in-disgrace-amid-allegations-he-faked -data-on-commonality-of-racism-had-6-papers-retracted?utm_campaign =64470.

39 Nick Anderson, Robert Barnes, Scott Clement, and Emily Guskin, "Over 6 in 10 Americans Favor Leaving Race Out of College Admissions, Post-Schar School Poll Finds," *Washington Post*, October 22, 2022, https://www.washingtonpost.com/education/2022/10/22 /race-college-admissions-poll-results.

40 *Reuters/Ipsos Poll: 2024 Primary Election, Debt Ceiling, Ukraine, University Admissions* (Washington, D.C.: Ipsos, 2023), 24, https: //www.ipsos.com/sites/default/files/ct/news/documents/2023–02 /Reuters%20Ipsos%20Large%20Sample%20Survey%20 2024%20Primary_%20Debt%20Ceiling_Ukraine_University%20 Admissions_%2002%2023%202023.pdf.

41 Alice Wender, "Resolution Letter: University of North Carolina, Chapel Hill, NC," U.S. Department of Education, November 27, 2012, https://www2.ed.gov/about/offices/list/ocr/docs/investigations /11072016-a.pdf.

42 "A Large Black-White Scoring Gap Persists on the SAT," *Journal of Blacks in Higher Education*, 2006, https://www.jbhe.com/features/53 _SAT.html.

43 The Harvard class of 2026 is just 42.5 percent white (see "Harvard Gussies Up Its Asian Admissions Numbers," Students for Fair Admissions, July 8, 2022, https://studentsforfairadmissions.org /harvard-gussies-up-its-asian-admissions-numbers). If we assume the same 43 percent of connected admissions (athletes, donors' kids, faculty relatives) were comprised of whites, this implies the "merit" admissions of whites is just 24.2 percent versus about 12.5 percent of African Americans admitted by merit, only about a 2–1 ratio. Asian Americans admitted under this standard would have been 23.5 percent (see "Public High School Graduates, by Race/Ethnicity: 1998–99 through 2025–26," National Center for Education Statistics, 2015, https://nces.ed.gov/programs/digest/d15/tables/dt15_219.30.asp).

Even if we make the assumption, asserted by the study authors, that 25 percent of these connected applicants would have been admitted regardless, this leads to 28.7 percent whites, 13 percent African Americans, 24.5 percent Asian Americans, and 10.6 percent Hispanics. Native Americans made up 3.6 percent of the class (see "Public and Private School Comparison," National Center for Education Statistics, https://nces.ed.gov/fastfacts/display.asp?id=55). In 2022 when this data was observed, 51.4 percent of public high school graduates were white and 53 percent overall graduates were white. Harvard was 11.9 percent Hispanic (a group that made up 23.5 percent of high school graduates that year, the only group similarly underrepresented to whites—but, of course, the academic profile of whites was dramatically better than that of Hispanics).

44 "UChicago Biased against 'Middle-Class White Kids,' Student Says," The College Fix, June 27, 2022, https://www.thecollegefix.com /bulletin-board/uchicago-biased-against-middle-class-white-kids-student -says.

45 Steve Hsu, "SAT Score Distributions in Michigan," *Information Processing* (blog), October 4, 2022, https://infoproc.blogspot.com /2022/10/sat-score-distributions-in-michigan.html.

46 Of note, the Michigan white population scored significantly lower than the national white population as a whole (see "Total and Section Score User Group Percentile Ranks by Gender and Race/Ethnicity," College Board, 2020, https://satsuite.collegeboard.org/media/pdf/sat -percentile-ranks-gender-race-ethnicity.pdf) and the Asian-American population slightly better.

47 "Appendix Report, Demographic Diversity of University of Michigan Constituencies from 2016–2021," University of Michigan, Ann Arbor, https://web.archive.org/web/20230119043218/https://report.dei .umich.edu/wp-content/uploads/2023/01/demographic-diversity.pdf.

48 "Public High School Graduates, by Race/Ethnicity: 1998–99 through 2025–26," National Center for Education Statistics, 2015, https://nces .ed.gov/programs/digest/d15/tables/dt15_219.30.asp.

49 Renata Kaminski, "The number of Latinos in high school and higher ed has increased in recent years," *Al Día*, July 11, 2022, https: //aldianews.com/en/education/education/more-latinos-hscollege.

50 Elaine Gunthorpe, "Nevada Implements 'Equitable Grading' in Schools," Hot Air, June 2, 2023, https://hotair.com/headlines/2023 /06/02/nevada-implements-equitable-grading-in-schools-n555010.

51 Sarah Randazzo, "Schools Are Ditching Homework, Deadlines in Favor of 'Equitable Grading,'" *Wall Street Journal*, April 26, 2023, https://www.wsj.com/articles/schools-are-ditching-homework -deadlines-in-favor-of-equitable-grading-dcef7c3e?mod=hp_trending _now_article_pos2.

52 Robert Stark, "LA's Brentwood School: Ground-Zero for Elite Ethno-Masochism," Robert Stark's Newsletter (Substack), March 29, 2022, https://robertstark.substack.com/p/las-brentwood-school-ground-zero.

53 Cesar Alesi Perez, Hans Johnson, and Vicki Hsieh, "Geography of Educational Attainment in California," PPIC, April 6, 2021, https: //www.ppic.org/blog/geography-of-educational-attainment-in -california; Andrew Depietro, "Median Household Income in California," September 27, 2022, https://www.creditkarma.com /insights/i/california-median-household-income.

54 Teresa Watanabe, "California Banned Affirmative Action in 1996. Inside the UC Struggle for Diversity," *Los Angeles Times*, October 31, 2022, https://archive.ph/i1PIA.

55 Jill Barshay, "Texas 10% Policy Didn't Expand Number of High Schools Feeding Students to Top Universities," The Hechinger Report, July 8, 2019, https://hechingerreport.org/texas-top-10-policy-didnt -expand-number-of-high-schools-feeding-students-to-top-universities.

56 Tarah Jean, "Tucker Carlson says FSU scholarship promotes 'race hatred'; university updates language," Tallahassee Democrat, February 8, 2023, https://www.tallahassee.com/story/news/local /fsu-news/2023/02/08/fox-news-host-tucker-carlson-calls-out-fsu-for -minority-scholarship/69880934007.

57 Kat Tretina and Alicia Hahn, "10 Scholarships for Minorities That Can Help Pay for College," Forbes, January 26, 2022, https://www .forbes.com/advisor/student-loans/scholarships-for-minorities.

58 Kelly Meyerhofer, "Conservative law firm to appeal judge's dismissal of lawsuit arguing minority retention grant discriminates against white students, others," *Milwaukee Journal Sentinel*, September 26, 2022, https://www.jsonline.com/story/news/education/2022/09/26 /will-lawsuit-targeting-wisconsin-college-grant-students-color -tossed/8092310001.

59 Scott Jaschik, "Does the Supreme Court Order Apply to Financial Aid?," Inside Higher Ed, July 5, 2023, https://www.insidehighered .com/news/admissions/2023/07/05/missouri-attorney-general-orders -colleges-drop-minority-scholarships.

60 Roy Hadley Jr., "Historic Levels of Federal Funding Available for HBCUs," Adams and Reese LLP, March 29, 2023, https://www .adamsandreese.com/news-knowledge/hbcu-federal-funding-hadley -williams-maynard.

## Chapter 6: The Erasure of History

1 Celine Da Silva, "Take Down the Statue of Christopher Columbus," Change.org, July 17, 2020, https://www.change.org/p/city-of -elizabeth-take-down-the-statue-of-christopher-columbus.

2 "Trump's Columbus Day Proclamation Includes Stark Warnings," WTTW, October 11, 2020, https://news.wttw.com/2020/10/11 /trumps-columbus-day-proclamation-includes-stark-warnings.

3 Niesha Davis, "A Love Letter to Marsha, the Spontaneous Statue of Trans-Activist Marsha P. Johnson, Gets a New Home at the Center in New York," Bust, May 5, 2022, https://bust.com/feminism/198802 -marsha-p-johnson-statue-love-letter-to-marsha-moves-to-the-center .html.

4 Paris L., "The Untold Truth of Marsha P. Johnson," Grunge, February 27, 2023, https://www.grunge.com/877449/the-untold-truth-of-marsha -p-johnson.

5 Julia Jacobs, "Two Transgender Activists Are Getting a Monument in New York," *New York Times*, May 29, 2019, https://www.nytimes .com/2019/05/29/arts/transgender-monument-stonewall.html.

6 Steve Watson, "Stonewall 1979: The Drag of Politics," *The Village Voice*, June 15, 1979, https://www.villagevoice.com/stonewall-1979 -the-drag-of-politics.

7 Ibid.

8 Tyler Born, "Marsha 'Pay It No Mind' Johnson," OutHistory.com, n.d., https://outhistory.org/exhibits/show/tgi-bios/marsha-p-johnson.

9 Michael Kasino, *Pay It No Mind—The Life and Times of Marsha P. Johnson*, Redux Pictures, 2012, https://www.youtube.com/watch?v =rjN9W2KstqE.

10 John Jay, "Federalist Papers No. 2: Concerning Dangers from Foreign Force and Influence for the Independent Journal," Lillian Goldman Law Library, accessed December 1, 2023, https://avalon.law.yale.edu /18th_century/fed02.asp.

11 "Our First President Knew Assimilation Is Critical," *Cape Cod Times*, May 15, 2017, https://www.capecodtimes.com/story/opinion/letters /2017/05/15/our-first-president-knew-assimilation/21043746007.

12 Mary Kay Linge and John Levine, "Founding Father James Madison Sidelined by Woke History in His Own Home," *New York Post*, July 16, 2022, https://nypost.com/2022/07/16/james-madison-sidelined-by-woke-history-in-his-own-home.

13 Mary Kay Linge and John Levine, "Monticello Is Going Woke—and Trashing Thomas Jefferson's Legacy in the Process," *New York Post*, July 9, 2022, https://nypost.com/2022/07/09/monticello-draws-criticism-after-trashing-thomas-jefferson.

14 Ibid.

15 Ibid.

16 Amy Nelson, "Visitor to Thomas Jefferson's Monticello Estate Calls Out New 'Woke' Tours: 'Depressing and Demoralizing,'" Fox News, July 11, 2022, https://www.foxnews.com/media/visitor-thomas-jefferson-monticello-estate-calls-new-woke-tours-depressing-demoralizing.

17 Ibid.

18 Linge and Levine, "Monticello Is Going Woke—and Trashing Thomas Jefferson's Legacy in the Process."

19 Ibid.

20 Samantha Willis, "Thomas Jefferson Owned Hundreds of Slaves—Now a Black Woman Will Run His Foundation," *Glamour*, June 29, 2018, https://www.glamour.com/story/melody-barnes-thomas-jefferson-foundation-chairman-monticello.

21 Andrew Lee, "Rethink the Founding Fathers.," Anti-Racism Daily, June 2, 2021, https://the-ard.com/2021/07/02/rethink-the-founding-fathers-anti-racism-daily.

22 Ibid.

23 Jarrett Stepman, "Celebrating Founding Fathers Is 'Structural Racism,' National Archives Says," Daily Signal, July 29, 2021, https://www.dailysignal.com/2021/06/29/celebrating-founding-fathers-is-structural-racism-national-archives-says.

24 Sarah Williams, "Founders' Lives, Fortunes, and Sacred Honor Still Our Foundation," Daily Signal, August 3, 2020, https://www.dailysignal.com/2020/08/03/founders-lives-fortunes-and-sacred-honor-still-our-foundation, and Stepman, Ibid.

25 Brittany Raymer, "National Archives Rotunda, Where Declaration of Independence Is Housed, Is Deemed 'Structurally Racist' and Should Have 'Trigger Warnings,'" Daily Citizen, June 28, 2021, https://dailycitizen.focusonthefamily.com/national-archives-rotunda-where-declaration-of-independence-is-housed-is-deemed-structurally-racist-and-should-have-trigger-warnings.

26　"The Arc of the Moral Universe Is Long, But It Bends Toward Justice," Quote Investigator, November 15, 2012, https://quoteinvestigator.com/2012/11/15/arc-of-universe.

27　Kevin Levin, "Why Non-Slaveholders Will Fight For Slavery," Kevin M. Levin, January 26, 2023, https://cwmemory.com/2013/01/26/why-non-slaveholders-will-fight-for-slavery.

28　Maya Rhodan, "Protestors Throw a Confederate Flag on the Grill in New Orleans," *Time*, July 4, 2015, https://time.com/3945856/confederate-flag-burning-new-orleans/; Jay Croft, "A Confederate Statue Is Coming Down Today in the Virginia City of Deadly 'Unite the Right' Violence," CNN.com, September 12, 2020, https://www.cnn.com/2020/09/12/us/charlottesville-albermarle-virginia-confederate-statue-trnd/index.html.

29　Robert Farley, "Trump Has Condemned White Supremacists," FactCheck.org, February 11, 2020, https://www.factcheck.org/2020/02/trump-has-condemned-white-supremacists.

30　Astead W. Herndon, "Charlottesville Inspired Biden to Run. Now It Has a Message for Him," *New York Times*, January 21, 2021, https://www.nytimes.com/2021/01/21/us/politics/charlottesville-attack-biden.html.

31　Bonnie Berkowitz and Adrian Blanco, "A Record Number of Confederate Monuments Fell in 2020, but Hundreds Still Stand. Here's Where," *Washington Post*, March 12, 2021, https://www.washingtonpost.com/graphics/2020/national/confederate-monuments/?nid=top_pb_signin.

32　"Procedure for Consideration of Renaming Requests," Yale University, n.d., https://ogc.yale.edu/governance/historic-documents/renaming-procedure.

33　Ken Masugi, "Who Will Free the Enslavers?" American Greatness, January 4, 2023, https://amgreatness.com/2023/01/04/who-will-free-the-enslavers/?fbclid=IwAR16Uw0abcVMzItGk34ZVVKQbjQwOWCapj1GXKTapG8Qn9ZBqurmCT0ajdE.

34　Ken Masugi, "Can the Constitution be Colorblind? On the Farsighted Constitutionalist, Justice John M. Harlan," Teaching American History, October 26, 2021, https://teachingamericanhistory.org/blog/can-the-constitution-be-colorblind-on-the-farsighted-constitutionalist-justice-john-m-harlan.

35　*Plessy v. Ferguson* 163 US 537 (1896), https://www.oyez.org/cases/1850–1900/163us537.

36　Jesse James Deconto and Alan Blinder, "'Silent Sam' Confederate Statue Is Toppled at University of North Carolina," *New York Times*, August 21, 2018, https://www.nytimes.com/2018/08/21/us/unc-silent-sam-monument-toppled.html.

37 Will Michaels, Elizabeth Baier, and Lisa Philip, "On Her Way Out, UNC Chancellor Orders Removal Of 'Silent Sam' Pedestal," NPR, January 15, 2019, https://www.npr.org/2019/01/15/685442684 /on-her-way-out-unc-chancellor-authorizes-removal-of-silent-sam-pedestal.

38 Michael Levenson, "Toppled but Not Gone: U.N.C. Grapples Anew with the Fate of Silent Sam," *New York Times*, February 14, 2020, https://www.nytimes.com/2020/02/14/us/unc-silent-sam-statue-settle ment.html.

39 "Museum Proposes Melting Lee Statue to Make New Artwork," Associated Press, October 21, 2021, https://apnews.com/article/race -and-ethnicity-virginia-charlottesville-public-art-82967e27bfe3a0fe bd9b584bde381a99.

40 Tim Fitzsimons, "San Francisco Board Halts Process to Rename Washington, Lincoln and Feinstein Schools," NBC News, April 7, 2021, https://www.nbcnews.com/news/us-news/san-francisco-board- halts-process-rename-washington-lincoln-feinstein-schools-n1263337.

41 Mélissa Godin, "George Washington Statue Toppled by Portland Protesters on the Eve of Juneteenth," *Time*, June 19, 2020, https://time .com/5856329/washington-statue-toppled-portland.

42 "Pioneer Statues Toppled amid Protest at University of Oregon," Oregon Live, June 14, 2020.

43 Leah Asmelash, "Statues of Christopher Columbus are being dismounted across the country," June 10, 2020, https://www.cnn .com/2020/06/10/us/christopher-columbus-statues-down-trnd/index .html.

44 "Results of SurveyUSA News Poll #25384," Survey USA, n.d., https://www.surveyusa.com/client/PollReport.aspx?g=b9ba83d6–156e -44e3–9d3a-0e88b5b0a595.

45 Adam E. Zielinski, "Allies and Enemies: British and American Attitudes towards Native Americans during the Revolution," American Battlefield Trust, March 18, 2020, https://www.battlefields .org/learn/articles/allies-and-enemies.

46 See *The Land that God Made* for a thorough discussion of this in the context of early American history.

47 "A Short History of Jamestown," National Park Service, n.d., https: //www.nps.gov/jame/learn/historyculture/a-short-history-of-jamestown .htm.

48 North Carolina History Project, "The Tuscarora War," North carolinahistory.org, https://northcarolinahistory.org/encyclopedia/tuscarora -war/.

49 Skeptic Research Center Team (@SkepResCenter), "How much do you agree: 'Prior to the arrival of the European settlers, Native American/ Indigenous tribes lived in peace and harmony' . . .," Twitter, May 30,

2023, 4:40 p.m., https://twitter.com/SkepResCenter/status/16636465
33336588295.

50 James S. Robbins, *Erasing America: Losing Our Future by
Destroying Our Past* (Washington, D.C.: Regnery, 2018), 182–83.

51 Ibid., 189.

52 "Race of the Population of the U.S. by States: 1960 (Supplementary
Reports, 1960 Census of Population)," United States Census Bureau,
1961, https://www2.census.gov/library/publications/decennial/1960
/pc-s1-supplementary-reports/pc-s1–10.pdf.

53 Campbell Gibson and Kay Jung, "Historical Census Statistics on
Population Totals by Race, 1790 to 1990, and by Hispanic Origin,
1970 to 1990, for the United States, Regions, Divisions, and States"
(working paper, U.S. Census Bureau, September 2002), https:
//mapmaker.rutgers.edu/REFERENCE/Hist_Pop_stats.pdf.

54 Department of Commerce and Labor, *Thirteenth Census of the
United States: 1910* (n.p.: Bureau of the Census, 1910), https://www2
.census.gov/library/publications/decennial/1910/bulletins
/demographics/369-population-us-abstract-color-race-nativity
-parentage-sex.pdf.

55 "Great Migration (African American)," Wikipedia, n.d., https://en
.wikipedia.org/wiki/Great_Migration_(African_American).

56 Gibson and Jung, "Historical Census Statistics on Population Totals
By Race, 1790 to 1990, and by Hispanic Origin, 1970 to 1990, for the
United States, Regions, Divisions, and States."

57 "Colonial and Pre-Federal Statistics," Census.gov, n.d., https://www2
.census.gov/prod2/statcomp/documents/CT1970p2–13.pdf.

**Chapter 7: Immigration: When the Walls Come Tumbling Down**

1 Portions of this chapter appeared in different form in *The American
Mind*.

2 "Homeland Security Fighting Terrorism Since 1492 Native Tee,"
Amazon, n.d., https://www.amazon.com/Homeland-Security-Fighting
-Terrorism-Native/dp/B07P9KJVQ1; "Native American We Should
Have Built A Wall Headdress T-Shirt," Amazon, n.d., https://www
.amazon.com/dp/B08FC6KHWM/ref=sspa_dk_detail_2?ie=UTF8&s
=apparel&sp_csd=d2lkZ2V0TmFtZT1zcF9kZXRhaWxfdGhlbWF
0aWM&pd_rd_i=B08FC6KHWM&pd_rd_w=GZLcP&content
-id=amzn1.sym.a53ea610-e450–44d1–897e-68c0c718bf50&pf
_rd_p=a53ea610-e450–44d1–897e-68c0c718bf50&pf_rd_r
=DS9BVACVFGYYMGB9Y2J1&pd_rd_wg=ncwZz&pd_rd_r
=b862022d-832b-437b-881a-3d70802038b1&customId=B0752XJY
NL&customizationToken=MC_Assembly_1%23B0752XJYNL&th
=1&psc=1.

3   "American Indians and Alaska Natives: Key Demographics and Characteristics," NCOA, January 10, 2023, https://www.ncoa.org /article/american-indians-and-alaska-natives-key-demographics -and-characteristics.

4   *Oklahoma v. Castro-Huerta,* 597 U. S. (2022), https://www.supreme court.gov/opinions/21pdf/21–429_806a.pdf; Nina Totenberg, "Supreme Court Hands Defeat to Native American Tribes in Oklahoma." NPR, June 29, 2022, https://www.npr.org/2022/06/29/1108717407/supreme -court-narrows-native-americans-oklahoma.

5   Peter Heather, "Migration at the end of Empire," Yalebooks, October 5, 2023, https://yalebooks.yale.edu/2023/10/05/migration-and-the-end -of-empire/.

6   Peter Walker, "Cop26 Failure Could Mean Mass Migration and Food Shortages, Says Boris Johnson," *The Guardian,* October 30, 2021, https://www.theguardian.com/environment/2021/oct/30/cop26-failure -could-mean-mass-migration-and-food-shortages-says-boris-johnson.

7   Annalisa Merelli, "1,700 Years Ago, the Mismanagement of a Migrant Crisis Cost Rome Its Empire," Quartz, May 7, 2016, https: //qz.com/677380/1700-years-ago-the-mismanagement-of-a-migrant -crisis-cost-rome-its-empire.

8   Rod Dreher, "Miguel Monjardino's República," *American Conservative,* June 28, 2018, https://www.theamericanconservative .com/miguel-monjardino-republica/.

9   Remco Zwetsloot and Dahlia Peterson, "The US-China Tech Wars: China's Immigration Disadvantage," The Diplomat, December 31, 2019, https://thediplomat.com/2019/12/the-us-china-tech-wars-chinas -immigration-disadvantage.

10   Jessie Yeung and Junko Ogura, "Japan Says One in 10 Residents Are Aged 80 or Above As Nation Turns Gray," CNN, September 19, 2023, https://www.cnn.com/2023/09/18/asia/japan-elderly-population -workforce-intl-hnk/index.html; "Number of Registered Foreign Residents Living in Japan from 2012 to 2021," Statista, December 2022, https: //www.statista.com/statistics/687809/japan-foreign-residents-total-number.

11   "Mexico," *Latin American Economic Outlook,* 1, https://www.oecd .org/dev/americas/44535802.pdf.

12   Ramesh Ponnuru, "Why Obama's 'Coalition of the Ascendant' Crashed," Bloomberg, November 5, 2014, https://www.bloomberg .com/view/articles/2014–11-05/why-obama-s-coalition-of-the-ascendant -crashed.

13   Maria Lauret, "Americanization Now and Then: The 'Nation of Immigrants' in the Early Twentieth and Twenty-First Centuries," *Journal of American Studies* 50, no. 2 (May 2016): 434, https://www .jstor.org/stable/44162777.

14　Jeremy Carl, "A Nation of Sellers," The American Mind, September 1, 2022, https://americanmind.org/features/rule-not-by-lies/a-nation-of-settlers.

15　"Death at Jamestown," PBS, May 28, 2014, https://www.pbs.org/wnet/secrets/death-jamestown-clues-evidence/1435.

16　Robert Stephens, "11 Lesser-Known Facts about the *Mayflower* and Thanksgiving," UFC Today, November 15, 2023, https://www.ucf.edu/news/11-lesser-known-facts-about-the-mayflower-and-thanksgiving.

17　Betsy McCaughey, "Biden's Welcome Program for Illegal Immigrants," *New York Post*, https://nypost.com/2022/04/12/bidens-welcome-program-for-illegal-immigrants; Melissa Goldin, "Phones Given to US Immigrants Have Limited Uses," Associated Press, May 24, 2023, https://apnews.com/article/fact-check-immigrant-phone-internet-texting-521577996794; Andrew Hensel, "More Taxpayer Funds Going toward Migrant Meals," *Cleburne Times-Review*, December 6, 2023, https://www.cleburnetimesreview.com/cnhi_network/more-taxpayer-funds-going-toward-migrant-meals/article_edac68ff-d50c-53c2-9e43-6f51f39da96e.html; Kristin Tate, "Your Taxpayer Dollars Are Footing the Spiraling Costs of Illegal Immigration," *The Hill*, April 21, 2019, https://thehill.com/opinion/immigration/439930-your-taxpayer-dollars-are-footing-the-spiraling-costs-of-illegal-immigration.

18　Raymond L. Cohn, "Immigration to the United States," Economic History Association, n.d., https://eh.net/encyclopedia/immigration-to-the-united-states.

19　Andrew Lawrence Crown, "Noble Savages and Barbarized Slaves: Tocqueville on Native Americans and African Americanss in Democracy in America," Voegelin View, August 10, 2021, https://voegelinview.com/noble-savages-and-barbarized-slaves-tocqueville-on-native-americans-and-african-americans-in-democracy-in-america.

20　Hank Burchard, "Pocahontas: A Maiden's Voyage," *Washington Post*, December 16, 1994, https://www.washingtonpost.com/archive/lifestyle/1994/12/16/pocahontas-a-maidens-voyage/8fce99f4-888f-4a08-bddd-36557f904175.

21　Cohn, "Immigration to the United States."

22　Israel Zangwill, *The Melting Pot*, https://archive.org/stream/themeltingpot23893gut/23893.txt.

23　Karen Seiber, "Israel Zangwill and the Melting Pot," Theodore Roosevelt Center, June 24, 2020, https://www.theodorerooseveltcenter.org/Blog/Item/Melting%20Pot.

24　"Early Immigration Policies," U.S. Citizenship and Immigrations Services, n.d., https://www.uscis.gov/about-us/our-history/explore-agency

-history/overview-of-agency-history/early-american-immigration
-policies.

25 James R. Rogers, "Know-Nothings and the Republican Coalition,"
*First Things*, March 1, 2016, https://www.firstthings.com/blogs/first
thoughts/2016/03/know-nothings-and-the-republican-coalition.

26 "Following the Frontier Line, 1790 to 1890," United States Census
Bureau, https://www.census.gov/dataviz/visualizations/001.

27 Ansel Adams, "The Closing of the American Wilderness," PBS, n.d.,
https://www.pbs.org/wgbh/americanexperience/features/ansel-closing
-american-wilderness.

28 See John F. Kennedy's 1958 book, *A Nation of Immigrants*.

29 Douglas S Massey and Karen A. Pren, "Unintended Consequences of
US Immigration Policy: Explaining the Post-1965 Surge from Latin
America," National Library of Medicine, July 30, 2012, https://www
.ncbi.nlm.nih.gov/pmc/articles/PMC3407978.

30 Cohn, "Immigration to the United States."

31 Ibid.

32 Alex Shashkevich, "New Stanford Research Explores Immigrants'
Decision to Return to Europe during Historical Age of Mass
Migration," *Stanford News*, September 12, 2017, https://news.stanford
.edu/2017/09/12/returning-home-age-mass-migration.

33 Josh Zeitz, "The 1965 Law That Gave the Republican Party Its
Race Problem," Politico, August 20, 2016, https://www.politico.com
/magazine/story/2016/08/immigration-1965-law-donald-trump-gop
-214179.

34 Paola Giuliano and Marco Tabellini, "The Seeds of Ideology:
Historical Immigration and Political Preferences in the United States,"
IZA Institute of Labor Economics, May 2020, https://ideas.repec.org
/p/iza/izadps/dp13268.html.

35 Helen Andrews, "How Early Immigration Shifted Our Politics
Permanently to the Left," *American Conservative*, June 12, 2020,
https://www.theamericanconservative.com/how-early-immigration-shifted
-our-politics-permanently-to-the-left.

36 Ibid.

37 Ibid.

38 Michael H. Keller and David D. Kirkpatrick, "Their America Is
Vanishing. Like Trump, They Insist They Were Cheated," *New York
Times*, October 23, 2022, https://www.nytimes.com/2022/10/23/us
/politics/republican-election-objectors-demographics.html.

39 "Mapping the Latinx Great Migrations (Part 2)," America's Great
Migrations Project, n.d., https://depts.washington.edu/moving1/map
_latinx_migration.shtml.

40 "Bhicaji Balsara," Wikipedia, n.d., https://en.wikipedia.org/wiki
/Bhicaji_Balsara.

41 "Asian Alone or in Any Combination by Selected Groups," United States Census Bureau, 2015, https://archive.ph/20200214011110/https://fact finder.census.gov/faces/tableservices/jsf/pages/productview.xhtml?pid =ACS_15_1YR_B02018&prodType=table#selection-263.0–260.3.

42 "Jane Lorenzi and Jeanne Batalova, "Sub-Saharan African Immigrants in the United States," Migration Policy Institute, May 11, 2022, https://www.migrationpolicy.org/article/sub-saharan-african -immigrants-united-states.

43 Timothy Noah, "What We Didn't Overcome, Part 2," Slate, November 12, 2008, https://slate.com/news-and-politics/2008/11/what-we-didn -t-overcome-part-2.html.

44 Jerry Kammer, "The Hart-Celler Immigration Act of 1965," Center for Immigration Studies, September 30, 2015, https://cis.org/Report /HartCeller-Immigration-Act-1965.

45 Ibid.

46 Otis L. Graham, *Unguarded Gates: A History of America's Immigration Crisis* (Lanham, Maryland: Rowman & Littlefield Publishers, 2004), 89, 92; https://www.google.com/books/edition /Unguarded_Gates/6I48qQTmW8kC?hl=en&gbpv=1&dq= %22congressmen+don%27t+want+to+look+like+racists.%22+new +york+times&pg=PA92&printsec=frontcover.

47 Kramer, "The Hart-Celler Immigration Act of 1965."

48 William Clinton, "Commencement Address at Portland State University in Portland, Oregon," The American Presidency Project," June 13, 1998, https://www.presidency.ucsb.edu/documents/commence ment-address-portland-state-university-portland-oregon.

49 "How Groups Voted in 1976," Roper Center, n.d., https://roper center.cornell.edu/how-groups-voted-1976; "National Exit Poll for Presidential Results," CBS News, December 14, 2020, https://www .cbsnews.com/elections/2020/united-states/president/exit-poll.

50 "National Exit Poll for Presidential Results"; Aaron O'Neill, "Share of Popular Votes for Major Parties in US Presidential Elections 1860–2020," Statista, May 23, 2023, https://www.statista.com /statistics/1035521 /popular-votes-republican-democratic-parties-since-1828.

51 "On This Day, Supreme Court Reviews Redistricting," National Constitution Center, March 26, 2023, https://constitutioncenter.org /blog/on-this-day-supreme-court-reviews-redistricting.

52 The Founders' Constitution, Volume 2, Article 1, Section 8, Clause 4 (Citizenship), Document 8, http://press-pubs.uchicago.edu/founders /documents/a1_8_4_citizenships8.html.

53 Ibid.

54 Ibid.

55  "From George Washington to John Adams, 15 November 1794,"
    Founders Online, November 15, 1794, https://founders.archives.gov
    /documents/Washington/05–17-02–0112.

56  Michael Anton, "That's Not Happening and It's Good That It Is,"
    The American Mind, July 26, 2021, https://americanmind.org/salvo
    /thats-not-happening-and-its-good-that-it-is.

57  Eric Jensen, Nicholas Jones, Megan Rabe, Beverly Pratt, Lauren
    Medina, Kimberly Orozco, and Lindsay Spell, "2020 U.S. Population
    More Racially and Ethnically Diverse Than Measured in 2010,"
    United States Census Bureau, August 12, 2021, https://www.census
    .gov/library/stories/2021/08/2020-united-states-population-more
    -racially-ethnically-diverse-than-2010.html.

58  U.S. Department of Commerce, *1960 Census of Population*
    (Washington, D.C.: Bureau of the Census, 1961), 3, https://www2
    .census.gov/library/publications/decennial/1960/pc-s1-supplementary
    -reports/pc-s1–10.pdf.

59  Jeffrey S. Passel and Marta Tienda, "From Native to Immigrant and
    Back Again: A Historical and Prospective Analysis of Generational
    Changes in the Latino Population, 1960–2030" (working paper,
    Urban Institute, Washington, D.C., and Princeton University,
    Princeton, New Jersey), https://paa2005.populationassociation.org
    /papers/51541.

60  *1960 Census of Population*, 3.

61  HUD Public Affairs, " HUD Launches Inaugural Latino Task Force
    During Hispanic Heritage Month 2023," U.S Department of Housing
    And Urban Development, Washington, DC, March 2023, https:
    //www.hud.gov/press/press_releases_media_advisories/hud_no_23_236
    #:~:text=The%20U.S.%20Hispanic%20population%20stands,
    minority%20group%20in%20the%20country. https://www.commerce
    .gov/news/blog/2023/05/us-census-bureau-releases-key-stats-honor
    -2023-asian-american-native-hawaiian-and

62  U.S. Department of Commerce, "U.S. Census Bureau Releases Key
    Stats in Honor of 2023 Asian American, Native Hawaiian, and Pacific
    Islander Heritage Month," Commerce.gov, May 1st 2003, https:
    //www.pewresearch.org/short-reads/2022/01/27/key-findings-about-
    black-immigrants-in-the-u-s/#:~:text=Between%202000%20and%20
    2019%2C%20the,from%20just%2023%25%20in%202000.

63  Christine Tamir, "Key Findings about Black Immigrants in the U.S.,"
    Pew Research Center, January 27, 2022, https://www.pewresearch.org
    /short-reads/2022/01/27/key-findings-about-black-immigrants-in-the
    -u-s/

64  Nicole Ward and Jeanne Batalova, "Frequently Requested Statistics on
    Immigrants and Immigration in the United States," Migration Policy
    Institute, March 14, 2023, https://www.migrationpolicy.org/article

/frequently-requested-statistics-immigrants-and-immigration-united
-states.

65  "Chapter 5: U.S. Foreign-Born Population Trends" in *Modern
Immigration Wave Brings 59 Million to U.S., Driving Population
Growth and Change Through 2065* (Washington, D.C.: Pew Research
Center, 2015), https://www.pewresearch.org/hispanic/2015/09/28
/chapter-5-u-s-foreign-born-population-trends.

66  "Chapter 5: U.S. Foreign-Born Population Trends," Pew Research
Center, Pewresearch.org, Sept, 28, 2015, https://www.pewresearch
.org/hispanic/2015/09/28/chapter-5-u-s-foreign-born-population-trends
/#:~:text=In%201960%2C%208.2%20million%20immigrants,to%20
10.7%20million%20in%202013.

67  "Update on Diversity Visa (DV) Program 2023," Travel.State.gov,
September 7, 2023, https://travel.state.gov/content/travel/en/News
/visas-news/update-on-diversity-visa-dv-program-2023.html.

68  Marco Rubio Senate, "Senate Democrats Block Rubio Resolution
Calling on Biden to Revoke Visas of Hamas Sympathizers," press
release, October 18, 2023, https://www.rubio.senate.gov/english
-espanol-senate-democrats-block-rubio-resolution-calling-on-biden-to
-revoke-visas-of-hamas-sympathizers.

69  Dara Lind and P. R. Lockhart, "The Diversity Visa Donald Trump
Hates, Explained," Vox, December 15, 2017, https://www.vox.com
/explainers/2017/11/2/16591118/diversity-visa-explained; "Senate
Democrats Block Rubio Resolution Calling on Biden to Revoke Visas
of Hamas Sympathizers."

70  Daniel de Visé, "America's White Majority Is Aging Out," August 7,
2023, https://thehill.com/homenews/race-politics/4138228-americas
-white-majority-is-aging-out.

71  "Demographic Background," Childstats, accessed December 13,
2023, https://www.childstats.gov/americaschildren/demo.asp.

72  Vivek Ramaswamy (@VivekGRamaswamy), "Can't make this stuff
up. . . .," Twitter, December 4, 2023, 11:07 p.m., https://twitter.com
/VivekGRamaswamy/status/1731888060848132097.

73  John Leo, "Bowling with Our Own," *City Journal*, June 25, 2007,
https://www.city-journal.org/article/bowling-with-our-own.

74  John Wahala, "Immigration and Social Trust," September 8, 2020,
https://cis.org/Wahala/Immigration-and-Social-Trust.

75  Peter Thisted Dinesen, Merlin Schaeffer, and Kim Mannemar
Sønderskov, "Ethnic Diversity and Social Trust: A Narrative and
Meta-Analytical Review," *Annual Review of Political Science* 23
(2020): 441–65, https://www.annualreviews.org/doi/pdf/10.1146
/annurev-polisci-052918- 020708#:~:text=We%20find%20a%20
statistically%20significant,diversity%20is%20measured%20
more%20locally.

76 Jason Wilson and Aaron Flanagan, "The Racist 'Great Replacement' Conspiracy Theory Explained," Southern Poverty Law Center, May 17, 2022, https://www.splcenter.org/hatewatch/2022/05/17/racist -great-replacement-conspiracy-theory-explained; "'The Great Replacement:' An Explainer," Anti-Defamation League, April 19, 2021, https://www.adl.org/resources/backgrounder/great-replacement -explainer.

77 "Great Replacement," Wikipedia, n.d., https://en.wikipedia.org/wiki /Great_Replacement.

78 Michelle Goldberg, "We Can Replace Them," *New York Times*, October 29, 2018, https://www.nytimes.com/2018/10/29/opinion /stacey-abrams-georgia-governor-election-brian-kemp.html; Charles M. Blow, "It Was a Terrifying Census for White Nationalists," *New York Times*, August 15, 2021, https://www.nytimes.com/2021/08/15 /opinion/united-states-census-white.html.

79 Domenico Montanaro, "How the 'Replacement' Theory Went Mainstream on the Political Right," NPR, May 17, 2022, https: //www.npr.org/2022/05/17/1099223012/how-the-replacement-theory -went-mainstream-on-the-political-right.

80 Mkay (@JoyAnnReid), "Watching all the bitter old white guys on the Republican side as #KBJ makes history is making me strangely giddy, honestly. May their Dixiecrat anger burn deep and long. History has defied their precious founders, who never, ever intended this day to be. We will revel in our joy!," Twitter, April 7, 2022, 2:07 p.m., https: //twitter.com/JoyAnnReid/status/1512129851167281155; Peter Wehner, "Obama's 'Coalition of the Ascendant' Is Collapsing," The Trinity Forum, December 6, 2013, https://www.ttf.org /obamas-coalition-of-the-ascendant-is-collapsing.

81 William H. Frey and Fred Dews, "White Decline and Increased Diversity in America's Aging Population," Brookings, October 1, 2021, https: //www.brookings.edu/articles/white-decline-and-increased-diversity -in-americas-aging-population; "The Vanishing White American," CNN, June 30, 2018, https://www.cnn.com/videos/tv/2018/06/30 /the-vanishing-white-american.cnn.

82 Adam Shaw, "Flashback: Biden Praised 'Constant,' 'Unrelenting' Stream of Immigration into US," Fox News, December 12, 2020, https://www.foxnews.com/politics/flashback-joe-biden-constant -unrelenting-immigration.

83 Razib Khan, "Hungarians as the Ghost of the Magyar Confederacy," Razib Khan's Unsupervised Learning, August 14, 2021, https://www .razibkhan.com/p/hungarians-as-the-ghost-of-the-magyar.

**Chapter 8: That's Entertainment?**

1  Johnny Walfisz, "Culture Re-View: 'Birth of a Nation' One of the Most Controversial Films Ever Is Released," Euronews, August 2, 2023, https://www.euronews.com/culture/2023/02/08/culture-re -view-birth-of-a-nation-one-of-the-most-controversial-films-ever-is -released.

2  Duncan Campbell, "Film Directors Strip Award of Link to Klan Epic," *The Guardian*, March 10, 2000, https://www.theguardian.com /film/2000/mar/11/world.news.

3  Roger Ebert, "The Birth of a Nation," RogerEbert.com, March 30, 2003, https://www.rogerebert.com/reviews/great-movie-the-birth-of-a -nation-1915.

4  "AFI's 100 Years . . . 100 Stars," American Film Institute, n.d., https: //www.afi.com/afis-100-years-100-stars.

5  Stephen P Powers, David J. Rothman, and Stanley Rothman, *Hollywood's America: Social and Political Themes In Motion Pictures* (London: Routledge, 2018), https://www.amazon.com /Hollywoods-America-Social-Political-Pictures-ebook/dp/B079X4VM96 /ref=tmm_kin_swatch_0?_encoding=UTF8&qid=&sr=.

6  True Discipline (@TruueDiscipline), "By the mid 60s, minorities were portrayed more favorably than whites in films . . .," Twitter, October 22, 2022, 8:23 p.m., https://twitter.com/TruueDiscipline/status /1583977408893358081.

7  Zuleka Zevallos, "Hollywood Racism: The Magical Negro Trope," The Other Sociologist, January 24, 2012, https://othersociologist .com/2012/01/24/hollywood-racism/.

8  "A Composite from a Variety of Comms and Posts," Live Journal, n.d., https://blackhistory.livejournal.com/74963.html.

9  Eric Deggans, "Opinion: Tom Hanks Is a Non-Racist. It's Time for Him To Be Anti-Racist," NPR, June 13, 2021, https://www.npr.org /2021/06/13/1005725990/tom-hanks-is-a-non-racist-its-time-for-him -to-be-anti-racist.

10  "Inequality in 1,300 Popular Films: Examining Portrayals of Gender, Race/Ethnicity, LGBTQ & Disability from 2007 to 2019," USC Annenberg Inclusion Initative, 2020, 3, https://assets.uscannenberg.org /docs/aii-inequality_1300_popular_films_09–08-2020.pdf.

11  *Inequality across 1,300 Popular Films: Examining Portrayals of Gender, Race/Ethnicity, LGBTQ and Disability from 2007 to 2019* (Los Angeles: USC Annenberg Inclusion Initiative, 2020), 5, https: //assets.uscannenberg.org/docs/aii-inequality_1300_popular_films _09–08-2020.pdf.

12  Ibid., 3–28.

13  James Barragan, "Column: Not Everyone in Austin Was Cheering for Richard Linklater," *Austin-American Statesmen*, October 12, 2016,

https://www.statesman.com/story/news/2016/10/12/column-not-everyone-in-austin-was-cheering-for-richard-linklater/9906344007; Emma Guinness, "Tim Burton Explained Why His Projects Are Full of White People as Netflix's Wednesday Is Accused of Being 'Racist,'" Unilad, December 2, 2022, https://www.unilad.com/film-and-tv/tim -burton-white-people-explained-netflix-wednesday-racist-699352 –20221202; Ed Guerrero, "Spike Lee: A New Black Wave of Cinema," ACMI, December 28, 2016, https://www.acmi.net.au/stories-and -ideas/spike-lee.

14  Jacqueline Keeler, "Sacheen Littlefeather Was a Native American Icon. Her Sisters Say She Was an Ethnic Fraud," *San Francisco Chronicle*, October 25, 2022, https://www.sfchronicle.com/opinion/openforum /article/Sacheen-Littlefeather-oscar-Native-pretendian-17520648.php.

15  "Academy Establishes Representation and Inclusion Standards for Oscars® Eligibility," Oscars, September 8, 2020, https://www.oscars .org/news/academy-establishes-representation-and-inclusion-standards -oscarsr-eligibility.

16  Dean Cain (@RealDeanCain), "How about we judge on this criteria—which film was the BEST PICTURE? . . . ," Twitter, September 8, 2020, 9:06 p.m., https://twitter.com/RealDeanCain/status /1303499933853515776?s=20.

17  Steve Chiotakis, "Film Editor Accused of 'Anti-White Racism' for Connecting Black Colleagues with Jobs," KCRW, June 25, 2020, https://www.kcrw.com/news/shows/greater-la/jose-huizar-race-film -fritz-coleman/black-editors-hollywood.

18  Ibid.

19  Caroline Graham, "Hollywood's Identity Crisis: Actors, Writers and Producers Warn of 'Reverse Racism' in the Film Industry Which Has Created a 'Toxic' Climate for Anyone Who Is a White, Middle-Age Man," *Daily Mail*, July 11, 2020, https://www.dailymail.co.uk/news /article-8513727/Actors-writers-producers-warn-reverse-racism-film -industry.html.

20  Isaac Simpson, "Mini Rooms in the Longhouse," The American Mind, May 10, 2023, https://americanmind.org/salvo/mini-rooms-in -the-longhouse.

21  John Loftus, "Hollywood's New Era of McCarthyism," *National Review*, June 22, 2020, https://www.nationalreview.com/2020/07 /hollywoods-new-era-of-mccarthyism.

22  Graham, "Hollywood's Identity Crisis."

23  Chris Gardner, "Jordan Peele on Making Movies After 'Us': 'I Don't See Myself Casting a White Dude As the Lead,'" The Hollywood Reporter, March 26, 2019, https://www.hollywoodreporter.com /news/general-news/jordan-peele-says-i-dont-see-myself-casting-a -white-dude-as-lead-us-1197021.

24  Armond White, "Return of the Get-Whitey Movie," *National Review*, February 24, 2017, https://www.nationalreview.com/2017/02/jordan -peeles-get-out-trite-get-whitey-movie.

25  Ibid.

26  Carol H. Hood, "This Is Why 'Get Out' Is Freaking Out White People," Dame, February 28, 2017, https://www.damemagazine.com /2017/02/28/why-get-out-freaking-out-white-people.

27  Ibid.

28  Michael Knowles, "No WHITES Allowed! Racist Black Panther Movie TikTok," YouTube video, October 28, 2022, https://www .youtube.com/watch?v=hBdypach3Ts.

29  Lonnae O'Neal, "She Didn't Want to Watch 'Black Panther' with Whites on Opening Night, but Then Why Was She Surprised More of Them Didn't Show Up?," Andscape, February 19, 2018, https: //andscape.com/features/watching-black-panther-commentary-sharing -wakanda-guarding-against-cultural-appropriation.

30  "'Black Panther' Box Office Numbers Show Representation Pays Off," CBS News, February 19, 2018, https://www.cbsnews.com/news /black-panther-box-office-numbers-show-representation-pays-off.

31  Becca Lewis and Kinjal Dave, "Black Panther and the Far Right," Medium, March 22, 2018, https://medium.com/@MediaManipulation /black-panther-and-the-far-right-e83facb735bb.

32  Ben Shapiro, "'Black Panther' Is A Very Good Movie. It's Also Chock Full of Radical Politics.," The Daily Wire, February 19, 2018, https://www.dailywire.com/news/review-black-panther-very-good -movie-its-also-ben-shapiro.

33  Lewis and Dave, "Black Panther and the Far Right."

34  "Fruitvale Station—Plot," IMDb, n.d., https://www.imdb.com/title /tt2334649/plotsummary.

35  Sandhya Dirks, "It Started with Oscar Grant: A Police Shooting in Oakland, and the Making of a Movement," KQED, July 5, 2020, https://www.kqed.org/news/11823246/it-started-with-oscar-grant-a -police-shooting-in-oakland-and-the-making-of-a-movement-2.

36  Maura Dolan, "Father of Oscar Grant Loses Lawsuit against BART Officer," *Los Angeles Times*, July 1, 2014, https://www.latimes.com /local/lanow/la-me-ln-bart-lawsuit-20140701-story.html.

37  Jana J. Monji, "'Black Panther: Wakanda Forever': Is Black Superiority Better Than White Superiority?," *Age of the Geek* (blog), November 8, 2022, https://ageofthegeek.org/2022/11/08/black- panther-wakanda-forever-is-black-superiority-better-than -white-superiority-%E2%AD%90%EF%B8%8F%E2%AD%90%EF %B8%8F.

38  Armond White, "*Wakanda Forever* Exploits Racial Politics," *National Review*, November 11, 2022, https://www.nationalreview .com/2022/11/wakanda-forever-exploits-commercial-politics.

39 "Top Lifetime Grosses," Box Office Mojo, accessed December 2, 2023, https://www.boxofficemojo.com/chart/top_lifetime_gross/?ref_=bo_cso_ac.

40 Erin Texeira, "Multiracial Scenes Now Common in TV Ads," NBC News, February 15, 2005, https://www.nbcnews.com/id/wbna6975669.

41 Erin Hackenmuller, The (Mis)representation of Interracial Couples in Television Advertising," University of Alabama, 2020, 39, https://ir.ua.edu/items/284d462d-04b1-4400-bfd0-b35cd94eee27/full.

42 Ibid.

43 Deborah Block, "Americans See More Interracial Relationships in Advertising," Voa, March 7, 2021, https://www.voanews.com/a/usa_race-america_americans-see-more-interracial-relationships-advertising/6202928.html.

44 Gretchen Livingston and Anna Brown, "Trends and Patterns in Intermarriage," Pew Research Center, May 18, 2017, https://www.pewresearch.org/social-trends/2017/05/18/1-trends-and-patterns-in-intermarriage.

45 Mohammed El Hazzouri, Kelley Main, and Sergio Carvalho, "Do Minorities Prefer Ads with White People?," The Conversation, n.d., https://theconversation.com/do-minorities-prefer-ads-with-white-people-82882.

46 Rob Rhode, "Let's Talk about Forced Diversity in TV Commercials," *The Cranky Creative*, January 5, 2022, https://thecrankycreative.com/what-happened-to-white-people-in-tv-commercials.

47 Mark Duffy, "Copyranter: The Go-to Ad Joke Is—Still—the White Male Moron," Digiday, March 25, 2016, https://digiday.com/marketing/copyranter-go-ad-joke-still-white-male-moron.

48 The account can be reached here: https://twitter.com/StupidWhiteAds.

49 Jessica Smith, "Hamilton Box Office: How Much Would A Theatrical Movie Have Made?," Screen Rant, September 17, 2022, https://screenrant.com/hamilton-musical-movie-box-office-performance-how-much.

50 Emi P. Cummings, "Unpopular Opinion: Color-Blind Casting Isn't 'Woke'—It's Racist," The Crimson, December 9, 2020, https://www.thecrimson.com/article/2020/12/9/unpop-opinion-color-blind-casting.

51 Samantha Vincenty, "*Hamilton*'s Jonathan Groff Is More Than Just the Spitting King George," Oprah Daily, July 7, 2020, https://www.oprahdaily.com/entertainment/tv-movies/a33234629/jonathan-groff-hamilton-king-george.

52 Christine Jeske, "Why White Kids Need *Hamilton* More Than Ever," Sapiens, August 25, 2020, https://www.sapiens.org/culture/hamilton-white-kids.

53 Eric Kohn, "How 'Hamilton' Became a Color-Conscious Casting Trailblazer, before It Was Cool," Indie Wire, July 4, 2020, https:

//www.indiewire.com/features/general/hamilton-cast-casting-directors
-diversity-1234571127.

54 "Creating and Convening Coalitions," Hispanic Federation, August
24, 2017, https://www.hispanicfederation.org/media/pinata/24Aug2017
/building_and_strengthening_coalitions.

55 Eriq Gardner, "White Actors Suing 'Hamilton' for Discrimination?
Supreme Court Hears Warning," *The Hollywood Reporter*, March
19, 2019, https://www.hollywoodreporter.com/business/business-news
/white-actors-suing-hamilton-discrimination-supreme-court-hears
-warning-1195755.

56 "Charter Communications Inc. v. National Association of African
American-Owned Media," SCOTUSBlog, n.d., https://www.scotusblog
.com/case-files/cases/charter-communications-inc-v-national-association
-of-african-american-owned-media.

57 Samantha Williams, "Coloring outside the Lines: A Look into Color-
Conscious, Colorblind, and For Us By Us Casting Practices," EXCEL
log, January 25, 2021, https://umexcelsmtd.com/2021/01/25/race
-in-casting-part-1.

58 Heather Mac Donald, *When Race Trumps Merit: How the Pursuit of
Equity Sacrifices Excellence, Destroys Beauty, and Threatens Lives*
(Augusta, Georgia: DW Books, 2023), 75.

59 Ibid.,76.

60 Ibid., 77

61 Ibid., 121

62 Yang (@SheluyangPang), "The shortlist for the National Book Award
this year is book after book of what I call 'marginalized group torture
porn'. Note that the biggest buyers of these books are actually affluent
white liberals. They want to hear about suffering because it makes
them feel virtuous." Twitter, September 18, 2023, 11:56 a.m., https:
//twitter.com/SheluyangPeng/status/1703800089158828425/photo/1.

63 Jeremy Carl, "*Democracy in Chains* and the Scandal of Tonight's
National Book Awards," *National Review*, November 15, 2017, https:
//www.nationalreview.com/corner/truth-chains-democracy-chains
-and-scandal-tonights-national-book-awards.

64 Quoted in Corrine Segal, "Why a White Male Poet Was Just
Published in 'The Best American Poetry 2015' as 'Yi-Fen Chou,'"
PBS, September 8, 2015, https://www.pbs.org/newshour/arts
/white-male-poet-just-published-best-american-poetry-2015-yi
-fen-chou.

65 Hua Hsu, "The End of White America?," *The Atlantic*, January–
February 2009, https://www.theatlantic.com/magazine/archive/2009
/01/the-end-of-white-america/307208.

66 Ibid.

67 Ibid.

68 Ibid.
69 Ibid.
70 Ibid.
71 Ibid.
72 Ibid.
73 Ibid.
74 Ibid.
75 Ibid.

## Chapter 9: The Unbearable Whiteness of the Green Movement

1 Rebecca Beitsch and Rachel Frazin, "OVERNIGHT ENERGY: Interior Official Called Black Lives Matter 'Racist,' Defended Alleged Kenosha Shooter | Trump Signs Bipartisan Bill Funding Conservation Grants," *The Hill*, October 30, 2020, https://thehill.com/policy /energy-environment/overnights/523697-overnight-energy-interior -official-called-black-lives.

2 Ayanna Pressley (@AyannaPressley), "A 17 year old white supremacist domestic terrorist drove across state lines, armed with an AR 15 . . . ," Twitter, August 26, 2020, 8:33 p.m., https://twitter.com/Ayanna Pressley/status/1298780540431224832.

3 Jerry Kammer, "Raul Grijalva: From Chicano Radical to Congressman," Center for Immigration Studies, October 17, 2009, https://cis.org/Raul-Grijalva-Chicano-Radical-Congressman.

4 Ibid.

5 Ibid.

6 Ibid.

7 Ian Brickey, "Sierra Club Condemns Racism at Interior," Sierra Club, October 27, 2020, https://www.sierraclub.org/press-releases/2020/12 /sierra-club-condemns-racism-interior.

8 "Trash at the Border Highlights the Environmental Cost of Illegal Immigration," Center for Immigration, September 19, 2018, https://cis .org/Immigration-Studies/Trash-Border-Highlights-Environmental -Cost-Illegal-Immigration.

9 Erik Ortiz, "'The Numbers Don't Lie': The Green Movement Remains Overwhelmingly White, Report Finds," NBC News, January 13, 2021, https://www.nbcnews.com/news/us-news/numbers-don-t-lie -green-movement-remains-overwhelmingly-white-report-n1253972.

10 David Bier, "New Study Links Anti-Immigration Groups to Pro-Population Control Environmentalists," Competitive Enterprise Institute, January 29, 2013, https://cei.org/blog/new-study-links-anti -immigration-groups-to-pro-population-control-environmentalists/.

11 Michelle Nijhuis, "Immigration Controversy Engulfs Sierra Club Board Election," Grist, March 2, 2004, https://grist.org/article /nijhuis-sierra.

12  Ibid.

13  Ibid.

14  Ibid.

15  Felicity Barringer, "Establishment Candidates Defeat Challengers in Sierra Club Voting," *New York Times*, April 22, 2004, https://www .nytimes.com/2004/04/22/us/establishment-candidates-defeat -challengers-in-sierra-club-voting.html.

16  Sierra Club (@SierraClub), "The only crisis on the border is the one the Trump administration is causing . . . ," Twitter, January 8, 2019, 9:22 p.m., https://twitter.com/SierraClub/status/10828248 52195688454.

17  "A Brief Chronology of the Sierra Club's Retreat from the Immigration-Population Connection (Updated)," Center for Immigration Studies, August 14, 2018, https://cis.org/Immigration-Studies/Brief-Chronology-Sierra-Clubs-Retreat-Immigration Population-Connection-Updated.

18  "Environmental Groups' Opposition to the Border Wall Is Disappointing, but Not Surprising," Center for Immigration Studies, October 18, 2018, https://cis.org/Immigration-Studies/Environmental -Groups-Opposition-Border-Wall-Disappointing-Not-Surprising.

19  Michael Brune, "From Outrage to Justice," Sierra Club, May 29, 2020, https://www.sierraclub.org/michael-brune/2020/05/christian -cooper-antiracism-outdoors.

20  Ibid.

21  Ibid.

22  Michael Brune, "Pulling Down Our Monuments," Sierra Club, July 22, 2020, https://www.sierraclub.org/michael-brune/2020/07/john-muir -early-history-sierra-club.

23  Ibid.

24  Ibid.

25  Michael Brune, "Why the Sierra Club Supports Reparations," Sierra Club, June 23, 2020, https://www.sierraclub.org/michael-brune/2021 /06/why-sierra-club-supports-reparations.

26  "CO$_2$ Emissions by Country 2023," World Population Review, n.d., https://worldpopulationreview.com/country-rankings/co2-emissions-by -country; Seth Borenstein, "World Carbon Dioxide Emissions Increase Again, Driven by China, India and Aviation," AP News, December 4, 2023, https://apnews.com/article/carbon -dioxide-climate-change-china-india-aa25e5a4271aa45810c43528 0bb97879.

27  Benjamin Storrow, "U.S. Carbon Emissions Fall for First Time in Biden Era," E&E News, July 7, 2023, https://www.eenews.net /articles/u-s-carbon-emissions-fall-for-first-time-in-biden-era/.

28 "Based on Science: Is It Possible to Achieve Net-Zero Emissions?" National Academies, October 27, 2021, https://www.national academies.org/based-on-science/is-it-possible-to-achieve-net-zero -emissions#:~:text=To%20achieve%20net%2Dzero%20emissions %20across%20the%20entire%20United%20States,gas%20 emissions%20by%20about%2010%25.

29 Michael Brune, "This Country Needs Dreamers," Sierra Club, June 18, 2020, https://www.sierraclub.org/michael-brune/2020/06/DACA -dreamers-Supreme-Court.

30 Alleen Brown, "Sierra Club Executive Director Resigns amid Upheaval around Race, Gender, and Abuses," The Intercept, August 19, 2021, https://theintercept.com/2021/08/19/sierra-club-resignation -internal-report.

31 Ibid.

32 Ibid.

33 "Meet Ben Jealous," Sierra Club, n.d., https://www.sierraclub.org /meet-ben-jealous.

34 Sierra Club, IRS Form 990 for 2020, Public Disclosure Copy, https: //www.sierraclub.org/sites/default/files/2023–11/2022-Sierra-Club -990.pdf.

35 Robin Bravender, "Sierra Club Announces Layoffs, Restructuring," E&E News, April 28, 2023, https://www.eenews.net/articles/sierra -club-announces-layoffs-restructuring.

36 Maxine Joselow, "The Sierra Club Hired Its First Black leader. Turmoil over Racial Equity Followed," *Washington Post,* September 7, 2023, https://www.washingtonpost.com/climate-environment/2023 /09/07/sierra-club-racial-equity/.

37 Ortiz, "'The Numbers Don't Lie.'"

38 Sarah Jaquette Ray, "Climate Anxiety Is an Overwhelmingly White Phenomenon," *Scientific American*, March 21, 2021, https://www .scientificamerican.com/article/the-unbearable-whiteness-of-climate -anxiety.

39 Ibid.

40 Ibid.

41 Ambika Chawla, "Why Is Environmentalism So Homogenous, and How to Cultivate Genuine Diversity?," GreenBiz, August 13, 2020, https://www.greenbiz.com/article/why-environmentalism-so -homogenous-and-how-cultivate-genuine-diversity.

42 Ibid.

43 Rachel Jones, "The Environmental Movement Is Very White. These Leaders Want to Change That.," *National Geographic,* July 29, 2020, https://www.nationalgeographic.com/history/article/environmental -movement-very-white-these-leaders-want-change-that.

44 *Department of Justice Report Regarding the Criminal Investigation into the Shooting Death of Michael Brown by Ferguson, Missouri Police Officer Darren Wilson*, March 4, 2015, https://www.justice .gov/sites/default/files/opa/press-releases/attachments/2015/03/04/doj _report_on_shooting_of_michael_brown_1.pdf.

45 Jones, "The Environmental Movement Is Very White."

46 Ibid.

47 James Edward Mills, "Here's How National Parks Are Working to Fight Racism," *National Geographic*, June 23, 2020, https://www .nationalgeographic.com/travel/national-parks/article/more-diversity -how-to-make-national-parks-anti-racist.

48 Ibid.

49 Ibid.

50 "Presidential Memorandum—Promoting Diversity and Inclusion in Our National Parks, National Forests, and Other Public Lands and Waters," Obama White House, January 12, 2017, https://obamawhite house.archives.gov/the-press-office/2017/01/12/presidential-memorandum -promoting-diversity-and-inclusion-our-national.

51 Ibid.

52 Emma Paterson, "Juneteenth: The Forgotten Holiday," Newport This Week, June 15, 2023, https://www.newportthisweek.com/articles /juneteenth-the-forgotten-holiday/#:~:text=Although%20the%20 day%20is%20important,little%20bit%E2%80%9D%20about%20 the%20holiday.

53 Jeremy Carl, "Parks and Devastation," The American Mind, October 5, 2022, https://americanmind.org/features/saving-the-environment -from-environmentalists/parks-and-devastation.

54 Ibid.

55 "The History of Palisades Tahoe and the Olympic Triumph," Red Wolf Lodge at Olympic Valley, n.d., https://www.redwolfolympic valley.com/olympic-valley-history/#:~:text=The%20ski%20resort %20is%20now,the%20name%2C%20so%20are%20we.

56 Carl, "Parks and Devastation."

57 "Going-to-the-Sun Road Seasonal Closure," National Park Service, last update April 21, 2023; "Glacier Visitation by Year," NationalParked, n.d., https://www.nationalparked.com/glacier /visitation-statistics; "Going-to-the-Sun Chalets," National Park Lodge Architecture Society," 2009, https://nplas.org/goingtothesun. html; "Historic Lodging in and around Glacier National Park," National Park Service eHistory Library, n.d., http://npshistory.com /brochures/glac/historic-lodging.pdf.

58 Alexander Hall, "Biden Roasted for Sending South Africa $8 Billion to Shut Down Coal Plants: 'Weapon-Grade Lunacy,'" Fox News, December 15, 2022, https://www.foxnews.com/media/biden-roasted -sending-south-africa-8-billion-shut-coal-weapon-grade-lunacy.

59 Joel B. Pollak, "Johannesburg to Follow Cape Town, Break from State Power Company," Breitbart, May 24, 2022, https://www.breitbart .com/africa/2022/05/24/johannesburg-to-follow-cape-town-break -from-state-power-company.

60 "Climate Change Is a Racial Justice Issue," *At Liberty* (podcast), ACLU, September 30, 2021, https://www.aclu.org/podcast/climate -change-is-a-racial-justice-issue.

61 Jeremy Williams, "Why Climate Change Is Inherently Racist," BBC, May 31, 2022, https://www.bbc.com/future/article/20220125-why -climate-change-is-inherently-racist.

62 Ibid.

63 "CO2 Emissions of All World Countries," EDGAR, European Commission, n.d., https://edgar.jrc.ec.europa.eu/report_2022.

64 Saifaddin Galal, "Africa's Share in Global Carbon Dioxide ($CO_2$) Emissions from 2000 to 2021," Statista, September 22, 2023, https: //www.statista.com/statistics/1287508/africa-share-in-global-co2 -emissions.

65 Williams, "Why Climate Changes Is Inherently Racist."

66 "The Global Climate Crisis Is a Racial Justice Crisis: UN Expert," United Nations Office of the High Commissioner Rights, October 31, 2022, https://www.ohchr.org/en/press-releases/2022/11/global-climate -crisis-racial-justice-crisis-un-expert.

67 "Carbon Footprint by Country 2023," World Population Review, n.d., https://worldpopulationreview.com/country-rankings/carbon-footprint -by-country.

68 Beth Gardiner, "Unequal Impact: The Deep Links between Racism and Climate Change," Yale Environment 360, June 9, 2020, https: //e360.yale.edu/features/unequal-impact-the-deep-links-between -inequality-and-climate-change.

69 Jim F. Couch, Peter M. Williams, Jon Halvorson, and Keith Malone, "Of Racism and Rubbish: The Geography of Race and Pollution in Mississippi," *Independent Review* 8, no. 2 (Fall 2003): 235–47, 240, https://www.independent.org/pdf/tir/tir_08_2_4_couch.pdf.

70 Ibid.

71 Climate Refugees, https://www.climate-refugees.org.

72 Zachary Faria, "Biden Goes All In on the UN's 'Climate Reparations' Scam," *Washington Examiner*, November 22, 2022, https://www.washington examiner.com/opinion/biden-all-in-on-un-climate-reparations-scam.

## Chapter 10: Big Business, Big Tech, and Big Discrimination

1 Thomas Pynchon, *Gravity's Rainbow* (New York: Penguin Press, 2012).

2 George Orwell, *Nineteen Eighty-Four* (London: Penguin Books, 1987), 65.

3 Thornton McEnery, "Jamie Dimon Drops into Mt. Kisco Chase Branch, Takes a Knee with Staff," *New York Post*, June 5, 2020,

https://nypost.com/2020/06/05/mending-jpm-chief-drops-into-mt
-kisco-chase-branch.

4   Tal Axelrod, "JPMorgan CEO Tells Employees He Is 'Disgusted by
    Racism,' after NY Times Report," *The Hill*, December 13, 2019,
    https://thehill.com/policy/finance/474554-jp-morgan-ceo-tells
    -employees-he-is-disgusted-by-racism-after-ny-times-report.

5   McEnery, "Jamie Dimon Drops into Mt. Kisco Chase Branch."

6   Jamie Dimon and Brian Lamb, "Message from Jamie Dimon and
    Brian Lamb," JPMorgan Chase & Co., n.d., https://www.jpmorgan
    chase.com/news-stories/message-from-jamie-dimon-and-brian-lamb.

7   "Largest American Companies by Market Capitalization,"
    CompaniesMarketCap.com, 2023, https://companiesmarketcap.com
    /usa/largest-companies-in-the-usa-by-market-cap.

8   Jessica Wohl, "McDonald's Issues a Silent Video Statement in Tribute
    to George Floyd and Others," *AdAge*, June 4, 2020, https://adage.com
    /creativity/work/mcdonalds-silent-video/2260721.

9   Bill Chappell, "Starbucks Closes More Than 8,000 Stores Today for
    Racial Bias Training," NPR, May 29, 2018, https://www.npr.org
    /sections/thetwo-way/2018/05/29/615119351/starbucks-closes-more
    -than-8–000-stores-today-for-racial-bias-training.

10  Michael Lee, "Coca-Cola Has Employees Take Training on How to
    'Be Less White' to Combat Racism," *Washington Examiner*, February
    20, 2021, https://www.washingtonexaminer.com/news/coca-cola
    -training-be-less-white.

11  Tracy Jan, Jena McGregor, and Meghan Hoyer, "Corporate America's
    $50 Billion Promise," *Washington Post*, August 23, 2021, https:
    //www.washingtonpost.com/business/interactive/2021/george
    -floyd-corporate-america-racial-justice.

12  "Americans Deserve to Know Who Funded BLM Riots," *Newsweek*,
    March 14, 2023, https://www.newsweek.com/
    americans-deserve-know-who-funded-blm-riots-opinion-1787460.

13  Jan, McGregor, and Hoyer, "Corporate America's $50 Billion
    Promise." See also "Consumer Financial Protection Bureau
    Issues Advisory Opinion to Help Expand Fair, Equitable, and
    Nondiscriminatory Access to Credit," Consumer Financial Protection
    Bureau, December 21, 2010, https://www.consumerfinance.gov
    /about-us/newsroom/consumer-financial-protection-bureau-issues
    -advisory-opinion-to-help-expand-fair-equitable-and-nondis
    criminatory-access-to-credit.

14  "Using Special Purpose Credit Programs to Expand Equality,"
    National Fair Housing Alliance, November 4, 2020, https://national
    fairhousing.org/using-spcps-blog.

15  Ingrid Jacques, "Do You Have a Good Credit Score? Biden Wants to
    Punish You for It," *USA Today*, May 4, 2023, https://www.usatoday

.com/story/opinion/columnist/2023/05/04/biden-mortgage-rule-credit
-score-cost-homebuyers-more/70179031007; Sabrina Karl, "Average
Credit Scores by Race," Investopedia, July 18, 2023, https://www
.investopedia.com/average-credit-scores-by-race-5214521.

16 "Police Reform," Business Roundtable, n.d., https://www.business
roundtable.org/policereform; Jan, McGregor, and Hoyer, "Corporate
America's $50 Billion Promise."

17 Sarah Dong, "The History and Growth of the Diversity, Equity, and
Inclusion Profession," GRC Insights, June 2, 2021, https://insights
.grcglobalgroup.com/the-history-and-growth-of-the-diversity-equity
-and-inclusion-profession.

18 Kira Lussier, "What the History of Diversity Training Reveals
about Its Future," The Conversation, September 7, 2020, https:
//theconversation.com/what-the-history-of-diversity-training-reveals
-about-its-future-143984.

19 Hans von Spakovsky and Abigail Carr, "California's Unconstitutional,
Morally Repugnant Racist Quotas Thrown Out by Federal Court,"
*Washington Times*, May 30, 2023, https://www.washingtontimes.com
/news/2023/may/30/californias-unconstitutional-morally-repugnant
-rac.

20 Vicki L. Bogan, Ekaterina Potemkina, and Scott E. Yonker, "What
Drives Racial Diversity on U.S. Corporate Boards?," Harvard Law
School Forum on Corporate Governance, January 17, 2022, https:
//corpgov.law.harvard.edu/2022/01/17/what-drives-racial-diversity
-on-u-s-corporate-boards.

21 Brett J. Miller and Sarah L. Nirenberg, "Are Employers' Diversity
Efforts Risking 'Reverse Discrimination' Lawsuits?," Butzel Attorneys
and Counselors, July 13, 2021, https://www.butzel.com/alert-Are
-Employers-Diversity-Efforts-Risking-Reverse-Discrimination
-Lawsuits.

22 Dana Kennedy, "Denver Councilwoman Candi CdeBaca Says White-
Owned Businesses Should Pay Reparations," *New York Post*, May 6,
2023, https://nypost.com/2023/05/06/candi-cdebaca-white
-businesses-should-pay-reparations/

23 "Corporate America Promised to Hire a Lot More People of Color. It
Actually Did," Bloomberg, September 26, 2023, https://www
.bloomberg.com/graphics/2023-black-lives-matter-equal-opportunity
-corporate-diversity.

24 Ed Shanahan, "White Starbucks Manager Fired amid Furor over
Racism Wins $25 Million," *New York Times*, June 13, 2023, https:
//www.nytimes.com/2023/06/13/nyregion/starbucks-pay-manager
-rittenhouse-square.html.

25 Jeremy Carl, "Towards a Republican Counter-Elite," *American
Conservative*, May 19, 2022, https://www.theamericanconservative

.com/towards-a-republican-counter-elite; Ali Tamaseb, *Super Founders: What Data Reveals about Billion-Dollar Startups* (New York: PublicAffairs, 2021), https://www.amazon.com/Super-Founders -Reveals-Billion-Dollar-Startups/dp/1541768426; David Teten and Katherine Boe Heuck, "The Iconic VC-Backed Founders Are All White & Asian Men. So Why Invest in Diversity?" David Teten, November 2, 2021, https://teten.com/the-iconic-vc-backed-founders- are-all-white-asian-men-why-invest-in-diversity.

26 Kenny Herzog, "Why Are Venture Capitalists Still Funding Mostly White, Male Entrepreneurs?," *Entrepreneur*, February 11, 2021, https://www.entrepreneur.com/growing-a-business/why-are-venture -capitalists-still-funding-mostly-white/365079.

27 Callum Booth, "Here's How Male (and White) VC Firms Are," TNW, January 25, 2019, https://thenextweb.com/news/male-white -venture-capitalist-gender-diversity.

28 Bismarck Analysis (@bismarckanlys), "India has the third-highest number of unicorn startups worth over $1 billion, after the U.S. and China. . . . ," Twitter, June 18, 2023, 10:13 a.m., https://twitter.com /bismarckanlys/status/1670434559081455617.

29 Richard Waters, "Boom Times for Silicon Valley's Elite Investors," *Financial Times*, July 15, 2021, https://www.ft.com/content /bde4697e-3eb7–4a69-b099-fdf14dcd2dfa.

30 Joseph Geha, "Silicon Valley Pain Index Shows 'White Supremacy' Prevalent across Institutions," Mercury News, June 23, 2020, https: //www.mercurynews.com/2020/06/23/silicon-valley-pain-index -shows-white-supremacy-prevalent-across-institutions.

31 Ibid.

32 Richard Watson, "In Silicon Valley, Young White Males Are Stealing the Future from Everyone Else," *The Guardian*, May 27, 2016, https: //www.theguardian.com/commentisfree/2016/may/27/in-silicon -valley-young-white-males-are-stealing-the-future-from-everyone-else.

33 mthree, *Diversity in Tech: 2021 U.S. Report* (New York: Wiley, 2021), https://www.wiley.com/edge/site/assets/files/2689/diversity_ in_tech_2021_us_report_by_mthree.pdf; Shawna Chen, "4. Tech's Troubled History with Asian Workers," Axios, October 16, 2021, https://www.axios.com/2021/10/16/tech-asian-workers-racism-equity; Neil G. Ruiz, Luis, Noe-Bustamante, and Sono Shah, "Appendix: Demographic Profile of Asian American Results," Pew Research Center, May 8, 2023, https://www.pewresearch.org/race -ethnicity/2023/05/08/asian-american-identity-appendix-demographic -profile-of-asian-american-adults.

34 Kate Rooney and Yasmin Khorram, "Tech Companies Say They Value Diversity, but Reports Show Little Change in Last Six Years," CNBC, June 12, 2020, https://www.cnbc.com/2020/06/12/six-years-into -diversity-reports-big-tech-has-made-little-progress.html.

35 Ibid.; Ari Levy, "Tech Companies and Execs Announce over $20 Million in Donations after Killing of George Floyd," CNBC, June 2, 2020, https://www.cnbc.com/2020/06/02/tech-companies-donate -over-20-million-after-death-of-george-floyd.html.

36 Dakin Campbell, "The Definitive Account of How WeWork Went from a $47 Billion Valuation to a Basket Case in Just 6 Weeks," Business Insider, November 2, 2023, https://www.businessinsider.com /weworks-nightmare-ipo.

37 Rooney and Khorram, "Tech Companies Say They Value Diversity."

38 Aaron Levie (@levie), "We have profound racial injustice in our society. George Floyd. Ahmaud Arbery. Breonna Taylor. Enough is enough. @joelle_emerson and I are committing $500,000 to support organizations that are doing important work in this space. Let us know if you have any orgs to recommend.," Twitter, May 29, 2020, 1:38 p.m., https://twitter.com/levie/status/1266423713257287680 ?lang=en.

39 "BLM Funding Database," The Claremont Institute Center for the American Way of Life, n.d., https://dc.claremont.org/blm-funding -database.

40 Brian Heater, "Tech Companies Respond to George Floyd's Death, Ensuing Protests and Systemic Racism," Tech Crunch, June 1, 2020, https://techcrunch.com/2020/06/01/tech-co-protests.

41 Ibid.

42 Ibid.; "Tech Firms Say They Support George Floyd Protests—Here's What's Happening," CNET, June 10, 2020, https://www.cnet.com /culture/tech-companies-say-they-support-george-floyd-protests-heres -whats-happening.

43 Chen, "4. Tech's Troubled History with Asian Workers."

44 "About," Bay Area Equity Atlas, n.d., https://bayareaequityatlas.org /about#us.

45 Malkia Devich-Cyril, "Banning White Supremacy Isn't Censorship, It's Accountability," *Wired*, January 31, 2021, https://www.wired.com /story/banning-white-supremacy-censorship-accountability.

46 Chas Danner, "Amazon, Apple, and Google Cut Off Parler, Citing Its Failure to Moderate Extremist Content," Intelligencer, January 10, 2021, https://nymag.com/intelligencer/2021/01/amazon-apple-and -google-axe-parler-the-right-wing-twitter.html; Sarah E. Needleman, "Conservative Social-Media App Parler Has Returned to Apple's App Store. Here's What That Means.," *Wall Street Journal*, May 17, 2021, https://www.wsj.com/articles/what-is-parler-app-apple -android-11610478890.

47 Devich-Cyril, "Banning White Supremacy Isn't Censorship"; Craig Timberg and Drew Harwell, "QAnon and Pro-Trump Online Forums Are Fracturing and Struggling in Aftermath of the U.S. Capitol Siege,"

*Washington Post*, January 22, 2021, https://www.washingtonpost
.com/technology/2021/01/22/trump-twitter-capitol-qanon.

48 Devich-Cyril, "Banning White Supremacy Isn't Censorship, It's
Accountability."

49 Ibid.; Morgan Brinlee, "More Black Women Are Killed in America
Than Any Other Race," Bustle, July 22, 2017, https://www.bustle
.com/p/more-black-women-are-killed-in-america-than-any-other-race
-a-new-cdc-report-says-71955.

50 "2019 Crime in the United States: Expanded Homicide Data Table 6,"
FBI, 2019, https://ucr.fbi.gov/crime-in-the-u.s/2019/crime-in-the
-u.s.-2019/topic-pages/tables/expanded-homicide-data-table-6.xls.

51 Joseph De Avila, "The People Permanently Banned from Twitter: See
the List," *Wall Street Journal*, November 3, 2022, https://www.wsj.
com/story/the-people-permanently-banned-from-twitter-52b85992.

52 Dan Milmo, "Banned from Twitter: Accounts That May be Reprieved
after Musk Takeover," *The Guardian*, April 26, 2022,
https://www.theguardian.com/technology/2022/apr/26/banned-from
-twitter-accounts-reprieve-elon-musk.

53 "Louis Farrakhan," Southern Poverty Law Center, n.d., https://www
.splcenter.org/fighting-hate/extremist-files/individual/louis-farrakhan.

54 Steven Overly, "Twitter Maintains Ban on Candidate Laura Loomer,"
*Politico*, August 19, 2020, https://www.politico.com/news
/2020/08/19/twitter-keeps-ban-laura-loomer-398695; Aila Slisco,
"Far-Right Activist Laura Loomer Refuses to Concede, Sobs about
Voter Fraud," *Newsweek*, August 24, 2022, https://www.newsweek
.com/far-right-activist-laura-loomer-refuses-concede-sobs-about-voter
-fraud-1736325; Gavin Haynes, "How Corporations Can Delete Your
Existence," UnHerd, October 29, 2020, https://unherd.com/2020/10
/how-corporations-can-delete-your-existence/.

55 Laurie Wastell, "Google, Defender of the BLM Narrative," Spiked,
February 3, 2023, https://www.spiked-online.com/2023/02/03/google
-defender-of-the-blm-narrative.

56 "Moonshot & ADL Project Finds Anti-Black, Antisemitic, White
Supremacist Internet Searches Peaked in Conjunction with Major
Offline Events," Homeland Security Today, June 20, 2021, https:
//www.hstoday.us/subject-matter-areas/counterterrorism/moonshot-
adl-project-finds-anti-black-antisemitic-white-supremacist-internet
-searches-peaked-in-conjunction-with-major-offline-events.

57 "How Google Is Disappearing Anti-White Racism in SA," Politicsweb,
June 23, 2021, https://www.politicsweb.co.za/opinion/how-google
-sends-antiwhite-racism-down-the-memory-.

58 Christopher F. Rufo, "Don't Be Evil," *City Journal*, September 8,
2021, https://www.city-journal.org/article/dont-be-evil.

59 Elizabeth Weise, "Ex-Google Engineer Damore Sues Alleging Discrimination against White, Conservative Men," *USA Today*, January 9, 2018, https://www.usatoday.com/story/tech/news/2018/01/08/ex-google-engineer-damore-sues-alleging-discrimination-against-white-conservative-men/1013024001.

60 Lisa Ryan, "Anti-Diversity Memo Dude Sues Google for Discriminating against White Men," The Cut, January 8, 2018, https://www.thecut.com/2018/01/james-damore-google-discrimination-lawsuit-white-men.html.

61 Madison Malone Kircher, "Alex Jones Is Reportedly Banned From Google (and Other Things We Learned From James Damore's Class-action Lawsuit)," *New York*, January 8, 2019, https://nymag.com/intelligencer/2018/01/most-interesting-parts-of-james-damores-class-action-filing.html.

62 Joe Nocera, "Google Has a Diversity Problem. And a Lawsuit Problem.," Bloomberg, March 7, 2018, https://www.bloomberg.com/view/articles/2018–03-07/discriminating-against-white-men-isn-t-google-s-big-diversity-problem.

63 Ibid.

64 Christopher Tremoglie, "Poll Shows Hiring Managers Discriminating against White Men," *Washington Examiner*, November 11, 2022, https://www.washingtonexaminer.com/opinion/poll-shows-hiring-managers-discriminating-against-white-men; "1 in 6 Hiring Managers Have Been Told to Stop Hiring White Men," Resume Builder, January 19, 2023, https://www.resumebuilder.com/1-in-6-hiring-managers-have-been-told-to-stop-hiring-white-men.

65 Ian Miller, "Tech Company CEO Implies Layoffs Targeted White People First," Outkick, September 15, 2022, https://www.outkick.com/tech-company-ceo-implies-layoffs-targeted-white-people-first.

66 Ibid.

67 Sakshi Udavant, "Tech Layoffs Disproportionately Affect Marginalized Communities," PRISM, April 3, 2023, https://prismreports.org/2023/04/03/tech-layoffs-marginalized-communities.

68 Joe Guzzardi, "Tech Layoffs May Give U.S. IT Workers Opportunities," *Gilmer Mirror*, November 13, 2022, https://www.gilmermirror.com/2022/11/13/tech-layoffs-may-give-u-s-it-workers-opportunities.

69 Nicole Torres, "The H-1B Visa Debate, Explained," *Harvard Business Review*, May 4, 2017, https://hbr.org/2017/05/the-h-1b-visa-debate-explained.

70 Kirk Doran, Alexander Gelber, and Adam Isen, "The Effects of High-Skilled Immigration Policy on Firms: Evidence from H-1B Visa Lotteries," National Buraeau of Economic Research, November 2014,

https://www.nber.org/system/files/working_papers/w20668/revisions/w20668.rev2.pdf.

71 Zach Dorfman, "How Silicon Valley Became a Den of Spies," Politico, July 27, 2018, https://www.politico.com/magazine/story/2018/07/27/silicon-valley-spies-china-russia-219071.

72 Kevin Lynn, "Once Again We Were Attacked by the SPLC," Institute for Sound Public Policy, February 9, 2020, https://institute forsoundpublicpolicy.org/splc-attacks-group-standing-up-for-working-men-and-women; "Workers Organization Shares Staff, Cash with Anti-Immigrant Groups," Southern Poverty Law Center, January 31, 2020, https://www.splcenter.org/hatewatch/2020/01/31/workers-organization-shares-staff-cash-anti-immigrant-groups.

73 "Santa Clara County," Bay Area Census, n.d., http://www.bayareacensus.ca.gov/counties/SantaClaraCounty70.htm.

74 Ibid.

75 "Quick Facts: Santa Clara County, California, United States Census Bureau, April 1, 2020, https://www.census.gov/quickfacts/fact/dash board/santaclaracountycalifornia/POP010220#POP010220.

76 "All Data: Santa Clara County," Kids Data, n.d., https://www.kidsdata.org/region/59/santa-clara-county/results.

77 "Intermarriage across the U.S. by Metro Area," Pew Research Center, May 18, 2017, https://www.pewresearch.org/social-trends/interactives/intermarriage-across-the-u-s-by-metro-area.

78 "Santa Clara County," Bay Area Census, n.d., http://www.bayareacensus.ca.gov/counties/SantaClaraCounty50.htm

79 "Quick Facts: San Mateo County, California, United States Census Bureau, July 1, 2022, https://www.census.gov/quickfacts/fact/table/sanmateocountycalifornia/PST045222.

80 http://www.bayareacensus.ca.gov/counties/SanMateoCounty50.htm.

81 http://www.bayareacensus.ca.gov/counties/SanMateoCounty50.htm.

82 Eric McGhee, Jennifer Paluch, and Vicki Hsieh, "California's Children Offer a Window into a More Diverse Future," PPIC, January 11, 2022, https://www.ppic.org/blog/californias-children-offer-a-window-into-a-more-diverse-future.

83 Kimberly Cataudella, "Voting in California is Easier, but Large Disparities in Turnout Remain," Center for Public Integrity, October 6, 2022, https://publicintegrity.org/politics/elections/who-counts/voting-in-california-is-easier-but-large-disparities-in-turnout-remain.

84 Matt Levin, "California's Growing Senior Population by the Numbers," *Mercury News*, May 27, 2019, https://www.mercurynews.com/2019/05/27/californias-growing-senior-population-by-the-numbers/#.

## Chapter 11: Unhealthy Disrespect

1   "What Is Healthy Equity?," CDC.gov, n.d., https://www.cdc.gov /healthequity/whatis/index.html.

2   Latoya Hill, Nambi Ndugga, and Samantha Artiga, "Key Data on Health and Health Care by Race and Ethnicity," Kaiser Family Foundation, March 15, 2023, https://www.kff.org/racial-equity-and -health-policy/report/key-data-on-health-and-health-care-by-race -and-ethnicity/.

3   "What Is Health Equity?"

4   For this statement, see "Race and Medicine," *The New England Journal of Medicine*, n.d., https://www.nejm.org/race-and-medicine.

5   Alan Weil, "Tracking Author Demographics to Increase Equitable Participation," *Health Affairs*, January 11, 2022, https://www.health affairs.org/content/forefront/tracking-author-demographics-increase -equitable-participation.

6   Sally Satel, "Do No Harm: Critical Race Theory and Medicine," AEI, July 9, 2021, https://www.aei.org/research-products/ journal-publication/do-no-harm-critical-race-theory-and-medicine.

7   Alec Schemmel, "HHS Allows Doctors Implementing 'Anti-Racism Plan' to Charge More for Services," ABC 7, December 17, 2021, https: //katv.com/news/nation-world/hhs-allows-doctors-implementing-anti -racism-plan-to-charge-more-for-services.

8   Usha Lee McFarling, "NIH Releases a Plan to Confront Structural Racism. Critics Say It's Not Enough," STAT, June 10, 2021, https: //www.statnews.com/2021/06/10/nih-releases-plan-to-confront-structural -racism-critics-say-its-not-enough.

9   Ibid.

10  "Intramural Research Program Personnel Demographics (End FY20)," National Institutes of Health, n.d., https://oir.nih.gov/sourcebook /personnel/irp-demographics/intramural-research-program-personnel -demographics-end-fy20.

11  Usha Lee McFarling, "'Health Equity Tourists': How White Scholars Are Colonizing Research on Health Disparities," STAT, September 23, 2021, https://www.statnews.com/2021/09/23/health -equity-tourists-white-scholars-colonizing-health-disparities-research.

12  Ibid.

13  Ibid.

14  Ibid.

15  Ibid.

16  Ibid.

17  McFarling, "NIH Releases a Plan to Confront Structural Racism. Critics Say It's Not Enough."

18  McFarling, "'Health Equity Tourists': How White Scholars Are Colonizing Research on Health Disparities."

19 "Foundation History," The Commonwealth Fund, n.d., https://www
.commonwealthfund.org/about-us/foundation-history.

20 McFarling, "'Health Equity Tourists': How White Scholars Are
Colonizing Research on Health Disparities."

21 Ibid.

22 Ibid.

23 Ibid. Also see https://www.citeblackwomencollective.org.

24 McFarling, "'Health Equity Tourists': How White Scholars Are
Colonizing Research on Health Disparities."

25 Rhea W. Boyd, Edwin G. Lindo, Lachelle D. Weeks, and Monica
R. McLemore, "On Racism: A New Standard for Publishing on Racial
Health Inequities," *Health Affairs*, July 2, 2020, https://www.health
affairs.org/content/forefront/racism-new-standard-publishing
-racial-health-inequities.

26 Akriti Pokhrel, Adeniran Olayemi, Stephanie Ogbonda, Kiron Nair,
and Jen Chin Wang, "Racial and Ethnic Differences in Sickle Cell
Disease within the United States: From Demographics to Outcomes,"
*European Journal of Haematology* (May 2023): 554–63, https://doi
.org/10.1111/ejh.13936; "Why Are Some Genetic Conditions More
Common in Particular Ethnic Groups?," Medicine Plus, n.d., https:
//medlineplus.gov/genetics/understanding/inheritance/ethnicgroup.

27 McFarling, "'Health Equity Tourists': How White Scholars Are
Colonizing Research on Health Disparities."

28 Ibid.

29 Usha Lee McFarling, "Troubling Podcast Puts JAMA, the 'Voice of
Medicine,' under Fire for Its Mishandling of Race," Stat, April 6,
2021, https://www.statnews.com/2021/04/06
/podcast-puts-jama-under-fire-for-mishandling-of-race.

30 Stacy Weiner, "Medical Schools Overhaul Curricula to Fight
Inequities," AAMC, May 25, 2021, https://www.aamc.org/news
/medical-schools-overhaul-curricula-fight-inequities.

31 "About *The Lancet Infectious Diseases*," *The Lancet*, 2023, https:
//www.thelancet.com/laninf/about#:~:text=With%20an%20Impact
%20Factor%20of,Reports%20%C2%AE%2C%20Clarivate%20
2023.

32 "Clearing the Myths of Time: Tuskegee Revisited," *The Lancet
Infectious Diseases 5*, no. 3 (March 2005): https://www.thelancet.com
/journals/laninf/article/PIIS1473–3099(05)01286–7/fulltext.

33 Ibid.

34 Ibid.

35 April Dembosky, "Stop Blaming Tuskegee, Critics Say. It's Not an
'Excuse' for Current Medical Racism," NPR, March 23, 2021, https:
//www.npr.org/sections/health-shots/2021/03/23/974059870/stop-
blaming-tuskegee-critics-say-its-not-an-excuse-for-current-medical
-racism.

36 Benita Cotton-Orr and Dr. Stanley Goldfarb, "A Woke Panic on Maternal Mortality," Do No Harm, November 18, 2022, https://donoharmmedicine.org/in-the-news/2022/11/18/a-woke-panic-on-maternal-mortality.

37 "Heart Disease Facts," Centers for Disease Control and Prevention, May 15, 2023, https://www.cdc.gov/heartdisease/facts.htm#:~:text=Heart%20disease%20is%20the%20leading,groups%20in%20the%20United%20States.

38 "Structural Racism and Health Equity Language Guide," American Heart Association, May 2023, https://professional.heart.org/-/media/PHD-Files-2/Science-News/s/structural_racism_and_health_equity_language_guide.pdf.

39 Daniel Tan and Paulette Cha, "Race, Health, and the Risk of COVID-19 Complications," PPIC, April 17, 2020, https://www.ppic.org/blog/race-health-and-the-risk-of-covid-19-complications; Anahad O'Connor, "Why Do South Asians Have Such High Rates of Heart Disease?," *New York Times*, February 12, 2019, https://www.nytimes.com/2019/02/12/well/live/why-do-south-asians-have-such-high-rates-of-heart-disease.html.

40 Volgman et al., "Atherosclerotic Cardiovascular Disease in South Asians in the United States: Epidemiology, Risk Factors, and Treatments," *Circulation* (July 2018): e14–e21, https://doi.org/10.1161/CIR.0000000000000580.

41 "Face Masks," American Public Health Association, 2023, https://www.apha.org/news-and-media/multimedia/infographics/masks-text; Tom Jefferson et al., "Physical Interventions to Interrupt or Reduce the Spread of Respiratory Viruses," Cochrane Library, January 30, 2023, https://www.cochranelibrary.com/cdsr/doi/10.1002/14651858.CD006207.pub6/full.

42 *Structural Racism and Health Equity Language Guide* (American Heart Association, 2023), 5, https://professional.heart.org/-/media/PHD-Files-2/Science-News/s/structural_racism_and_health_equity_language_guide.pdf.

43 "COVID-19—Vermont Health Equity Initiative," Vermont Health Equity Initiative, n.d., https://www.vermonthealthequity.org/covid19.

44 Riis L. Williams, "Native American Deaths from COVID-19 Highest among Racial Groups," Princeton.edu, December 2, 2021, https://spia.princeton.edu/news/native-american-deaths-covid-19-highest-among-racial-groups; Mary Van Beusekom, "Native Americans at Outsized Risk of Severe COVID-19, Death," Center for Infectious Disease Research and Policy, University of Minnesota, August 30, 2023, https://www.cidrap.umn.edu/covid-19/native-americans-outsized-risk-severe-covid-19-death.

45 Michael Price, "European Diseases Left a Genetic Mark on Native Americans," *Science*, November 15, 2016, https://www.science.org /content/article/european-diseases-left-genetic-mark-native-americans.

46 Cameron K. Ormiston, Jolyna Chiangong, and Faustine Williams, "The COVID-19 Pandemic and Hispanic/Latina/o Immigrant Mental Health: Why More Needs to Be Done," *Health Equity* 7, no. 1 (January 2023): https://www.ncbi.nlm.nih.gov/pmc/articles /PMC9892920.

47 "COVID-19—Vermont Health Equity Initiative."

48 Harold Schmidt, Lawrence O. Gostin, Michelle A. Williams, "Is It Lawful and Ethical to Prioritize Racial Minorities for COVID-19 Vaccines?," *Journal of the American Medical Association* 324, no. 20 (October 2020): https://jamanetwork.com/journals/jama/full article/2771874.

49 Preeti Vankar, "Distribution of Medicaid/CHIP Enrollees in the United States in 2021, by Ethnicity," Statista, September 27, 2023, https://www.statista.com/statistics/1289100/medicaid-chip-enrollees -share-by-ethnicity; Smiljanic Stasha, "27+ Affordable Care Act Statistics and Facts (Updated 2023)," PolicyAdvice, July 24, 2023, https://policyadvice.net/insurance/insights/affordable -care-act-statistics.

50 "Analysis of Recent US Medicaid Spending," US Government Spending, n.d., https://www.usgovernmentspending.com/ medicaid_spending_analysis.

51 "Federal Subsidies for Health Insurance: 2023–2033, Congressional Budget Office, Washington D.C., 2023, https://www.cbo.gov/system /files/2023–09/59273-health-coverage.pdf.

52 Bowen Garrett and Anuj Gangopadhyaya, *Who Gained Health Insurance Coverage under the ACA, and Where Do They Live?* (Urban Institute, 2016), 2, https://www.urban.org/sites/default/files /publication/86761/2001041-who-gained-health-insurance-coverage -under-the-aca-and-where-do-they-live.pdf.

53 Kevin Fiscella, "Why Do So Many White Americans Oppose the Affordable Care Act?," *The American Journal of Medicine* 129, no. 5 (May 2015): https://www.amjmed.com/article/S0002–9343(15)00930–4 /fulltext.

54 "Medicare Beneficiary Enrollment Trends and Demographic Characteristics," Office of Health Policy, March 2, 2022, https: //aspe.hhs.gov/sites/default/files/documents/f81aafbba0b331c71c6e8bc 66512e25d/medicare-beneficiary-enrollment-ib.pdf.

55 Vijay Chokal-Ingam, "Racism Against Asian Americans and Whites in Med School Admissions Continues . . . ," Almost Black, August 23, 2016, https://almostblack.com/medical-schools-discriminate-asian -american-white-applicants-dont-try-hide.

56 Brendan Murphy, "MCAT Scores and Medical School Success: Do They Correlate?," AMA, February 24, 2022, https://www.ama-assn .org/medical-students/preparing-medical-school/mcat-scores-and -medical-school-success-do-they-correlate.

57 Nia Evans and Diana Halloran, "It's Time to Scrap the MCAT," Slate, September 11, 2020, https://slate.com/technology/2020/09/get-rid-of -the-mcat.html.

58 "Table B-3: Total U.S. MD-Granting Medical School Enrollment by Race/Ethnicity (Alone) and Gender, 2019–2020 through 2023–2024," AAMC, November 14, 2023, https://www.aamc.org/media/6116 /download.

59 Gabrielle Redford, "AAMC Renames Prestigious Abraham Flexner Award in Light of Racist and Sexist Writings," AAMC, November 17, 2020, https://www.aamc.org/news-insights/aamc-renames-prestigious- abraham-flexner-award-light-racist-and-sexist-writings.

60 Eui Young Kim, "Yale Prof Proposes Replacing MCAT in Med School Admissions," Yale News, September 11, 2018, https://yaledailynews .com/blog/2018/09/11/yale-prof-proposes-replacing-mcat-in-med -school-admissions.

61 Rohan Jotwani, "Medical Schools That Don't Require the MCAT: What You Should Know," Inspira Advantage, July 19, 2023, https://www.inspiraadvantage.com/blog/medical-schools-that-dont -require-the-mcat-what-you-should-know.

62 Mark J. Perry, "New Chart Illustrates Graphically the Racial Preferences for Blacks, Hispanics Being Admitted to US Medical Schools," AEI, June 25, 2017, https://www.aei.org/carpe-diem/new -chart-illustrates-graphically-racial-preferences-for-blacks-and-hispanics -being-admitted-to-us-medical-schools.

63 Ibid.

64 Tanya Albert Henry, "High Court Shouldn't Impede Efforts to Diversify Medical Schools," AMA, August 24, 2022, https: //www.ama-assn.org/education/medical-school-diversity /high-court-shouldn-t-impede-efforts-diversify-medical-schools.

65 "Racism in Medicine Report Helps Build Antiracism Curriculum at BUSM," Boston University Chobanian & Avedisian School of Medicine, August 17, 2021, https://www.bumc.bu.edu/ camed/2021/08/17/racism -in-medicine-report-helps-build-antiracism-curriculum-at-busm.

66 Stanley Goldfarb, "Keep Politics Out of the Doctor's Office," *Wall Street Journal*, April 18, 2022, https://www.wsj.com/articles/keep -politics-out-of-the-doctors-office-racism-woke-ideology-crt-critical-race -theory-medical-care-minorities-systemic-racism-covid-19-regulation -11650308028?mod=article_inline.

67 Ibid.

68   "Forced to Take Implicit Bias Training? Here's How to Respond," Do No Harm, October 5, 2022, https://donoharmmedicine.org/2022 /10/05/forced-to-take-implicit-bias-training-heres-how-to-respond.

69   "Ralph Waldo Emerson, 1803–82," Oxford Reference, n.d., https://www.oxfordreference.com/display/10.1093/acref/9780191826719 .001.0001/q-oro-ed4–00004155.

**Chapter 12: Not Everyone Who Says, "Lord, Lord"**

1    "Nietzsche's Moral and Political Philosophy," Stanford Encyclopedia of Philosophy, February 27, 2020, https://plato.stanford.edu/entries /nietzsche-moral-political.

2    Ryan P. Burge, "Mainline Protestants Are Still Declining, But That's Not Good News for Evangelicals," *Christianity Today*, July 13, 2021, https://www.christianitytoday.com/news/2021/july/mainline-protestant -evangelical-decline-survey-us-nones.html.

3    Greg Smith, "The UCC Is Missing 1.3 Million People! (#2054)," So What Faith, June 13, 2023, https://sowhatfaith.com/2023/06/13 /the-ucc-is-missing-1–3-million-people.

4    "Racial Justice," United Church of Christ, n.d., https://www.ucc.org /justice_racism.

5    Ibid.

6    UCC Leadership, "Build on the Love, Join the Movement," United Church of Christ, May 3, 2021, https://www.ucc.org/build-on-the -love-join-the-movement.

7    Ibid.

8    Greg Smith, "UCC Membership Decline: 2,193,593 to 773,539 (#1974)," So What Faith, February 20, 2022, https://sowhatfaith.com /2022/02/20/ucc-membership-decline-from-2193593-to-773539.

9    Ibid.

10   Ibid.

11   United Church of Christ, *A Statistical Profile 2021* (CARDD, 2021), 8, https://www.ucc.org/wp-content/uploads/2022/01/2021statisticalreport .vfweb_.pdf.

12   Rick Jones, "PC(USA) 2021 Statistics Continue to Show Declining Membership," Presbyterian Church USA, April 25, 2022, https://www.pcusa.org/news/2022/4/25/pcusa-2021-statistics-continue -show-declining-memb.

13   "Comparative Summaries of Statistics," Presbyterian Church USA, 2021, https://pcusa.org/site_media/media/uploads/oga/pdf/2021_stats _comparativesummary_update06_2022.pdf.

14   PC (USA) General Assembly, "On Recognition That Israel's Laws, Policies, and Practices Constitute Apartheid Against the Palestinian People," 225th General Assembly, 2022, https://www.pc-biz.org/# /search/3000773; Jackie Subar, "The Presbyterian Church's Lost

Moral Compass on Israel," ADL.ORG, July 7, 2022, https://www.adl
.org/resources/news/presbyterian-churchs-lost-moral-compass-israel.

15 *A Statistical Profile 2021*, 46.

16 Ibid., 47.

17 Ibid., 47.

18 Mark Tooley, "Don't Celebrate the Decline," *Juicy Ecumenism* (blog),
April 26, 2022, https://juicyecumenism.com/2022/04/26/dont
-celebrate-mainline-decline.

19 Ibid.

20 Collin Bastian, "Mainline Churches Call for Equity over Equality in
Reparations," *Juicy Ecumenism* (blog), February 28, 2022, https:
//juicyecumenism.com/2022/02/28/church-reparations-for-slavery.

21 Ibid.

22 Jeffrey Walton, "Attendance Crash as COVID Restrictions Take Toll
on Episcopal Church," *Juicy Ecumenism* (blog), November 22, 2022,
https://juicyecumenism.com/2022/11/22/episcopal-church-attendance
-crash.

23 Ibid.

24 Caleb Greggsen, "Evangelical Celebrity and the Root Problem behind
'Big Eva,'" The Gospel Coalition, October 18, 2019, https://www
.thegospelcoalition.org/article/evangelical-celebrity-problem-big-eva.

25 Brett McCracken (@brettmccracken), "White Christians in America
must partner with, listen to, defer to nonwhite & nonwestern
Christian leaders. We need humility, hope, revival.," Twitter,
November 9, 2016, 1:48 a.m., https://twitter.com/brettmccracken
/status/796243146594058240.

26 *Department of Justice Report regarding the Criminal Investigation
into the Shooting Death of Michael Brown by Ferguson, Missouri
Police Officer Darren Wilson* (Washington, D.C.: Department of
Justice, 2015), 5, https://www.justice.gov/sites/default/files/opa/press
-releases/attachments/2015/03/04/doj_report_on_shooting_of
_michael_brown_1.pdf.

27 Chuck Raasch, "Michael Brown's Mother Appears at Democratic
National Convention, Prompting Police Ire," *St. Louis Post-Dispatch*,
July 27, 2016, https://www.stltoday.com/news/local/metro
/michael-browns-mother-appears-at-democratic-national-convention
-prompting-police-ire/article_4b4e6e1a-55c7–5267-828a-e74472b0a7ee
.html.

28 Darryl G. Hart, "How to Fight Racism by Jemar Tisby," The
Orthodox Presbyterian Church, August–September 2021, https://opc
.org/os.html?article_id=907; Bob Smietana, "How Evangelical Writer
Jemar Tisby Became a Radioactive Symbol of 'Wokeness,'" The Roys
Report, May 30, 2023, https://julieroys.com/how-evangelical-writer
-jemar-tisby-became-a-radioactive-symbol-of-wokeness.

29 "Jemar Tisby Keynote Speaker," The Harry Walker Agency, n.d., https://www.harrywalker.com/speakers/jemar-tisby.

30 Preston Perry, "Dear Mike Brown," The Gospel Coalition, April 7, 2018, https://www.thegospelcoalition.org/conference_media/dear-mike -brown.

31 James Riley, "Broke and 'Woke' Hirelings," JPR, March 16, 2019, https://www.jamespatrickriley.com/index.php/broke-woke-hirelings.

32 Voddie Baucham, *Fault Lines: The Social Justice Movement and Evangelicalism's Looming Catastrophe* (Washington, D.C.: Salem Books, 2021), 5.

33 Ibid., 25.

34 Ibid., 36.

35 Ibid., 223

36 Ibid., 44.

37 Ibid., 56.

38 Ibid., 215.

39 Ibid., 67.

40 Tom Ascol, "Matthew Hall's Rejection of Critical Race Theory," Founders Ministries, n.d., https://founders.org/articles/matthew-halls- rejection-of-critical-race-theory/; see also Matthew Hall, "'I Am a Racist'—Matthew Hall, Provost at Southern Seminary," YouTube video, https://www.youtube.com/watch?v=1IiKCYSevDU.

41 "About Matthew Hall," Biola University, n.d., https://www.biola.edu /office-of-the-provost/about.

42 Matthew J. Hall, "'For He Is Our Peace': The Centrality of the Gospel of Christ in Racial Reconciliation," November 26, 2019, https://equip .sbts.edu/article/peace-centrality-gospel-christ-racial-reconciliation.

43 Associated Press, "Southern Baptists Elect Leader Focused on Bridging the Racial Divide," NBCNews.com, June 15, 2021, https:// www.nbcnews.com/news/religion/southern-baptists-elect-leader -focused-bridging-racial-divide-n1270973.

44 Baucham, *Fault Lines*, 111.

45 Daniel Silliman, "Died: Tim Keller, New York City Pastor Who Modeled Winsome Witness," *Christianity Today*, May 19, 2023, https://www.christianitytoday.com/news/2023/may/tim-keller-dead -redeemer-new-york-pastor-cancer.html.

46 Baucham, *Fault Lines*, 66.

47 Ibid., 87.

48 Ibid., 209.

49 Ibid., 210.

50 Tia Noelle Pratt, "Augustine's African Heritage Matters," U.S. Catholic, April 28, 2023, https://uscatholic.org/articles/202304/augustines-african -heritage-matters.

51 Rachel Hart Winter, "Anti-Racism, the Catholic Church, and the Sin of White Supremacy," Dominican University, n.d., https://www .dom.edu/arts-minds/st-catherine-siena-center/past-events/anti-racism -catholic-church-and-sin-white-supremacy.

52 "Anti-Racism Initiative," The Roman Cathlic Archdiocese of Washington, n.d., https://adw.org/living-the-faith/our-cultures/anti-racism -initiative.

53 Ryan Burge, "Catholic Mass Attendance Has Fallen by Half," Graphs about Religion, May 7, 2023, https://www.graphsaboutreligion.com/p /catholic-mass-attendance-has-fallen.

54 Jema Gatdula, "The Future of Catholicism Is with the Traditional Latin Mass," BusinessWorld, February 16, 2023, https://www .bworldonline.com/opinion/2023/02/16/505264/the-future-of -catholicism-is-with-the-traditional-latin-mass.

55 Brittany Wilmes and Stephanie Yeagle, "An anti-racism reading list from NCR," *National Catholic Reporter*, June 16, 2020, https://www .ncronline.org/opinion/ncr-today/anti-racism-reading-list-ncr.

56 Andrew Lyke, "Dear White Catholics: It's Time to Be Anti-Racist and Leave White Fragility Behind.," *America*, November 30, 2020, https://www.americamagazine.org/faith/2020/11/30/white-fragility -catholics-anti-racism-racial-justice-239097.

57 Fay S. Joyce, "Jackson Admits Saying 'Hymie' and Apologizes at a Synagogue," *New York Times*, February 27, 1984, https://www .nytimes.com/1984/02/27/us/jackson-admits-saying-hymie-and-apologizes -at-a-synagogue.html; Mark Higgins, "Rev. Jesse Jackson to Amazon: You Have the Power to Lift Up Our Youth, Diversify Boardroom," *Seattle Times*, June 4, 2018, https://www.seattletimes.com/opinion /rev-jesse-jackson-to-amazon-you-have-the-power-to-lift-up-our -youth-diversify-boardroom; Sasha Jones, "Jesse Jackson Demands Memphis Increase Contracts for Black Businesses," Action News 5, May 10, 2017, https://www.actionnews5.com/story/35387485/jesse- jackson-demands-memphis-increase-contracts-for-black-businesses.

58 Elizabeth MacDonald, "People Jailed for Owing Less Taxes Than Al Sharpton," Fox Business, February 5, 2016, https://www.foxbusiness. com/features/people-jailed-for-owing-less-taxes-than-al-sharpton; Peter Wallsten, "Obama's New Partner: Al Sharpton," *Wall Street Journal*, March 17, 2010, https://www.wsj.com/articles/SB100014240 52748704588404575123404191464126.

59 "Obama's Pastor: God Damn America, U.S. to Blame for 9/11," ABC News, March 13, 2008, https://abcnews.go.com/Blotter /DemocraticDebate/story?id=4443788&page=1.

60 Ibid.

61 Valerie Richardson, "Bill Clinton Slammed for Sharing Stage with Louis Farrakhan at Aretha Franklin Funeral," Associated Press,

September 2, 2018, https://apnews.com/article/entertainment-music
-religion-bill-clinton-race-and-ethnicity-4f9bf2f93650939a
093be8e189bd1e8c.

62 "WOKE PREACHER MONTAGE: Fire Up the Hammond Organ for
Ketanji Brown Jackson!," YouTube video, April 1, 2022, https://www
.youtube.com/watch?v=YkadCZe-5a8.

63 "Jewish Americans in 2020," Pew Research Center, May 11, 2021,
https://www.pewresearch.org/religion/2021/05/11/jewish-americans-in
-2020.

64 Ari Goldman, "Jewish Group Faces Reorganization," *New York
Times*, February 13, 1990, https://www.nytimes.com/1990/02/13/us
/jewish-group-faces-reorganization.html.

65 Ibid.

66 "Jewish Americans in 2020."

67 "Racial Justice," Religious Action Center, n.d., https://rac.org/issues
/racial-justice.

68 Ibid.

69 See https://native-land.ca.

70 "Racial Equity, Diversity and Inclusion Resources," Religious Action
Center, n.d., https://rac.org/issues/racial-justice/racial-justice-campaign
/racial-equity-diversity-and-inclusion-resources-our-racial-justice
-campaign.

71 "Reconsidering Being 'Colorblind,'" Union for Reform Judaism, n.d.,
https://urj.org/sites/default/files/ahcolorblindness-microaggression
handout_final.pdf.

72 Rachel Klein, "An Al Cheit for Asylum Seekers, Refugees, and All
Those Seeking Safety," Religious Action Center, September 29, 2022,
https://rac.org/blog/al-cheit-asylum-seekers-refugees-and-all-those
-seeking-safety.

73 Shayna Han, "Reflections on the 1-Year Anniversary of the Atlanta
Shootings," Religious Action Center, March 9, 2022, https://rac.org
/blog/reflections-1-year-anniversary-atlanta-shootings.

74 Kat Chow, "'Model Minority' Myth again Used as a Racial Wedge
between Asians And Blacks," NPR, April 19, 2017, https://www
.npr.org/sections/codeswitch/2017/04/19/524571669/model-minority
-myth-again-used-as-a-racial-wedge-between-asians-and-blacks;
Adrian Horton, "John Oliver: 'The Model Minority Myth Is a Tool of
White Supremacy and a Trap,'" *The Guardian*, June 7, 2021, https:
//www.theguardian.com/tv-and-radio/2021/jun/07/john-oliver-the
-model-minority-myth-is-a-tool-of-white-supremacy-and-a-trap.

75 Ali Rosenblatt, "Justice Delayed, Justice Denied, for Far Too Many,"
Religious Action Center, June 4, 2020, https://rac.org/blog/justice
-delayed-justice-denied-far-too-many.

76 Richard Fausset, "What We Know about the Shooting Death of Ahmaud Arbery," *New York Times*, August 8, 2022, https://www .nytimes.com/article/ahmaud-arbery-shooting-georgia.html.

77 Jacob Greenblatt, "Racism Is a Public Health Crisis," Religious Action Center, July 2, 2020, https://rac.org/blog/racism-public-health-crisis.

78 Rabbi Jocee Hudson, "Our Neighbor's Blood Calls to Us from the Ground," Religious Action Center, June 11, 2020, https://rac.org/blog /our-neighbors-blood-calls-us-ground.

79 Ibid.

80 Molly Meisels, "On Being Anti-Racist in an Orthodox World," *YU Observer*, June 7, 2020, https://yuobserver.org/2020/06/on-being -anti-racist-in-an-orthodox-world.

## Chapter 13: Apocalypse Now: The Anti-White Military

1 Helen Andrews, "Racial Trouble in the Vietnam Era," *American Conservative*, August 25, 2023, https://archive.is/pzGM8.

2 Sujata Gupta, "Military Towns Are the Most Racially Integrated Places in the U.S. Here's Why," *ScienceNews*, February 8, 2022, https://www.sciencenews.org/article/military-towns-integration -segregation-united-states.

3 Gerald F. Goodwin, "Black and White in Vietnam," *New York Times*, July 18, 2017, https://www.nytimes.com/2017/07/18/opinion/racism -vietnam-war.html.

4 Ibid.

5 Andrews, "Racial Trouble in the Vietnam Era."

6 M. James Littig, *Vietnam War Stats* (Alexandria, Virginia: Congressional Strategies, n.d.), 3, https://post3legion.org/Vietnam _Statistics.pdf.

7 "Myths of the Vietnam War," Vietnam Veterans of America, n.d., https://www.vva310.org/myths-of-the-vietnam-war.

8 Thomas C. Wilson, "Vietnam-Era Military Service: A Test of the Class-Bias Thesis," *Armed Forces & Society* 21, no. 3 (spring 1995), 461–71.

9 Ibid; "Myths of the Vietnam War."

10 *Da 5 Bloods*, directed by Spike Lee (Los Gatos, California: Netflix, 2020).

11 Tony Perry, "Whites Account for Most of Military's Fatalities," *Los Angeles Times*, September 24, 2005, https://www.latimes.com /archives/la-xpm-2005-sep-24-na-dead24-story.html.

12 Ibid.

13 "Young Adult Population Ages 18 to 24 by Race and Ethnicity in United States," The Anne E. Casey Foundation, July 2023, https: //datacenter.aecf.org/data/tables/11207-young-adult-population-ages -18-to-24-by-race-and-ethnicity#detailed/1/any/false/2048,574,1729, 37,871,870,573,869,36,868/68,69,67,12,70,66,71,7983/21595,21596.

14  "Special Forces Officer Demographics and Statistics in the US," Zippia, n.d., https://www.zippia.com/special-forces-officer-jobs /demographics.

15  Tom Vanden Brook, "Pentagon's Elite Forces Lack Diversity," *USA Today*, August 6, 2015, https://www.usatoday.com/story/news /nation/2015/08/05/diversity-seals-green-berets/31122851.

16  Caitlin Doornbos, "GOPers Press Pentagon on 'Woke' School Admin Who Made Anti-White Comments," *New York Post*, January 31, 2023, https://nypost.com/2023/01/31/gopers-press-pentagon-on-woke -school-admin-who-made-anti-white-comments.

17  Karen Jowers, "DoD Schools Diversity Chief Responds to 'Racism' Claims," *Military Times*, February 10, 2023, https://www.military times.com/news/your-military/2023/02/10/dod-schools-diversity-chief -responds-to-racism-claims.

18  Jacqueline Feldscher, "Hundreds of Troops Complain about 'Woke' Racism, Extremism Training, Cotton Claims," Defense One, June 11, 2021, https://www.defenseone.com/policy/2021/06/hundreds -troops-complain-about-woke-racism-extremism-training-cotton -claims/174672.

19  Chelsey Cox, "Gen. Mark Milley Fires Back against GOP Criticism of Critical Race Theory," Yahoo!Life, June 24, 2021, https://www .yahoo.com/lifestyle/gen-mark-milley-fires-back-012602609.html.

20  Will Thibeau, "Merit in the Armed Forces," *American Mind*, September 9, 2023, https://americanmind.org/salvo/ merit-in-the-armed-forces.

21  Tom Cotton, "Memorandum," June 10, 2021, https://www.govexec .com/media/gbc/docs/pdfs_edit/memorandum_for_recordv2jb.pdf.

22  Ibid.

23  Leo Shane III, "Lawmakers Accuse Army of Ignoring 'Woke' Policies That Hurt Recruiting," *Army Times*, February 23, 2023, https://www .armytimes.com/news/pentagon-congress/2023/02/23/lawmakers -accuse-army-of-ignoring-woke-policies-that-hurt-recruiting.

24  "Executive Summary of the 2023 Index of U.S. Military Strength," The Heritage Foundation, October 18, 2022, https://www.heritage .org/military-strength/executive-summary.

25  "What Is Most Significant in the Pentagon's China Military Report?," Reuters, October 20, 2023, https://www.reuters.com /world/what-is-most-significant-pentagons-china-military-report -2023–10-21; "World's Largest Army, Navy: How China Has Ramped Up Its Defense Capabilities," *Economic Times*, March 5, 2023, https://economictimes.indiatimes.com/news/how-to/worlds-largest-army -navy-how-china-has-ramped-up-its-defense-capabilities/ articleshow/98426138.cms#.

26 Meghann Myers, "DoD Testing Extremism Questions on Command Climate Surveys," *Military Times*, May 3, 2021, https://www. militarytimes.com/news/your-military/2021/05/03 /optional-extremism-questions-added-to-command-climate-surveys.

27 David Vergun, "DOD Issues Guidance on Plans to Counter Extremist Activity in the Force," U.S. Department of Defense, December 20, 2021, https://www.defense.gov/News/News-Stories/Article/Article /2880115/dod-issues-guidance-on-plans-to-counter-extremist-activity -in-the-force.

28 U.S. Department of Homeland Security, *Homeland Threat Assessment* (Washington, D.C.: U.S. Department of Homeland Security, October 2020), 18, https://www.dhs.gov/sites/default/files /publications/2020_10_06_homeland-threat-assessment.pdf.

29 Katharine Lackey, "Fort Hood Shooter Asks to Be 'Citizen' of Islamic State," *USA Today*, August 29, 2014, https://www.usatoday.com/story /news/nation/2014/08/29/fort-hood-shooter-islamic-state/14790297; Matthew Levitt, "Fort Hood: A Terrorist Attack on U.S. Soil," The Washington Institute, October 7, 2023, https://www.washingtoninstitute .org/policy-analysis/fort-hood-terrorist-attack-us-soil.

30 Will Dunham, "Army Chief Fears Backlash for Muslim U.S. Soldiers," Reuters, November 8, 2009, https://www.reuters.com/article/idUSTRE5 A71AJ.

31 Stephen Losey, "Goldfein: 'Every American Should Be Outraged' at Police Conduct in Death of George Floyd," *Air Force Times*, June 2, 2020, https://www.airforcetimes.com/news/your-air-force/2020/06/02 /goldfein-every-american-should-be-outraged-at-police-conduct-in-death -of-george-floyd; Zach England, Kyle Rempfer, Geoff Ziezulewicz, and Diana Stancy Correll, "Top Military Leaders Speak Out about Racism in Wake of George Floyd's Death in Police Custody," *Military Times*, June 3, 2020, https://www.militarytimes.com/2020/06/03/army-navy -leaders-latest-to-speak-out-about-racism-in-wake-of-george-floyds -death-in-police-custody.

32 JoAnne S. Bass (@cmsaf_official), "Who am I? I am a Black man who happens to be the Chief Master Sergeant of the Air Force. . . . " (thread), Twitter, June 1, 2020, 5:42 p.m., https://twitter.com/cmsaf _official/status/1267572332907954177.

33 Ibid.

34 Gina Harkins, "Top Marine Explains Why He's Banning Confederate Flags on Bases," Military.com, March 6, 2020, https://www.military .com/daily-news/2020/03/06/top-marine-explains-why-hes-banning -confederate-flags-bases.html.

35 Robbie Gramer, "Blinken Authorizes U.S. Embassies Worldwide to Display BLM Flags," Foreign Policy, May 25, 2021, https://foreign policy.com/2021/05/25/black-lives-matter-blm-state-department -embassies-flags-blinken-diplomacy-racial-injustice.

36 Hank Berrien, "Secretary of Veteran Affairs Authorizes All VA-Owned Facilities to Fly Pride Flag for up to 30 Days," The Daily Wire, June 2, 2023, https://www.dailywire.com/news/secretary-of-veteran-affairs-authorizes-all-va-owned-facilities-to-fly-pride-flag-for-up-to-30-days.

37 Leo Shane III, "Troops: White Nationalism a National Security Threat Equal to ISIS, Al-Qaida," *Military Times*, September 3, 2020, https://www.militarytimes.com/news/pentagon-congress/2020/09/03/troops-white-nationalism-a-national-security-threat-equal-to-isis-al-qaeda.

38 Allison Abbe, Diversity as Strategic Asset: How Asian-Americans Strengthen the Force," War Room, May 12, 2022, https://warroom.armywarcollege.edu/articles/asian-americans.

39 Irene Loewenson, "If Supreme Court Ends Affirmative Action, How Will the Military Adapt?," *Military Times*, October 26, 2022, https://www.militarytimes.com/news/your-military/2022/10/26/if-supreme-court-ends-affirmative-action-how-will-the-military-adapt; Brief for the United States as *Amicus Curiae* Supporting Respondent, *Students for Fair Admissions v. Harvard*, 600 U.S. 181, https://www.supremecourt.gov/DocketPDF/20/20–1199/232539/20220801205901633_20–1199%20Harvard%20FINAL%20Revised.pdf.

40 Ibid.; Brief of Veterans for Fairness and Merit as *Amicus Curiae* Supporting Petitioner, *Students for Fair Admissions v. Harvard*, 600 U.S. 181, May 9, 2022, https://www.supremecourt.gov/DocketPDF/20/20–1199/222848/20220509154943084_Amicus%20Brief%20of%20Veterans%20for%20Fairness%20and%20Merit%20Supp%20Petitioner.pdf.

41 Ronald R. Fogleman and Claude M. McQuarrie III, "No, Affirmative Action in The Military Doesn't Boost National Security, It Erodes It," The Federalist, October 25, 2022, https://thefederalist.com/2022/10/25/no-affirmative-action-in-the-military-doesnt-boost-national-security-it-erodes-it/?utm_source=rss&utm_medium=rss&utm_campaign=no-affirmative-action-in-the-military-doesnt-boost-national-security-it-erodes-it.

42 U.S. Navy, *Task Force One Navy Final Report* (Washington, D.C.: U.S. Navy, 2021), https://media.defense.gov/2021/Jan/26/2002570959/-1/-1/1/TASK%20FORCE%20ONE%20NAVY%20FINAL%20REPORT.PDF.

43 Christine Hauser, "Target of Racist Graffiti Wrote It, Air Force Academy Says," *New York Times*, November 8, 2017, https://www.nytimes.com/2017/11/08/us/air-force-academy-racist.html.

44 Tom Roeder, "Air Force Academy Finds Cadet Candidate Responsible for Racist Messages," *The Gazette*, November 7, 2017, https://gazette.com/air-force-academy-finds-cadet-candidate-responsible-for-racist-messages/article_e0abd653-e47b-5b6f-837b-d793a8369e34.html.

45 Ben Kesling, "Cadets, Midshipmen Were Not Flashing 'White Power' Signs, Probe Finds," *Wall Street Journal*, December 20, 2019, https://www.wsj.com/articles/cadets-midshipmen-were-not-flashing-white-power-signs-investigators-found-11576864999.

46 Will Thibeau, "Arms Must Cede," *American Conservative*, June 26, 2023, https://www.theamericanconservative.com/arms-must-cede.

47 "'Diversity & Inclusion Strategic Plan' Will Weaken Special Operations Forces," Center for Military Readiness, April 22, 2021, https://www.cmrlink.org/issues/full/diversity-and-inclusion-strategic-plan-will-weaken-special-operations-forces.

48 Ibid.

49 Ibid.

50 Ibid.

51 "DEI Executive Order Expands Diversity Industrial Complex," Center for Military Readiness, April 25, 2023, https://cmrlink.org/issues/full/dei-executive-order-expands-diversity-industrial-complex.

52 Ibid.

53 Gregory Newbold, "A Retired Marine 3-Star General Explains 'Critical Military Theory,'" Task & Purpose, February 10, 2022, https://taskandpurpose.com/news/critical-military-theory; Dakota Wood, "Identity Politics and Critical Race Theory Have No Place in U.S. Military," The Heritage Foundation, March 29, 2021, https://www.heritage.org/defense/commentary/identity-politics-and-critical-race-theory-have-no-place-us-military.

54 Patrick H. Brady and Mike Waltz, "The Military Should Reject DEI and CRT," *Wall Street Journal*, March 24, 2023, https://www.wsj.com/articles/the-military-should-stay-colorblind-race-dod-army-navy-air-force-racial-preferences-dei-e64ead41.

55 Elaine Donnelly, "Biden's 'Racial Equity' Order Threatens the Meritocracy That Makes Our Military Great," The Federalist, April 20, 2023, https://thefederalist.com/2023/04/20/bidens-racial-equity-order-threatens-the-meritocracy-that-makes-our-military-great/.

56 Chelsey Cox, "Gen. Mark Milley Fires Back against GOP Criticism of Critical Race Theory," *USA Today*, June 23, 2021, https://www.usatoday.com/story/news/politics/2021/06/23/top-general-defends-critical-race-theory-against-gop-lawmakers/5327404001.

## Chapter 14: The End Game: Reparations and Expropriation

1 Christina Zhao, "Joe Biden Asked about Responsibility for Slavery during Democratic Debate, Answers about Venezuela," *Newsweek*, September 12, 2019, https://www.newsweek.com/joe-biden-asked-about-responsibility-slavery-during-democratic-debate-answers-about-venezuela-1459065.

2   William H. Frey, "The Nation Is Diversifying Even Faster Than Predicted, according to New Census Data," The Brookings Institution, July 1, 2020, https://www.brookings.edu/articles/new -census-data-shows-the-nation-is-diversifying-even-faster-than -predicted; William H. Frey, "The US Will Become 'Minority White' in 2045, Census Projects," The Brookings Institution, March 14, 2018, https://www.brookings.edu /articles/the-us-will-become-minority-white-in-2045-census-projects.

3   Ibram X. Kendi, "Pass an Anti-Racist Constitutional Amendment," *Politico*, 2019, https://www.politico.com/interactives/2019/how-to-fix -politics-in-america/inequality/pass-an-anti-racist-constitutional -amendment.

4   Ibid.

5   "Ibram X. Kendi," Boston University, n.d., https://www.bu.edu /history/profile/ibram-x-kendi.

6   Sarah Weissman, "Ibram X. Kendi Defends Boston University Center after Layoffs," Inside Higher Ed, September 25, 2023, https://www .insidehighered.com/news/quick-takes/2023/09/25/ibram-x-kendi -defends-antiracism-center-after-layoffs; Michelle Goldberg, "Ibram X. Kendi and the Problem of Celebrity Fund-Raising," *New York Times*, September 25, 2023, https://www.nytimes.com/2023/09/25 /opinion/columnists/kendi-center-antiracist-research.html.

7   Portions of this section appeared in a different form in *The American Mind*.

8   Ta-Nehisi Coates, "The Case for Reparations," *The Atlantic*, June 2014, https://www.theatlantic.com/magazine/archive/2014/06/the -case-for-reparations/361631.

9   Kiran Misra, "Illinois City's Reparations Plan Was Heralded—but Locals Say It's a Cautionary Tale," *The Guardian*, August 18, 2021, https://www.theguardian.com/us-news/2021/aug/18/evanston-illinois -reparations-plan-cautionary-tale; Cheyanne M. Daniels, "Inside a California Proposal to Pay $1.2 Million in Reparations to Black Americans," *The Hill*, May 4, 2023, https://thehill.com/homenews /state-watch/3988577-inside-a-california-proposal-to-pay-1-2-million -in-reparations-to-black-americans; Associated Press, "San Francisco Board Open to Reparations with $5M Payouts," NBC News, March 14, 2023, https://www.nbcnews.com/news/nbcblk/san-francisco -decide-black-reparations-plan-5m-person-rcna74873.

10  Michael T. Nietzel, "College Endowments Took a Big Hit in Fiscal Year 2022," *Forbes*, February 18, 2023, https://www.forbes.com/sites /michaeltnietzel/2023/02/18/college-endowments-hit-the-skids-in -fiscal-year-2022/?sh=74af48711986.

11 "Statistics from the Civil War," Facing History and Ourselves, August 12, 2022, https://www.facinghistory.org/resource-library/statistics -civil-war.

12 Elsie Freeman, Wynell Burroughs Schamel, and Jean West, "The Fight for Equal Rights: A Recruiting Poster for Black Soldiers in the Civil War," *Social Education 56*, no. 2 (February 1992): 118–20, https: //www.archives.gov/education/lessons/blacks-civil-war. [Revised and updated in 1999 by Budge Weidman.]

13 "Civil War Casualties," American Battlefield Trust, September 15, 2023, https://www.battlefields.org/learn/articles/civil-war-casualties.

14 Christine Tamir, "Key Findings about Black Immigrants in the U.S.," Pew Research Center, January 27, 2022, https://www.pewresearch .org/short-reads/2022/01/27/key-findings-about-black-immigrants-in -the-u-s.

15 Ellen Barry, "How Kamala Harris's Immigrant Parents Found a Home, and Each Other, in a Black Study Group," *New York Times*, October 6, 2020, https://www.nytimes.com/2020/09/13/us/kamala -harris-parents.html.

16 Edmund Sanders, "From the Archives: Obama and His Kenyan Father: So Alike and Yet So Different," *Los Angeles Times*, July 23, 2015, https://www.latimes.com/world/africa/la-fg-obama-kenyan -father-20080717-story.html.

17 Faustine Ngila, "Over Half of Africa's Young Adults Want to Emigrate," Quartz, June 20, 2022, https://qz.com/africa/2179954 /world-refugee-day-why-africas-youth-want-to-emigrate-to-europe -and-us.

18 Roy E. Finkenbine, "The Grandchildren of Slaves Are Dying," History News Network, n.d., https://historynewsnetwork.org/article/164515.

19 "Daniel Smith, Believed to Be the Last Child of Enslaved People, Dies at 90," Equal Justice Initiative, October 21, 2022, https://eji.org /news/daniel-smith-believed-to-be-the-last-child-of-enslaved-people -dies-at-90.

20 Ryan King, "Black People Should Get $350,000 Each in Reparations, Landmark California Committee Hears," *Washington Examiner*, December 15, 2022, https://www.washingtonexaminer.com/restoring -america/community-family/black-people-get-350000-reparations -california-committee; Associated Press, "San Francisco Board Open to Reparations with $5M Payouts."

21 William La Jeunesse, "San Francisco Reparations Proposal Makes Waves: 'American Must Admit Its Sin,'" Fox News, January 18, 2023, https://www.foxnews.com/us/san-francisco-reparations-proposal -makes-waves-america-must-admit-sin.

22 Jacob Berkman, "At Least 139 of the Forbes 400 Are Jewish," Jewish Telegraphic Agency," October 5, 2009, https://www.jta.org

/2009/10/05/united-states/at-least-139-of-the-forbes-400-are-jewish; "The Size of the U.S. Jewish Population," Pew Research Center, May 11, 2021, https://www.pewresearch.org/religion/2021/05/11/the-size -of-the-u-s-jewish-population.

23 "Income and Wealth in the United States: An Overview of Recent Data," Peter G. Peterson Foundation, November 9, 2023, https: //www.pgpf.org/blog/2023/11/income-and-wealth-in-the-united -states-an-overview-of-recent-data.

24 "America's Black Upper Class," *Deutsche Welle*, March 11, 2022, https://www.dw.com/en/americas-black-upper-class-rich-successful -empowered/a-60787979.

25 Thomas Sowell, "The Quest for Cosmic Justice," Hoover Institution, January 30, 2000, https://www.hoover.org/research/quest-cosmic-justice.

26 "San Francisco's Insane 'Reparations' Program" (editorial), *National Review*, January 18, 2023, https://www.nationalreview.com/2023/01 /san-franciscos-insane-reparations-program.

27 Jeremy Carl, "Prescription for Disaster," *American Mind*, March 1, 2023, https://americanmind.org/salvo/prescription-for-disaster.

28 Graham Lee Brewer, "The Supreme Court Gave States More Power over Tribal Land. Tribes Say That Undermines Their Autonomy," NBC News, June 30, 2022, https://www.nbcnews.com/news/us-news /supreme-court-oklahoma-castro-huerta-decision-tribal-sovereignty -rcna35872.

29 "Land Acknowledgements," Princeton University, 2023, https://inclusive .princeton.edu/initiatives/building-community/native-american -indigenous-inclusion/land-acknowledgements.

30 Christopher Tremoglie, "Genocide, Slavery, and Rape: Let's Remember the Atrocities of Indigenous Peoples," *Washington Examiner*, October 11, 2021, https://www.washingtonexaminer.com/opinion/genocide -slavery-and-rape-lets-remember-the-atrocities-of-indigenous-peoples.

31 Kristen Inbody, "Chasing Broken Montana Homestead Dreams in the Missouri Breaks," *Great Falls Tribune*, October 11, 2017, https: //www.greatfallstribune.com/story/life/2017/10/11/chasing-broken -montana-homestead-dreams-missouri-breaks/739996001.

32 Harmeet Kaur, "Indigenous People across the US Want Their Land Back—and the Movement Is Gaining Momentum," CNN, November 26, 2020, https://www.cnn.com/2020/11/25/us/indigenous-people -reclaiming-their-lands-trnd/index.html.

33 "Secretary of Interior Orders Mashpee Wampanoag Reservation 'Disestablished,' Tribe Says," WBUR, March 28, 2020, https: //www.wbur.org/news/2020/03/28/mashpee-wampanoag-reservation -secretary-interior-land-trust; Valerie Richardson, "Elizabeth Warren Aids Mashpee Wampanoag Tribe in Taunton, Massachusetts Casino Bid," *Washington Times*, May 10, 2018, https://www.washingtontimes

.com/news/2018/may/10/elizabeth-warren-aids-mashpee-wampanoag
-tribe-taun.

34 Kristofer Rios, Ashley Riegle, and Allie Yang, "Mexican Americans
Seek Atonement for Ancestral Lands That Were Taken over
Generations," ABC News, September 30, 2020, https://abcnews
.go.com/US/mexican-americans-seek-atonement-ancestral-lands
-generations/story?id=73320792.

35 Brackets and ellipsis original. Ibid.

36 Ibid.

37 Priscilla Solis Ybarra, "The Forgotten History of Wilderness, and a
Possible Future," *High Country News*, March 15, 2022, https://www
.hcn.org/articles/books-wilderness-is-stolen-land.

38 Joy Diaz, "Some Mexican Leaders Want to Revisit the Treaty That
Made Texas a Part of the U.S.," *Texas Standard*, April 12, 2017,
https://www.texasstandard.org/stories/some-mexican-leaders-want-to
-revisit-the-treaty-that-made-texas-a-part-of-the-u-s.

39 Enrique Krauze, "Will Mexico Get Half of Its Territory Back?," *New
York Times*, April 6, 2017, https://www.nytimes.com/2017/04/06
/opinion/will-mexico-get-half-of-its-territory-back.html.

## Chapter 15: Finding Our Way Home

1 Dustin McGladrey, "'It's Okay To Be White' Was a Planned Hate
Crime from 4chan Internet Trolls," CFWE, November 1, 2017,
https://web.archive.org/web/20180625104237/http:/www.cfweradio
.ca/on-air/blogs/dustin-mcgladrey/post/its-okay-to-be-white-was-a
-planned-hate-crime-from-4chan-internet-trolls.

2 Bradford Richardson, "'It's OK to Be White' Campaign Rankles
Higher Education," *Washington Times*, November 10, 2017, https:
//www.washingtontimes.com/news/2017/nov/10/its-ok-be-white
-campaign-rankles-higher-education.

3 Donna St. George, "Signs Saying 'It's Okay to Be White' Found at
Maryland High School," *Washington Post*, November 1, 2017, https:
//www.washingtonpost.com/local/education/signs-saying-its-okay
-to-be-white-found-at-maryland-high-school/2017/11/01/92013a26
-bf3b-11e7-959c-fe2b598d8c00_story.html; Michael Edison Hayden,
"It's OK to Be White: How Fox News Is Helping to Spread Neo-Nazi
Propaganda," *Newsweek*, November 19, 2017, https://www
.newsweek.com/neo-nazi-david-duke-backed-meme-was-reported-
tucker-carlson-without-context-714655; "'It's Okay to Be White'
Fliers Target Campuses Nationwide," Anti-Defamation League,
November 5, 2018, https://www.adl.org/resources/blog/its-okay-be
-white-fliers-target-campuses-nationwide.

4   "Fox News Tucker Carlson—It's Okay to Be White Goes National," YouTube, November 3, 2017, https://www.youtube.com/watch?v=aYE_Q9gslVo.

5   Paul Bedard, "'It's OK to Be White,' Agree 72%, Including 53% of Black People," *Washington Examiner*, https://www.washington examiner.com/news/washington-secrets/its-ok-to-be-white-agree-72-including-53-of-blacks.

6   Taylor Nadauld, "'It's Okay to Be White' Posters Spark Mixed Responses," *Spokesman-Review*, November 30, 2017, https://www.spokesman.com/stories/2017/nov/30/its-okay-to-be-white-posters-spark-mixed-responses.

7   Maia Szalavitz, "No, Native Americans Aren't Genetically More Susceptible to Alcoholism," The Verge, October 2, 2015, https://www.theverge.com/2015/10/2/9428659/firewater-racist-myth-alcoholism-native-americans.

8   Anne Case and Angus Deaton, "Rising Morbidity and Mortality in Midlife among White Non-Hispanic Americans in the 21st Century," PNAS, November 2, 2015, https://www.pnas.org/doi/10.1073/pnas.1518393112.

9   Ibid.

10  Elena Lesley, "Cultural Impairment and the Genocidal Potential of Intoxicants: Alcohol Use in Colonial North America," *Genocide Studies and Prevention* 13, no 1 (2019): https://digitalcommons.usf.edu/gsp/vol13/iss1/10.

11  William H. Frey, "Even as Metropolitan Areas Diversify, White Americans Still Live in Mostly White Neighborhoods," Brookings.edu, March 23, 2020, https://www.brookings.edu/articles/even-as-metropolitan-areas-diversify-white-americans-still-live-in-mostly-white-neighborhoods.

12  Ibid.

13  Hansi Lo Wang, "New 'Latino' and 'Middle Eastern or North African' Checkboxes Proposed for U.S. Forms," NPR, April 7, 2023, https://www.npr.org/2023/01/26/1151608403/mena-race-categories-us-census-middle-eastern-latino-hispanic.

14  "2020 Census Failures Cost Red States House Seats and Funds—*Wall Street Journal* Calls for Investigation," Christian Broadcasting Network, May 24, 2022, https://www2.cbn.com/news/us/2020-census-failures-cost-red-states-house-seats-and-funds-wall-street-journal-calls.

15  Mike Gonzalez, "Even the Census Bureau Is Trying to Promote Radical Gender Ideology," *Washington Examiner*, November 16, 2023, https://www.washingtonexaminer.com/restoring-america/equality-not-elitism/census-bureau-trying-to-promote-radical-gender-ideology.

16  Nicholas Jones, Rachel Marks, Roberto Ramirez, and Merarys Ríos-Vargas, "2020 Census Illuminates Racial and Ethnic Composition of the Country," United States Census Bureau, August 12, 2021, https://www.census.gov/library/stories/2021/08/improved-race-ethnicity-measures-reveal-united-states-population-much-more-multiracial.html.

17  "Hispanic Family Facts: More Than 1 in 4 Hispanic Newlyweds Marry Someone of Another Race," Hispanic Research Center, February 14, 2019, https://www.hispanicresearchcenter.org/hisp-family-facts/hispanic-family-facts-more-than-1-in-4-hispanic-newlyweds-marry-someone-of-another-race.

18  "Fertility Rate, Total (Births per Woman)," The World Bank, n.d., https://data.worldbank.org/indicator/SP.DYN.TFRT.IN?locations=MX.

19  "Hispanic Population to Reach 111 Million by 2060," United States Census Bureau, October 9, 2018, https://www.census.gov/library/visualizations/2018/comm/hispanic-projected-pop.html.

20  Katarzyna Bryc, Eric Y. Durand, J. Michael Macpherson, David Reich, and Joanna L. Mountain, "The Genetic Ancestry of African Americans, Latinos, and European Americans across the United States," *American Journal of Human Genetics* 96, no. 1 (January 2015): https://www.ncbi.nlm.nih.gov/pmc/articles/PMC4289685.

21  Kim Parker, Juliana Menasce Horowitz, Rich Morin, and Mark Hugo Lopez, "Chapter 1: Race and Multiracial Americans in the U.S. census," Pew Research Center, June 11, 2015, https://www.pewresearch.org/social-trends/2015/06/11/chapter-1-race-and-multiracial-americans-in-the-u-s-census.

22  Kimmy Yam, "Asian Americans Voted for Biden 63% to 31%, but the Reality Is More Complex," NBC News, November 9, 2020, https://www.nbcnews.com/news/asian-america/asian-americans-voted-biden-63-31-reality-more-complex-n1247171.

23  See, for example, "The National Council of Asian Pacific Americans Statement in Solidarity with the Black Community," National Council of Asian Pacific Americans, May 28, 2020, https://www.ncapaonline.org/ncapa-statement-in-solidarity-with-the-black-community/.

24  Christine Tamir, "Key Findings about Black Immigrants in the U.S.," Pew Research Center, January 27, 2022, https://www.pewresearch.org/short-reads/2022/01/27/key-findings-about-black-immigrants-in-the-u-s.

25  Zach Goldberg, "America's White Saviors," Tablet, June 5, 2019, https://www.tabletmag.com/sections/news/articles/americas-white-saviors.

26  Michael I. Norton and Samuel R. Sommers, "Whites See Racism as a Zero-Sum Game That They Are Now Losing," *Perspectives on Psychological Science* 6, no. 3 (2011): https://www.hbs.edu/ris/Publication%20Files/norton%20sommers%20whites%20see%20racism_ca92b4be-cab9-491d-8a87-cf1c6ff244ad.pdf.

27 FischerKing (@FischerKing64), "The United States won't be in a position to right the ship until white people can say all the things that minorities can say without personal consequences. GOP creates surrogates to say what whites can't say without ruining their lives and that tells you everything.," Twitter, April 20, 2023, 8:50 p.m., https://twitter.com/FischerKing64/status/1649213866776363008.

28 Frederick Douglass, "West India Emancipation," speech delivered at Canandaigua, New York, August 3, 1857, https://rbscp.lib.rochester.edu/4398.

29 Max Zahn, "The Boycott against Bud Light Is Hammering Sales. Experts Explain Why.," ABC News, May 23, 2023, https://abcnews.go.com/Business/boycott-bud-light-hammering-sales-experts-explain/story?id=99505649

30 Timur Kuran, "True Lies," *New Republic*, December 25, 1995, https://newrepublic.com/article/63480/true-lies.

31 Steve Sailer, "Americans First," *American Conservative*, February 13, 2006, https://www.theamericanconservative.com/americans-first.

32 Stephen Miller (@StephenM), "Are you white or Asian? Were you denied a job, raise or promotion due to your race? Were you disciplined, harassed or unfairly treated based on your skin color? Please contact America First Legal at 1–877-AFL-5454 or equality@AFLegal.org Learn more at http://AFLegal.org/equality," Twitter, June 15, 2023, 10:18 a.m., https://twitter.com/StephenM/status/1669348632523575296.

33 Max Zahn, "Starbucks Discrimination Lawsuit Awarded White Employee $25 million: Legal Experts Weigh In," ABC News, June 16, 2023, https://abcnews.go.com/Business/starbucks-discrimination-lawsuit-awarded-white-employee-25-million/story?id=100104620.

34 "Former Philadelphia School District Employees Win $2.96 Million 'Reverse' Race Discrimination Verdict," Flaster Greenberg, n.d., https://www.flastergreenberg.com/experience-Former_Philadelphia_School_District_Employees_Win_2_96_Million_Reverse_Race_Discrimination_Verdict.html.

35 Amy Howe, "Supreme Court Strikes Down Affirmative Action Programs in College Admissions," SCOTUS blog, January 29, 2023, https://www.scotusblog.com/2023/06/supreme-court-strikes-down-affirmative-action-programs-in-college-admissions.

36 "Autumn 1942 (Age 68)," International Churchill Society, March 12, 2016, https://winstonchurchill.org/the-life-of-churchill/war-leader/1940–1942/autumn-1942-age-68.

37 Jack Stripling, "DeSantis Signs Bill to Defund DEI Programs at Florida's Public Colleges," *Washington Post*, May 15, 2023, https://archive.is/6yzy8.

38 Ahmed al-Tunis (@altunisahmed), "Florida's farmers, waitresses, and truck drivers should not be subsidizing a permanent bureaucracy of

left-wing activists who hate them and hate their values. . . ," Twitter, May 15, 2023, 11:57 a.m., https://twitter.com/altunisahmed /status/1658139675117203456.

39 James Madison, "Letter to Jacob De La Motta" in *Letters and Other Writings of James Madison*, vol. iii (Philadelphia: J. B. Lippincott & co., 1867), 179.

40 Elisabeth Zerofsky, "How the Claremont Institute Became a Nerve Center of the American Right," *New York Times*, August 3, 2022, https://www.nytimes.com/2022/08/03/magazine/claremont-institute -conservative.html.

# INDEX